Essentials of UK Politics

Essentials of UK Politics

Second Edition

Andrew Heywood

palgrave
macmillan

First edition 2008
Second edition 2011

Published by PALGRAVE MACMILLAN

Palgrave Macmillan in the UK is an imprint of Macmillan Publishers Limited,
registered in England, company number 785998, of Houndmills, Basingstoke,
Hampshire RG21 6XS.

Palgrave Macmillan in the US is a division of St Martin's Press LLC,
175 Fifth Avenue, New York, NY 10010.

Palgrave Macmillan is the global academic imprint of the above companies
and has companies and representatives throughout the world.

Palgrave® and Macmillan® are registered trademarks in the United States,
the United Kingdom, Europe and other countries.

ISBN 978-0-230-28562-0

This book is printed on paper suitable for recycling and made from fully
managed and sustained forest sources. Logging, pulping and manufacturing
processes are expected to conform to the environmental regulations of the
country of origin.

A catalogue record for this book is available from the British Library.

A catalog record for this book is available from the Library of Congress.

10   9   8   7   6   5   4   3   2   1
20   19   18   17   16   15   14   13   12   11

Printed and bound in China

For David, Anne, Daniel and Kelly

Brief Contents

Contents

List of Illustrative Material

Focus on

Who is

Differences between

By comparison

For or against?

Acknowledgements

The author and publishers would like to thank the Press Association for permission for the use of copyright illustrative material on pages 5, 31, 63, 99, 123, 129, 137, 169, 191, 193, 223, 237, 250, 275, 303.

Preface

This second edition of *Essentials in UK Politics* attempts to take account of the implications of the Conservative–Liberal Democrat coalition after its first full year in existence. As the UK's first peacetime coalition government since the 1930s, the coalition has far-reaching significance. Amongst other things, it reflects ideological trends in both coalitions parties that have substantially (but not completely) narrowed the political divide between them, making this very much an ideological 'coalition of the willing'. However, whether this constitutes a tactical manoeuvre or a strategic adjustment for the parties concerned, and whether it is linked to a long-term shift in the UK party system, remains to be seen. Similarly, the coalition has been used very astutely by Cameron both to reduce his dependence on the Conservative right and to deflect attention from the Conservative Party's failure under his leadership to win a parliamentary majority at a fourth consecutive general election.

Most importantly, the end (whether temporary or permanent) of single-party majority government and the traditional two-party system has major ramifications for the institutional landscape of UK politics. Topics ranging from the democratic system and the constitution to the balance between the executive and Parliament and the extent of prime ministerial power now have to be understood within the framework of coalition government. Nevertheless, this framework is not a fixed structure, but one that is fluid and developing. It is important to remember that coalitions have different implications in different circumstances and at different points in time, not least because of shifts in the balance between unity and distinctiveness between coalition partners. The implications of coalition government for UK politics may thus be very different in, say, 2014–15 from what they were in 2010–11. That is part of the joy of studying UK politics!

I would like to thank Steven Kennedy, my publisher at Palgrave Macmillan, and, as ever, an indefatigable source of encouragement, and also Helen Caunce, for her work in selecting suitable photographs among other things. Discussions with friends and colleagues, notably Gerald and Michelle Walton and June and George Clements, have also sharpened the arguments and ideas outlined in this book.

ANDREW HEYWOOD

How to Use this Book

This textbook has been written specifically to meet the needs of students who are studying AS level Government and Politics, though it will hopefully be useful for anyone approaching the subject for the first time. It provides a lively, accessible and comprehensive introduction to the 'essentials' of the subject and covers the key topics and themes on the Edexcel, AQA and OCR specifications for examinations after 2008 (see below for more details).

Features of the book

The book has a number of features that are designed to aid understanding and to support examination performance. (The boxed features are cross-referenced throughout.)

▶ **Previews**. These appear at the beginning of each chapter. They provide an introduction to the topic of the chapter and highlight the key issues that it addresses.

▶ **Getting you thinking**. Also appearing at the beginning of each chapter, these focus on a significant event or development from recent years that raises interesting questions about the topic being studied.

▶ **On-page definitions**. These provide single-sentence definitions of key terms at appropriate points in each chapter. (You can search for defined terms by looking for bold entries in the index. They also appear on the website; see Online support.)

▶ **'What is' boxes**. These provide fuller explanations of significant political ideas and concepts.

▶ **'Focus on' boxes**. These supplement information that is found in the main text by providing fuller or more detailed explanations of important political processes.

▶ **'Who is' boxes**. These provide brief biographies of major figures in contemporary UK politics, mainly prime ministers.

▶ **'Differences between' boxes**. These highlight differences between terms and concepts that are sometimes confused.

▶ **'By comparison' boxes**. These aim to strengthen the understanding of UK politics by providing comparative information about the USA. (In many AS topics, explicit comparisons with US politics can help candidates to demonstrate a deeper level of understanding.)

▶ **'Debating' boxes**. These provide an overview of the main arguments for and against a particular topic. (One of the important skills that AS students need to demonstrate is the ability to show an awareness of competing viewpoints and to be able to evaluate political arguments.)

▶ **Weblinks**. Found at appropriate points in each chapter, these provide information about useful websites that offer up-to-date comment and more information on the issue under discussion.

▶ **What you should know**. These appear at the end of each chapter and provide a summary of the key information that is contained in the chapter.

▶ **Test yourself**. Also appearing at the end of each chapter, these consist of a set of questions that can be used to check your understanding and to help to prepare you for the examination.

▶ **Online support**. The website associated with this book provides clickable weblinks and a searchable glossary of all the on-page definitions. See **www.palgrave.com/politics/essentials**.

The specifications

The following provides an overview of the AS Government and Politics specifications of each of the three main boards and shows, topic by topic, how this book supports their study.

EDEXCEL Government and Politics (8GP 01)	
Topic	Chapter
Introduction to the subject	1
Unit 1: People and politics	
Democracy and participation	2
Elections	3

Topic	Chapter
Party policies and ideas	4
Pressure groups	5
Unit 2: Governing the UK	
The constitution	6
Parliament	7
Prime minister and cabinet	8
Judges and civil liberties	9

Chapter 10 (on devolution and Europe) contains useful background information that is relevant to a variety of other topics

AQA Government and Politics (2150)

Main topic	Subtopic	Chapter
Introduction to the subject		1
Unit 1: People, politics and participation		
Participation and voting behaviour	Nature of participation	2
	Participation through elections	3
Electoral systems	Types of electoral system	3
	Nature of representation	2
Political parties	Role of parties in a democracy	4
Pressure groups and protest movements	Importance of groups	5
	Pressure group behaviour	5
Unit 2: Governing modern Britain		
The British constitution	Nature of the constitution	6
	The judiciary	9
Parliament	Role of Parliament	7
	Parliament and government	7
The core executive	Prime minister and cabinet	8
	Ministers and civil servants	8
Multilevel governance	Local and devolved bodies	10
	The European Union	10

OCR Government and Politics (H095)

Topic	Chapter
Introduction to the subject	1
Unit F851: Contemporary Politics in the UK	
Background knowledge of key concepts	2

Topic	Chapter
Political parties (mandatory)	4
Pressure groups (mandatory)	5
Electoral systems and referendums	2 and 3
UK parliamentary elections	3
Voting behaviour in the UK	3
Unit F852: Contemporary Governing of the UK	
The constitution	6
The executive (mandatory)	8
The legislature (mandatory)	7
The judiciary	9
The European Union	10

Maximizing performance

How can you ensure that your performance in Government and Politics is as good as it can be? How can you ensure exam success? Below are some helpful hints on how you can maximize your performance as you study the subject and as you prepare for the examination.

Studying the subject

▶ **Keep up-to-date with current affairs.** This will both make the subject more interesting to study (politics never stands still) and give you useful ammunition to use in the examination. Your knowledge needs to be as up-to-date as possible, and examiners are particularly looking to reward *contemporary* knowledge and understanding. Use websites, read a 'quality' newspaper (many of which can be accessed online) and articles in journals such as *Politics Review*, and watch the news and current affairs programmes on television.

▶ **Understand key terms and concepts.** Much of political understanding is based on a grasp of major terms and concepts – democracy, representation, parliamentary sovereignty, civil liberties, and so on. Make sure you have a thorough grasp of these terms, and be sure that you can define and explain them reliably in the examination itself.

▶ **Be aware of competing viewpoints.** Just about every issue in politics is the subject of debate and discussion. You need to show an awareness of the different sides of an argument – almost every statement you make in politics could be followed by 'However…'. But you also need to develop your own views, which means being able to support a particular viewpoint on the basis of *evidence* – make a point and prove it.

Preparing for the examination

▶ **Draw up a revision plan.** Revision is seldom done effectively if it is left until 'the mood takes you'. Draw up a plan of which topics you are going to revise and when – and then stick to it!

▶ **Know your specification inside out.** You have an outline above of the main topics covered in each unit. But the specification itself, as well as supporting materials provided by the awarding body for students, provides you with greater detail, including the identification of key concepts and an outline of the content.

▶ **Be familiar with past papers, marking schemes and examiners' reports.** These are all provided by awarding bodies, and they contain invaluable information about the kind of questions that will come up and the level of performance that will be expected.

▶ **Have as much exam practice as possible.** In the run-up to the examination, frequently practise answering examination questions in examination conditions and within examination timescales. If nothing else, this will ensure that your do not get your timings wrong – the silliest of all reasons for poor exam performance.

▶ **Pay attention to 'command words' and key terms in questions.** These are words such as 'define', 'explain', analyse', 'assess' or 'evaluate'. You need to know what each of these words means to ensure that you carry out the 'right' task in answering each question. For example:

> ▶ *Define* – say what a word or phrase means
> ▶ *Features* – the parts that define what a thing *is*
> ▶ *Functions* – the roles that highlight what a thing *does*
> ▶ *Explain* – show how something works, often by identifying causes and effects
> ▶ *Analyse* – break something into its component parts and show how they relate to one another
> ▶ *Evaluate* – make judgements about something's value, its strengths and weaknesses
> ▶ *Assess* – 'weigh up' a statement, showing an awareness of arguments in favour and against.

▶ **Be aware of what you get marks for.** This is spelled out in the three assessment objectives that are relevant to Government and Politics. These are:

> ▶ AO1: *knowledge and understanding* (e.g. 'Outline…', 'Define…', 'Distinguish…', 'How…', 'In what ways…')
>
> ▶ AO2: *analysis, evaluation and parallels or similarities/differences* (e.g. 'Why…', 'Analyse…', Compare…', 'Contrast…', 'Assess…', 'Evaluate…', 'To what extent…', 'Discuss…')
>
> ▶ AO3: *communication* (this covers (1) the quality of your written communication, (2) the use of appropriate political vocabulary, and (3) your ability to organize your ideas and arguments in a clear and structured way).

▶ **Answer the *precise* question set.** The most common reason for exam under-performance is a failure to 'target' the question set. Common mistakes include providing a pre-prepared answer to a question from a previous examination, and writing generally about the topic of the question, rather than addressing the particular question itself. To help to avoid these mistakes, get in the habit of regularly using the terms from the question in your answers.

Part **1**

People and Politics

Chapter 1

Introducing Politics and Government

Beginning the study of politics

Politics is exciting because people disagree. They disagree about how they should live – what rules or principles should guide our behaviour. They disagree about the distribution of power and other resources – who should get what. They disagree about how society should be organized – should society be based on co-operation or competition. And so on. Debate and disagreement therefore lie at the very heart of politics. This affects not only the practice of politics, but also how the subject should be studied. Politics is not a subject of absolute 'rights' or absolute 'wrongs'; it is a subject of rival viewpoints and competing opinions. By definition, there are more answers than questions in politics. But this does not mean that politics consists of nothing more than a collection of opinions. If all opinions were 'equal', they would be equally worthless. The challenge of politics is to develop your own views and opinions in the light of the viewpoints and perspectives available to you. This means, above all, thinking for yourself.

This chapter provides you with a general introduction to the study of UK Government and Politics. It does this in three ways. First, it discusses what the subject is all about. In particular, what is politics? But also, what is government, and why are politics and government usually linked? Second, it examines the context of UK politics, and considers the factors that make UK politics distinctive, even unique. All political systems are shaped by a set of historical, social, international and other factors. What are the factors that have shaped UK politics? Third, it provides an overview of the political system itself. How does the larger political system work? What are the major issues and key themes in contemporary UK politics?

- ■ **What is politics?**
- ■ **What is government?**
- ■ **How has UK politics been shaped by its historical, social and external context?**
- ■ **What are the main features of UK government and politics?**
- ■ **What are the main themes in contemporary UK politics?**

GETTING YOU THINKING

Only in it for the money?

Before starting the chapter, read this passage and briefly consider the questions on the next page.

On 8 May 2008, the *Daily Telegraph* published the first in a series of extracts from leaked documents containing details of MPs' expenses claims. This was the beginning of an expenses scandal that raged during the spring and summer of 2008 as more information came out. Amongst the most news-worthy revelations were claims for a duck house, for clearing a moat and, in at least two cases, for mortgages that had already been paid off. Many of the claims that attracted criticism related to MPs' second homes (which were, sometimes, not being used as such) and for a wide range of domestic items (food, routine repairs, household goods, furniture and the like). By May 2009, MPs and peers had promised to repay over £100,000 of falsely claimed taxpayers' money.

In the wake of the expenses scandal, trust in politics hit an all-time low. In an opinion poll in 2009, two-thirds of people agreed with the statement that 'most MPs make a lot of money by using their public office improperly'. The 2010 British Social Attitudes survey found that 4 in 10 people 'almost never' trust politicians to put the national interest first, and a majority of voters believe that MPs never tell the truth. But what does the expenses scandal tell us about the nature of politics and politicians? Some argue that it simply reflects the fact that people are selfish and that those in power will always, given the chance, act in their own interests rather than the public interest. The problem, in short, is human nature. Others argue that the scandal reflects more recent developments, namely the fact that people nowadays tend to enter politics as a way of 'getting on', when, in the past, politics was a kind of public service. Still others blame the media for creating the impression that politics is a gravy train by giving massive publicity to the flaws and failings of a minority of politicians.

A protest in 2009 against the misuse by MPs of their expenses system — but is this a fair reflection of their general behaviour?

What issues do such developments raise?

▶▶▶   Why do you think most politicians go into politics?

▶▶▶   Should elected politicians be expected to behave better than other people?

▶▶▶   Are modern politicians less honourable and trustworthy than previous generations of politicians?

▶▶▶   Does power inevitably corrupt those who hold it?

▶▶▶   If power tends to corrupt, would we be better off without government?

Understanding politics

Whenever you begin the study of a new academic subject, it is usual to be introduced to the nature of the subject itself. This happens for two main reasons. First, you need to know what the study of the subject is going to involve. If you like, you need to know what 'you are in for'. Second, it is helpful to be introduced to some of the basic ideas and concepts of the subject, the building blocks for later understanding. This section therefore looks at:

▶▶▶   What is politics?
▶▶▶   What is government?

What is politics?

Although the question 'What is Politics?' has sometimes stimulated fierce debate and disagreement (whole books have even been written on the subject), politics has a clear basic character. Politics can be defined as follows:

> Politics is the activity though which people make, uphold and
> revise the general rules under which they live.

At first sight, this definition is simple and straightforward. However, when looked at further, at least three other questions emerge:

▶▶▶   In what sense are these rules 'general'?
▶▶▶   Why are such rules needed?
▶▶▶   How are these rules made and upheld?

What are 'general' rules?

General rules are rules that affect how we interact more widely with other members of society. In other words, they are the rules that affect how we behave within the community, rather than how we behave in our personal life; that is, within our families or just with close friends. This highlights an important distinction in politics: the difference between 'public' life and 'private' life. *Public* life is the realm of politics. It deals with issues that affect all members of the community, such as law and order, the economy, defence, social welfare, and so on. *Private* life, by contrast, is an arena in which we are, or should be, free to act as we wish. It includes, for example, decisions about who to marry, what to buy, religious belief, and so forth. However, this is where problems begin. Quite simply, there is no agreement about the proper balance between public and private life. This was the point of the example of MPs' expenses, looked at at the beginning of the chapter.

Why are general rules needed?

Conflict: Competition between opposing forces, based on the existence of different opinions, wants and needs.

General rules are needed because of the problem of **conflict**. Politics, in short, exists because people disagree. If everybody had the same views and opinions, and agreed about how their society should work, there would be no politics. In a world of universal harmony and agreement, people would not need rules to guide their behaviour or the behaviour of others. They would 'naturally' know what to do, and how and when to do it. Sadly, such a society does not exist, and probably never has. Most basically, people disagree about how the wealth and other resources in society should be distributed – they disagree about who gets what. However, politics is not just about conflict. It is also about finding ways of resolving conflict, ways of allowing people with different opinions, wants and needs to live together within the same society. This is what the 'general rules' of society seek to do.

How are the rules made?

Power: The *ability* to influence the behaviour of others, usually through rewards or punishment.

Authority: The *right* to influence the behaviour of others, based on an acknowledged duty to obey.

As we shall see later, the general rules in society are made in different ways depending on the system of government in existence. Each of these systems nevertheless has one thing in common. They each operate on the basis of **power**. Power is a vital ingredient of politics. It is the factor that determines who gets what, when and how. If politics is a struggle over scarce resources, power is the means through which the struggle is conducted. However, **authority** is often more important in politics than power. Authority can be defined as 'legitimate power' – power that people believe they *should* obey, rather than obey through fear or intimidation.

Legitimacy: Rightfulness; legitimacy confers on a command or order an authoritative or binding character, meaning that it should be obeyed.

In the classic formulation advanced by the German sociologist, Max Weber, there are three types of authority: *traditional* authority (based on history and the belief that something has 'always happened'), *charismatic* authority (based on personality) and, the most common form in modern politics, *legal-rational* authority (based on formal and impersonal rules). All political systems try to turn power into authority, and they do so through a quest for **legitimacy**. As legitimacy establishes a 'right to rule' that encourages citizens willingly to obey the state, it is crucial to the maintenance of political stability. But some political systems are more successful in building legitimacy than others.

What is government?

Politics and government invariably go together. The subject, after all, is called Government and Politics. But why are the two linked? Government can be defined as follows:

FOCUS ON . . .

Types of power

Power is exercised whenever A gets B to do something that B would not otherwise have done. In this sense, it refers to 'power *over*' people. However, A can influence B in a variety of ways.

Stephen Lukes (2004) identified three types of power:

▶ Power as *decision-making* – the ability to affect the content of public policy (what governments actually do)
▶ Power as *agenda-setting* – the ability to influence the issues and proposals that are discussed (what is on, or off, the political agenda)

▶ Power as *thought control* – the ability to shape popular beliefs, values and ideas (what people think).

It has become increasingly common to distinguish between 'hard' power and 'soft' power, especially in international or global politics:

▶ *Hard* power is the ability to exert influence through the use of threats or rewards, e.g. the use of military force or the control of jobs and investment.
▶ *Soft* power is the ability to exert influence through attraction rather than coercion, e.g. the use of film, radio and TV to affect people's values and aspirations.

Government is a set of institutions through which the general rules of society (usually called laws) are made and enforced.

In other words, government is the machinery through which politics operates. Its central features are the ability to make collective decisions and the ability to enforce them. A form of government can therefore be identified in almost all social institutions: families, schools, businesses, trade unions, and so on. As far as the government of a society is concerned, government consists of three parts. These parts are responsible for:

▶ Making laws – legislation
▶ Carrying out laws – execution
▶ Interpreting laws – adjudication.

Although all systems of government set out to ensure 'ordered rule', they do this in very different ways. Government, therefore, has taken a wide variety of shapes and forms. Two ways of classifying different forms of government are on the basis of how powerful government is and who controls the government.

How powerful is government?

The issue of government power – and how far government can *affect* ordinary citizens – highlights the difference between limited government and authoritarian government. In the case of *limited* government (as the terms suggests), government operates within a framework of checks or constraints. These are meant to protect individual freedom by preventing over-mighty government. The main ways of limiting government power are through constitutions (rules that govern the government itself) and by fragmenting government through the creation of a number of institutions which can check one another. On the other hand, *authoritarian* government imposes rules on the people regardless of checks or limitations. In effect, authoritarian governments can do whatever they wish. Such governments have usually been seen as a recipe for tyranny and oppression.

Who controls the government?

The issue of control over government highlights the difference between democracies and autocracies. In the case of *democratic* government (more fully discussed in Chapter 2), power lies with the people. Government is meant to be carried out *by* the people. In practical terms, this means that government is based on the principle of elections – those who hold government power are chosen through a process of regular and competitive elections. This is designed to ensure that government acts *for* the people; that is, in the public interest. At the other extreme is *autocratic* government, a form of government in which all power is held by one person. **Autocracy** usually goes hand in hand with **authoritarianism**. Examples of such regimes include absolute monarchies, empires and dictatorships of various kinds. By the same token, limited government and democracy are often found together, most commonly in the form of so-called liberal democracies. Liberal democracy (see p. 10) has become the most popular type of regime in the modern world. By 2003, 63 per cent of countries, accounting for about 70 per cent of the world's population, exhibited some of the key features of liberal democracy. The UK is often seen as a classic example of a liberal democracy. However, as we shall see later, some critics regard it as an untypical, or incomplete, liberal democracy.

Autocracy: Literally, self-rule; rule by a single person who exercises his or her power in an arbitrary manner.

Authoritarianism: The practice of rule 'from above'; government that is imposed on citizens regardless of their consent.

UK politics in context

Having gained a general understanding of the nature of politics and government, we now need to turn our attention to the UK. In particular, we need to see what is distinctive about how government and politics work in the UK. Politics does not take place in a vacuum; it is shaped by a wide variety of factors – historical, social, cultural, international, and so on. Each political system therefore operates in a

What is . . . liberal democracy

Liberal democracy is an indirect and representative form of democracy (see p. 00). In a liberal democracy, the right to rule is gained through success in regular and competitive elections, conducted on the basis of political equality ('one person, one vote'). Liberal democratic regimes attempt to combine the 'liberal' goal of limited government with a 'democratic' commitment to elections and popular participation.

The core features of a liberal democracy are:

▶ Free, fair and regular elections that respect the principle of **universal suffrage**
▶ Competition for power between a number of candidates and a number of parties
▶ Guaranteed civil liberties and individual rights
▶ Constitutional government based on formal, usually legal, rules
▶ A healthy **civil society**, in which the media is free and groups enjoy independence from government
▶ A capitalist or private-enterprise economy.

Universal suffrage: The right of all adult citizens to vote (however 'adulthood' is defined).

Civil society: A 'private' realm in which individuals and groups enjoy independence from government; civil society includes businesses, clubs, families, and so on.

different context, and it is this context that makes the political system distinctive, even unique. What is the context of UK politics?

Historical context

This brief historical overview highlights three important developments that have helped to shape the modern UK:

▶▶ Crown and Parliament
▶▶ The rise of industrialization
▶▶ Politics since 1945.

Crown and Parliament

The UK has had an unusually stable and peaceful political history. Wars and revolutions have rarely visited British shores, unlike much of continental Europe. The exception, however, is an important one. The English Revolution of the 17th century is often viewed as the first modern political revolution. Ideas that surfaced during the English Revolution helped to influence the American Revolution of 1776 and the French Revolution of 1789. The English Revolution was a struggle for power between the monarchy and Parliament. It commenced with the outbreak of a civil war in 1642 and led to the execution of King Charles I in 1649. A brief republic was then formed under the military dictatorship of Oliver Cromwell, 1649–60. Cromwell's death nevertheless weakened the republic and eventually the monarchy was restored, under Charles II. This period of political

Map 1.1 **The UK**

FOCUS ON . . .
The Glorious Revolution

The Glorious Revolution refers to a series of events that took place in 1688 and 1689, which led to the exile of James II and the accession to the throne of his daughter Mary and her husband William of Orange. However, William and Mary agreed to be monarchs of a new kind: they were constitutional monarchs who accepted that they ruled within constraints established by Parliament. The Act of Settlement, 1701, for example, established that Parliament could alter the succession to the throne.

The Glorious Revolution was (arguably) the key moment in Britain's constitutional history:

▶ It provided the basis for the principle of parliamentary sovereignty (see p. 180), through which Parliament came to exercise unlimited legal authority.

▶ In establishing the idea of representative government, it laid the grounds for the later spread of democracy in the UK.

upheaval and civil strife ended in the Glorious Revolution of 1689, which established a new relationship between the Crown and Parliament, and provided the basis for Britain's later constitutional development. The English Revolution threw up radical political ideas of many kinds, even communist and anarchist political thinking. However, its enduring legacy, in Britain and elsewhere, was the establishment of the ideas of individual rights and representative government.

The rise of industrialization

The UK was the world's first industrialized state. The Industrial Revolution started in the mid-18th century and by the mid-19th century it had made the UK the 'workshop of the world', producing two-thirds of the world's coal, half its steel, half its cotton goods and virtually all its machine goods. Industrialization changed Britain internally and externally. *Internally*, it transformed the class structure, producing a rising middle class of industrialists and business men, and a growing industrial working class. This, in turn, created powerful pressure to widen political participation beyond the narrow ranks of the aristocracy or upper classes. A consequence of this was the Great Reform Act of 1832, which started the process through which the right to vote was expanded until universal adult suffrage was eventually achieved when women gained equal voting rights in 1928. The advance of democracy in the 19th century helped to establish the UK's parliamentary system of government, by making ministers accountable to Parliament rather than the monarch. *Externally*, industrialization made the UK the world's leading economic power, a fact that fuelled imperial expansion during the late 19th century. By 1918, the British Empire included about one-quarter of the world's population.

The post-1945 period

The political and ideological twists and turns of the post-1945 period are examined much more closely in Chapter 4. However, it is helpful to have an overview of such developments at the outset, as they affect many aspects of the contemporary political scene. UK politics since the Second World War has usually been divided into three distinct periods:

▶ The post-war consensus: 1945–79
▶ Thatcherism: 1979–97
▶ The post-Thatcherite consensus: since 1997.

Although such divisions are simplistic and, in many ways, misleading, they nevertheless help to illustrate some important trends in post-1945 UK politics. From this perspective, the post-war period has been defined by two radical, reforming governments:

▶ Clement Attlee's Labour governments, 1945–51
▶ Margaret Thatcher's Conservative governments, 1979–90.

Keynesianism: An economic strategy (developed by J. M. Keynes) in which growth is stimulated by allowing government spending to exceed tax revenues, so creating a budget deficit.

Butskellism: A term made up from the names of the Conservative chancellor R. A. Butler and the Labour leader Hugh Gaitskell, indicating an overlap in party policies.

The Attlee Labour governments established a new approach to economic and social policy-making. It sought to 'roll forward' the state, and it did this in a number of ways. Major industries, such as coal, steel, gas, electricity and shipbuilding, were nationalized. The economy was 'managed' by the government with the aim of ensuring steady growth and full employment using **Keynesian** techniques. The welfare state was expanded, with the creation of a comprehensive system of social security and the National Health Service (NHS). These policies aimed to promote social justice and to establish general prosperity, in line with the principles of social democracy (see p. 114). The fact that the Conservative Party was quickly converted to a broad acceptance of these social-democratic policies led to a period of consensus politics in the 1950s and 1960s. This is sometimes seen as the period of **Butskellism**, highlighting the extent to which the major two parties agreed on key economic and social priorities.

The social-democratic consensus nevertheless started to break down in the 1970s, as the economy began to suffer from renewed economic problems, notably rising inflation and growing unemployment. The clearest break with post-war social democracy, however, came with the election of the Thatcher Conservative government in 1979. Although the 'Thatcher revolution' only took shape gradually during the 1980s, its hallmark was the attempt to 'roll back' the state. This meant reversing many of the social-democratic reforms of the earlier post-war period. Industries that had been nationalized were privatized. Low inflation rather than full employment became the main goal of economic policy. Attempts were made to reform the welfare state, to increase efficiency and to tackle what was seen as the problem of 'welfare dependency'. What quickly became known as 'Thatcherism' (see p. 116) amounted to a counter-revolution against the values and policies of the social-democratic period. Its main theme was an emphasis on market competition and faith in self-reliance and personal aspiration.

However, the election of Tony Blair (see p. 223) and so-called New Labour in 1997 brought about a further shift in the direction of post-war politics. Although this shift was not as radical as those brought about by the Attlee and Thatcher governments, it was nevertheless significant. In styling his party as 'New' Labour, Blair had indicated that the Labour Party had no intention of returning to the post-war social democracy of 'old' Labour. Instead, it built on Thatcherism in accepting the need for a greater emphasis on markets, competition and enterprise. But this was not simply a continuation of Thatcherism by other means. Important changes were made. For example, the Blair government initiated a series of major constitutional reforms and, especially after 1999, introduced unprecedented increases in government spending, in particular in health and education. These changes, moreover, were not just confined to the Labour Party. Just as Thatcherism had helped to transform Labour in the 1980s and 1990s, so the success of 'Blairism' after 1997 stimulated a process of change within the Conservative Party. Under David Cameron (see p. 123), Blair's blend of free-market policies and continued welfare provision came to be broadly accepted by the Conservatives. This resulted in a 'post-Thatcherite' consensus in UK politics, in which all the major parties appeared to be competing for the overcrowded political 'centre ground'.

However, the May 2010 general election and the formation of a coalition between the Conservatives and the Liberal Democrats, with Cameron as prime minister, marked an important new trend within the post-Thatcherite consensus. Some have even argued that these developments may indicate the beginning of a distinctive new phase in post-war UK political history. This could apply in at least two respects. In the first place, the Conservative–Liberal Democrat coalition speedily embarked on the most radical programme of public spending cuts for a generation, leading some to believe that it was carrying out a wholesale restructuring of the state, even attempting to complete the 'Thatcher revolution' of the 1980s. This programme of cuts, ushering in what Cameron called an 'age of austerity', can be traced back to political divisions that started to open up in response to the dramatic deepening of the global financial crisis in 2008 and the onset of a sharp recession. The Brown Labour government responded to the financial crisis by carrying out the semi-nationalisation of a clutch of ailing banks, and also tried to revive growth through a Keynesian-style policy of 'fiscal stimulus', which allowed the budget deficit to expand to record levels. Cameron and the Conservatives, however, responded to the mounting debt crisis in increasingly Thatcherite terms, making the need for a swift and robust reduction of the budget deficit the cornerstone of their economic strategy.

Although differences between Labour and the Conservatives over the deficit can be exaggerated, the electorate was offered a real economic choice on 6 May 2010, and the willingness of Nick Clegg (see p. 193) and the Liberal Democrats to participate in a coalition with the Conservatives determined the outcome of that choice.

The second significant development related to the 2010 general election concerns the nature of the government that was formed. The Conservative–Liberal Democrat coalition was the UK's first peacetime **coalition government** since the 1930s. In the light of declining support for the two major parties (only two-thirds of the electorate voted for the Conservative and Labour parties in 2010) and the increased possibility of a reform of the Westminster electoral system, coalition government may be in the process of replacing single-party majority government as the norm in the UK, just as it is across most of continental Europe. However, views about the implications of coalition government are hotly contested (see p. 16).

Coalition government:
A government in which power is shared between two or more parties, based on the distribution among them of ministerial posts (see p. 79).

Table 1.1	Elections and outcomes since 1945			
Election	**Government**	**Prime Minister**	**Majority**	**Turnout**
1945	Labour	Clement Attlee	147	73%
1950	Labour	Clement Attlee	6	81%
1951	Conservative	Winston Churchill	16	83%
1955	Conservative	Anthony Eden	59	77%
1959	Conservative	Harold Macmillan	99	79%
1964	Labour	Harold Wilson	5	77%
1966	Labour	Harold Wilson	97	76%
1970	Conservative	Edward Heath	31	72%
1974 (Feb)	Labour	Harold Wilson	−32	79%
1974 (Oct)	Labour	Harold Wilson	4	73%
1979	Conservative	Margaret Thatcher	44	72%
1983	Conservative	Margaret Thatcher	143	73%
1987	Conservative	Margaret Thatcher	100	75%
1992	Conservative	John Major	22	78%
1997	Labour	Tony Blair	178	71%
2001	Labour	Tony Blair	166	59%
2005	Labour	Tony Blair	65	61%
2010	Con–Lib Dem	David Cameron	77	65%

Note: majorities take account of the Speaker, who does not vote.

Social context

At almost every level, politics is linked to society. Social factors affect how we vote; party policies and ideas are tailored to the make-up of society; and, to a large extent, political conflicts reflect underlying social and economic tensions.

FOR OR AGAINST?

COALITION GOVERNMENT

FOR	AGAINST
Effective coalitions. Much criticism of coalition government stems from misconceptions about how they operate elsewhere, often sustained by unrepresentative examples (Italy). Coalition governments are commonplace across continental Europe and, in most cases, they are stable and cohesive. This particularly occurs as political parties adjust to a culture of partnership and compromise. There is no reason why UK parties cannot adjust to such a culture, enabling them to form effective coalitions.	**Weak government**. Coalition governments cannot easily guarantee parliamentary approval for their programme of policies. Much of the government's energies have to be devoted to resolving tensions and conflicts between coalition partners. More seriously, internal disagreement, in government or in Parliament, can lead to paralysis, making it perhaps impossible for a coalition government to exercise bold policy leadership.
Broad, popular government. As they are formed by two or more parties, coalitions represent a wider range of views and interests than do single-party governments. Similarly, there is a greater likelihood that the combined electoral support for all the coalition partners will exceed 50 per cent. This means that coalitions, unlike most single-party governments in the UK, can genuinely claim to have a popular mandate.	**Unstable government**. Coalition governments, generally, do not last as long as single-party governments. They are fragile because the defection of one coalition partner will usually bring the government down, and coalition parties are encouraged to threaten such defections in the hope of exerting greater influence. More frequent general elections, and more regular changes in government, risk creating a general climate of instability.
End of adversarialism. Single-party government tends to operate in the context of a two-party system, in which politics degenerates into an ongoing electoral battle between government and opposition. Instead of incessant disagreement and conflict, coalitions allow for the emergence of the 'new politics'. Released from adversarialism (so-called 'yaa-boo' politics), parties are able to form alliances and work together on matters of common concern.	**Democracy undermined**. Deals that are done after the election inevitably mean that coalition parties abandon some of the policies on which they fought the election and accept some policies they had criticized. Not only may some voters therefore feel betrayed, but no one has a chance to accept or reject the coalition's eventual programme for government. There is also no guarantee that parties' influence within the coalition will reflect their electoral strength.
Wider pool of talent. One of the drawbacks of single-party government is that ministers can only be selected from the ranks of a single party's MPs or peers. Coalition governments, by contrast, can access a wider range of talent, drawing on the expertise and experience of two or more parties. Coalitions therefore come closer to the ideal of a 'government of all the talents'.	**Confused ideological direction**. Whereas individual parties attempt to develop coherent policy programmes based on clear ideological visions, coalition governments' policy programmes are often unclear or inconsistent. They are shaped not by a single ideological vision but by the attempt to reconcile two (or more) contrasting visions.

The decline of class?

A social class is, broadly, a group of people who share a similar social and economic position. A common way of distinguishing between different social classes is on the basis of occupation. Official government statistics in the UK distinguish between the social classes shown in Table 1.2.

Table 1.2	Social classes in the UK
Class A	higher managerial and professional workers
Class B	middle managers and professionals
Class C1	clerical workers
Class C2	skilled manual workers
Class D	semi-skilled and unskilled workers
Class E	unemployed, pensioners and people unable to work

During the 1950s and 1960s, UK politics appeared to be all about social class. Middle-class voters (A, B and C1 voters) tended to support the Conservative Party, and working class voters (C2, D and E voters) tended to support Labour. This, in turn, shaped the ideas, values and cultures of the main two parties and ensured that UK politics was a battle between conservatism and socialism. However, since the 1970s the UK's class system has changed in significant ways. The size of the traditional working class has roughly halved, going down from two-thirds of the electorate in the 1960s to about one-third. On the other hand, the professional middle class has steadily grown, and now accounts for almost 40 per cent of the electorate. Class divisions have also become less stark, due to factors such as the expansion of home ownership, the decline of trade union membership and the general spread of individualist and materialist values. This has nevertheless occurred despite little evidence that the UK is becoming a more socially equal society. Social mobility levels have not risen since the late 1970s, and the UK is unusual amongst advanced industrial societies in having witnessed a growing gap between the rich and the poor since the 1980s.

Gender and politics

Feminism: A commitment to an improvement in the social role of women, usually reflected in a sense to promote sexual equality.

The political importance of gender was established by the emergence of the women's movement in the 1960s and early 1970s, and the growth of **feminism**. The main object of feminist criticism was the exclusion of women from public and political life, and certainly from senior positions in political parties, businesses and the unions. Key reforms that have taken place include the legalization of abortion in 1967, the introduction of equal pay legislation through the Sex Discrimination Act 1975 and the creation of an Equal Opportunities Commission. Two underlying trends have nevertheless been significant. Since the late 1970s there has been a steady increase in the number of working women, who now outnumber men in the economy as a whole, and a 'gender' gap has opened up in education whereby girls out-perform boys at every level in the educational system. On the other hand, sexual equality is still a long way from being achieved. Men continue to dominate senior positions in all professions, companies and political bodies; and, despite legislation, women's pay still lags well behind men's pay. In 2007, women earned 17 per cent less than men and 42 per cent less if they were part-time workers.

A multicultural society?

Ethnicity: A sense of loyalty towards a particular population or territorial area; ethnic bonds are cultural rather than racial.

Race and **ethnicity** first became significant in UK national politics as a result of increased immigration in the 1950s and 1960s from the country's former colonies. The number of refugees and asylum seekers arriving in the UK rose steeply during the 1990s due to political conflict and civil strife in various parts of the world, notably the former-Yugoslavia, Afghanistan, Iraq and parts of Africa, with asylum applications averaging over 37,000 a year. Further immigration has resulted from the expansion of the EU to include ten new states in 2004. Just how multicultural is the UK? In 2010, 9 per cent of the total population were non-white. However, some areas are substantially more multicultural than others. Almost half of all ethnic minority Britons live in London, which has a unique ethnic and cultural mix that makes it genuinely a 'global city'. Although the UK has never practised an official policy of **multiculturalism** (unlike countries such as Canada, Australia and New Zealand), since the 1980s it has broadly been accepted as an approach to the issue of cultural diversity. This has been reflected in an emphasis on equality and diversity in education and in public life generally, and in campaigns against discrimination and **racism**. Race and ethnicity have nevertheless been kept on the political agenda since the 1990s by the issue of asylum, and by 9/11 and the 'war on terror' generally. This latter development has led to attacks on multiculturalism in the name of community cohesion and public safety. On the other hand, such trends have also led to allegations of 'Islamophobia' and fears that 'tough' counter-terrorism measures may only end up radicalizing young Muslims.

Multiculturalism: The belief that different cultural groups have the right to respect and recognition; a positive approach to cultural diversity.

Racism: Prejudice or hostility towards others based on their ethnic or racial origins.

The UK and the world

Nation-state: A state in which the population have a shared national identity, based (usually) on the same language, religion, traditions and history.

Although the **nation-state** continues to be the main focus of political activity, all states are affected by their external environment. Indeed, it is widely argued that, in the modern 'global village', what goes on in one country is increasingly affected by actions and decisions taken in other countries or by a range of increasingly influential international organizations. In the case of UK politics, we can identify a European context and a global context.

European context

Since the UK joined what was then called the European Community in 1973, it has been impossible to discuss British politics except within a European context. Since the 1970s, the 'European project' has gone through significant changes.

Founding members (1952 ECSC; 1958 EEC and Euratom): Belgium, France, (West) Germany, Italy, Luxembourg, Netherlands. The territory of the German Democratic Republic (East Germany) was incorporated into a united Germany in 1990.

First enlargement (1973): Denmark, Ireland, United Kingdom.

Mediterranean enlargement: Greece (1981); Portugal, Spain (1986).

EFTA enlargement (1995): Austria, Finland, Sweden.

2004 enlargement: Cyprus, Czech Republic, Estonia, Hungary, Latvia, Lithuania, Malta, Poland, Slovakia, Slovenia.

2007: Bulgaria, Romania.

Key
1 Croatia
2 Bosnia and Herzegovina
3 Serbia
4 Montenegro
5 Former Yugoslav Republic of Macedonia
6 Albania
7 Switzerland
8 Moldova
9 Slovenia

Map 1.2 **Europe and EU membership**

Table 1.3   Key dates in British political history

1066	Norman conquest
1215	Magna Carta signed
1265	Simon de Montfort convened first British Parliament
1536–42	Union with Wales
1642–49	English Civil War
1688	The Glorious Revolution
1707	Union with Scotland
1801	Legislative union with Ireland
1832	Great Reform Act (beginning of the expansion of the franchise)
1914–18	First World War
1918	Votes for women (middle-class women over 30)
1922	Irish independence (Northern Ireland remained in the UK)
1928	All women given the right to vote
1939–45	Second World War
1947	Independence of India and Pakistan
1952	Queen Elizabeth II succeeds to the throne
1957–70	Independence of most of the UK's colonies
1973	The UK joins the European Community
1979	Margaret Thatcher wins first of three elections
1982	The Falklands War
1991	The Gulf War
1997 (May)	Tony Blair wins first of three elections
1997 (Sept)	Referendums in Scotland and Wales support devolution
1998	Referendum in Northern Ireland approves the Good Friday Agreement
2003 (Mar)	Beginning of the Iraq War
2005 (July)	7/7 terrorist attack on London
2008 (Sept)	The global financial crisis deepens
2010 (May)	David Cameron forms Conservative–Liberal Democrat coalition

The most important of these have been greater *integration*, through which power has been transferred from national governments to European institutions; and a continued process of *expansion*, which has seen the original six-member Community grow into an organization of 27 states, extending into post-communist Eastern Europe. The transformation of the European Community into the European Union in 1993 marked the birth of a political union with common citizenship rights, and (for most member states) monetary union in the form of the euro. EU membership has affected UK politics in a number of ways. For example:

▶ A growing body of legislation is made by EU bodies
▶ European law is now 'higher' than UK statute law, meaning that Parliament is no longer legally sovereign
▶ The European Court of Justice is now the highest court of appeal, not the House of Lords.

Nevertheless, the UK's relationship to Europe has remained problematic. The UK has remained the 'awkward partner'. Not only does the UK not participate fully in all aspects of the EU, especially through its 'opt-out' on the single currency, but (uniquely amongst EU states) there is continuing debate between and within major parties over whether European integration has gone too far. The UK, in other words, has yet to be properly reconciled to its European identity. The relationship between the UK and the EU is discussed in greater depth in Chapter 10.

Global context

Superpower: A state with overwhelming nuclear military capacity and global territorial influence; the term is usually reserved for the USA and the Soviet Union.

'Special relationship': A strong and close relationship between the UK and the USA, supposedly based on language, cultural similarities and common support for the values of capitalism and representative government.

Humanitarian intervention: Military intervention in the affairs of another state for humanitarian rather than strategic reasons.

The UK's world role has declined significantly since 1945. Once one of the 'Big Three' (the USA, the Soviet Union and the UK) that resisted Nazi aggression in the Second World War, the UK lost influence during the '**superpower** era' and as a result of de-colonization in the post-1945 period. In the famous words of the former US Secretary of State, Dean Acheson: 'Britain had lost an empire but failed to find a role'. The enduring theme in the UK's post-1945 foreign policy is the so-called '**special relationship**' between the UK and the USA. The special relationship with the USA was not a relationship of equals, however. The USA was the 'coming power'; the UK was the 'going power'. This was clearly demonstrated by the humiliation of the Suez Crisis in 1956, when UK troops were withdrawn from Egypt once the USA indicated that it did not support the joint UK, French and Israeli invasion. The Falklands War of 1982 only went ahead because of covert political and technical support that was provided by Washington. The fall of the Soviet Union in 1989–91, and the emergence of the USA as the world's only superpower, has only strengthened Atlanticist tendencies in UK foreign policy. This was reflected, for instance, in the strong support that Blair gave to the USA in the aftermath of 9/11 and, in particular, in the UK's involvement in the 2003 Iraq War. The progress of this war has nevertheless presented future UK governments with the challenge of how to maintain the special relationship without merely becoming an instrument of US foreign policy. However, Cameron's role in advocating **humanitarian intervention** in Libya in 2011 showed that the UK's foreign involvements are now not necessarily dependent on US global leadership.

World politics, however, has changed in important ways in recent decades. Instead of countries acting as separate and independent entities, they have increasingly been enmeshed in a web of interconnectedness. National borders have therefore become less significant. This process is usually called globalization. Economic globalization has created, to a greater or lesser extent, an interlocking global economy. Economic developments on the other side of the globe can therefore have a dramatic and almost immediate impact on the UK. Most obviously, this applies in the case of stock market crashes, which ripple through global financial markets as quickly as computer screens are able to register price changes. A further aspect of this is cultural globalization, often fuelled by the so-called information revolution, the spread of satellite communication, telecommunications

What is ... globalization

Globalization is the development of a complex web of interconnectedness that means that our lives are increasingly shaped by events that occur at a great distance from us. The central feature of globalization is that geographical distance is of declining relevance. Territorial boundaries, particularly those between nation-states, have also become less important; states have become 'permeable'.

Globalization has taken three contrasting forms:

▶ *Economic* globalization is the absorption of national economies into a single global economy
▶ *Cultural* globalization is the process whereby cultural differences between nations and regions tend to be 'flattened out'
▶ *Political* globalization reflects the growing importance of international bodies and organizations.

Global governance: The capacity of international bodies such as the UN, NATO, the World Bank and the WTO to co-ordinate world affairs and influence the actions of states.

networks, information technology and the Internet, and global media corporations. This has greatly increased people's awareness of, and interest in, political developments in other parts of the world. A final 'face' of globalization is political globalization, reflected in the growth of **global governance**. The World Trade Organization (WTO), for instance, has become a particularly controversial institution through its role in promoting free trade.

Globalization has affected UK politics in a variety of ways. For example:

▶ Business group power has increased as major corporations have been able to relocate production and investments more easily.
▶ Increased global competition has created pressure to cut business taxes, reduce welfare spending and increase the flexibility of labour markets.
▶ Neo-liberal or free-market economic ideas have been accepted by all major parties.
▶ Issues such as climate change and global poverty have become more prominent, helping to create influential protest movements.

UK Politics: an overview

The Westminster model

The UK has traditionally been viewed as the classical example of 'Westminster model' government. It is a model that it has exported, to a greater or lesser extent, to other countries, especially former colonies. The Westminster model is so called because Parliament is central to the constitutional structure of the UK, and Parliament is located at Westminster. Most importantly, government governs in

What is ... the Westminster model

The Westminster model is a form of government in which there is a 'fusion' of power between the executive and the legislature. Although all forms of parliamentary government are sometimes called 'Westminster systems', the Westminster model goes further in concentrating government decision-making within a single body (Parliament or, in practice, the House of Commons). The main battleground of politics in the Westminster model is between the government (composed of the leaders of the largest party in the Commons) and the opposition (composed of the second largest party in the House of Commons).

and through Parliament. Government is drawn from Parliament (all ministers must be MPs or peers) and it is accountable to Parliament (Parliament can remove ministers, individually or collectively). UK government is therefore parliamentary government (see p. 213). The focal point of political conflict in the UK has traditionally been the House of Commons (the elected chamber of Parliament), where the government does battle with the opposition.

The Westminster model in the UK is upheld by a number of factors:

▶ The UK's uncodified or 'unwritten' constitution means that Parliament is legally supreme: it can make, unmake and amend any law it wishes.
▶ Ministers are accountable to, and removable by, Parliament.
▶ The 'first-past-the-post' voting system usually creates strong, single-party government.
▶ The unelected House of Lords has weak powers and cannot effectively challenge the Commons.
▶ Local government is firmly subordinate to central government.
▶ There is a limited role for judges, who certainly cannot challenge Parliament's authority.

However, since the 1980s, a variety of developments have tended to move the UK political system away from its traditional focus on the 'Westminster village'. New political arenas and processes have developed to complement or compete with the party-political battle in the Commons. The UK political system therefore has become increasingly complex and pluralized. This has occurred not least through the constitutional reforms that were introduced by the Labour governments 1997–2010, and those introduced by the Conservative-led coalition since 2010 (see Chapter 6). The most important of these trends include the following:

▶ As prime ministers have become more 'presidential', they have distanced themselves from Parliament and their party.

▶ European integration has allowed a growing range of policies to be made by EU institutions, rather than national governments.

▶ Devolution to Scotland, Wales and Northern Ireland has meant that important decisions are increasingly made by devolved bodies, not by the Westminster Parliament.

▶ The beginning of the reform of the House of Lords has encouraged the Lords to be more assertive in challenging the Commons, with a growing prospect of more radical reform.

▶ The wider use of referendums has allowed the public to take decision-making authority away from Parliament.

▶ More proportional electoral systems have been introduced for devolved and other bodies, with the Westminster electoral system coming under greater pressure.

▶ Judges have been more willing to challenge ministers and even question Acts of Parliament.

Key themes in UK politics

Two major and interconnected themes have emerged in contemporary UK politics. These themes link the various chapters and parts of this book. They are:

▶▶ The decline of civic engagement
▶▶ The changing constitutional structure.

Declining civic engagement

Concerns about civic engagement in the UK have largely arisen from the fact that fewer and fewer people are bothering to vote. The 2001 and 2005 general elections saw the lowest turnout levels (at 59 per cent and 61 per cent, respectively) since 1918. Although the turnout rose in the 2010 general election to 65 per cent, this remains low by historical standards. In the case of 2005, the combination of a low turnout and declining support for the Labour Party meant that only just over one-fifth of the electorate voted for the government of the day. Further evidence of growing apathy and a disillusionment with conventional politics can be found in a steady decline in the number of people joining political parties and in opinion polls that show falling levels of trust in government and in politicians generally.

Such trends and how they can be countered are themes that link the chapters in this part of the book. These chapters consider the so-called 'participation crisis' in UK politics and the idea of democratic renewal in the UK (Chapter 2); the role of elections (Chapter 3); the nature of party politics, and the ideas and policies of the major parties (Chapter 4); and the role and significance of pressure groups (Chapter 5).

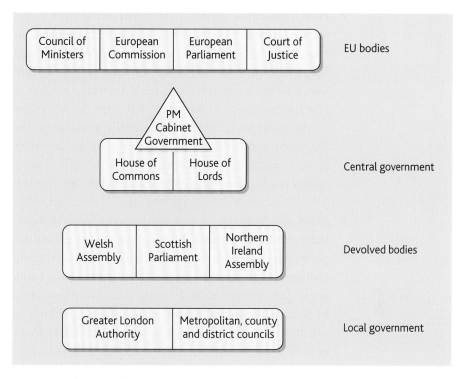

Figure 1.1 **The UK political system**

Changing constitutional structure

UK politics is currently in an unusual state of flux. Since 1997, the UK political system has changed more rapidly than at any time since the 17th century. Devolved assemblies have been introduced, creating a kind of 'quasi-federal' structure within the UK. The process of reforming the House of Lords has been started, and, having been started, further reform now appears to be inevitable (even if the timing is questionable). Referendums have been more widely used, leading to the expectation that future constitutional changes will be approved directly by the people and not just by Parliament. Proportional voting systems are now widely used in different parts of the UK. The Human Rights Act 1998 has given the UK, for the first time, a framework of individual rights that are written into statute law. The list goes on.

Such reforms have already changed the relationships between and among the institutions of government in significant, and permanent, ways. But they have also created a momentum for change that may be irresistible – constitutional reform is a process, not an event. However, two significant questions have been raised by these developments:

▶ **How fragmented should government power be?** On the one hand, there are those who favour fragmented or divided government on the grounds that it creates a network of checks and balances (see p. 186) that protect freedom and keep government 'off our backs'. On the other hand, there are those who warn that fragmented government leads to weakness and confusion, leaving a government that is at war with itself. This debate is relevant, amongst other things, to the relationship between Parliament and the executive, and between the Lords and the Commons (Chapter 7), to the relationship between the prime minister and the cabinet (Chapter 8), and to the relationship between central government and devolved assemblies and the EU (Chapter 10).

▶ **What should be the relationship between law and politics?** On the one hand, there are those who wish to strengthen the role of law, in order to ensure that government power is not abused and, in particular, that individual rights and civil liberties (see p. 286) are protected. On the other hand, there are those who argue that politics should always take precedence over law, quite simply because politicians are elected whereas judges are both unelected and socially unrepresentative. This debate is relevant, amongst other things, to the nature of the constitution and the idea of a codified constitution (Chapter 6); and the role of the judiciary and the possibility of a UK bill of rights (Chapter 9).

WHAT YOU SHOULD KNOW

▶▶ Politics, most broadly, is the activity through which people make, uphold and revise the general rules under which they live. Politics arises from the basic fact of conflict. It seeks to provide ways in which people with different ideas, values and interests can live together peacefully within the same society.

▶▶ Government is a set of institutions through which the general rules of society are made and enforced. Systems of government can be categorized as either limited or authoritarian, or as democratic or autocratic. Liberal democracy has become the form of government most commonly found in the modern world.

▶▶ UK politics has been shaped by major historical forces. These have included the transfer of constitutional supremacy from the Crown to Parliament in the 17th century and the advance of democracy in the 19th and early 20th centuries (under the pressures generated by industrialization). The post-1945 period has been characterized by a series of phases: the establishment of the social-democratic consensus (1945–79); the rise of Thatcherism (1979–97); and the emergence of a post-Thatcherite consensus (since 1997). The election of the Conservative-led coalition in 2010 may mark a further phase, both in terms of a shift back to anti-state policies and the greater likelihood of coalition government in the future.

▶▶ The social context of UK politics has traditionally been shaped by the impact of social class, influencing voting behaviour and the party system in particular. However, the importance of social class has declined since the 1970s, and other issues have become more prominent. These include those related to gender and the social role of women and to culture and ethnicity.

▶▶ The global context of UK politics has been increasingly influenced by Europe, especially as the EC/EU has become larger and more integrated. UK foreign policy, since 1945, has consistently stressed the importance of the 'special relationship' with the USA. However, the pressures of globalization have exposed the UK to a broader range of economic, cultural and political influences. These have tended to reduce the significance of state and geographical borders.

▶▶ Although the UK can broadly be classified as a liberal democracy, it conforms to a 'Westminster model' of government. This reflects a 'fusion' of power between the executive and Parliament. The main battleground of politics is therefore the House of Commons, where the government and the opposition confront one another. However, recent constitutional and political changes have made the UK political system increasingly complex and pluralized, bringing the Westminster model into question. The decline in civic engagement and the ongoing process of constitutional change are important themes in contemporary UK politics.

Chapter 2

Democracy and participation

PREVIEW

Defining democracy

What is democracy? Most people will have an answer to this question. After all, democracy is one of those rare political issues over which everyone seems to agree: we are all democrats. Very few of us, and even fewer politicians, are prepared to say that they are *against* democracy. But what is it that we all support? Is democracy in danger of becoming simply a 'good thing' – something we all think we believe in, but have little idea about what it is?

Democracy is, in fact, a difficult issue. On the one hand, it seems deceptively simple. Democracy is 'government *by* the people'. *Demos* is the Greek word for 'the people' or 'the many', and 'cracy' comes from *kratos*, meaning rule or power. But what does this mean in practice? What would popular rule actually look like? One problem with democracy is that there is no agreement about the form it should take. There are various models of democracy, the most common being 'direct democracy' and 'representative democracy'. Not only do these offer quite different ways in which popular rule can and should take place, but each has its own supporters and critics. What is the best form of democracy?

Further problems arise when we apply democracy to the UK. Some commentators view the UK as a model of democratic government, an example for other countries to follow. Others, however, argue that the democratic revolution has always been incomplete in the UK. They either argue that the UK political system still contains important non-democratic features, or they warn that democracy in the UK is being eroded. Who is right? And if democracy in the UK is weak or under threat, how can it be strengthened?

KEY ISSUES

- How does direct democracy differ from representative democracy?
- How does democracy work in the UK?
- What are the strengths and weaknesses of the UK's democratic system?
- Has the UK become more or less democratic in recent years?
- How could democracy in the UK be enhanced?

GETTING YOU THINKING

Birth of the 'new politics'?

Before starting the chapter, read this passage and briefly consider the questions on the next page.

The May 2010 general election resulted in the formation of a coalition government between the Conservative and Liberal Democrat parties. This was the UK's first peacetime coalition government since 1931. Do coalitions strengthen democratic rule, or undermine it? Supporters of the coalition claimed that it marked the birth of the 'new politics' in the UK. By this, they meant a form of politics that places the national interest ahead of the narrow interests of just one political party. In this view, coalitions draw people together rather than pull them apart; they force the government to respond to a wider range of views and opinions. This image is strengthened by the breadth of electoral support enjoyed by the Conservative–Liberal Democrat coalition. Between them, the coalition parties won an overall majority of votes cast in 2010 (59 per cent), something that had not been achieved in the UK since 1935.

However, while the majority of electors voted for one or other of the parties that are now in government, it is questionable whether most voters supported the formation of a coalition or its policy programme. During the election campaign, the Conservatives, Labour and the Liberal Democrats each defended their own manifestos and looked to form a government on their own. The coalition was formed *after* the election and inevitably involved a process of 'horse trading' through which the coalition partners negotiated a compromised set of policies. Each abandoned some of the policies on which it had fought the election, and also accepted certain policies that it had actively criticized. What no one knows is how many electors may have switched their votes had they been aware of the policy changes that were going to be made. The formation of a coalition undoubtedly created the impression that the government enjoys broad popular support, but this is nevertheless far from a straightforward reflection of the electoral outcome of May 2010.

One of the televised, pre-election leaders' debates in 2010 — but how meaningful did the choices on offer turn out to be?

What issues do these developments raise?

▶▶▶   How are elections supposed to bring about democracy?

▶▶▶   What is a coalition government?

▶▶▶   In what sense do coalitions strengthen democracy?

▶▶▶   How, and to what extent, do coalitions weaken democracy?

▶▶▶   Did the May 2010 general election have a 'democratic' outcome?

IN THIS CHAPTER:

Types of democracy • Democracy in the UK • Enhancing democracy

Types of democracy

Democracy is an answer to the question: who rules? Most political systems throughout history have been based either on rule by one person (monarchies, empires and dictatorships) or rule by a small group of people (elites and oligarchies). Democracy, on the other hand, is rule by the *demos*, or the people. As such, it is a revolutionary idea. Democracy means giving power to the people. In its simplest sense, democracy is 'people power'. A political system is therefore democratic if the major decisions that affect society are made, directly or indirectly, by the people themselves, with each citizen having an equal right to have a say and to make his or her opinion count (Beetham, 2005). Such an idea can be applied to any group of people in any circumstances.

For example, if a group of friends were discussing where to go in the evening, their decision would be 'democratic' if:

1 Each of them could speak freely and think for themselves
2 The views of each of them carried the same weight
3 In the event of disagreement, they decided to go where the majority of them wanted to go.

The task of understanding democracy is made more difficult by the fact that democracy comes in such a variety of shapes and forms. People talk about 'liberal democracy', 'parliamentary democracy', 'pluralist democracy'; in fact, all kinds of democracy. However, the two main types of democracy are:

▶▶ Direct democracy
▶▶ Representative democracy

Direct democracy

Direct democracy is associated with the origins of democracy itself, which are usually traced back to ancient Greece, and notably to its pre-eminent city state, or *polis*, Athens. From about 500 to 322 BCE a form of democracy operated in Athens that has served ever since as the model of 'classical' democracy. Athenian democracy (see p. 35), however, was a very particular form of democracy, quite different from the forms that are found in the modern world. In particular, it relied on a very high level of popular participation in government. Athenian citizens governed themselves through a system of popular mass meetings. Nevertheless,

What is ... democracy

Democracy is most simply defined as 'rule by the people'. Democracy is therefore based on two core principles:

▶ *Political participation*: key political decisions are made by the people. This is reflected in the idea of government *by* the people.
▶ *Political equality*: each citizen has a free and equal opportunity to influence political decisions. This is reflected in the idea of equal citizenship (see p. 54).

In practice, there are a number of competing models of democracy. Although democracy comes in a wide variety of different forms, the key distinction is between direct democracy and representative democracy (see Figure 2.1):

▶ In *direct* democracy (see p. 34), the people make political decisions themselves. The effectiveness of direct democracy is based on the extent of *popular participation* in government.
▶ In *representative* democracy (see p. 37), the people simply choose who will make decisions on their behalf. The effectiveness of representative democracy is based on the extent of *popular control* over government.

ancient Athens was, in other respects, starkly undemocratic by modern standards. The 'citizens' of Athens constituted only a tiny minority of those who lived within the city state. The groups excluded from political influence included women, men classified as 'immigrants' (despite the fact that many of them came from families that had lived in Athens for many generations) and slaves, who made up at least three-fifths of the population of Athens.

Such a form of democracy is widely considered to be quite unworkable in modern political conditions. Athenian citizens devoted a great deal of time and energy to political activity. They were also able to meet together in a single place. How can such a high level of face-to-face interaction be achieved in societies that are composed of tens or hundreds of millions of people? If citizens are expected to carry out all the tasks of government, how can they find time to engage in other activities? The answer in ancient Athens was simple: foreigners and slaves did the bulk of the work, and women looked after family life. However, the classical model of direct participation in political life has been kept alive in local government in certain parts of the world. Examples of this include township meetings in New England in the USA and the communal assemblies that operate in the smaller Swiss cantons.

Direct democracy is used in modern politics to supplement rather than replace representative democracy. However, recent years have witnessed a steady trend, evident in the UK and elsewhere, towards the wider use of direct democracy. This has occurred as representative democracies have been seen to suffer from

What is . . . direct democracy

Direct democracy (sometimes known as 'classical', 'participatory' or 'radical' democracy) is a form of democracy that is based on the direct, unmediated and continuous participation of citizens in the tasks of government. As such, it obliterates the distinction between government and the people. It is therefore a system of popular *self*-government.

The key features of direct democracy are:

▶ Popular participation is *direct* in that the people 'make' policy decisions — they do not merely choose who will rule on their behalf

▶ Popular participation is *unmediated* in that the people 'are' the government — there is no separate class of professional politicians

▶ Popular participation is *continuous* in that people engage in politics on a regular and ongoing basis — all decisions are made by the people.

Historical examples of direct democracy were found in ancient Athens and in the Paris Commune of 1871, both of which operated as forms of government by mass meeting. The most common modern form of direct democracy is the use of the **referendum**, although this is used to supplement representative democracy rather than to replace it.

Referendum: A popular vote on an issue of public policy (see p. 45).

Apathy: The absence of interest in or enthusiasm about a subject, usually reflected in inactivity.

increased voter **apathy** and growing popular disillusionment with politics. The great advantage of direct democracy is that it strengthens popular participation in government, making participation seem *meaningful* because it places power directly in the hands of the public (see Benefits of direct democracy, p. 36). An increased interest in direct democracy is apparent in the wider use of referendums in recent years and in proposals to increase popular participation through, for example, citizens' juries or electronic or digital democracy. Such trends are discussed more fully later in the chapter.

Representative democracy

Representative democracy is electoral democracy — it is a way of deciding who should decide. In a representative democracy, people acquire the power to make political decisions by means of a competitive struggle for the people's vote. Those who win elections can claim to 'represent' the people. It is therefore a form of rule by professional politicians. Whereas direct democracy is based on the principle of popular participation, representative democracy operates on the basis of popular control — ways of ensuring that professional politicians represent the people and not themselves. This is the role of elections (see Chapter 3). The public chooses, through the ballot box, who will rule on their behalf. Most importantly, this makes it possible to 'kick the rascals out'. Politicians therefore know that they can

FOCUS ON . . .
Democracy in ancient Athens

▸ The sovereign body in the Athenian system of government was the Assembly, or *Ecclesia*. This met at least 40 times a year and was composed entirely of male citizens over 20 years of age. All major issues were debated and decided at these meetings, ranging from matters of public order and taxation to foreign policy and military affairs. The size of the Assembly dwarfed modern legislatures: it had a **quorum** of 6,000.

▸ When full-time officials were needed, they were chosen on the basis of lot or rota (an idea maintained in the '**jury principle**'), to ensure that they resembled as closely as possible the larger body of citizens. Terms of office were also typically kept short to allow as many citizens as possible to hold them.

▸ A Council consisting of 500 citizens acted as the executive or steering committee of the Assembly, and a 50-strong Committee, in turn, made proposals to the Council. The President of the Committee held office for only a single day, and no Athenian could hold this honour more than once in his lifetime.

Quorum: The minimum number of people whose presence is required for proper or valid decisions to be taken.

Jury principle: The idea that a randomly chosen group of people can express the views of the wider public (their peers).

only win or retain power if they serve the people. If they fail to do so, they will be removed. But not all elections are 'democratic' elections.

The basic condition for representative democracy is the existence of democratic elections. These are elections that are based on the following rules:

▸ Free, fair and regular elections: voters can express their own views
▸ Universal suffrage: all adults can vote
▸ Party and candidate competition: voters have a choice.

Representative democracy is the dominant form of democracy in the modern world. It is, in fact, the core feature of liberal democracy (see p. 10), the most

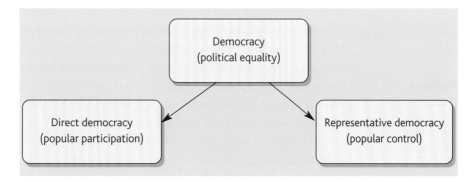

Figure 2.1 Types of democracy

FOCUS ON . . .
Benefits of direct democracy

▶ **Genuine democracy:** Direct democracy is the only pure form of democracy, as it ensures that people only obey laws that they make themselves. Popular participation in government is the very stuff of freedom: it is how the people determine their collective destiny, their 'general will'. Representative democracy always means that there is a gulf between government and the people.

▶ **Personal development:** Direct democracy creates better informed and more knowledgeable citizens. In this sense, it has educational benefits. Direct and regular popular participation in government encourages people to take more interest in politics and to better understand their own society – both how it works and how it *should* work.

▶ **End of professional politics:** Direct democracy reduces, or removes, the public's dependence on self-serving professional politicians. Representative democracy places too much faith in politicians, who are always liable to distort public opinion by imposing their own views and preferences on it. It therefore amounts to 'government by politicians', acting only in the *name* of the people.

▶ **Legitimate government:** Direct democracy ensures that rule is legitimate, in the sense that people are more likely to accept decisions that they have made themselves. When citizens make political decisions directly, they have to take responsibility for them – there is no one else to blame. This helps to ensure stable government.

Constitutional democracy: A form of democracy that operates within a clear constitutional framework that both disperses government power and protects minorities and individuals (see p. 48).

Majoritarian democracy: A form of democracy that is based on the principle of majority rule and emphasizes the general or collective interests of society, rather than particular interests (see p. 48).

common type of regime in contemporary politics. Liberal democracy is better thought of as a special form of representative democracy. It is 'representative democracy plus limited government'. Liberal democracy balances the need for popular government (democracy) against the desire to protect the individual (freedom). However, liberal democracy is a broad idea and encompasses a range of different democratic forms, depending on the balance between democracy and freedom (see Figure 2.2). On the one hand, there is **constitutional democracy**, which places particular emphasis on upholding individual freedom and minority rights. This can be illustrated by the form of democracy that operates in the USA (see p. 51). On the other hand, there is **majoritarian democracy**, in which the views of the majority take precedence over those of the minority, and the majority effectively speaks for the people. As will be discussed later, the UK's democratic system has traditionally had clear majoritarian features.

The strength of representative democracy is that it places ultimate power in the hands of the public – the power to decide who governs – while leaving day-to-day policy-making in the hands of experts (professional politicians). It is therefore based on a compromise between the need for 'government *by* the people' (popular

What is ... representative democracy

Representative democracy (sometimes known as indirect democracy) is a limited and indirect form of democracy. It operates through the ability of representatives to speak for, or act on behalf of, the people. At the heart of representative democracy is the process through which representatives are chosen and can be removed. In practice, this is usually done through regular and popular elections.

The key features of representative democracy are:

▶ Popular participation is *indirect* — the public do not exercise power themselves; they choose (usually by election) who will rule on their behalf
▶ Popular participation is *mediated* — the people are linked to government through representative institutions
▶ Popular participation in government is *limited* — it is infrequent and brief, being restricted to the act of voting every few years.

Representative democracy usually operates though the mechanism of elections. Its effectiveness is therefore based on the extent to which the electoral process gives the people control over government.

participation) and the need for 'government *for* the people' (government in the public interest) (see Benefits of representative democracy, p. 38). However, critics allege that representative democracy is merely a form of facade democracy. The act of voting every few years is, at best, a democratic ritual; and, at worst, it benefits the government more than the people. As the anarchist slogan put it: 'Don't vote – the government always wins!'. Governments therefore govern in the name of the people, but, in practice, the people may have little meaningful control over government. Further concerns about representative democracy have arisen from confusion over exactly how representatives do their jobs. How do they 'represent'

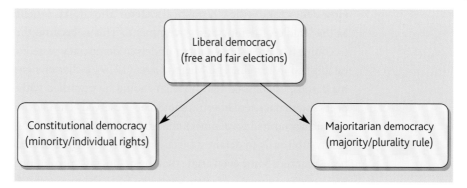

Figure 2.2 **Types of representative democracy**

FOCUS ON . . .

Benefits of representative democracy

▶ **Practicable democracy:** Direct democracy is only achievable in relatively small communities, especially in the form of government by mass meeting. Representative democracy is the only form of democracy that can operate in large, modern societies. It is therefore a practical solution to the problem of popular rule.

▶ **Government by experts:** Representative democracy places decision-making in the hands of politicians who have better education and greater expertise than the mass of the people. They can therefore govern for the people using their superior understanding to act in the public interest.

▶ **Division of labour in politics:** One of the drawbacks of direct democracy is that it

means that politics is the job for *all* citizens, restricting their ability to carry out other duties and activities. Representative democracy is more efficient because ordinary citizens are relieved of the burden of day-to-day decision-making – they simply have to choose who they want to govern them.

▶ **Political stability:** Representative democracy maintains political stability by helping to distance ordinary citizens from politics, thereby encouraging them to accept compromise. The more involved in decision-making citizens are, the more passionate and committed they may become. A certain level of apathy is helpful in maintaining political stability.

the public? By acting in their interests? By carrying out the policies on which they won the election? Or by resembling (looking like) them? The nature of representation is discussed more fully in Chapter 3.

Democracy in the UK

How democratic is the UK political system? The UK has sometimes been thought of as the 'cradle of democratic government'. This is because the political rights and freedoms that are usually said to underpin democracy were, for the most part, first established in Britain. The Magna Carta (1215), a charter signed by King John and his barons, established that no man should be punished without a trial before his peers and that ancient liberties should be preserved. The Glorious Revolution (see p. 12) further limited royal power and, for example, placed limits on the government's ability arbitrarily to detain subjects. However, the UK's democratic system has also been attacked. Some even argue that the democratic revolution in the UK has always remained incomplete – power was taken from the monarchy, but it was transferred not to the people but to ministers accountable to Parliament. This section looks at:

▶▶ The features of the UK's democratic system
▶▶ The kind of democracy that operates in the UK
▶▶ Whether the UK is suffering from a 'participation crisis'.

Features of the UK's democratic system

As a representative democracy, the effectiveness of democracy in the UK can be judged on the basis of the *control* that the public exerts over its politicians. To what extent are UK governments **publicly accountable?** However, as with much else in UK politics, the democratic system has undergone significant change in recent years. Whereas it was once possible to describe democracy in the UK largely through the role of elections and Parliament, the democratic process is now more complex and diffuse.

Public accountability: The process through which politicians are forced to answer for their actions to the public or its elected representatives; account-ability implies politicians can be removed.

Democracy in the UK has a number of features (some of which are discussed more fully in later chapters):

Core features:

▶▶ Democratic elections (see also Chapter 3)
▶▶ Parliament (see also Chapter 7)
▶▶ Pressure groups (see also Chapter 5).

Supplementary features:

▶▶ Referendums
▶▶ Devolution (see also Chapter 10)
▶▶ The European Parliament (see also Chapter 10).

Democratic elections

Elections in the UK are democratic to the extent that they are:

▶▶ Free and fair
▶▶ Based on universal suffrage
▶▶ Competitive and provide electoral choice.

Free and fair elections

The basis for free and fair elections in Britain was laid by the gradual extension of political rights and freedoms. By the end of the 18th century, the basic civil liber-ties (see p. 286) of freedom of speech, conscience and assembly were widely accepted in the UK. As electoral democracy developed in the 19th century, these ensured that voters could think for themselves and express their own views at elec-tion time. This was supported by:

Secret ballot: A ballot in which the casting of votes is private and protected from public scrutiny.

▶ The introduction in 1872 of the **secret ballot,** which helped to bring an end to intimidation at election time.

▶ The final establishment of 'one person, one vote' in 1948, through the abolition of plural voting for business ratepayers and graduates of Oxford and Cambridge universities.

▶ The use of proportional representation (see pp. 71–8) for elections to the political bodies that have been created since 1997.

▶ The establishment in 2000 of the Electoral Commission, whose aim is to ensure the integrity of, and public confidence in, the UK's democratic processes.

Fixed-term Parliaments: A parliamentary term whose length is fixed, meaning that the date of the next general election is pre-determined.

▶ The proposed introduction of **fixed-term Parliaments** to prevent governments from calling general elections at times that favour their own prospects of winning, although their democratic credentials have been questioned (see p. 267).

However, the fairness of the electoral process in the UK has also been questioned:

▶ *Non-elected bodies.* Some key political posts in the UK are not filled through elections. The most obvious examples are the monarchy and the House of Lords, neither of which enjoy democratic legitimacy.

▶ *The Westminster voting system.* The 'first-past-the-post' system used for elections to the House of Commons has been criticized for distorting electoral preferences and creating a system of plurality rule (in which governments win fewer than half of the votes cast).

▶ *Electoral malpractice.* The use of postal ballots in general elections and local elections in recent years has been associated with more frequent allegations of electoral malpractice.

Universal suffrage

Elections in the UK became democratic through the progressive extension of the franchise, until the eventual achievement of universal adult suffrage in 1928. The main steps on the UK's road to democracy are shown below.

Table 2.1	The UK's road to democracy
1832	The Great Reform Act abolished 'rotten boroughs', with either no electors or a few electors controlled by a rich patron and granted voting rights to middle-class property owners (before 1832, fewer than 5 per cent of people could vote)
1867	The vote was extended to many skilled male manual workers
1884	The vote was extended to virtually all male householders and tenants
1918	All men over 21 and middle-class women over the age of 30 could vote
1928	Equal voting rights for women and men
1969	The voting age was reduced from 21 to 18

FOCUS ON . . .
The Electoral Commission

The Electoral Commission was established by the Political Parties, Elections and Referendums Act 2000 (PPERA). It is an independent body, charged both with reviewing the operation of the UK's democratic processes and with making recommendations for strengthening democracy. The Electoral Commission has a number of key responsibilities. It:

▶ Reports on elections and referendums
▶ Sets the standards for running elections and reports on how well this is done
▶ Must be consulted on changes to election law and electoral procedures
▶ Comments on the intelligibility of referendum questions and oversees their conduct

▶ Registers political parties
▶ Makes sure people understand and follow the rules on election finance, as outlined in the PPERA and elsewhere
▶ Publishes details of where parties and candidates get money from and how they spend it
▶ Makes sure people understand it is important to register to vote and know how to vote.

Weblink ■ www.aboutmyvote.co.uk

Use this website to find out more about the role, objectives and achievements of the Electoral Commission.

However, the extent of universal suffrage in the UK has also been questioned:

▶ *The 'unenfranchised'.* Until recently, the requirement that people on the electoral register have a home effectively prevented homeless people from voting. Members of the House of Lords, imprisoned convicts (although this has been challenged by the European Court of Human Rights) and the mentally incapable are legally ineligible to vote.
▶ *Non-voting.* A universal *right* to vote does not ensure universal participation. The quality of democracy is impaired by the fact that non-voting is most common amongst the poor and the disadvantaged, and by declining turnout levels in recent years, as discussed later.

Electoral choice

Electoral choice is vital to democracy as it allows electors to vote for the people or policies that they most prefer. No choice or little choice means that electors have to vote for what is available. Electoral choice is ensured through competition between candidates and parties. The UK has a long tradition of competitive party politics. The Conservative and Liberal parties developed during the 19th century, with the Labour Party emerging at the beginning of the 20th century. Since the 1960s, there has been a proliferation of political parties, with, for example, the strengthening of the Scottish National Party (SNP) and Plaid Cymru, and the emergence of parties such as the Greens and the UK Independence Party (UKIP). Multiparty political systems now exist in many parts of the UK – for example, in Scotland, Wales, Northern Ireland and London.

However, the effectiveness of party competition in promoting democracy has also been questioned:

▶ *The two-party system*. Voters have little effective choice in general elections because a two-party system has usually existed at Westminster. Labour and Conservative parties have been the main parties of government.

▶ *Consensus politics*. The tendency in the UK towards consensus politics (discussed in Chapter 4) means that there may be very little to choose between the policies of the major parties.

Parliament

As the only popularly elected institution in UK central government, Parliament lies (in theory at least) at the heart of the democratic process. The UK is therefore a parliamentary democracy (see p. 43). Parliament is the main institution that links government to the people. It does this by upholding what is called representative and responsible government. Parliament ensures *representative* government because the dominant chamber of Parliament, the House of Commons, is elected. MPs are meant to represent their constituencies, and the House of Commons serves as the debating chamber of the nation. One of the virtues of Parliament is therefore that it maintains **deliberative democracy**. Parliament ensures *responsible* government in that it oversees and scrutinizes the actions of government. Governments only survive if they continue to enjoy the support of the House of Commons.

However, the effectiveness of Parliament in promoting democracy has also been questioned:

▶ *The House of Lords*. The second chamber of Parliament, the House of Lords, is entirely unelected. This weakens the representative role of Parliament.

▶ *The party system*. Party discipline prevents MPs from using their own judgement in representing their constituents. It also restricts freedom of debate and voting in the House of Commons (see How party unity is maintained, p. 216).

▶ *Executive control*. Parliament's ability to scrutinize the executive is weak because the government of the day usually has majority control of the House of Commons.

Pressure groups

Pressure groups (see p. 139) link government to the governed in a variety of ways. For example:

▶ They give a political voice to minorities that are ignored by the majoritarian parliamentary system

Deliberative democracy: A form of democracy in which the public interest is decided through debate, discussion and argument, amongst either representatives or private citizens.

What is... parliamentary democracy

Parliamentary democracy is a form of democracy that operates through a popularly elected deliberative assembly, which establishes an indirect link between government and the governed. Democracy, in this sense, is essentially a system of representative and responsible government. Parliamentary democracy balances popular participation against elite rule. Government is accountable not directly to the public but to the public's elected representatives (see Figure 2.3).

▶ They provide a way in which citizens can exert influence between elections
▶ They provide an important vehicle for political participation beyond the ritualistic act of voting.

In these ways, pressure groups help to supplement forms of democracy that operate through elections and Parliament. Some, indeed, go further and argue that **pluralist democracy** may be in the process of displacing parliamentary democracy in the UK. While turnout in elections is falling, the membership of pressure groups has been steadily rising since the 1960s.

However, the effectiveness of pressure groups in promoting democracy has also been questioned (see pp. 158–62 for a fuller discussion of pressure groups and democracy):

▶ *Concentrated power.* Pressure groups may concentrate political power, rather than distribute it more widely. Financially powerful pressure groups may be able to 'buy' influence through funding political parties. Particular concern has been expressed about the power of business groups.

Pluralist democracy:
A form of democracy that operates through the capacity of organized groups to articulate popular demands and ensure government responsiveness (see p. 158).

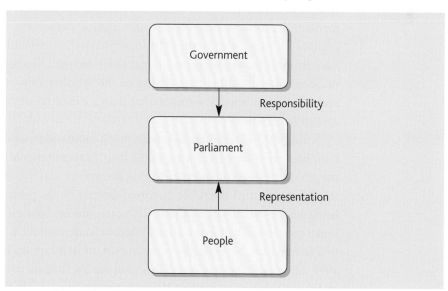

Figure 2.3 **Parliamentary democracy**

Table 2.2 Major referendums since 1997

When	Where	Issue	Result	Turnout
1997	Scotland	Establishment of a Scottish Parliament	'Yes' (74%)	60%
		Give the Parliament tax varying powers	'Yes' (64%)	
1997	Wales	Establishment of a National Assembly for Wales	'Yes' (50%)	50%
1998	Northern Ireland	Belfast (or Good Friday) Agreement, including establishment of a Northern Ireland Assembly	'Yes' (72%)	80%
1998	London	Establishment of a Greater London Authority	'Yes' (72%)	34%
2004	Northeast England	Establishment of an elected assembly for Northeast England	'No' (78%)	48%
2011	Wales	Give the Welsh Assembly primary legislative powers	'Yes' (63%)	35%
2011	UK	Introduction of AV for Westminster elections	'No' (68%)	42%

▶ *Undermining of Parliament.* Pressure groups often bypass Parliament and so undermine the representative process. This weakens the role of elected MPs.

▶ *Unaccountable power.* Pressure group leaders are not elected, meaning that they are not democratically accountable. Also, few pressure groups are internally democratic.

Referendums

The use of referendums was traditionally frowned upon in the UK. They were seen as somehow 'not British', because they conflicted with the principles of parliamentary democracy. Referendums diminished Parliament and undermined its popular authority. On the other hand, supporters of referendums argue that they have strong advantages over elections. These include allowing the public to make decisions directly, rather than relying on the 'wisdom' of professional politicians; and focusing on specific issues, rather than a broad set of policies. (See For and against referendums p. 53.)

Since 1997, referendums have been much more widely used in the UK. This has been because of the prominence of the issue of constitutional reform, especially in the period 1997–2001, and the growing acceptance that major changes to the way the UK is governed should be endorsed directly by the public rather than simply being left for Parliament to decide. This may, indeed, have created a new constitutional convention that major constitutional changes should in future always be put to a referendum. Nevertheless, some important referendums had been held before 1997. The most important one ever held in the UK (both in terms of its implications and the fact that it was the first UK-wide referendum) was the 1975 referendum on continued membership of the European Community. This referendum also illus-

What is ... a referendum

Plebiscite: Literally, a popular vote; equivalent to a referendum.

A referendum (sometimes called a **plebiscite**) is a vote in which the electorate can express a view on a particular issue of public policy. It differs from an election in that the latter is essentially a means of filling a public office and does not provide a direct or reliable method of influencing the content of policy. The referendum is therefore a device of direct democracy.

Referendums may be either advisory or binding. They may be used to raise issues for discussion rather than to decide or confirm policy questions, in which case they have been called 'propositions'. Whereas most referendums are called by the government, '**initiatives**' (used especially in Switzerland and California) are a form of referendum that can be brought about by citizens.

Initiative: A procedure, usually using a petition, through which the public can call a referendum or force politicians to consider a legislative proposal.

trated the fact that the decision to call a referendum is never unrelated to considerations of political advantage. For the then Prime Minister, Harold Wilson, the 1975 EC referendum was, in part, a device to hold together a Labour Party that was deeply divided over Europe. Referendums were also held in Scotland and Wales in 1979, in an unsuccessful attempt to introduce devolution.

The election in 2010 of a Conservative–Liberal Democrat coalition gave renewed impetus to the use of referendums. The coalition's programme for government, published in May 2010 contained commitments to hold referendums on five issues. These were:

▶ The introduction of the alternative vote (AV) (see p. 80) system for Westminster elections, in place of the 'first-past-the-post' system
▶ Any further transfer of power to Brussels (presumably through new EU treaties, although this is unclear)
▶ Further Welsh devolution, specifically giving the Welsh Assembly primary legislative powers
▶ The creation of directly elected mayors in the 12 largest English cities
▶ The possibility of local referendums on any local issue, instigated by residents.

Why have referendums once again become more common? Part of the answer is that the participation of the Liberal Democrats in the coalition ensured that there would be revived interest in the issue of constitutional reform; and, in the light of practice since 1997, any significant constitutional reforms will need to be publicly endorsed. The Liberal Democrats have also been more openly committed than either the Labour or Conservative parties to the use of referendums on principled grounds, linked to the promotion of democracy. However, these commitments on referendums were not merely a consequence of constitutional or principled considerations. Concerns about practical issues, notably those related to coalition management, were at least as important.

For example, in the case of the AV referendum, its attraction for Liberal Democrats was that it created the possibility that the 'first-past-the-post' electoral system could be replaced, whereas for many Conservatives the referendum had the advantage that a 'no' vote would allow 'first-past-the-post' to survive. Similarly, support in the Conservative Party for a referendum on any further transfer of power to Brussels is based on the desire to slow down, or block, the process of European integration, by imposing a so-called 'referendum lock' that would prevent a UK government from ratifying an EU treaty without holding a referendum. Liberal Democrats, on the other hand, have generally favoured the idea of such referendums on the grounds that they may help to build public support for further EU integration. In other words, the coalition partners may be united in their desire to hold a referendum, but be divided over the desired outcome. The referendum may therefore, once again, serve as a mechanism for holding together a divided governing party or, in this case, a coalition government containing rival goals or aspirations.

Devolution

The creation in 1998 of a Scottish Parliament, a Welsh Assembly and, as part of the Good Friday Agreement, a Northern Ireland Assembly strengthened democracy in three main ways:

▶ It gave the constituent nations of the UK their own political voice for the first time. The representation of distinctive Scottish, Welsh and Northern Irish interests through Parliament was always inadequate because English MPs dominate the House of Commons.
▶ It refined representative democracy by allowing voters in Scotland, Wales and Northern Ireland separately to express views about 'national' issues (via devolved bodies) and about 'state' or UK issues (via Parliament).
▶ It widened the opportunities available for political participation and, in so doing, strengthened civic engagement and political education.

However, the effectiveness of devolution in promoting democracy has also been questioned:

▶ *Limited powers*. Devolution stops well short of 'home rule' or full self-government. Although the powers of devolved bodies have, in some cases, widened (see Chapter 10), major economic and foreign policy decisions are still made at Westminster and in Whitehall.
▶ *The English question*. Devolution has done nothing to advance representative democracy in England, where about 84 per cent of the UK's population live.

The European Parliament

The final feature of the UK's democratic system is the opportunity UK citizens have to exert popular influence within the European Union. This is done through elections to the European Parliament. Direct elections to the European Parliament were introduced in 1979, and these are fixed-term elections that take place every five years. Moreover, since 1999 European Parliament elections have been conducted on the basis of a proportional electoral system that represents parties more fairly and gives small parties (such as the Greens and UKIP) a better chance of being elected.

However, the effectiveness of European Parliament elections in promoting democracy in the UK has been questioned:

▶ *Democratic deficit*. The European Parliament is the weakest of the EU institutions, with little policy-making influence and only limited effective control over the European Commission. The EU therefore suffers from a 'democratic deficit' (see p. 323).

▶ *Rule from Brussels*. Growing EU influence over UK politics has been interpreted as a threat to the sovereign power of Parliament and thus to the capacity of the UK to function as an independent democratic state.

Weblink ■ www.democraticaudit.com

Use this website to follow debates over democracy in the modern UK. Democratic Audit is a research and advocacy organization that monitors the effectiveness of democracy and human rights in the UK and internationally.

What kind of democracy?

It is very difficult to monitor the health of democracy in the UK. This is because of confusions over the nature of democracy itself. If democracy is 'being threatened' or 'being promoted', what *kind* of democracy is being referred to? This is illustrated by the issue of 'new politics', examined at the beginning of the chapter.

The UK has traditionally conformed to the principles of majoritarian democracy. The 'majoritarian' bias in UK politics occurs for a number of reasons. It is largely a consequence of the UK's Westminster model (see p. 23) of government, and the tendency for power to be concentrated in the hands of ministers accountable to Parliament. Once a government has majority control over the House of Commons, little stands in the way of its interpretation of the public interest. When he was home secretary in 2006, Jack Straw dubbed this form of democracy 'executive democracy'.

However, when democracy in the UK is criticized, it is often from the perspective of constitutional democracy. Although the UK system is effective in ensuring **majority rule** – or, because of the Westminster electoral system, 'plurality rule' –

Majority rule: The rule that the views or interests of the majority should take precedence over those of the minority, as the majority speak for the people.

Differences between . . .

MAJORITARIANISM AND CONSTITUTIONAL DEMOCRACY

Majoritarian democracy	Constitutional democracy
Protects society	Protects the individual
Parliamentary sovereignty	Divided sovereignty
Majoritarian elections	Proportional elections
Single-party rule	Coalitions
Centralized government	Fragmented government

it is less effective in protecting minority groups or individual freedom. This can be seen in the issue of terrorism, where public order has, since 2001, been protected by a series of anti-terror laws, but these have (arguably) threatened the interests of the Muslim community and violated civil liberties (such issues are discussed further in Chapter 9). Debates over democracy in the UK are therefore often debates about the respective merits of majoritarian and constitutional democracy.

A participation crisis?

Perhaps the main modern concern about democracy in the UK stems from evidence of growing political apathy. Some have seen this as nothing less than a 'participation crisis'. How can democracy be healthy when, despite opportunities for participation, more and more citizens seem to be uninterested or unwilling to engage in political life? This has been most evident in the declining rates of voter turnout and falling levels of party membership.

Trends in voter turnout have highlighted particular concerns:

▸ In the period between 1945 and 1992, the average turnout in UK general elections usually remained above 75 per cent, with a post-war high of 84 per cent being achieved in 1950.

▸ In 1997, the turnout was 71 per cent, which meant the Blair government's 'landslide' victory was won with half a million fewer votes than John Major's 21-seat victory in 1992.

▸ The 2001 general election recorded a turnout of 59 per cent, the lowest figure since 1918.

▸ The turnout in 2005 rose marginally to 61 per cent, probably as a consequence of the widespread use of postal voting. It, anyway, constituted the second lowest turnout figure since 1918.

▸ Although the turnout in 2010 rose again, to 65 per cent, this was still more than 10 per cent below the 1945–92 average and occurred despite (by contrast with 2001 and 2005) the closeness of the contest and the first use of televised leaders' debates.

Similar trends are also apparent in the membership of the UK's main political parties:

▶ Labour Party membership has fallen from more than 1 million in the mid-1950s to around 166,000 in 2009.

▶ Conservative Party membership has fallen from an estimated 2.8 million in the mid-1950s to around 250,000 in 2009.

▶ By 2007, fewer than 1 per cent of people across the UK belonged to political parties, down from 7 per cent some 50 years before.

Declining party membership is also mirrored by a decline in the voters' loyalty towards political parties and the extent to which they 'identify' with them. The trend towards what is called partisan dealignment (see p. 89) has seen a significant shift from regular and habitual voting patterns in the UK to more volatile and less predictable ones.

However, the idea of a 'participation crisis' in UK politics has also been criticized. The problem may not so much be a decline in the overall level of political participation but, rather, that there has been a shift from one kind of participation to another. In particular, as disillusionment and cynicism with party politics have grown, there has been an upsurge of interest in pressure-group politics and protest movements. Such trends are looked at more closely in Chapters 5 and 6. Nevertheless, voter apathy cannot be dismissed so lightly. As a representative democracy, elections are the cornerstone of democracy in the UK. The level of electoral turnout must therefore be an important indication of the health of the larger democratic system.

Explaining declining participation

Who, or what, is to blame for declining participation rates, and particularly for falling electoral turnout? A number of possible explanations have been advanced. It is possible to blame the public, the mass media and the politicians. (The issue of declining voter turnout is discussed more fully on pp. 92–4.)

▶ **Blame the public.** Are 'we' the problem? This is certainly suggested by the fact that in recent years almost all mature democracies have, to a greater or lesser extent, experienced difficulties in mobilizing their electorates. A widely discussed explanation for growing disengagement with politics is the idea that '**social capital**' (Putnam, 2000) has declined. This reflects the impact of the growth of individualism and materialism in an increasingly consumerist society. People are more concerned about themselves and their family and friends, and less concerned about the larger society – and, indeed, other people. Falling party membership and electoral turnout may therefore simply be part of a larger process that has seen, for example, steady declines in church attendance and union membership.

Social capital: The levels of trust and sense of social connectedness that help to promote stability, cohesion and prosperity; what turns the 'I' into the 'we'.

▶ **Blame the media.** The mass media is sometimes charged with having created a climate of cynicism amongst the public, leading to a growing popular disenchantment with politics generally, and a lack of trust in governments and politicians of all complexions (Lloyd, 2004). The UK, indeed, is often seen as the most advanced example of a media-driven 'culture of contempt', best reflected in the tabloid press. This has occurred, at least in part, because increasingly intense commercial pressures have forced the media to make their coverage of politics 'sexy' and attention-grabbing. Routine political debate and policy analysis therefore receive less and less attention, as the media focus instead on – or 'hype' – scandals of various kinds and allegations of incompetence, policy failure or simple inertia. Leading politicians have, as a result, simply become fodder for either 'good news' or, more commonly, 'bad news' stories.

▶ **Blame the politicians.** The most common explanation of political disengagement is that it is caused by politicians themselves. But why are modern politicians held in such low regard? A variety of explanations have been put forward:

> ▶ *Lack of vision.* It is often argued that modern politicians and political parties now believe in nothing except getting elected. Politics has become an end in itself, and being a politician has become just another professional career. Modern politicians lack vision, a sense of moral purpose and direction. This reflects the shift from programmatic political parties to so-called 'catch-all' parties, as discussed in Chapter 4.

> ▶ *Age of 'spin'.* One of the consequences of the modern media-obsessed age is that politicians have become over-concerned about communication and news management. This is reflected in the growth of so-called '**spin**'. Modern politics is therefore all about presentation – how things *appear*, not how they *are*. This, in turn, creates at least the impression that politicians are less trustworthy, more willing to be 'economical with the truth'.

> ▶ *Lack of choice.* Interest in politics generally, and in voting in particular, may be influenced by the political and ideological divide between the major parties. Does the outcome of the election matter? In this light, declining participation rates may be linked to the growth of 'consensus politics'. This has happened as both the Labour and Conservative parties have distanced themselves from their traditional ideologies and increasingly respond to the same group of 'middle England' voters.

> ▶ *Electoral strategies.* The growing tendency for political parties to 'target' key voters and key seats in an election (discussed in Chapter 3) may also have contributed to declining overall levels of turnout. Although there is evidence that such strategies are effective, they also mean that the mass of voters in the majority of seats are increasingly ignored by parties at election time.

Spin: A biased portrayal of an event or information designed to elicit a favourable or unfavourable response.

BY COMPARISON . . .

Democracy in the USA

The US democratic system differs from the UK's in a number of ways. These include the following:

- The USA has a system of so-called 'Madisonian democracy' (named after James Madison (1751–1836), one of the 'founding fathers' of the US Constitution). This attempts to make government responsive to competing minorities by creating a network of checks and balances among elected bodies. These are the House of Representatives and the Senate, the two chambers of Congress, the presidency and the (now 50) state governments. None of these bodies can claim a monopoly of popular authority; the public interest is established through competition between and amongst them.

- The 'liberal' features of US liberal democracy are more prominent than its 'democratic' features. The effectiveness of democracy in the USA is undermined by factors such as the relatively recent arrival of universal suffrage (many Southern blacks could not vote until the 1960s); traditionally low electoral turnouts (barely 50 per cent in presidential elections), with non-voting being highest among black and poor Americans; and electoral choice being restricted to but two ideologically similar parties, the Republicans and the Democrats.

- The USA nevertheless has a strong tradition of grass-roots democracy. This is reflected in the election of a wide range of local officials (from judges to, sometimes, dog catchers), the provision in some states for recall elections and the increasingly wide use of popular initiatives and propositions.

Enhancing democracy

As criticisms of the UK's democratic system have increased, a growing debate has emerged about how democracy can best be protected or enhanced. In particular, how can the decline in electoral turnout and other forms of participation be reversed? Some of the proposed reforms are discussed in other chapters. This applies, for instance, to the issue of electoral reform (discussed in Chapter 3) and the possibility of an elected second chamber (discussed in Chapter 7). Other key proposals include:

▶▶ Referendums and other forms of direct participation
▶▶ Lowering the voting age
▶▶ Compulsory voting
▶▶ Digital democracy.

Referendums and other forms of direct participation

Many supporters of direct democracy argue that the best way of getting greater popular involvement in politics is through the wider use of referendums or initiatives. One of the current weaknesses of referendums is the absence of popular control over when and where they will be used. This creates the suspicion that governments will only call referendums on issues which they support and when they are confident of winning. For example, the promised referendums on an alternative to the Westminster electoral system (in Labour's 1997 manifesto) and the referendum on the EU constitutional reform treaty, which became the Lisbon Treaty (in Labour's 2005 manifesto), never took place. However, this problem can be overcome by establishing processes through which citizens can initiate referendums, usually by getting the required number of signatures on a petition. Such initiatives have been increasingly widely used in the USA. They can be used either to give the public the power of veto over legislation or to force legislators to consider policy proposals.

However, referendums are by no means the only form of direct democracy available. The Labour governments, 1997–2010; have placed an increasing emphasis on the use of **focus groups** and opinion polls. These can be viewed as devices of direct democracy, in that they both rely on the views of a small sample

Focus group: A small cross-section of people who are used to gain insight into the wider public views.

FOR OR AGAINST?

REFERENDUMS

FOR	AGAINST
Direct democracy. Being a device of direct democracy, referendums give the general public direct and unmediated control over government decision-making. This ensures that the public's views and interests are properly and accurately articulated, and not distorted by politicians who claim to 'represent' them.	**Ill-informed decisions**. By comparison with elected politicians, the general public is ill-informed, poorly educated and lacks political experience. The public's interests are therefore best safeguarded by a system of 'government by politicians' rather than any form of popular self-government.
Political education. By widening the opportunities for political participation, and allowing debate to focus on a particular issue, referendums help to create a better informed, more educated and more politically engaged electorate. Members of the public have a stronger incentive to think and act politically.	**Weakens Parliament**. The use of referendums does not strengthen democracy; rather, at best, it substitutes direct democracy for parliamentary democracy. This not merely undermines the vital principle of parliamentary sovereignty (see p. 180), but also means that decisions are not made on the basis of careful deliberation and debate.
Responsive government. Referendums make government more responsive by forcing them to listen to public opinion between elections. Moreover, they allow public opinion to be expressed on a particular issue, something that is difficult to achieve via elections and impossible to achieve if all parties agree on an issue.	**Irresponsible government**. Referendums allow governments to absolve themselves of responsibility by handing decisions over to the electorate. As governments are elected to govern, they should both make policy decisions and be made publicly accountable for their decisions.
Reduced government power. Referendums provide a much needed check on government power, because the government has less control over their outcome than it does over Parliament. Citizens are therefore protected against the danger of over-mighty government.	**Strengthens government**. Referendums may extend government power in a variety of ways. Not only do governments decide whether, when and over what issues to call referendums, they also frame the question asked ('yes' responses are usually preferred to 'no' responses) and can also dominate the publicity campaign. (However, such matters are now 'policed' by the Electoral Commission.)
Constitutional changes. It is particularly appropriate that constitutional changes should be popularly endorsed via referendums because constitutional rules affect the way the country is governed, and so are more important than ordinary laws. This also ensures that any newly created body has democratic legitimacy.	**Unreliable views**. Referendums provide only a snapshot of public opinion at one point in time. They are therefore an unreliable guide to the public interest. This also makes them particularly inappropriate for making or endorsing constitutional decisions, as these have long-term and far-reaching implications.

What is ... citizenship

Citizenship is a relationship between the individual and the state, in which the two are bound together by reciprocal rights and duties (citizens, most simply, are members of the state). The rights implied by citizenship include:

▶ *Civil* rights: the right to live and work within a state
▶ *Political* rights: the right to vote and stand for public office
▶ *Social* rights: the right of access to social security and public services.

Citizenship is linked to the ideas of freedom and democracy. Its link to freedom reflects its emphasis on rights. Its link to democracy reflects its emphasis on participation, often seen as a duty rather than as a right. In fact, democracy could be defined as full and equal citizenship.

Citizens' jury: A panel of non-specialists, often randomly chosen, used to deliberate on and express views about issues of public policy.

of the population chosen to represent the larger society. A cross-section, or microcosm, of society therefore speaks for the whole of society. Nevertheless, government has used these methods less as a way of widening citizens' involvement in politics and more as a means of gauging public opinion and 'pre-testing' government policies. A more important development is the wider use of 'citizens' forums' or '**citizens' juries**', increasingly used in the USA and in countries such as Germany, Denmark and the Netherlands.

One of the major advantages of citizens' juries is that, unlike referendums and opinion polls (and also voting), they operate through deliberation and debate. Participants are not just asked to express opinions. Instead, they are required to engage in discussion, possibly assisted by a neutral advisor, and have the opportunity to scrutinize information and even to cross-examine witnesses. Through such mechanisms, an informed and 'mature' sense of public opinion is developed. This significantly widens the traditional view of citizenship, helping to overcome one of the key drawbacks traditionally associated with direct democracy (the public's lack of knowledge and understanding).

Recall election: A special election (usually) precipitated by a popular partition that forces an official to seek re-election (and possibly be removed) before the end of his or her term in office.

Primary election: An intra-party election held to select a candidate to contest a subsequent 'official' election; primaries may be either 'open' to all voters or 'closed' (restricted to registered supporters of a party).

Since 2010, the Conservative–Liberal Democrat coalition has, in addition to the wider use of referendums (discussed earlier), proposed that direct popular participation be expanded in a number of ways. These include the introduction of **recall elections** for MPs. This would allow voters to force a by-election where an MP is found to have engaged in serious wrong-doing and a petition for a by-election has been signed by 10 per cent of his or her constituents. The coalition government also favours moves towards the introduction of US-style **primary elections** in the UK. This is evident in the proposal to fund 200 all-postal primaries during the current Parliament, targeting seats that have not changed hands in many years. This money will be available to all parties that take up seats in Parliament, in proportion to their electoral strength at the last general election.

Further proposed reforms aim to strengthen the link between Parliament and the public by creating opportunities for the public to influence parliamentary debate. Citizens would gain the ability to initiate parliamentary debates through the proposal that any petition that secures 100,000 signatures would be eligible for formal debate in Parliament, the petition with the most signatures being tabled as a bill eligible to be voted on in Parliament. The idea of a 'public reading stage' would give the public an opportunity to comment on proposed legislation online, while a 'public reading day' within a bill's committee stage would enable comments and suggestions from the public to be debated and, potentially, incorporated into the bill. Proposals have also been made to strengthen local democracy, including the idea of giving local residents the ability to block excessive council tax increases. Critics, on the other hand, remain sceptical. They argue that such proposals, like those before for citizens' juries, are just a form of 'fig leaf democracy', designed to give the impression that government is listening to the public without genuinely having to share policy-making power with them.

Reducing the voting age

Age of majority: The age at which adulthood begins, in the eyes of the law; reflecting the idea that a person has 'majority control' over him- or herself.

Views about the **age of majority** have changed over time. Traditionally, adulthood, and therefore the right to vote, was believed to commence at 21. However, as the 20th century progressed, this was gradually reduced in most parts of the world to 18. In the UK, the voting age was reduced from 21 to 18 in 1969, by the Wilson Labour government. Examples of voting ages higher than 18 are now rare. They include Singapore, Malaysia, Lebanon and Fiji, where the voting age remains at 21; and Italy where, although the general voting age is 18, voters must be 25 to elect the Senate.

Nevertheless, there are also examples of states with lower voting ages. For example, voting can take place at 17 in Sudan, Seychelles and Indonesia, and at 16 in Cuba, Nicaragua, the Isle of Man (changed from 18 in 2006) and in certain state elections in Germany. In the UK, there has been a growing campaign to lower the voting age, either to 17 or, more usually, to 16. The Liberal Democrats, Scottish Nationalists, Plaid Cymru and the Green Party all back lowering the voting age as well as reducing the candidacy age. In the 2010 general election, the Labour Party supported a 'free vote' in Parliament on lowering the voting age to 16. Such ideas have been endorsed by independent commissions such as the Electoral Commission (see p. 41), the Commission on Local Governance in England and the Human Rights Commission in Northern Ireland. The issue has also been made more prominent by a number of youth and democracy organizations, notably the 'Votes at 16' campaign which was launched in 2003.

Weblink ■ www.votesat16.org.uk

Use this website to find out more about the campaign to lower the voting age in the UK. Votes At 16 is a campaigning organization.

FOR OR AGAINST?

LOWERING THE VOTING AGE

FOR	AGAINST

Responsibilities without rights. The UK has a blurred 'age of majority', with the minimum age for various activities being lower than 18. The case for votes at 16 is based on the fact that this is the age at which young people can leave education, enter full-time education, have sex, and (with parental consent) join the army, get married or leave home.

Youth interests ignored. The lack of political representation for young people between 16 and 18 means that their needs, views and interests are routinely marginalized or ignored. Lowering the voting age may therefore give greater attention to, and stimulate fresher thinking on, issues such as education, drugs policy and social morality generally.

Stronger political engagement. Concern about declining civic engagement focuses particularly on the young, as 18–24 year olds have the lowest turnout rates. Lowering the voting age would re-engage such voters in two ways. First, it would strengthen their interest and understanding, and, second, it would help to reorientate politics around issues more meaningful to younger voters.

Irrational cut-off age. The notion that the current voting age is a reflection of intellectual and educational development is flawed. It both ignores the steady rise in educational standards and the fact that no restrictions are applied to ignorant and poorly educated adults. If 16- or 17-year-olds are being excluded from politics on the grounds of their knowledge and level of understanding, the principle is being very inconsistently applied.

Immature voters. The main argument against lowering the voting age is that until 18 most young people are in full-time education and continue to live with their parents. This means that they are not full citizens, and their educational development, even though they can leave school, remains incomplete. Most 16–18 year olds are unlikely to be interested in, or have knowledge of, politics.

Preserving 'childhood'. The campaign to lower the voting age is a symptom of a larger trend to erode childhood by forcing adult responsibilities and choices on children and young people. Adolescence should be a period during which young people can concentrate on school, enjoyment and personal development, without having weighty political matters placed on their shoulders.

Deferred representation. To regard the lack of representation of 16–18 year olds as a political injustice is absurd. Unlike women and the working classes of old, young people are not permanently denied political representation.
Their representation is only delayed or deferred. Moreover, 18 year olds are also likely to be broadly in touch with the interests of 16 and 17 year olds.

Undermining turnout. There is a possibility that, by lowering the voting age, turnout rates may decline. As young voters are less likely to vote than older voters, many, and possibly most, 16–18 year olds may choose not to vote. As voters who do not vote in their first eligible election are the most unreliable voters, this may create a generation of abstainers.

Compulsory voting

Electoral choice in the UK currently extends not only to a choice of candidates and parties, but also to the (perhaps more fundamental) issue of whether or not to vote. Anxiety about declining electoral turnout in the UK is therefore anxiety about voters *choosing* not to vote. The UK is undoubtedly in the majority amongst modern democracies in allowing voters not to vote. However, there are important examples of states in which voting is compulsory. In 2007, voting was compulsory in some 32 states, including Australia, Spain, Italy and France (for Senate elections only). In the case of Italy and France, the compulsion to vote is more symbolic than legal, as voting is not enforced through the punishment of non-voters. Elsewhere, enforcement normally consists of a small fine. In Australia, where compulsory voting was first introduced in Queensland in 1915 and in federal elections in 1924, it is compulsory for voters not only to attend a polling station and have their names marked off the certified list, but also to mark a ballot paper, fold it and place it in the ballot box. The current fine for non-voting in Australia is $20, payable within 21 days; however, the enforcement of the fine is by no means strict. (See For and against compulsory voting, p. 93.)

Digital democracy

An alternative to compulsory voting would be to make voting easier and more convenient. Moves in this direction have already been taken in the UK. Experiments in postal-only elections were conducted in 16 council wards in the 2002 local elections, and a much greater emphasis was placed on postal voting in the 2005 general election. Other ways of making voting more convenient would include revising the siting of polling stations (for example, placing them in supermarkets) and a switch in the voting day (from Thursday to probably Sunday, often used in continental Europe). More radical alternatives would include exploiting the democratic potential embodied in 'new' information and communication technology, notably mobile phones and the Internet. This is the sphere of digital democracy, sometimes called 'cyber democracy' or 'e-democracy'. Digital democracy could operate through interactive television, the Internet and online voting, enabling private citizens to both receive information, perhaps by watching parliamentary and other debates, and to express their views either through voting to elect representatives or via online referendums.

Weblink ■ www.hansardsociety.org.uk

Use this website to find out more about initiatives in digital democracy. The Hansard Society runs an e-democracy programme that examines ways of using interactive technologies to reinvigorate links between Parliament and citizens.

FOR OR AGAINST?

DIGITAL DEMOCRACY

FOR	AGAINST
Easier participation. E-democracy enables citizens to express their views easily and conveniently without having to leave home. It is thus likely to have a positive impact on participation rates and, in turn, on levels of political education. Falling electoral turnout may thus simply be a consequence of the failure of the democratic process to keep up to date with how citizens in an 'information society' wish to participate in politics.	**Electoral malpractice**. One problem with any attempt to make political participation easier and more convenient – via voting, telephone, the Internet and so on – is that scrutiny and control of the process become weaker. Wider postal voting in the UK led to growing allegations of malpractice and corruption. The great advantage of physical participation is, after all, that people's identities can be effectively checked and the process of voting can be properly 'policed'.
Access to information. 'New' technology massively enlarges citizens' access to information, making possible, for the first time, a truly free exchange of ideas and views. The Internet already makes available to private citizens specialist information that was once only available to governments. E-democracy could create a genuinely two-way democratic process, in which citizens become active participants in politics rather than passive recipients.	**'Virtual' democracy**. A deeper criticism of e-democracy is that it threatens to turn the democratic process into a series of push-button referendums while citizens sit alone in their own living rooms. This would further erode the 'public' dimension of political participation, reducing democratic citizenship to a series of consumer choices. This would demean politics, turning it into something resembling voting in *Big Brother*.
Ease of organization. One of the disadvantages of the wider use of referendums is the significant time, cost and resources that go into their organization. Referendums currently have to be organized months in advance. On the other hand, 'virtual' referendums using electronic democracy would be cheaper and easier to organize, and so could be held much more frequently.	**Digital divide**. A final argument against e-democracy is that it is difficult to square with the democratic notion of political equality. Access to 'new' information and communication technology is not universal. Placing greater emphasis on electronic participation would only give rise to new patterns of political inequality, as the 'information rich' came to dominate the 'information poor'.

WHAT YOU NEED TO KNOW

▶▶ Democracy, put most simply, means 'rule by the people'. Its core principles are political equality – an equal distribution of political power and influence, and political participation – popular involvement in the processes of government. The two main types of democracy are direct democracy and representative democracy.

▶▶ Direct democracy is based on the direct, unmediated and continuous participation of citizens in the task of government. In effect, the people *become* the government, and there is no need for a separate class of professional politicians. Examples include ancient Athens, which amounted to a form of government by mass meetings, and referendums.

▶▶ Representative democracy is a limited and indirect form of democracy. It operates through the ability of representatives to speak for, or act on behalf of, the people, usually ensured by regular and competitive elections. The key principle of representative democracy is popular control, operating through forms of public accountability that ultimately allow unpopular politicians and governments to be removed.

▶▶ The UK has a system of representative democracy, supplemented by limited forms of direct democracy. Its central features are democratic elections (free and fair elections, based on universal suffrage and party competition), Parliament's ability to deliver representative and responsible government, and the role of pressure groups in widening access to political power.

▶▶ The effectiveness of democracy in the UK has been criticized for a number of reasons. These include: the impact of the Westminster voting system, the weakness of Parliament and the concentration of power in the hands of influential pressure groups. The UK is a better example of majoritarian democracy than constitutional democracy.

▶▶ Democracy in the UK has been strengthened in recent years by developments such as the introduction of devolution in Scotland, Wales and Northern Ireland; the wider use of proportional representation (PR) electoral systems; and a greater willingness to use referendums, especially on issues of constitutional reform.

▶▶ A decline in political participation (electoral turnout and party membership in particular) in recent years has stimulated concerns about the effectiveness of democracy in the UK. Possible explanations for this 'crisis' include the decline in 'social capital', the impact of the mass media and politicians' lack of vision caused by the declining influence of traditional ideologies.

▶▶ A variety of reforms intended to strengthen democracy in the UK, and in particular promote political participation, have been proposed. These include: the wider use of forms of grass-roots or direct democracy, such as referendums and citizens' juries; providing more opportunities for the public to influence MPs and parliamentary debate; a reduction in the voting age; the introduction of compulsory voting; the wider use of digital democracy.

59

Test yourself

Short questions:

1 What is democracy?
2 Define direct democracy.
3 Outline *two* key features of representative democracy?
4 Outline the differences between direct democracy and representative democracy.
5 Identify *three* ways in which citizens can participate in politics.
6 What is a referendum?
7 How do referendums differ from elections?

Medium questions:

8 Explain the advantages of direct democracy.
9 Explain the advantages of representative democracy.
10 How do elections promote democracy?
11 Why is political participation important to democracy?
12 What are the main forms of political participation in the UK?
13 Explain the main features of representative democracy in the UK.
14 Explain the circumstances in which referendums have been used in the UK.
15 Why have some people advocated a reduction in the voting age?
16 Explain the disadvantages of compulsory voting?

Extended questions:

17 Assess the advantages of direct democracy.
18 Assess the advantages of representative democracy.
19 To what extent is the UK political system democratic?
20 Why has democracy in the UK been criticized?
21 To what extent does the UK suffer from a 'participation crisis'?
22 How could the UK political system be made more democratic?
23 What would be the most effective ways of improving political participation in the UK?
24 Should referendums be more widely used in the UK?

Chapter 3

Elections and Voting

Elections and democracy

Elections are often seen as the practical face of democratic government. They are, in effect, democracy in action. When voters cast their ballots, they, rather than politicians or government, are 'pulling the strings'. This is why, for instance, the suffragettes in the early years of the 20th century risked imprisonment, endured force-feeding and even sacrificed their lives to win the right to vote. However, does voting change anything? Are elections really the heart of the political process, or are they merely a democratic fig leaf? As the anarchist slogan put it, 'If voting changed anything, they would abolish it'.

However, the closer we look at elections the more complicated they appear. The task of electing representatives can be done in a wide variety of ways, and each has its strengths and weaknesses. In fact, no fewer than five voting systems are currently in operation in different parts of the UK. Which of these systems is the best? Which one is the most democratic? Such issues are particularly controversial when they are applied to the oldest and most important voting system in the UK, the Westminster electoral system. As this is the system that is used for general elections, any change to it would affect almost every aspect of how the political system works. Nevertheless, elections are not just about rules and procedures. They are also about voters and how they behave at election time. Why do voters vote as they do? And have the factors influencing their voting behaviour changed over time?

KEY ISSUES

- What are the functions of elections?
- How does representation work?
- How do the UK's voting systems differ?
- Which voting system is best, and why?
- How can voting best be explained?
- What factors influence voting behaviour in the modern UK?

GETTING YOU THINKING

'A fairer electoral system?'

Before starting the chapter, read this passage and briefly consider the questions on the next page.

On 5 May 2011, a referendum was held on whether to replace the 'first-past-the-post' (FPTP) electoral system for Westminster elections with the alternative vote (AV) system. Although the proposal was defeated, with 68 per cent of the electorate voting 'no', the referendum gave unprecedented attention to the issue of electoral reform. In particular, the campaign highlighted the drawbacks of FPTP. These include that, under FPTP, winning candidates need only gain a 'plurality' of votes; that is, more votes than any other single candidate. More people may therefore vote against the winning candidate than vote in favour. In AV elections, candidates can only win if they gain 50 per cent or more of votes cast. Furthermore, voters in FPTP elections may feel that their vote is 'wasted' if they do not support one of the leading contenders. Under AV, electors' votes would have been more likely to 'count' because they vote preferentially (ranking candidates in order, 1, 2, 3, and so on) and these votes can be redistributed until one candidate gains 50 per cent.

However, AV has critics on both sides of the electoral reform debate. Advocates of electoral reform, including a large proportion of Liberal Democrats, argue that AV would do little to redress the chief defect of FPTP. This is its tendency to 'over-represent' large parties and 'under-represent' small parties. In most cases, FPTP results in a single party having a majority of seats in the Commons, without having come close to winning a majority of votes in the election. Whatever else AV may have changed, it would not have changed this, meaning that neither FPTP nor AV can be seen as examples of 'fair voting'. Supporters of FPTP, who won the day in the referendum, argue that it has advantages over AV. These include that preferential voting may mean that the outcome of an elections is decided by supporters of fringe candidates or extremist parties, whose votes are the most likely to be redistributed.

David Cameron and John Reid, the former Labour minister, campaigning in 2011 against AV – but has the referendum finally settled the electoral reform debate?

What issues do such developments raise?

▶▶▶   How does the 'first-past-the-post' voting system work?

▶▶▶   Why was the AV referendum held?

▶▶▶   Why has the 'first-past-the-post' electoral system been so controversial?

▶▶▶   What would have been the benefits of introducing AV?

▶▶▶   What would constitute a 'fair' electoral system?

IN THIS CHAPTER:

Elections and representation • Voting systems and electoral reform • Voting behaviour

Elections and representation

Election: A method of filling an office or post through choices made by a designated body of people: the electorate.

Elections are central to the theory and practice of democracy in the UK. As we saw in the previous chapter, the UK's claim to be a democracy is largely based on the nature of its electoral system, and the fact that UK elections are based on:

▶ Universal adult suffrage
▶ One person, one vote
▶ The secret ballot
▶ Competition between candidates and parties.

Elections are therefore the main link between government and the people, meaning that voting is the most important form of political participation. The opportunities to vote in the UK have, in fact, increased significantly in recent years. Since 2000, the electoral process in the UK has been regulated by the Electoral Commission (see p. 41).

The main elections in the UK are:

▶ **General elections.** These are full parliamentary elections, in which all the seats in the House of Commons come up for re-election (Westminster elections). They have traditionally taken place within a five-year maximum term, the date being decided by the prime minister, but the Conservative-led coalition has changed these to five-year, fixed-term elections.

▶ **Devolved assembly elections.** These are elections to the Scottish Parliament, the Welsh Assembly and the Northern Ireland Assembly. They are fixed-term elections that take place every four years (first held in 1998 in Northern Ireland and in 1999 elsewhere).

▶ **European Parliament elections.** These are fixed-term elections that take place every five years (first held in 1979).

▶ **Local elections.** These are elections to district, borough and county councils. They include elections to the Greater London Assembly and for the London Mayor, with mayoral elections also taking place in some other local authorities. They are fixed-term elections that take place usually every four or five years.

Weblink ■ www.electoralcommission.org.uk

Use the Electoral Commission website for extensive information about the conduct of elections in the UK and for considering also ways of improving electoral democracy.

Differences between . . .
ELECTIONS AND REFERENDUMS

Election	Referendum
Fill office/form government	Make policy decisions
Vote for candidate/party	Select yes/no option
General issues	Specific issue
Regular (legally required)	Ad hoc (decided by government)
Representative democracy	Direct democracy

However, what role do elections play in the political system? And in what sense do elected politicians 'represent' the people?

Functions of elections

There are three main functions of elections. Elections serve to:

▶▶ Form governments
▶▶ Ensure representation
▶▶ Uphold legitimacy

Forming governments

Elections are the principal way in which governments in the UK are formed. They therefore serve to transfer power from one government to the next. This is the function of a general election. In the UK, governments are formed from the leading members of the majority party in the House of Commons. As the results of the elections are usually clear (every general election since 1945, except those in February 1974 and May 2010, has produced a single, majority party), this usually takes place the day after the election. The leader of the majority party becomes the prime minister, and the prime minister's first task is to appoint the other ministers in his or her government.

However, elections in the UK may not always be successful in forming governments:

▶ As is discussed later in the chapter, where proportional electoral systems are used it is less likely that a single 'winning' party emerges from the election. As May 2010 demonstrated, this can also occur (although less frequently) when majoritarian electoral systems are used. Governments may therefore be formed through deals negotiated amongst two or more parties after the election has taken place. These deals may take days and, in some cases, weeks to negotiate.

Ensuring representation

Elections are also a vital channel of communication between government and the people. They carry out a representative function on two levels. First, they create a link between elected politicians and their constituents. This helps to ensure that constituents' concerns and grievances are properly articulated and addressed (although this 'constituency function' may be carried out more effectively by some electoral systems than by others). Second, they establish a more general link between the government of the day and **public opinion**. This occurs because elections make politicians, and therefore the government of the day, publicly accountable and ultimately removable. Elections therefore give the people final control over the government.

However, doubts have also been raised about the effectiveness of elections in ensuring representation:

▶ Four- or five-year electoral terms, as found in the UK, weaken the link between voters and representatives. Five-year, fixed-term Parliaments, as proposed in 2010, are longer than the equivalent in many other liberal democracies (see p. 267).

▶ There is considerable debate about how elected politicians can and should 'represent' their electors. This is reflected in competing theories of representation, as discussed below.

Upholding legitimacy

Elections play a crucial role in maintaining legitimacy. Legitimacy is important because it provides the key to maintaining political stability. It ensures that citizens recognize that they have an obligation to obey the law and respect their system of government. Elections uphold legitimacy by providing a ritualized means through which citizens 'consent' to being governed: the act of voting. Elections therefore confer democratic legitimacy on government.

However, elections in the UK may not always be successful in upholding legitimacy:

▶ Low turnout levels in the 2001, 2005 and 2010 general elections have cast doubt on the legitimacy of the UK political system. Voter apathy may be a way in which disillusioned citizens are withholding 'consent'.

▶ Falling support, since the 1970s, for the two 'governing' parties – Labour and the Conservatives – may indicate declining levels of popular satisfaction with the performance of the UK political system.

How does representation work?

How can one person be said to 'represent' another? What is it that he or she represents? Is it the public's *views*, their *interests*, the *groups* from which they come, or

Public opinion: Views shared by members of the public on political issues; the views of many or most voters.

What is . . . representation

As a political principle, representation is a relationship through which an individual or group stands for, or acts on behalf of, a larger body of people. Representation differs from democracy in that, while the former acknowledges a distinction between government and the people, the latter, at least in its classical sense, aspires to abolish this distinction and establish popular self-government. Representative democracy (see p. 37) may nevertheless constitute a limited and indirect form of democratic rule.

what? These questions are difficult to answer because there is no single, agreed theory of representation. Rather, there are a number of competing theories, and these competing theories are based on quite different assumptions about how representation can and should be carried out. How can politicians best 'serve' their voters?

The three main competing notions in debates about representation are:

▶▶ Trusteeship
▶▶ The doctrine of the mandate
▶▶ Descriptive representation.

Trusteeship

Delegate: A person who is chosen to act for another on the basis of clear guidance or instructions; delegates do not think for themselves.

Trustee: A person who has formal (and usually legal) responsibility for another's property or affairs.

Trusteeship is the traditional form of representation that is said to operate in UK politics. It is based on the idea that elected politicians should act not as **delegates** but as **trustees**. Trustees act on *behalf of* others, using their superior knowledge, better education or greater experience. This form of representation is sometimes called 'Burkean representation', as its classic expression was found in a speech that Edmund Burke (1729–97) gave to the electors of Bristol in 1774. Burke declared that, 'Your representative owes you, not his industry alone, but his judgement; and he betrays, instead of serving you, if he sacrifices it to your opinion'. In other words, representatives should think for themselves and use their own judgement because the mass of people may not know their own best interests. Until the 1950s, constitutional theory in the UK (despite changing political practice) held that MPs were Burkean representatives.

However, the idea of trusteeship has also attracted severe criticism:

▶ Allowing politicians to think for themselves creates a 'gap' between the views of ordinary citizens and the views of their representatives. This could mean that representatives act in their own interests, or in the interests of people like themselves (middle-class males, on the whole), rather than in the interests of the mass of the people. This 'gap' could be filled either by a shortening of electoral terms or by the introduction of recall elections.

▶ The trusteeship model is largely out of date. Since the development of the party system in the late 19th century, the scope MPs have had to think and act on the basis of their own 'mature judgement' has been very limited. Burkean representation is now applicable only in cases such as '**free votes**', or backbench revolts (see Chapter 7).

The doctrine of the mandate

The doctrine of the **mandate** is the most influential theory of representation in modern politics. It is based on the idea that, in winning an election, a party gains a 'popular' mandate that authorizes it to carry out the policies on which it fought the election. These are the policies that are contained in election **manifestos**. This implies that it is the party, rather than individual politicians, that carries out representation. If this is the case, the doctrine of a mandate model provides a clear justification for party unity and party discipline. In effect, politicians serve their constituents not by thinking for themselves, but by remaining loyal to their party and its policies. This leads to what can be called 'mandate democracy'. The strength of the mandate doctrine is that it takes account of the undoubted importance in modern politics of party labels and party policies. In UK elections, most voters on most occasions vote for a party and give little or no attention to the strengths or weaknesses of individual candidates.

However, the doctrine of the mandate has also been criticized:

▶ It is based on a highly questionable model of voting behaviour. As discussed in the final section of this chapter, there is little evidence that voters vote 'rationally', choosing between parties on the basis of their manifesto commitments. A variety of 'non-rational' factors affect how people vote.

▶ Even if voters are influenced by policies, a vote for a party is unlikely to indicate support for its *entire* manifesto, meaning that the doctrine of the mandate is, at best, a very blunt weapon.

▶ There is no way of forcing governments, once elected, to carry out their manifesto commitments. Manifestos often include 'vote-winning' policies that prove to be difficult to implement in practice.

▶ It is unclear who the mandate falls to: the party or the prime minister. There has been a growing tendency for prime ministers to claim a 'personal mandate', on the basis of their role in leading the party to power. However, the idea of a *personal* mandate may simply allow prime ministers to act however they wish. (This is discussed in Chapter 8, in relation to the rise of presidentialism.)

▶ If an election leads to the formation of a coalition government, the doctrine of the mandate may become unworkable, as post-election deals are negotiated between coalition partners, through which each party abandons certain manifesto promises.

Free vote: A vote in which there is no 'party line', allowing MPs to think for themselves and vote independently.

Mandate: An instruction or command that gives authority to a person or body to act in a particular way.

Manifesto: A pamphlet that outlines (in more or less detail) the policies or programme a party intends to introduce if elected to power.

Descriptive representation

Descriptive representation (sometimes called characteristic representation, microcosmic representation or the resemblance model of representation) is based on the idea that representatives should typify or resemble the group they claim to represent. This notion is embodied in the idea of a 'representative cross-section', as used by market researchers and opinion pollsters. By this standard, a representative government would constitute a **microcosm** of the larger society, containing members drawn from all groups and sections in society (in terms of social class, gender, religion, ethnicity, age, and so on), and in numbers that are proportional to the size of the groups in society at large. By this standard, there are significant concerns about the quality of representation across the UK political system, stemming in particular from the 'under-representation' of groups such as women, the working class and ethnic minorities. This certainly applies to Parliament, as discussed in Chapter 7, but also to the senior judiciary, discussed in Chapter 9. The basis for this kind of representation is that it is necessary for people to share the experiences of a particular group in order to be fully able to identify with its interests. They must have 'walked in their shoes'.

However, concerns have also been expressed about the value of descriptive representation:

▶ If all representatives simply advance the interests of the groups from which they come, representation becomes exclusive or narrow, with no one being able to defend the common good or advance a broader public interest.
▶ A government that is a microcosm of society would reflect that society's weaknesses as well its strengths. What would be the advantage, for example, of government resembling society if the majority of the population are apathetic, ill-informed and poorly educated?
▶ It is difficult to see how characteristic representation can be reconciled with electoral choice. For example, the Labour Party's attempt to boost female representation in Parliament through all-women shortlists of parliamentary candidates was declared to be illegal under equal opportunities legislation.

Microcosm: Literally a little world; a miniature version of a larger body, but exact in its features and proportions.

Electoral systems and electoral reform

Electoral systems

Why do electoral systems matter? Electoral systems are not simply a collection of technical rules about how the electorate is organized and who they are able to vote for. More importantly, different electoral systems have different political outcomes – electoral systems make a difference. It is quite possible for a party to win an election under one set of rules, but to lose it under another set of rules. Similarly, one electoral system may produce a single-party government, while

Table 3.1 UK electoral systems

Votong system	Where used	Type
'First past the post' (FPTP) (see p. 71)	• House of Commons, • Local government in England and Wales	Plurality system
Additional member system (AMS) (see p. 76)	• Scottish Parliament • Welsh Assembly • Greater London Assembly	Mixed system
Single transferable vote (STV) (see p. 77)	• Northern Ireland Assembly • Local government in Northern Ireland and Scotland	Quota system
Regional party list (see p. 78)	• European Parliament elections	List system
Supplementary vote (SV) Alternative vote (AV) (see p. 80)	• London mayoral elections • Local government by-elections in Scotland	Majority system Majority system

another would lead to coalition government. Electoral systems therefore have a major impact on political parties and on government, and therefore also on the quality of representation and the effectiveness of democracy.

For general purposes, the voting systems that are used in the UK can be divided into two broad categories on the basis of how they convert votes into seats:

Majoritarian system:
An electoral system that tends to 'over-represent' larger parties and usually results in single-party majority government.

▶ There are **majoritarian systems**, in which larger parties typically win a higher proportion of seats than the proportion of votes they gain in the election. This increases the chances of a single party gaining a parliamentary majority and being able to govern on its own. (Majoritarian systems are defined by their impact on the allocation of seats, not by the requirement that winning candidates must gain electoral majorities as in the case of AV and SV. These are called 'majority systems'.)

Proportional system:
An electoral system that tends to represent parties in-line with their electoral support, often portrayed as proportional representation.

▶ There are **proportional systems**, which guarantee an equal, or at least a close and reliable, relationship between the seats won by parties and the votes they gained in the election.

Weblink ■ www.electoral-reform.org.uk

Use the Electoral Reform Society website for detailed information on the workings of voting systems. The Electoral Reform Society is a long-time critic of FPTP and a supporter of STV.

Plurality: The largest number out of a collection of numbers; a 'simple' majority, not necessarily an 'absolute' majority.

'First-past-the-post'

The main majoritarian voting system used in the UK is 'first-past-the-post', sometimes called FPTP or the single-member **plurality** system (SMP). It is undoubtedly the most important electoral system used in the UK, as it is the system that is

FOCUS ON . . .

'First-past-the-post' voting system

Used: House of Commons and in England and Wales for local government.

Features:

▶ It is a **constituency** system. Currently, there are 646 parliamentary constituencies in the UK.

▶ Voters select a single candidate, and do so by marking his or her name with an 'X' on the ballot paper. This reflects the principle of 'one person, one vote'.

▶ Constituencies are of roughly equal size, which is ensured by reviews by the Electoral Commission and the Boundary Commissions for Scotland and Northern Ireland.

▶ Each constituency returns a single candidate. This is often seen as the 'winner-takes-all' effect. (However, there are still a small number of multimember constituencies in local government.)

▶ The winning candidate needs only to achieve a plurality of votes. This is the 'first-past-the-post' rule.

For example, if votes were cast as follows:

Candidate A = 30,000 votes
Candidate B = 22,000 votes
Candidate C = 26,000 votes

Candidate A would win, despite polling only 38 per cent of the vote.

(For advantages and disadvantages, see 'For and against the reform of the Westminster system', p. 82.)

Constituency: An electoral unit that returns one or more representatives, or the body of voters who are so represented.

used for elections to the House of Commons and therefore it serves to form UK governments. Hence it is known as the Westminster electoral system.

'First-past-the-post' has the following implications:

▶▶ Disproportionality
▶▶ Systematic biases
▶▶ Two-party system
▶▶ Single-party government
▶▶ The landslide effect.

Disproportionality

FPTP fails to establish a reliable link between the proportion of votes won by parties and the proportion of seats they gain. This happens because the system is primarily concerned with the election of individual members, not with the representation of political parties. An example of this is that it is possible with FPTP for the 'wrong' party to win an election. This is what happened in 1951, when the Conservatives formed a majority government but won fewer votes than Labour.

In February 1974 the tables were turned, with Labour forming a minority government (as the largest party in the House of Commons) but with fewer votes than the Conservatives.

Systematic biases

However, the disproportionality of FPTP is not random. Certain parties do well in FPTP elections, while others suffer, sometimes dramatically. There are two kinds of bias:

▶ **Size of party.** Large parties benefit at the expense of small parties. This happens for three reasons:

  ▶ The 'winner takes all' effect means that 100 per cent of representation is gained in each constituency by a single candidate, and therefore by a single party.

  ▶ Winning candidates tend to come from large parties, as these are the parties whose candidates are most likely to be 'first-past-the-post', in the sense of winning plurality support. By contrast, candidates from small parties that come, say, third or fourth in the election win nothing and gain no representation for their party. This is a particular curse for so-called 'third' parties, which often come second behind one or other of two larger parties.

  ▶ Voters are discouraged from supporting small parties because they know that they are unlikely to win seats, and even more unlikely to win the overall election, This is the problem of so-called '**wasted votes**'. A proportion of voters are therefore inclined to vote for large parties on the grounds that they are the 'least bad' of the two available, rather because they are their first preference party.

▶ **Distribution of support.** Parties whose support is geographically concentrated do better than ones with evenly distributed support. This occurs because geographical concentration makes a party's support more 'effective', in the sense that it is more likely to gain pluralities and thereby win seats. Similarly, such parties also have the advantage that where they are not winning seats they are 'wasting' fewer votes. The danger for parties with geographically evenly distributed support is that they come second or third in elections almost everywhere, picking up very few or perhaps no seats.

The Labour and Conservative parties have traditionally been 'over-represented' by FPTP because they have been both large parties and have tended to have geographically concentrated support thanks to the class basis of their voters (see Table 3.4, p. 87). The Liberal Democrats, by contrast, suffer the double disadvantage that they are smaller than the Labour and Conservative parties and also have

Wasted vote: A vote that does not affect the outcome of the election because it is cast for a 'losing' candidate or for a candidate who already has a plurality of votes.

less class-based and more geographically evenly spread support. The levels of **proportionality** and disproportionality that result from the use of FPTP can be illustrated by the outcomes of the general election of May 2010.

Proportionality: The degree to which the allocation of seats among parties reflects the distribution of the popular vote.

Table 3.2 General election results, 2010

Parties	No. seats	% seats	No. votes	% votes
Conservative Party	307	46.0	10,703,754	36.1
Labour Party	258	39.0	8,609,507	29.0
Liberal Democrats	57	8.8	6,836,824	23.0
Scottish National Party	6	1.0	491,386	1.7
Plaid Cymru	3	0.5	165,394	0.6

The 2010 general election nevertheless amounted to the second-best performance for the Liberal Democrats in the post-1945 period, in any of their incarnations (as, previously, the Liberal Party or the SDP–Liberal Alliance). Indeed, in 1983 the Alliance gained a mere 3.5 per cent of seats on the basis of 25.4 per cent of the vote. The improving position of the Liberal Democrats can be explained by two factors:

Tactical voting: Voting not for a preferred party but for a 'least bad' party or to defeat a 'worst' party

▶ The ruthless targeting of seats in election campaigns
▶ The growing tendency towards **tactical voting**.

Both of these tend artificially to concentrate a party's support and thus to make its votes more 'effective'. It is also worth noting that small parties are not always so dramatically 'under-represented'. The nationalist parties in Scotland and Wales fare proportionally better under FPTP than do the Liberal Democrats because they enjoy the benefit of geographically concentrated support.

Two-party system

An important implication of FPTP is a tendency for politics to be dominated by two 'major' parties. In other words, only two parties have sufficient parliamentary support to have a chance of winning general elections and forming governments. Clearly, this happens as a result of the biases discussed above. Since the First World War, the UK has had a two-party system, dominated by the Labour and Conservative parties. Although the proportion of votes gained by these parties has tended to fall, from over 95 per cent in the early 1950s to 65 per cent in 2010, they have continued to have a stranglehold on the House of Commons. Even in 2010, 85 per cent of MPs belonged to either the Labour or Conservative parties. This tendency for UK politics to be a 'two-horse race' may, indeed, have further implications. For example, it may discourage potential supporters of 'third' parties from voting for them, thinking that such votes would be 'wasted' because they would not affect the outcome of the election. The problem of wasted votes is all the greater because Labour and the Conservatives each have 'heartlands' in which most seats are **'safe' seats**. The outcome of a general election is therefore determined by what happens in a minority of seats, so-called **'marginal' seats**. The key 'marginals' may number as few as 100 out of 650 seats.

Safe seat: A seat or constituency that rarely changes hands and is consistently won by the same party.

Marginal seat: A seat or constituency with a small majority, which is therefore 'winnable' by more than one party.

Single-party government

The most important consequence of a two-party system is that the larger of the 'major' parties usually wins sufficient support to be able to govern alone. In the UK, this means that it usually wins a majority of seats in the House of Commons. The other 'major' party forms the opposition and therefore acts as a kind of 'government in waiting'. Not since 1935 has a party gained a majority of votes in a UK general election. However, only twice since then, in February 1974 and May 2010, has a party failed to gain a majority of seats in the House of Commons. Single-party government, in turn, has a wide range of consequences. Many of the arguments about electoral reform focus on the advantages of single-party government against those of coalition government (see p. 16).

Landslide effect

Not only does FPTP usually give the largest party majority control of the House of Commons, but it also tends to produce a 'winner's bonus'. This occurs as relatively small shifts in votes can lead to dramatic changes in the seats the parties gain. One of the consequences of this is that parties can win 'landslide' victories on the basis of relatively modest electoral support. This is a tendency that has become increasingly pronounced from the 1980s onwards through the decline in combined Labour–Conservative electoral support. This can bring about a dramatic decline in the representation of the second 'major' party, resulting in an artificial 'landslide' victory for the winning party. For example, in 1983, the Conservatives won a 143-seat majority, up from 44 seats in 1979, despite the fact that Conservative support fell by 0.5 per cent. This also applied to Labour in 1997 and again in 2001, when its electoral support of 43 per cent and 41 per cent produced parliamentary majorities of 178 and 166 respectively.

Proportional systems

Proportional representation: The principle that parties should be represented in an assembly or parliament in direct proportion to their overall electoral strength.

The other four electoral systems used in the UK broadly conform to the principle of **proportional representation**. These systems are:

▶ The *additional member system* (AMS), sometimes called the mixed-member proportional system (MMP), is used for elections to the Scottish Parliament, the Welsh Assembly, the Northern Ireland Assembly and the Greater London

Figure 3.1 **The majoritarian–proportional spectrum**

Assembly. As such, it is the second most significant electoral system in the UK after FPTP.

▶ The *single transferable vote* system, or STV, has been used since 1973 for local government elections in Northern Ireland. It is the system that has been used since 1998 to elect the Northern Ireland Assembly. It is also used for local elections in Northern Ireland and Scotland.

▶ The *regional party list* has been used for elections to the European Parliament since 1999 (except in Northern Ireland, where STV is used). This brought the UK into line with the EU requirement that elections to the European Parliament should be proportional (even though the particular system used is left to each member state).

▶ The *supplementary vote*, or SV, has been used since 1999 for the election of the London mayor. It is the least proportional of the new voting systems, but it is usually more proportional than FPTP. SV is derived from the *alternative vote*, or AV, which is used for local government by-elections in Scotland and was rejected as an alternative to FPTP in a referendum in 2011.

(For more details on each of these systems see the 'Focus on . . .' boxes on pp. 76–80.)

Proportional voting systems have, to a greater or lesser extent, the following implications:

▶▶ Greater proportionality
▶▶ Multiparty systems
▶▶ Coalition or minority government
▶▶ Consensus-building.

Greater proportionality

The regional party list, AMS and STV all deliver a high and reliable level of proportionality. The 'over-representation' of large parties and the so-called winner's bonus or landslide effect of FPTP are absent, or greatly reduced, when these systems are used. For example, in the 2007 Scottish Parliament elections, although Labour won

FOCUS ON . . .
Additional member system (AMS)

Used: Scottish Parliament, Welsh Assembly, Greater London Assembly.

Features:

▶ It is a 'mixed' system, made up of constituency and party-list elements.

▶ A proportion of seats are filled by 'first past the post', using single-member constituencies. In Scotland and London, 56 per cent of representatives are elected in this way. In Wales, this figure is 66 per cent.

▶ The remaining seats are filled using a 'closed' party-list system (see p. 78).

▶ Electors cast two votes: one for a candidate in a constituency election and the other for a party in a list election.

▶ The party-list element in AMS is used to 'top up' the constituency results. This is done 'correctively', using the D'Hondt method (devised by the Belgian mathematician Victor D'Hondt), to achieve the most proportional overall outcome.

Advantages:

▶ The mixed character of this system balances the need for constituency representation against the need for electoral fairness.

▶ Although the system is broadly proportional in terms of its outcomes, it keeps alive the possibility of single-party government.

▶ It allows voters to make wider and more considered choices. For example, they can vote for different parties in the constituency and list elections.

Disadvantages:

▶ The retention of single-member constituencies reduces the likelihood of high levels of proportionality.

▶ The system creates confusion by having two classes of representative.

▶ Constituency representation will be less effective than it is in FPTP, because of the larger size of constituencies and because a proportion of representatives have no constituency duties.

just over half the constituency seats (37 out of 63) on the basis of 32 per cent of the vote, its overall representation in the Scottish Parliament was 'corrected' by the distribution of party-list seats. This gave Labour 36 per cent of the total seats, leaving it in second place behind the Scottish National Party. Similarly, in the 2011 Welsh Assembly election Labour gained a clear majority of constituency seats (28 out of 40) with 42 per cent of the vote, but won only 43 per cent of the total seats in the Welsh Assembly because it gained only two regional seats.

Multiparty systems

Minor parties that are denied representation by FPTP are more likely to win seats in the other voting systems. This substantially broadens the basis of party

FOCUS ON . . .
Single transferable vote (STV)

Used: Northern Ireland Assembly, in Northern Ireland and Scotland for local government, and in Northern Ireland only for European Parliament.

Features:

▶ There are multimember constituencies. The Northern Ireland Assembly has 18 constituencies, each returning 6 members. In local elections in Northern Ireland there is a mixture of 5–6- and 7-member constituencies.

▶ Political parties are able to put up as many candidates as there are seats to fill in each constituency.

▶ Electors vote preferentially by ranking candidates in order (1, 2, 3, and so on).

▶ Candidates are elected if they achieve a quota of votes. This quota is calculated on the basis of the Droop formula, as follows:

$$\text{Quota} = \frac{\text{total number of votes cast}}{(\text{number of seats to be filled} + 1)} + 1$$

▶ Votes are counted, first, according to first preferences. If any candidate achieves the quota, additional votes for him or her are counted according to second or subsequent preferences.

▶ If this process still leaves some seats unfilled, the candidate with the fewest votes drops out and his or her votes are redistributed according to second or subsequent preferences.

Advantages:

▶ The system is capable of achieving highly proportional outcomes.

▶ Competition amongst candidates from the same party means that they can be judged on their individual records and personal strengths.

▶ The availability of several members means that constituents can choose who to take their grievances to.

Disadvantages:

▶ The degree of proportionality achieved in this system can vary, largely on the basis of the party system.

▶ Strong and stable single-party government is unlikely under STV.

▶ Multimember constituencies may be divisive because they encourage competition amongst members of the same party.

representation and creates multiparty systems. For example, until 2010 (when it won one seat), the Green Party had no representation at Westminster, despite having gained more than a quarter of a million votes in some previous general elections. However, the Greens were represented on most other bodies: two sit in the Scottish Parliament, two sit in the Greater London Assembly, and two sit in the European Parliament. The UK Independence Party (UKIP) won over 600,000 votes in the 2005 general election but gained no seats. On the other hand, UKIP has 13 seats in the European Parliament. Similarly, the Liberal Democrats,

FOCUS ON . . .
Regional party list

Used: European Parliament (except Northern Ireland).

Features:

▶ There are a number of large multimember constituencies. For European Parliament elections, the UK is divided into 12 regions, each returning 3–10 members (72 in total).

▶ Political parties compile lists of candidates to place before the electorate, in descending order of preference.

▶ Electors vote for parties not for candidates. The UK uses **'closed' list** elections.

▶ Parties are allocated seats in direct proportion to the votes they gain in each regional constituency. They fill these seats from their party list.

Advantages:

▶ It is the only potentially 'pure' system of proportional representation, and is therefore fair to all parties.

▶ The system tends to promote unity by encouraging electors to identify with a region rather than with a constituency.

▶ The system makes it easier for women and minority candidates to be elected, provided they feature on the party list.

Disadvantages:

▶ The existence of many small parties can lead to weak and unstable government.

▶ The link between representatives and constituencies is significantly weakened and may be broken altogether.

▶ Parties become more powerful, as they decide where candidates are placed on the party list.

Closed list: A version of the party-list system where voters only vote for political parties and have no influence over which individual candidates are elected, unlike 'open' lists.

Minority government: A government that does not have overall majority support in the assembly or parliament; minority governments are usually formed by single parties that are unable, or unwilling, to form coalitions.

condemned to 'third'-party status at Westminster by the systematic biases of FPTP, have greater representation where other voting systems are used, giving them, at times, considerable influence over the formation of governments.

Coalition or minority government

The tendency of more proportional voting systems to produce multiparty systems is also reflected in a greater likelihood of coalition governments or **minority governments**. This has been evident where all such electoral systems have been used in the UK. In the case of the Scottish Parliament, the SNP majority executive formed in 2011 is an exception, as the previous administrations were either Labour–Liberal Democrat coalitions or (in 2007) a minority SNP executive. In the case of the Welsh Assembly, Labour formed a brief minority executive after the 1999 election with a Labour–Liberal Democrat coalition executive being formed in 2000 and a grand coalition being formed in 2007 between Labour and Plaid Cymru, following four years of Labour minority

What is ... coalition government

A coalition is a grouping of rival political actors brought together through the recognition that their goals cannot be achieved by working separately. Coalition governments are formal agreements between two or more parties that involve a sharing of ministerial responsibilities. They are usually formed when no party has majority control of the legislature.

A 'national' government (sometimes called a 'grand coalition') comprises all major parties, but is usually formed only at times of national crisis (such as the National Governments which held office from 1931 until 1940). While supporters of coalition government highlight its breadth of representation and bias in favour of compromise and consensus-building, its critics warn that such governments tend to be weak and unstable.

rule. Although the Conservative–Liberal Democrat coalition at Westminster, formed in 2010, resulted from the use of FPTP, it, in effect, provides a laboratory which enables the implications of proportional representation to be studied.

Consensus-building

The shift from single-party majority government to coalition government leads to a different style of policy-making and to the adoption of different policies, described by David Cameron (see p. 123) and Nick Clegg (see p. 193) as the 'new politics'. In particular, whereas FPTP generally results in single-party governments that are supposedly able to 'drive' their policies through the House of Commons, other electoral systems lead to a policy process that emphasizes the need for compromise, negotiation and the development of a cross-party consensus. This occurs formally through the construction of coalition governments. Coalitions are usually based on post-election deals that share out posts in government and formulate legislation programmes that draw on the policy commitments of two or more parties. Consensus-building is also required in the case of single-party minority governments, which have to attract informal support from other parties in order to maintain control of their assembly or parliament. Policy, in any case, cannot be driven simply by the priorities of the leaders of a single party. The Scottish Parliament has thus broken with the Westminster Parliament on a number of key policy issues, despite Labour being the largest party in both institutions until it lost power in Scotland in 2007. Examples of this include higher education tuition fees and the provision of non-medical care for the elderly. The policy implications of devolution based on proportional voting systems are considered in greater detail in Chapter 10.

FOCUS ON . . .
Supplementary vote (SV)/Alternative vote (AV)

Used: London Mayor (SV), Scottish local government by-elections (AV).

Features:
▶ There are single-member constituencies.
▶ AV: electors vote preferrentially. SV: Electors have two votes: a first preference vote and a second, 'supplementary' vote.
▶ Winning candidates in the election must gain a minimum of 50 per cent of all votes cast.
▶ Votes are counted according to first preference. If no candidate reaches 50 per cent, under AV the bottom candidate drops out, and so on, until one candidate gains 50 per cent. Under SV, the top two candidates remain in the election and all other candidates drop out, their votes being redistributed on the basis of their supplementary vote (meaning that the winner must achieve 50 per cent).

Advantages:
▶ SV/AV ensures that fewer votes are 'wasted' than in FPTP.
▶ As winning candidates must secure at least 50 per cent support, a broader range of views and opinions influence the outcome of the election, with parties thus being drawn towards the centre ground.

Disadvantages:
▶ The outcome of the election may be determined by the preferences of those who support small, possibly extremist, parties.
▶ Winning candidates may enjoy little first-preference support and only succeed with the help of redistributed supplementary votes, making them only the least unpopular candidate.

Which electoral system is best?

Electoral reform: A change in the rules governing elections, usually involving the replacement of one electoral system by another; in the UK the term is invariably associated with the reform of FPTP and the adoption of a PR system.

The **electoral reform** debate in the UK has intensified since the mid-1970s. This is because of the revival in support for the Liberal Party and, later, the Alliance and the Liberal Democrats. Although more people voted for centre parties, they were unable to make an electoral breakthrough because of the biases implicit in the FPTP voting system. This was very clearly demonstrated in 1983, when the Alliance gained over one quarter of the vote but won only 23 seats, coming second in no fewer than 313 constituencies.

The prospects for electoral reform nevertheless brightened during the 1990s, as more and more members of the Labour Party were converted to the cause of PR. This occurred for two reasons:

▶ Having been defeated by the Conservatives in four general elections between

1979 and 1992, some Labour members had started to doubt if the party could win any more under FPTP.

▶ Many in the Labour Party anticipated returning to power probably as a member of a coalition government with the Liberal Democrats, and that would only be possible if they reached an agreement on electoral reform.

Growing sympathy towards electoral reform within the Labour Party was evident in two ways. First, Labour agreed that each of the devolved and other bodies that the party planned to introduce if it was returned to power would have a PR voting system. These new bodies, together with their various PR systems, were established from 1997 onwards. Second, Labour committed itself to the establishment of an Independent Commission on the Westminster voting system, chaired by the Liberal Democrat peer and former Labour minister, Lord Jenkins. The aim of the Commission was to develop an alternative to FPTP that could be put to a public vote through a referendum. However, although the Commission reported in 1998, proposing the adoption of a system called '**AV Plus**', the promised referendum was never held and the issue of electoral reform for Westminster elections was quietly forgotten. This occurred because support for PR within the Labour Party declined significantly once the 1997 election proved that Labour could still win, and indeed win handsomely, under FPTP rules.

> **AV plus**: A mixed voting system consisting of the alternative vote (AV) and the party list, which is used as a top-up; SV is a version of AV

Parties' positions on electoral reform have always been closely linked to calculations about political advantage. The Conservative Party, the UK's major party of government, has consistently opposed plans to reform an FPTP system that has only very rarely failed to 'over-represent' it. Labour, for its part, supported electoral reform for Westminster until 1945, when the party formed its first majority government, and its subsequent interest in electoral reform has tended to surface only when the party has been in opposition for a prolonged period or when it anticipates losing its majority at the next election. As a result, the prospects for electoral reform in the UK have always been linked to the possibility of a **'hung' Parliament**, in which a 'third' party, now the Liberal Democrats, holds the balance of power.

> **'Hung' Parliament**: A parliament in which no single party has majority control in the House of Commons.

This is precisely what occurred in 2010. The key aspect of the deal between the Conservatives and the Liberal Democrats through which the coalition government was formed was an agreement to hold a referendum on the introduction of AV for Westminster elections, with a commitment to impose a three-line whip on both parties in order to push the measure through the Commons in the event of a successful referendum. The decision to hold the AV referendum was clearly a compromise between the Liberal Democrats' preference for the proportional STV system (which would almost have tripled their representation in 2010, see Table 3.3), and Conservative support for the retention of FPTP. Ironically, the only

FOR OR AGAINST?

REFORMING WESTMINSTER ELECTIONS

FOR	AGAINST

FOR

Electoral fairness. Fairness dictates that a party's strength in Parliament *should* reflect its level of support in the country. Proportionality underpins the basic democratic principle of political equality. In PR, all people's votes have the same value, regardless of the party they support.

All votes count. In PR, no votes, or fewer votes, are 'wasted', in the sense that they are cast for candidates or parties who lose the election, or are surplus to the needs of winning candidates or parties. This should strengthen electoral turnout and promote civic engagement.

Majority government. Governments elected under PR will enjoy the support of at least 50 per cent of those who vote. These will be genuinely popular, broad-based governments. By contrast, FPTP results in plurality rule. Parliamentary majorities can be gained with as little as 35 per cent of the vote, as occurred in 2005.

Accountable government. PR has implications for the relationship between the executive and Parliament. FPTP leads to executive domination because a single party has majority control of the Commons. Under PR, governments have to listen to Parliament as they will generally need the support of two or more parties.

Consensus political culture. PR electoral systems distribute political power more widely. As a wider range of parties are involved in the formulation of policy, decision-making becomes a process of consultation, negotiation and compromise. 'Partnership politics' therefore replaces 'yaa-boo politics'.

AGAINST

Clear electoral choice. FPTP aids democracy because it clarifies the choices available to voters. It offers voters a clear and simple choice between potential parties of government, each committed to a different policy or ideological agenda. This makes elections and politics more meaningful to ordinary citizens.

Constituency representation. FPTP establishes a strong and reliable link between a representative and his or her constituency. When a single MP serves a single constituency, people know who represents their interests and who should take up their grievances.

Mandate democracy. In FPTP, voters get what they vote for: winning parties have the ability to carry out their manifesto promises. The doctrine of the mandate can therefore only operate in systems that produce single-party governments. Under PR, policies are decided through post-election deals not endorsed by the electorate.

Strong government. FPTP helps to ensure that governments can govern. This happens because the government of the day enjoys majority control of the House of Commons. Coalition governments, by contrast, are weak and ineffective because they have to seek legislative support from two or more parties.

Stable government. Single-party governments are stable and cohesive, and so are generally able to survive for a full term in office. This is because the government is united by common ideological loyalties and is subject to the same party disciplines. Coalition governments, by contrast, are often weak and unstable.

party that was committed to holding a referendum on AV in the 2010 election was the defeated Labour Party. AV, which is used in elections for the Australian House of Commons, has nevertheless long been viewed as a possible alternative to FPTP in the UK. A Royal Commission in 1909–10 proposed that AV be used for elections to the House of Commons, but without success. A bill to introduce AV passed the Commons in 1917, but was rejected by the Lords and was eventually withdrawn. And an attempt by the minority Labour government, 1929–31, to establish AV only failed when the government fell.

AV has some clear advantages as an alternative to FTPT. These include that it would involve the simplest change, requiring no alteration to the established constituency structures. It can also be seen to maintain some of the alleged benefits of FPTP – a firm link between an MP and his or her constituency; and the possibility of strong and stable government, achieved through the existence of a single majority party – whilst at the same time increasing voter choice (through preferential voting) and ensuring that MPs enjoy at least 50 per cent support in their constituency. Under FPTP, this did not occur in about two-thirds of parliamentary constituencies and, exceptionally, as in Inverness in 1992, seats can be won with as little as 26.6 per cent of the vote. However, AV also has drawbacks. Chief amongst these is that it would create little prospect of greater proportionality, and may even result in less proportional outcomes (it has been estimated, for instance, that, under AV, Labour's majority in 1997 would have been 245 instead of 178). Many therefore argued that the Conservatives could accept AV on the grounds that the Westminster electoral system would remain clearly majoritarian, while for many Liberal Democrats AV was only desirable as a stepping stone to 'proper' PR, preferably achieved through the introduction STV.

The defeat of the AV referendum in May 2011 brought to an end this most recent attempt to reform the Westminster electoral system. In so doing, it badly damaged the prospects for electoral reform in the near future. The size of AV's defeat (with a 'no' vote of 68 per cent), and the fact that AV represents the most modest version of electoral reform, appears to provide clear evidence of a lack of public support for the abandonment of FPTP. On the other hand, the outcome of the referendum may have had more to do with the unpopularity of the Liberal Democrats in 2011 than with the popularity of FPTP.

Weblink ■ www.electoral-reform.org.uk/downloads/What%20is%20AV web.pdf

Use this website to access an Electoral Reform Society's pamphlet on *What is AV?*

However, would the reform of the Westminster voting system be a 'good thing'? What is the best voting system? The simple fact is that there is no such thing as a 'best' electoral system. Each voting system is better at achieving different things: the

Table 3.3 Allocation of seats in 2010 election using different electoral systems

Parties	FPTP	AV	STV	'Pure' PR
Conservative Party	307	246	246	234
Labour Party	258	262	207	189
Liberal Democrats	57	79	162	150
Others	28	28	35	77

Source: Electoral Reform Society.

real question is which of these things are the most important? The electoral reform debate is, at heart, a debate about the desirable nature of government and the principles that underpin 'good' government. Is representative government, for instance, more important than effective government? Is a bias in favour of compromise and consensus preferable to one that favours conviction and principle? There are no objective answers to these questions, only competing viewpoints.

Weblink ■ www.makemyvotecount.org.uk

Use the Make My Vote Count site for a critical review of FPTP and its campaign to widen voter choice and strengthen representation.

Voting behaviour

How can we explain the outcome of elections? Why do people support one party rather than another? The study of voting behaviour is important because it helps us to explain the process of political change, not only changes in government but also changes in parties' policies and ideological beliefs (as will be discussed in Chapter 4). However, there is no agreement about how voting behaviour should be explained. Instead, there are three competing theories of voting:

▶ **Sociological model.** This links voting behaviour to group membership. It suggests that electors adopt a pattern of voting that reflects the economic and social position of the group (or groups) to which they belong. It therefore places emphasis on long-term social factors, such as social class, gender, ethnicity, religion and region.

▶ **Party identification model.** This sees voting as an expression of an emotional attachment that people have to a party. Electors 'identify' with a party in the sense of being a long-term supporter – the party is *their* party. Voting is therefore a manifestation of **partisanship**.

▶ **Issue-voting model.** This treats voters as if they are consumers, who cast their vote for the party they think is most likely to benefit them. Voting is therefore

Partisanship: A bias or preference in favour of a particular group or body, expressed through affection, loyalty and support.

an instrumental act: it is a means to an end. This suggests that long-term social or political factors are less important than the policies adopted by the various parties.

Long-term factors and voting

Voting in the UK has traditionally been explained in terms of long-term social and political factors. This is because, until the 1970s, voting patterns tended to be stable and habitual. Most voters could be classified as **'core' voters**, with only a minority (around one fifth) being so-called **'floating' voters**.

A variety of long-term factors influence voting:

Core voters: Voters who support the same party time and time again, reflecting a strong allegiance towards a particular party.

Floating (or swing) voters: Voters with few or no long-term party loyalties, who therefore vote for different parties in different elections.

Class voter: Either a working-class Labour voter or a middle-class Conservative voter.

▶ **Social class.** Until the 1970s, class was widely seen as the key to understanding voting behaviour in the UK. Peter Pulzer (1967) was able to declare, famously: 'Class is the basis of British party politics; all else is embellishment and detail'. The stable Conservative–Labour two-party system of the 1945–70 period was largely a reflection of what was called 'class alignment' (a link between class and voting). For example, in 1964–66, 64 per cent of working class or manual voters (classes C2, D and E, see p. 00) voted Labour, while 62 per cent of middle-class or non-manual voters (classes A, B and C1) voted Conservative. Overall, in 1966, 66 per cent of voters could be classified as **class voters**, in that they supported their 'natural' party. However, from the 1970s onwards, the UK has experienced an accelerating process of 'class dealignment' (see p. 88). This does not mean that social class has become irrelevant to voting behaviour, but only that the relationship between class and voting has weakened substantially. By 1979, just 51 per cent of all voters supported their 'natural' class party, and by 1987 this had fallen to a mere 44 per cent. The 2010 general election witnessed the weakest ever link between class and voting, with only 38 per cent of electors being 'class voters' (see Table 3.4).

Weblink ■ http://tutor2u.net/politics/topics/elections/class_voting.htm

Use this tutor2u website to find out more about social class and voting behaviour in the UK.

▶ **Party loyalty.** The second factor that explains the relatively stable, habitual voting patterns of the 1964–70 period is that most voters had a clear and enduring identification with a particular party. This was known as 'partisan alignment' (a link between voting and party identification). For instance, during 1964–66, 90 per cent of voters claimed to identify with a party, overwhelmingly with Labour or the Conservatives. What is more, many voters (44 per cent in 1964) saw themselves as 'very strong' identifiers with a party. Nevertheless, like social class, party loyalty has declined markedly since the 1970s, in this case through a process of 'partisan dealignment' (see p. 89). This has been most marked in relation to the strength of party identification. By 2005, a mere 10 per

BY COMPARISON . . .

Elections in the USA

- The USA has separate elections for the presidency and for Congress. The president and vice president are elected every four years on a single ticket. Members of the House of Representatives are re-elected every two years. Each Congressman or Congresswoman (as they are called), like each MP, represents a single district. Senators are re-elected every six years on a 'rolling' system, one third of them being re-elected every two years. Two Senators represent each state, regardless of population. Unlike the UK, US elections are fixed-term elections (presidential elections are held on the Tuesday after the first Monday in November every four years).

- Primary elections (internal party elections) and caucuses (party meetings) play a major role in the nomination of electoral candidates. The 'primary circuit' for presidential elections starts in January with the Iowa caucus and the New Hampshire primary. These play a disproportionate role in the nomination of presidential candidates because they create a 'band-wagon effect' – successful candidates attract greater media attention, more campaign finance, and so on. The nominations are effectively decided long before the national party conventions in the summer.

- Electoral turnout is low, with often only about 50 per cent voting in presidential elections. This is because of difficulties in registering to vote (only just over 75 per cent of adult Americans are 'registered voters'), many contests are uncompetitive with the incumbent candidate a 'certain' winner, and the electoral choice is narrow (usually only between Republican and Democrat). Non-voting is also closely related to income, and there is a disproportionately low level of turnout amongst most ethnic and racial minorities.

- The Democrats are more closely associated with those on low incomes, while the Republicans draw support from higher income groups. Nevertheless, like the UK, the USA has experienced a process of partisan dealignment, with a fall in the number of 'strong party identifiers' and a rise in the number of 'independents'. 'Split-ticket voting' (voting for different parties in different elections) has also become more common.

Table 3.4 Voting and social class in 2010

Category	Con	Lab	LD	Con lead over Lab
Class AB	36	29	28	+7
Class C1	42	26	26	+8
Class C2	39	22	24	+17
Class DE	28	44	15	−16

cent of voters claimed to be 'very strong' party identifiers, with only 9 per cent identifying very strongly with the Conservative or Labour parties.

▶ **Gender.** The main gender bias in UK voting has traditionally been a tendency for women voters to support the Conservatives. This became less pronounced under Margaret Thatcher (see p. 250), but reasserted itself under John Major. Nevertheless, the advent of Tony Blair (see p. 223) and New Labour had a major impact on this gender bias. In 1997, Labour was supported by an equal number of women and men (44 per cent), making this the first general election which Labour would have won with an all-female electorate. This trend continued in 2001 and 2005. In 2010, men in the 18–34 age range were clearly more likely to vote Conservative than women, and it was only amongst voters aged 55 or above that female Conservative voters outnumbered male voters (44 per cent to 39 per cent).

▶ **Age.** There is a general tendency for levels of Conservative support to increase with age. Even in 1997 and 2001, the party led Labour among the over-65s. Some explain this in terms of a tendency for people to become more conservative with age (either because they are better-off or because they become more fearful of change), while others use the idea of **political generations**. Labour, by contrast, tends to do better amongst young voters, although it suffered defections (usually to the Liberal Democrats) amongst 18–25 year olds in 2005. In 2010, the tendency for Conservative voting to increase with age was particularly evident amongst female voters.

Political generation: The (alleged) tendency for a generation of voters to remain loyal to the party that was dominant when they were young.

▶ **Religion and ethnicity.** Although the impact of religion on party affiliation weakened during the 20th century, the Conservatives still enjoyed a 9 per cent lead over Labour in 2005 amongst Church of England voters (the church was once seen as the 'Tory party at prayer'). Labour, on the other hand, has drawn disproportionate support from the Protestant non-conformists, and especially Methodists, and, to a lesser extent, from Catholics. Black and ethnic minority voters have also usually voted Labour. In 2001, Labour had a 67 per cent lead over the Conservatives among black voters and a 58 per cent lead amongst Asian voters. However, there were signs of a fracturing in the Asian vote in 2005 and 2010, with defections among some Muslim Asians from Labour, usually to the Liberal Democrats, over the Iraq War.

FOCUS ON . . .
Class dealignment

Class dealignment is the weakening of the relationship between social class and party support. Social class may nevertheless remain a significant factor influencing electoral choice. Class dealignment is reflected in a declining proportion of working-class voters supporting Labour, and a fall in the proportion of middle-class voters supporting the Conservatives. Among the consequences of class dealignment has been a shift in the policies and ideas of the major two parties (especially Labour) as they have been forced to seek votes from 'natural' supporters of other parties.

Suggested explanations for class dealignment include the following:

▶ **Changing class system.** The manual work force has shrunk (from 58 per cent in 1961 to 29 per cent in 2010), and the **'traditional' working class** has given way to the **'new' working class**.

▶ **Cross-class locations.** Social class has become less clear-cut, through, for instance, the decline in trade union membership and the rise in home ownership.

▶ **Embourgeoisement.** Growing affluence has encouraged some working-class voters to think of themselves as being middle-class. Affluent workers are less 'solidaristic' and may be more concerned about material self-interest.

▶ **Sectoral cleavages.** Voters have been increasingly affected by whether they work in the public sector or the private sector. These cleavages cut across class differences.

Traditional working class: Manual workers who tend to work in 'heavy' industries (e.g. coal, steel and shipbuilding), have high levels of union membership and are dependent on public services, including council housing.

New working class: Workers who tend to work in service or 'sunrise' industries, are less unionized and are often home-owners.

▶ **Region.** During the 1980s, it became increasingly topical to talk of a 'North–South divide' in UK politics. Labour held only a handful of seats south of a line from the Bristol Channel to the Wash, while Conservative support declined in the north of England and, for a period, the party held no seats in either Scotland or Wales. Although Labour made significant progress in traditionally Conservative areas in 1997 and 2001, these broad regional trends still persist. For example, Conservative gains in 2005 were made almost exclusively in the south. Liberal Democrat support also has a marked regional dimension, its support being strongest in the so-called **'Celtic fringe'**. Generalizations about regional party strength nevertheless conceal substantial intra-regional differences and are, anyway, largely a reflection of class factors and the impact of differences between urban (pro-Labour) and rural (pro-Conservative) areas.

Weblink ■ www.essex.ac.uk/bes

Use the British Election Study at the University of Essex for a detailed analysis of the 2005 general election and of matters influencing voting behaviour.

FOCUS ON . . .
Partisan dealignment

Partisan dealignment is a decline in the extent to which people align themselves with a party by identifying with it. What is seen as the 'normal' support of parties falls, and a growing number of electors become 'floating' voters. The main consequence of partisan dealignment has been greater electoral volatility. This has been reflected in increased uncertainty about electoral outcomes, as 'swings' from one party to another become larger and, perhaps, in the rise of new parties or the decline of old ones.

A variety of explanations have been advanced for partisan dealignment:

▶ **Increased education.** The expansion of education in recent decades has encouraged voters to question traditional, party-based loyalties, and perhaps to take policies and issues more seriously.

▶ **Impact of the media.** Voters have access to wider sources of political information, particularly through television. They are therefore less dependent on party-supporting newspapers.

▶ **Ideological change.** Shifts in parties' policies and ideological beliefs since the 1980s (often in response to class dealignment) have alienated some of their traditional supporters.

▶ **Decline in 'social capital'.** As post-industrial societies have become more diverse, fluid and consumer-orientated, social attachments and loyalties of all kinds have weakened.

Short-term factors and voting

In an 'age of dealignment' and greater electoral volatility, short-term factors have become more important in explaining the outcome of elections. A variety of short-term factors may be significant:

▶ **Policies.** Parties spend a great deal of time and effort formulating policies that will have wide electoral appeal. Having the 'wrong' policies can certainly damage a party, as Labour demonstrated in 1983 when its manifesto (famously described by a former Labour minister as the 'longest suicide note in history') contained commitments to extend nationalization, increase taxation and boost public spending. Labour's long road back to 'electability' started with a comprehensive policy review, which was initiated after its third successive election defeat in 1987. Since 2003, the Conservatives have similarly been trying to revive their electoral fortunes by revising their policies, notably on issues such as the environment and public services (see Chapter 4).

▶ **Performance.** The conventional wisdom on elections has long been that 'governments lose elections; oppositions do not win them'. This suggests that elections are largely decided by the performance of the government of the day, and particularly by its economic performance. As the reminder on the wall of Bill Clinton's office during the 1992 presidential election put it: 'It's the Economy, Stupid'. If the 2010 general election could be regarded as a 'referendum' on Labour's performance, the party was fatally damaged by the loss of its reputation for economic competence following the global financial crisis and the subsequent sharp recession. However, there is no simplistic link between economic performance and electoral outcomes. The Conservatives were badly defeated in 1997, despite several years of steady economic growth.

▶ **Leaders.** In an 'age of dealignment', parties place increasing faith in leaders and leadership to win elections. However, what makes for an effective leader in electoral terms? Successful leaders have to demonstrate a number of qualities:

  ▶ *Accessibility*. Leaders must be telegenic and demonstrate a relaxed 'like-ability'.
  ▶ *Trust*. Voters need to believe that what their leaders say is true.
  ▶ *Strength*. Leaders have to demonstrate that they can 'run the show'.

Tony Blair was widely believed to have been a considerable electoral asset for Labour in 1997 and 2001. By 2005, however, his personal appeal had diminished significantly. Nevertheless, it is difficult to argue that Blair had become an electoral liability, as neither of his main rivals (Michael Howard for the Conservatives and Charles Kennedy for the Liberal Democrats) were able to establish a lead over him, particularly on the issue of competence. In fact, Blair enjoyed a healthy 15 per cent lead over other party leaders when respondents were asked to choose who would make the best prime minister.

The importance of leaders was, potentially, greatly enhanced in 2010 by the introduction of US-style televised debates between the candidates of the three leading parties. The first debate undoubtedly transformed the fortunes of Nick Clegg, as polls taken in its aftermath were widely interpreted as evidence that 'Cleggmania' was sweeping the country. In the later debates, however, greater attention was given to less popular Liberal Democrat policies and the impact of the first debate faded, particularly as pro-Conservative newspapers sought to bolster the image of Cameron's performance. There is only modest evidence that the televised debates shifted anyone's opinion, even though they may have had a marginal impact on turnout. Of almost certainly greater significance, in terms of explaining the outcome in 2010, was the poor personal standing of Gordon Brown, who consistently lagged badly behind Cameron in opinion polls after the fiasco in the autumn of 2008 over the so-called 'election that never was' (when Brown eventually announced that he was not going to hold a 'snap' election after a summer during which his aides had deliberately played up the possibility of holding one).

▶ **Party image.** Associated with a party's policies and the appeal of its leader is the image that a party has in the minds of voters. For instance, Labour undoubtedly had an 'image problem' in the 1980s, still being seen as a 'cloth cap' party closely linked to the unions. During the 1990s, the Conservatives developed a reputation as the 'nasty party' (a description used in 2002 by the then Conservative chairman, Theresa May). The party was seen to be associated with a 'get rich quick' ethos and appeared to show little sympathy for the young, the poor, ethnic minorities, gays and lesbians, or women. After he became Conservative leader in December 2005, Cameron's strategy was largely devoted to 'detoxifying' the party's image. In this, he consciously drew on the example of Labour's rebranding ('New Labour') in the 1990s. In Cameron's case, this involved an emphasis on 'green' policies, a stress on a more inclusive appeal (aiming at the young, women and ethnic minority voters) and more open concern about the plight of the poor and the role of public services. Such image rebranding contributed significantly to the 5 per cent swing from Labour to the Conservatives in 2010. 'Rebranding' has therefore become an important electoral strategy for parties, as they try to create an image that will allow more voters to 'connect' with them. Names have been changed ('New Labour'), logos have been redesigned and leadership styles 'revamped'.

▶ **Campaigning.** Over £40 million was spent by parties during the 2005 election campaign. However, the net impact of national campaigning (via party-political broadcasts, newspaper advertising, media interviews, rallies and the like) may be less significant than, for example, getting the backing of major newspapers (especially the Murdoch group). Not uncommonly, party strength on polling day is often little different from what it was at the start of the three-week election campaign. On the other hand, there is clear evidence that local campaigning can make a difference. This has led to a growing tendency for parties to 'target' key seats as a means of artificially concentrating their support where it will have the greatest impact.

▶ **Tactical voting.** First used on a large scale in 1997, tactical voting occurs when two parties are sufficiently close to one another in policy and ideological terms for their supporters to be willing to vote for the 'other' party in order to keep their 'least preferred' party out of power. In 1997 and 2001, tactical voting favoured Labour and the Liberal Democrats and damaged the Conservatives. However, more complex patterns of tactical voting appear to have taken place in 2005 and 2010. Divisions between Labour and the Liberal Democrats over the Iraq War may have meant that fewer Liberal Democrat supporters were willing to 'lend' their vote to Labour, while former Labour supporters disaffected by the war were happy to switch their vote to the Liberal Democrats.

Weblink ■ www.ipsos-mori.com

Use Ipsos MORI for general information on UK voting behaviour and for the latest surveys on political issues.

Explaining declining turnout

The sharp declines in electoral turnout in 2001 and 2005 (the lowest two turnouts in any general election since 1918) stimulated anxiety about the state of political participation in the UK and led to a growing debate about how democracy can be 'renewed'. Although turnout increased in 2010, at 65 per cent it still remained well below the level of the 1950s and 1960s. Proposed solutions to this problem have included electoral reform, the use of e-democracy or digital democracy (see p. 58) and the introduction of compulsory voting (see p. 93). General explanations for declining electoral turnout and falling political participation are discussed in Chapter 2. But what light do the theories of voting behaviour throw on the issue?

Two sociological factors may be having an impact on turnout. The first is that there is a clear link between turnout and education: people with higher levels of education are more likely to vote than people who are less educated. However, this should have led to an increase, not a decrease, in turnout over time, as educational standards rise and participation rates in further and higher education continue to grow. The second factor is the changing size of the UK's ethnic minority population, amongst whom voting levels tend to be lower than in the wider society. The impact of this on recent turnout trends is highly questionable, however. Although the ethnic minority population has certainly grown, this has happened gradually over a number of decades; it did not happen abruptly in the post-1997 period. The same problem undermines partisan dealignment as an explanation for falling turnout. Partisan dealignment may undoubtedly be reflected in growing voter apathy, as declining party identification means that people may be less concerned about the outcome of elections. Nevertheless, partisanship started to decline in the 1970s, long before turnout levels began to cause alarm.

As none of these theories adequately explains what happened in 2001, 2005 and (albeit to a lesser extent) 2010, the answer may lie in the immediate political circumstances of these general elections. The simple fact may therefore be that there was little in 2001 and 2005 to encourage people to vote. In particular, a less-than-popular government faced an even more unpopular opposition, with the parties offering potential voters little choice in terms of policies or ideas. In 2010,

FOR OR AGAINST?

COMPULSORY VOTING

FOR	AGAINST
Increased participation. The almost certain consequence of introducing compulsory voting would be that turnout rates would increase. At a stroke, the UK's 'participation crisis' would be resolved. Indeed, a significant impetus for the introduction of compulsory voting in Australia was a decline in voter turnout, which had fallen to 60 per cent at the 1922 election.	**Abuse of freedom**. Compulsion, even in the name of democracy, remains compulsion: a violation of individual freedom. The right *not* to vote may be as significant as the right to choose who to vote for. Non-voting may, indeed, be entirely rational, reflecting, for instance, the absence of choice between parties or a principled rejection of the political system.
Greater legitimacy. Governments formed on the basis of compulsory voting would be much more likely to rest on a popular majority, not just an electoral majority. This has never occurred in a UK general election, and in 2005 the winning Labour Party's popular support was just 22 per cent. Compulsory voting would therefore strengthen the democratic legitimacy of UK governments.	**Cosmetic democracy**. Compulsory voting addresses the symptom but not the cause of the problem. Making voting compulsory would undoubtedly increase electoral turnout, but it would not address the deeper problems that account for a growing decline in civic engagement. Higher turnout levels brought about through compulsion may simply mask these problems.
Civic duty. Making voting compulsory would have wider educational implications in emphasizing, for voters and would-be non-voters alike, that political participation is a civic duty. The more people participate in politics, the more they will think and act as full citizens, as members of a political community.	**Worthless votes**. Generally, those who do not vote have the least interest in and understanding of politics. Forcing such would-be non-voters to vote would therefore simply increase the number of random and unthinking votes that are cast. This may be particularly the case as some voters may feel both resentful and aggrieved.
Stronger social justice. Voluntary voting effectively disadvantages the most vulnerable elements in society, the poor and less educated, those who are least likely to vote. The interests of the educated, articulate and well-off are thus represented at the expense of those who do not enjoy these advantages. Genuine political equality requires that not only that all *can* vote, but that all *do* vote.	**Distorted political focus**. A final problem with compulsory voting is that it may distort the strategies adopted by political parties, by encouraging them to frame policies designed to attract more volatile 'marginal' voters (would-be non-voters), rather than to focus on the interests of the mass of the electorate.

an unpopular prime minister, leading a government widely accused of economic failure, confronted an opposition that had only partially 'detoxified' its image and whose austerity package alarmed important sections of the electorate. If this is true, then the responsibility for increasing turnout appears to lie with the major parties themselves, and specifically with their capacity to regain public trust and credibility.

WHAT YOU SHOULD KNOW

▶▶ Elections are a method of filling an office or post through choices made by the electorate. The democratic character of elections is ensured by universal suffrage, political equality (in the form of one person, one vote), the secret ballot and electoral choice (provided by competition between candidates and parties).

▶▶ The main functions of elections are to form governments, ensure representation and maintain legitimacy. Representation is a relationship through which an individual or group stands for, or acts on behalf of, a larger body of people. The three main competing notions in debates about representation are trusteeship, the doctrine of the mandate and descriptive representation. Each notion of representation has been subject to criticism, however.

▶▶ There are five main voting systems currently in use in the UK: 'first-past-the-post', the additional member system, the single transferable vote, the regional party list and the supplementary/alternative vote. These systems can either be classified as majoritarian systems (which tend to 'over-represent' larger parties and usually result in single-party majority government) or as proportional systems (which guarantee an equal, or at least a more equal, relationship between the seats won by a party and the votes gained in the election).

▶▶ 'First-past-the-post', used for Westminster elections, has a range of important implications. These include systematic biases in favour of large parties, a tendency towards a two-party system and single-party government, and a trend in favour of landslide election victories.

▶▶ Proportional systems, as used for all elected bodies created since 1997 and the European Parliament, have quite different implications. These include greater proportionality, a tendency towards multiparty systems and coalition or minority government, and a trend in favour of policy being developed through compromise and consensus-building.

▶▶ Voting behaviour can be explained in three different ways. The sociological model focuses on the relationship between social factors and voting; the party-identification model considers voters' loyalty or attachment towards a party; and the issue model portrays voters as rationally self-interested actors.

▶▶ Voting is affected by long-term and short-term factors. The long-term factors include social class, age, race, gender, region and party loyalty, although these have been affected in recent years by the processes of class dealignment and partisan dealignment. The short-term factors include party policies, the performance and image of parties, the effectiveness of party leaders and tactical considerations.

Test yourself

Short questions:

1   What is an election?
2   Distinguish between an election and a referendum.
3   What is representation?
4   Identify *two* features of the 'first-past-the-post' electoral system.
5   Define proportional representation.
6   Briefly explain the meaning of class dealignment.
7   Briefly explain the meaning of partisan dealignment.

Medium questions:

8   Explain *two* functions of elections.
9   How do elections ensure representation?
10   Explain *three* ways in which elections promote democracy.
11   What are the limitations of the doctrine of the mandate?
12   Explain the workings of any *three* electoral systems used in the UK.
13   How does the 'first-past-the-post' differ from the other electoral systems used in the UK?
14   Why are marginal seats important under the 'first-past-the-post' system?
15   What influence does social class have on voting in the UK?

Extended questions:

16   To what extent do different electoral systems affect party representation and government?
17   To what extent has the use of more proportional electoral systems affected the political process in the UK?
18   Should proportional representation be introduced for Westminster elections?
19   Make a case against reforming the electoral system used for UK general elections.
20   'A link still exists between class and voting.' Discuss the extent to which class still influences voting behaviour in the UK.
21   To what extent have voting patterns in the UK become more volatile and less predictable?
22   Assess the impact of issue voting on the outcomes of recent UK general elections.

Chapter 4

Political Parties

Parties and politics

UK politics is party politics. When we vote, we vote for a political party – very few of us even know the name of the candidate we vote for. When governments are formed, they are formed *by* parties, and they govern very largely *as* parties: that is, through a process of party discipline. Parties dominate the lives of almost all of our politicians. Quite simply, they speak, vote and act (in most circumstances) as their parties tell them to. Gilbert and Sullivan's *HMS Pinafore* (1878) is no less true today than when it was first written: 'I always voted at my party's call, And I never thought of thinking for myself at all'. Parties are also responsible for developing the ideas and policies that dominate the political landscape in the UK. The battle of ideas is fought between rival political parties.

And yet, party politics in the UK appears to be in a sorry state. Somehow parties seem to be failing in one of their basic functions: getting people involved in political life. Turnout levels at elections have fallen; there has been a decline in party membership; and fewer voters claim to 'identify' with a particular party. In a media-obsessed age, leaders sometimes appear to be more important than their parties. Parties look to leaders to get them elected, rather than the other way round. The level of party competition has also changed. Instead of two mighty parties confronting one another, in many parts of the UK, three, four or even more parties jostle for power. What is more, the major two parties have come increasingly to resemble one another. Is the party-political battle any longer a battle of ideas?

- **What are the main functions of political parties?**
- **Where does power lie within parties?**
- **Is the two-party system any longer relevant?**
- **What are the main ideas and policies of the major parties?**
- **How much conflict is there between the major parties, and within them?**

GETTING YOU THINKING

An age of austerity: necessity or choice?

Before starting the chapter, read this passage and briefly consider the questions on the next page.

On 20 October 2010, the Chancellor, George Osborne, presented the government's spending review, which fixed the budgets for each government department up to 2014–15. By introducing the most radical programme of spending cuts in a generation, the spending review was a defining moment for the Conservative–Liberal Democrat coalition, probably marking out the dividing lines in UK politics for the current Parliament and possibly beyond. Much of the time and energy of the coalition had been devoted to negotiating these cuts ever since David Cameron, shortly after becoming prime minister, dubbed the new era the 'age of austerity'. Some £81 billion of spending cuts were mapped out over four years. This reflects, on average, a 19 per cent cut in departmental budgets, and will result in the loss of between half a million and three-quarters of a million of public sector jobs.

Why have these cuts been introduced? Osborne proclaimed that, in the light of the UK's record budget deficit (the extent to which government spending exceeds tax revenues), the purpose of the cuts was 'to bring sanity to our public finances and stability to our economy'. Referring to tackling the deficit, Cameron and Nick Clegg emphasised in the coalition's May 2010 programme for government that this 'is not what we came into politics to achieve'. These arguments are based on the assertion that a large budget deficit creates the ever-present danger of a financial crisis in which the pound collapses and the UK's 'credit rating' plummets. However, the Labour opposition and other critics of the coalition argued that the size, scale and timing of the government's cuts owes at least as much to an ideological desire to 'roll back' the state as it does to the need to appease financial markets. They point out that the fact that no other country in a similar position is adopting such a radical programme of cuts suggests that the cuts are being made by choice, not necessity.

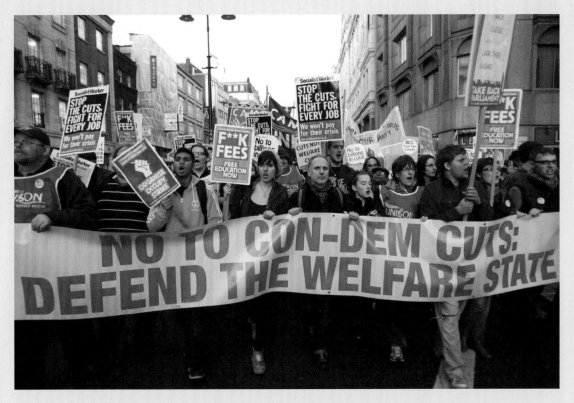

A demonstration against the coalition's programme of cuts – but is this simply a consequence of an inevitable need to reduce the budget deficit?

What issues do these developments raise?

▶▶▶ What was the chief purpose of the 2010 spending review?

▶▶▶ How has the coalition government justified its spending cuts?

▶▶▶ Why and how have the spending cuts been criticized?

▶▶▶ Why may 'rolling back' the state be seen as a desirable goal?

▶▶▶ How large should the state be? What should the state be responsible for?

IN THIS CHAPTER:

Parties and party politics • Parties: ideas and policies

Parties and party politics

Politics, it seems, cannot exist without political parties. The only political systems that have no parties are ones, such as military dictatorships, that suppress them by force. It would be a mistake, however, to assume that parties have always been with us. Parties, in the modern sense, only emerged during the 19th century, and were a product of the development of representative government and the extension of the franchise. Until then, there existed only '**factions**', which operated within the House of Commons, but which lacked the internal discipline of modern political parties as well as wider membership and organization outside of Parliament. In the early 19th century, the main factions in Parliament were the Whigs and Tories. These in due course developed, respectively, into the Liberal Party and the Conservative Party. The Labour Party was different, however. It developed not from a parliamentary faction but was created by pressures from beyond Parliament. It was established in 1900 by the trade union movement, in the hope of gaining working-class representation in the House of Commons.

Faction: A group of like-minded politicians, usually formed around a key leader or in support of a set of preferred policies.

Functions of parties

Why are parties so important to politics? Parties carry out a wide range of functions within the political system. However, in many cases, these have come under pressure in recent years, even allowing some commentators to speak of a 'crisis' in party politics.

Parties have the following functions:

▶▶▶ Representation
▶▶▶ Policy formulation
▶▶▶ Recruitment of leaders
▶▶▶ Organization of government
▶▶▶ Participation and mobilization of electorate.

Representation

Representation (see p. 67) is often seen as the primary function of parties in liberal democracies. Parties link government to the people by responding to and articulating public opinion. They do this by developing policies that appeal to the mass of the electorate. The major UK parties are therefore '**catch-all parties**'. The winning party in an election can thus claim a popular mandate to carry out its policies (see The doctrine of the mandate, p. 68). In this way, parties translate public opinion into government policy.

Catch-all party: A party that develops policies that will appeal to the widest range of voters, by contrast with a programmatic party.

What is . . . a political party

A political party is a group of people that is organized for the purpose of winning government power. In a democratic system, parties do this by putting candidates up for election, in the hope of gaining representation and ultimately forming (or participating in) government. Parties are often confused with pressure groups (see p. 139) or social movements.

Political parties have three main features:

▶ Parties aim to exercise government power by winning political office (small parties may nevertheless use elections more to gain a political platform than to win power)
▶ Parties typically adopt a broad issue focus, addressing each of the major areas of government policy (small parties, however, may have a narrower, or even a single, issue focus, thus resembling pressure groups)
▶ Members of political parties are usually united by shared political preferences and a general ideological identity, although these are often loose and broadly defined.

However, the effectiveness of parties in ensuring representation has also been questioned:

▶ The electorate is not always well-informed and rational in choosing between parties. Factors such as a party's image and the personality of its leader may be as important as its policies (see Chapter 3).
▶ Because of the 'first-past-the-post' electoral system (see p. 71), parties may only need the support of 35–40 per cent of the electorate to win a general election.

Differences between . . .
PROGRAMMATIC PARTIES AND CATCH-ALL PARTIES

Programmatic parties	Catch-all parties
Ideological	Pragmatic
Long-term goals	Short-term popularity
Fixed values	Flexible values
Shape public opinion	Follow public opinion
Traditional policies	Policy renewal
Class-based support	Classless support
Strong activist base	Weak activist base

Policy formulation

Political parties are one of the key means through which societies set collective goals and formulate public policy. In the process of seeking power, parties develop programmes of government (through party forums, annual conferences and, most importantly, in election manifestos). Not only does this mean that parties often *initiate* policy (come up with policy proposals), but they also *formulate* coherent sets of policy options that give the electorate a choice of realistic and achievable goals.

However, the effectiveness of parties in formulating policies has also been questioned:

▸ As the major parties have, in recent years, distanced themselves from their traditional ideologies, they have become less interested in formulating larger goals for society, and generally less interested in ideas. (This trend is discussed on pp. 121–2.)

▸ In a related development, parties have become more eager to *follow* public opinion (for example, by responding to opinion polls and the views of focus groups) than in trying to *shape* it by adopting clear ideological stances.

Weblink ■ www.epolitix.com

Use the ePolitix website to gain access to wide-ranging and up-to-date political news, comment and interviews.

Recruitment of leaders

All senior political careers start with the decision to join a political party. As a party member, a budding politician can gain experience of canvassing, debating issues and helping to run a constituency party. Most importantly, party membership opens the door to political office. Nomination as a parliamentary candidate can ultimately lead to Number 10 (where the prime minister lives: 10 Downing Street). Parties therefore both recruit and train the political leaders of the future.

However, the effectiveness of parties in recruiting and training leaders has also been questioned:

▸ As governments are appointed from the ranks of the majority party in the House of Commons, they rely on a relatively small pool of talent.

▸ Electioneering and other party activities may be poor training for running a large government department.

Organization of government

The operation of government relies on parties in many ways. Parties:

What is ... party government

Party government is a system through which single parties are able to form governments and carry through policy programmes.

Party government has a number of features:

▶ The major parties have clear ideological convictions and develop rival programmes of government, giving the electorate a meaningful choice between potential governments
▶ The governing party is able to claim a popular mandate and enjoys sufficient internal unity and ideological cohesion to be able to translate its manifesto commitments into government policy
▶ The government is accountable to the electorate through its mandate and by the existence of a credible opposition party, which acts as a balancing force.

▶ Help to form governments, meaning that the UK effectively has a system of 'party government'
▶ Give governments a degree of stability and coherence, especially as the members of the government are usually drawn from a single party and are therefore united by common sympathies and attachments
▶ Facilitate cooperation between the two major branches of government: Parliament and the executive
▶ Provide a source of opposition and criticism, helping to scrutinize government policy and provide a 'government in waiting'.

However, the effectiveness of parties in organizing government has also been questioned.

▶ The decline in party unity since the 1970s has tended to weaken the majority party's control of the Commons. (This tendency is discussed more fully in Chapter 7.)

Participation and mobilization

Political parties foster participation in two ways. Parties:

▶ Provide opportunities for citizens to join political parties and therefore help to shape party policy and, if they are lucky, government policy
▶ Help to educate and mobilize the electorate through a range of activities – canvassing, public meetings, advertising and poster campaigns, party broadcasts, and so on.

Such activities are designed to elicit support for a particular party, and for its policy and ideological agendas. This is the sense in which parties are, at heart, electoral machines, operating though the building up of loyalty and identification amongst the electorate.

However, the effectiveness of parties in ensuring participation and mobilization has also been questioned:

▶ Voters' loyalty towards, and identification with, parties has declined. Whereas 44 per cent of voters claimed to have a 'very strong' attachment to a party in 1964, this had fallen to a mere 10 per cent by 2005 through the process of partisan dealignment (see p. 89).

▶ Turnout in general elections has fallen sharply since 1997, with only 59 per cent voting in 2001, the lowest turnout since 1918, and 65 per cent voting in 2010, still about 10 per cent below the historical trend.

▶ The membership of parties in the UK has fallen – from over 3 million in the 1960s to around 800,000 in the early 2000s (see pp. 48–53 for more details).

Weblink ■ www.guardian.co.uk

Use the Guardian Unlimited website for news and comment on current affairs, with helpful links to other sites.

Who has power within parties?

As parties are important channels of communications between government and the people, the location of power within them is of great significance. Are parties really governing machines, centralized bodies that are controlled by a small group of parliamentary leaders? Or are they genuinely 'bottom-up' organizations that are responsive to pressure from members and extra-parliamentary bodies? What is significant here is not so much the formal structure of a political party but how, and by whom, its policies and political strategies are determined.

The main actors within a political party are:

▶▶ Party leaders
▶▶ Parliamentary parties
▶▶ Members and constituency parties
▶▶ Party backers.

Party leaders

In theory, Conservative leaders have greater authority than Labour leaders. Whereas few formal obstacles stand in the way of Conservative leaders, Labour leaders are supposed to be bound by decisions made by their annual conferences and, between conferences, by the views of the National Executive Committee (NEC). However, as McKenzie (1964) argued, for most practical purposes power is distributed in the same way in the two parties: parliamentary leaders dominate the rest of the party. This applies especially when the leader is the prime minister. Indeed, since the 1980s, party leaders have grown in importance in a number of respects. In an age of political celebrity, their public profiles dominate those of senior colleagues and even of their parties. Moreover, in line with the trend towards 'presidentialism' (examined in Chapter 8), leaders are increasingly expected to determine their parties' ideological direction and to deliver electoral success. However, they are by no means all-powerful. The fact that leaders act as a kind of 'brand image' for their parties is a source of vulnerability as well as strength. There is an increasing tendency for 'failed' leaders to be removed or encouraged to stand down. The Conservatives, for instance, have had no fewer than four leaders since John Major resigned after the 1997 general election – William Hague (1997–2001), Iain Duncan Smith (2001–03), Michael Howard (2003–05) and David Cameron (since 2005). The Liberal Democrats have had three leaders since 2005 – Charles Kennedy (until 2006), Sir Menzies Campbell (2006–07) and Nick Clegg (since 2007).

Parliamentary parties

The popular image of parliamentary parties is that, being subject to a system of party discipline, they are mere 'lobby fodder': troops ready to be pushed through the division lobbies on the instructions of their leaders. Nevertheless, trends dating back to the 1970s suggest that MPs have generally become less deferential and more independently minded. This has been reflected in a decline of party unity (as discussed in Chapter 7), which can lead to splits and divisions that, in turn, weaken the authority of the leader. Margaret Thatcher's removal in 1990 demonstrates the ultimate power than parliamentary parties have over their leaders, and Major's position was seriously undermined by a series of backbench revolts, mainly over Europe. The 1922 Committee (the committee of Conservative backbenchers) and the Parliamentary Labour Party (PLP) may therefore play a significant role in upholding or challenging the parliamentary leadership. As far as the PLP is concerned, it has the additional power of electing the members of Labour's shadow cabinet when the party is in opposition.

Members and constituency parties

The influence of constituency parties and party members is difficult to evaluate. On the one hand, falling membership and an associated decline in the ranks of party activists suggests that constituency parties are becoming less and less important. Furthermore, the growing tendency for the major parties to develop policy through policy committees, forums and task forces has generally strengthened the control that parliamentary leaders exercise over policy development, while creating an impression of consultation and wider debate. In the Labour Party, such strategies have effectively robbed the party conference of its traditional

FOCUS ON . . .
How party leaders are elected

Labour leaders are elected as follows:

▶ In the case of a vacancy, nominations must be supported by 12.5 per cent of the PLP. Where there is no vacancy, nominations must be supported by 20 per cent of the PLP.

▶ Voting takes place in three sections, each section having one third of the vote, using the alternative vote system, or AV (see p. 80). *Section 1* consists of Labour MPs and MEPs. *Section 2* consists of individual members of the Labour Party (since 1993, they have voted on the basis of one member, one vote, or OMOV). *Section 3* consists of members of affiliated organizations (trade unions and socialist societies).

▶ If no candidate receives more than half the vote, the least popular candidate drops out, with his or her votes being redistributed until one candidate achieves 50 per cent.

Conservative leaders are elected as follows:

▶ In the case of a vacancy, candidates can be nominated by any two Conservative MPs. Where there is no vacancy, a leadership contest can be initiated by the parliamentary party passing a vote of no confidence in the present leader. This is called if 15 per cent of

Conservative MPs write to the chairman of the 1922 Committee.

▶ If more than two candidates stand, MPs hold a series of ballots to reduce the number to two. On each round, the candidate with the fewest votes is eliminated. If two candidates stand, the election immediately proceeds to a ballot of all party members. If only one candidate stands (as happened in 2003), he or she is elected uncontested.

▶ All paid-up party members are then eligible to vote for one of the two remaining candidates. The candidate who tops the poll is declared the leader.

Liberal Democrat leaders are elected as follows:

▶ Candidates for the leadership of the Liberal Democrats must be supported by 10 per cent of the parliamentary party plus 200 party members drawn from at least 20 constituencies. There is no limit to the number of candidates and MPs can nominate more than one candidate.

▶ The election is decided by all individual members of the Liberal Democrats in a postal ballot.

▶ Voting is conducted on the basis of AV.

policy-making role. On the other hand, constituency parties and ordinary members have retained, or even enlarged, their power in other respects. Conservative constituency associations, for instance, have maintained a high degree of autonomy in the selection of parliamentary candidates, even though the process has become more centrally controlled in the Labour Party (not least through the imposition of all-women shortlists in half of all 'winnable' seats before the 1997 and 2005 elections). Nevertheless, the clearest demonstration of internal party democracy is in the role that individual party members now play in the election of party leaders.

Party backers

Some argue that the real power within political parties lies not with people who have formal positions of influence (leaders, MPs, constituency activists, and so on), but with the people who fund the party, those who provide campaign and political finance. Critics have long alleged that Labour has, in effect, been controlled by the trade unions that provide the bulk of the party's funds (Labour's dependence on the unions has significantly declined in recent years, but they still provide about one-third of the party's money). The Conservatives are similarly open to the allegation that their major business backers (such as brewers, tobacco companies and construction companies) exert undue influence over the process of policy development. Recurrent charges of 'sleaze' and corruption, levelled at both Conservative and Labour governments (for example, 'cash for questions' and 'cash for honours'), have also kept alive the idea that rich individuals can buy influence within parties. Such scandals have led to new rules on party funding, administered by the Electoral Commission (see p. 41), which, amongst other things, place limits on campaign spending and require the public disclosure of donations over £5,000. Others, nevertheless, argue that problems related to party finance can only properly be addressed by the introduction of state funding, as occurs widely in continental Europe (see State funding of political parties, p. 108).

The changing party system

Political parties are important not only because of the range of functions they carry out, but also because the relationships between and amongst them are crucial in structuring the way the political system works in practice. These relationships are called a party system. The traditional view of UK politics is that it is dominated by a two-party system (see p. 109). Just as the 19th century was characterized by a Conservative–Liberal two-party system, so the 20th century was characterized by a Conservative–Labour two-party system. In fact, this image has often been misleading. The Conservatives, for example, were the dominant party for much of the 20th century, with neither the Liberals nor Labour being able effectively to challenge them in the interwar period in particular. Nevertheless, an archetypal two-party system did exist between 1945 and 1970. During this period, Conservative and Labour parties consistently won over 90 per cent of the vote and also dominated the House of Commons with over 90 per cent of MPs. Power alternated four times, with the average electoral gap between the parties being only 4 per cent. However, even during this period, two-partyism was called into question during the 13 years of continuous Conservative rule during 1951–64.

FOCUS ON . . .
State funding of political parties

UK political parties receive relatively limited public funding for various purposes, including supporting long-term policy development and assisting opposition parties in carrying out their business. However, pressure to introduce a proper system of state funding has increased as funding and financial scandals have become more common. The issue, nevertheless, remains controversial.

Benefits of state funding:

▶ It would reduce parties' dependence on vested interests and allow them to be more responsive to the views of party members and voters. This would make parties more democratically responsive.

▶ It would create a more level playing field for the parties, removing the unfair advantages that some parties derive from the simple fact that they have wealthy backers.

▶ It would improve the performance of parties generally, allowing them to carry out their roles more effectively; and to waste less time and energy on fund raising.

Drawbacks of state funding:

▶ In providing parties with a reliable source of income, it may weaken their links to the larger society. These are brought about by the need to seek financial support as well as electoral support.

▶ It may create a bias in favour of existing parties if (as is usual) the level of state funding reflects past party performance.

▶ It may reduce the independence of parties, making them, in effect, part of the state machine and less likely to advance policies that run counter to the interests of important state bodies.

Two-party politics was once portrayed as the surest way of reconciling representative government with effective government. Its key advantage is that it makes possible a system of party government, supposedly characterized by stability, choice and accountability. The two major parties are able to offer the electorate a straightforward choice between rival programmes and alternative governments. Voters can support a party knowing that, if it wins the election, it will have the capacity to carry out its manifesto promises without having to negotiate or compromise with coalition partners. The two-party system was also praised for delivering strong but accountable government, based on competition between the governing and opposition parties. Two-partyism, moreover, created a bias in favour of moderation. As the two contenders for power battled for the support of 'floating' voters, they were drawn to the centre ground. This helps to explain why a social-democratic consensus prevailed in the UK in the 1950s and 1960s (as discussed later in the chapter).

What is . . . a two-party system

A two-party system is a system that is dominated by two 'major' parties that have a roughly equal prospect of winning government power. In its classical form, a two-party system can be identified by three features:

▶ Although a number of 'minor' parties may exist, only two parties enjoy sufficient electoral and parliamentary strength to have a realistic chance of winning government power

▶ The larger of the two parties is able to rule alone (usually on the basis of a parliamentary majority); the other party provides the opposition

▶ Power alternates regularly between these parties; both are 'electable', the opposition serving as a 'government in the wings'.

However, the two-party system started to break down from 1974 onwards, with revived support for the 'third' party (the Liberals, then the Liberal-SDP Alliance (1983–87) and finally the Liberal Democrats). This shift was signalled by the outcome of the February 1974 election, which resulted in a 'hung' Parliament and the formation of a minority Labour government. During 1974–97, the UK had a kind of two-and-a-half-party system. This occurred as a result of significant shifts in voting behaviour associated with class dealignment (see p. 88) and partisan dealignment (see p. 89). The impact of these electoral shifts was nevertheless masked by the majoritarian tendencies of the 'first-past-the-post' electoral system (see p. 71). Indeed, the main political manifestation of these shifts was the long period of Conservative rule during 1979–97. Conservative dominance during this time was largely a consequence of the divided nature of the non-Conservative vote. The Labour Party, in particular, appeared to be in long-term decline, not only losing the support of working-class voters, but also being damaged by the shrinkage of the 'traditional' working class.

Since 1997, two-partyism in the UK has given way to multiple or overlapping party systems, which operate in different ways at different levels. Many of these, moreover, are multiparty systems (see p. 110). Two-partyism continued (thanks to the Westminster electoral system) to operate within the House of Commons. But, even there, it is distorted by the fact that Labour was in power continuously between 1997 and 2010. Two-partyism nevertheless suffered a major blow when the 2010 general election led to a 'hung' Parliament and the formation of a coalition government (see p. 79). This reflected a long-term decline in combined support for the Conservative and Labour Parties, down to 65 per cent in 2010. Whereas in February 1974, there were just 38 MPs from parties other than Labour and the Conservatives, in 2010 there were 85. This means that to gain a Commons majority of just one, the Conservative and Labour parties need to secure 86 more seats than their rival. That has been achieved in only 8 out of the 18 elections since

1945. Elsewhere, the picture is more complex and diverse. This has happened for a number of reasons:

- Devolution has made nationalist parties more prominent, turning them from being 'minor' Westminster parties into 'major' parties in Scotland and Wales.
- The use of proportional electoral systems for newly created bodies since 1997 has improved 'third' and minor party representation, also underlining the extent to which two-partyism was maintained by 'first-past-the-post' elections.
- New issues have emerged that cut across traditional party-political battle lines, such as Europe, the environment and war. This has given impetus to parties such as the United Kingdom Independence Party (UKIP), the Green Party and, especially in 2005, Respect.

Evidence of multipartyism is now widespread. The 2008 European Parliament election saw MEPs being elected from ten different parties. The Scottish Parliament was controlled until 2007 by a Labour–Liberal Democrat coalition, and during 2007–11 a minority Scottish National Party administration was in power. The Welsh Assembly has had four different types of government: a majority Labour administration, a minority Labour administration, a Labour–Liberal Democrat coalition and a grand coalition between Labour and Plaid Cymru. In Northern Ireland, where quite different parties compete for power, a power sharing executive controlled by the Democratic Unionists and Sinn Fein was established in 2007 on the basis of a Northern Ireland Assembly in which no party has overall control.

What is... a multiparty system

A multiparty system is a party system in which more than two parties compete for power.

Multiparty systems can be identified by three factors:

- No single party enjoys sufficient electoral or parliamentary strength to have a realistic prospect of winning government power alone. This means that the distinction between 'major' and 'minor' parties often becomes irrelevant.
- Governments tend to be either coalitions (see p. 79) or minority administrations. This can either create a bias in favour of compromise and consensus-building or it can lead to fractured and unstable government.
- Government power can shift both following elections and between elections as coalition partnerships break down or are renegotiated.

Parties: ideas and policies

Left and right

Left: Political ideas that are based on generally optimistic views about human nature and favour social change; left-wingers tend to support liberty, equality and state intervention.

Right: Political ideas that tend to be pessimistic about human nature and oppose change; right-wingers typically favour order, authority and oppose state intervention.

Capitalism: An economic system in which wealth is owned privately and economic life is organized according to the market.

Ideology: An 'ism', a more or less coherent set of ideas, values and theories that help to explain the world and guide political action.

Political ideas and beliefs are often categorized on the basis that they are either 'left'-wing' or 'right'-wing'. These terms date back to the French Revolution and the seating arrangements adopted by the different groups at the first meeting of the Estates General (roughly equivalent to Parliament) in 1789. Supporters of the king and the traditional social order sat on the right of the assembly, and the opponents sat on the left. Although the terms left and right do not have exact meanings, they tend to summarize different attitudes to the economy and the role of the state. Left-wingers generally support social welfare and economic intervention, and in extreme cases (communists or the 'far left') they believe that all property should be owned collectively by the state. Right-wingers, by contrast, wish to 'roll back the state' and support a free-market or unregulated **capitalism**. This can be illustrated by the traditional, linear left/right political spectrum.

In the UK, the left/right divide has traditionally been portrayed as a battle between two contrasting **ideologies**: socialism (see p. 113) and conservatism (see p. 113). In turn, these ideologies have been represented by political parties that have dominated UK politics since the early 20th century, the Labour and Conservative parties. Socialism has traditionally been viewed as the ideology of the Labour Party, and conservatism has traditionally been seen as the ideology of the Conservative Party. These two parties therefore had, to a greater or lesser extent, a 'programmatic' character. They developed policies on the basis of a vision of how they believed society *should* be organized. This vision was always defined in very general terms, allowing both major parties to be 'broad churches' and, when in power, to respond more to practical pressures than to ideological beliefs. Nevertheless, both parties had a sense of what they 'stood for'. This was underpinned by the class basis of their support. As discussed in Chapter 3, working-class voters tended to vote Labour and middle-class voters tended to vote Conservative.

However, the relevance of this traditional left/right battle between socialism and conservatism has declined in recent years in a number of ways:

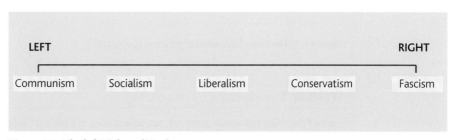

Figure 4.1 The left/right political spectrum

Conviction politics: A style of politics in which party policies are shaped by the ideological convictions of its leader.

▶ During the 1980s, the Conservative Party went through a period of major ideological upheaval. The party's traditionally non-ideological approach to politics was upset by an upsurge in '**conviction politics**' in the form of Thatcherism (see p. 116). Some within the party argued that this had led to an abandonment of traditional conservatism in favour of free-market or classical liberalism (see p. 127).

▶ The Labour Party has also changed, as a process of 'modernization' accelerated during the 1990s, leading to the birth of so-called New Labour. Many have asserted that New Labour, in effect, ditched the party's core values and broke any remaining link between the Labour Party and socialism.

▶ Ideology itself may have become less important. Labour and the Conservatives are no longer programmatic parties but 'post-ideological' catch-all parties. They are willing to adopt policies on the basis of 'what works' or 'what is popular', rather than on the basis of a long-term strategy or an ideological vision.

▶ Many modern political issues cut across the traditional left/right (pro-state versus anti-state) political spectrum. Examples include the environment, women's rights, homosexuality, abortion, cloning, multiculturalism, terrorism, and so on. Some therefore believe that an authoritarian/libertarian (strong state versus personal freedom) axis needs to be added to the left/right (state intervention versus the free market) spectrum:

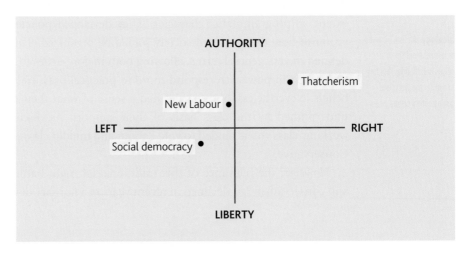

Figure 4.2 **The two-dimensional political spectrum**

Weblink ■ www.politicalcompass.org

Use the Political Compass website to test your own political views on a left/right and a libertarian/authoritarian spectrum.

What is... socialism

Socialism is an ideology that covers beliefs ranging from revolutionary communism to reformist social democracy (see p. 114). The central idea of socialism is that people are social creatures who are bound together by a common humanity. The defining values of traditional socialism are:

▶ Fraternity — literally, brotherhood; bonds of sympathy and comradeship between people.
▶ Cooperation — a preference for people working together rather than competing with one another.
▶ Equality — the desire to abolish or at least reduce class divisions.

There are two main kinds of socialism:

▶ *Fundamentalist* socialists (e.g. Marxists and communists) believe that capitalism should be abolished and replaced by a system based on the collective ownership of wealth
▶ *Revisionist* socialists (e.g. social democrats) believe that capitalism should be reformed through social and economic intervention.

Party ideology in the post-1945 period has gone through a number of phases:

▶▶ Post-war social democracy
▶▶ Thatcherism
▶▶ Post-Thatcherite consensus
▶▶ Ideas and policies in the 'age of austerity'.

What is... conservatism

Conservatism is an ideology that is defined by a 'desire to conserve'. It has traditionally been suspicious of abstract principles or developed theories, preferring instead to place its faith in tradition, experience and history.

The defining values of Conservativism are:

▶ Tradition — respect for ideas, practices and institutions that have been passed down from one generation to the next
▶ Human imperfection — the belief that people are security-seeking creatures and also morally flawed
▶ Hierarchy and authority — 'top-down' social organization is natural and beneficial.

There are two kinds of conservatism in the UK:

▶ *One Nation* conservatism (see p. 115)
▶ *Thatcherite* conservatism (see p. 116).

What is ... social democracy

Social democracy is an ideological stance that supports a broad balance between a capitalist or market economy on the one hand and state intervention on the other. Although some see social democracy as a betrayal of socialism (because it accepts the continuing need for capitalism), others view it as the only practicable form of socialism. The key goal of social democracy is reformed or 'humanized' capitalism, based on the economic efficiency that only capitalism can deliver and an enduring socialist belief in equality and social justice.

Post-war social democracy

The ideological identity of the Labour Party, and the nature of British socialism, were deeply influenced by the reforms enacted by the Attlee governments, 1945–51. These reforms gave rise to a particular brand of socialism, best referred to as social democracy. Social democracy is a 'revisionist', even 'watered down', form of socialism. Instead of trying to abolish capitalism, as socialists in the Marxist or communist tradition had wanted to do, social democrats sought instead to reform or 'humanize' it. Such a position was based on a kind of compromise – the social-democratic compromise – which recognized both the strengths and drawbacks of a capitalist or market economy. On the one hand, capitalism was accepted as the only reliable means of *generating* wealth (because of the profit motive, competition and incentives), but it was seen as a very poor means of *distributing* wealth (because the wealthy would get wealthier and the poor would get poorer). Therefore, socialism, in the form of social democracy, was reborn as an attempt to create greater equality within a capitalist society, by redistributing wealth from the rich to the poor. This is reflected in the overriding principle of social democracy: **social justice**.

Social democracy came to be associated with three key policies:

▶ **A mixed economy.** A programme of **nationalization** created a 'mixed' economy, an economy made up of both publicly and privately owned industries and enterprises. The Attlee government set out to nationalize what it called the 'commanding heights of the economy'. These industries included coal, steel, ship building, the railways, gas and electricity.

▶ **Economic management.** A managed economy is an economy that is regulated by the government. The idea that the economy should be managed was advanced by the economist John Maynard Keynes (1883–1946). Keynesianism reflects the belief that governments achieve full employment and stimulate growth by 'reflating' the economy through higher levels of public spending. These policies later became known as 'tax and spend' policies.

▶ **Comprehensive social welfare.** Under Attlee, the welfare state was expanded on the basis of the Beveridge Report (1942), written by the economist and

Social justice: A morally justifiable distribution of wealth, usually implying a desire to reduce material inequalities (rather than absolute equality).

Nationalization: The extension of state control over the economy through the transfer of industries from private ownership to public ownership.

What is... One Nation conservatism

One Nation conservatism is a pragmatic and paternalistic form of conservatism that was prominent during the 1950s and 1960s. One Nation ideas can be traced back to the early writings of Benjamin Disraeli, who was prime minister in 1867 and again in 1874–80. Disraeli warned against the danger of Britain being divided into 'two nations: the Rich and the Poor'. His call for social reform to narrow (but not remove) social inequalities was based on the principles of **paternalism**. The rich therefore have an obligation to attend to the needs of the poor.

Paternalism: Acting in the interests of others who are unable to make informed moral decisions, supposedly as fathers do in relation to children.

social reformer, William Beveridge (1879–1963). The Beveridge Report set out to attack the so-called 'five giants':

- ▶ Want (poverty)
- ▶ Disease (illness)
- ▶ Ignorance (lack of education)
- ▶ Squalor (poor housing)
- ▶ Idleness (unemployment).

The expanded welfare state, based on a comprehensive system of social security and a National Health Service (NHS), sought to protect citizens 'from the cradle to the grave'. It brought about a major redistribution of wealth, as it was funded by a system of **progressive taxation**.

Progressive taxation: A system of taxation in which the rich pay proportionally more in tax than the poor, usually based on graduated direct taxes.

Weblink ■ http://fabians.org.uk

Use the Fabian Society website for 'left of centre' comment on contemporary UK policies and issues. The Fabian Society is affiliated to the Labour Party.

Consensus politics: An overlap of ideological positions between two or more political parties; an agreement about fundamental policy goals that permits disagreement on matters of detail or emphasis.

However, these social democratic ideas and policies were soon accepted across the political spectrum in the UK. By 1950, the Conservatives had come to accept the key reforms introduced by the Attlee Labour governments. This created a period of **consensus politics** that lasted through the 1950s and 1960s. This ideological shift was brought about by the prominence of One Nation thinking within the party, making the Conservatives more sympathetic to social reform, having a pragmatic approach to economic policy. The central idea in Conservative politics during this period was the notion of the 'middle way', championed in the writings of Harold Macmillan who later became prime minister, 1957–63. The 'middle way' rejected the two ideological extremes, free-

What is . . . Thatcherism

Thatcherism is an ideological agenda that was associated with the ideas and values of Margaret Thatcher (see p. 250) and the policies of her government, 1979–90. Thatcherism does not so much constitute a coherent and systematic philosophy as an attempt to marry two distinct traditions. Although there is political and ideological tension between these two traditions, they can be combined in support of the goal of a strong but minimal state: in Andrew Gamble's (1994) words, 'the free economy and the strong state'.

The two elements within Thatcherism are:

▶ *Neoliberalism* (sometimes called 'economic Thatcherism'). This is an updated version of classical liberalism. Its central pillars are the **free market** and the self-reliant individual.
▶ *Neoconservatism* (sometimes called 'social Thatcherism'). This is a form of authoritarian conservatism that calls for a restoration of order, authority and discipline in society.

Free market: The principle or policy of unrestricted market competition, free from government interference.

Individualism: A belief in the primacy of the human individual, implying that people are self-interested and largely self-reliant.

Collectivism: A belief in people working together and supporting one another, often (but not necessarily) linked to state intervention.

market liberalism and socialist state planning, attempting to draw a balance between rampant **individualism** and overbearing **collectivism**.

Thatcherism

The post-1945 social-democratic consensus broke down during the 1970s as the 'long boom' of the 1950s and 1960s came to an end and the UK suffered from renewed economic problems. Unemployment rose and prices also increased, creating the problem of so-called 'stagflation' (a combination of economic stagnation and inflation). This brought about the so-called 'Thatcherite revolution', initiated by the Thatcher governments of 1979–90, and consolidated by the Major governments of 1990–97. What became known as the New Right, and in the UK was more commonly called 'Thatcherism', amounted to a kind of counter-revolution against both the post-war drift towards state intervention and the spread of liberal or progressive social values. It constituted the most important shift in the ideological balance of UK politics since 1945.

The principal goal of Thatcherism was to 'roll back the frontiers of the state', in the belief that unregulated capitalism would lead to efficiency, growth and widespread prosperity. It wished to remove the 'dead hand' of government from economic life. Its other enemy was the 'nanny state', the welfare system that undermines hard work and initiative by creating a culture of dependency. The 'Thatcherite revolution' set out to overturn the key features of post-war social democracy.

The central themes of 'economic Thatcherism' were:

Privatization: The selling off of nationalized industries and other state assets, transferring them from the public to the private sector.

▶ **Privatization.** The 'mixed' economy was transformed by the **privatization** of most of the industries that had been nationalized during the 20th century;

examples included telecommunications, gas, electricity, water, steel, buses and railways. The state, therefore, lost direct control of major UK industries.

▶ **Reduced union power.** The 'problem' of trade union power was tackled by a series of laws that restricted the ability of unions to take industrial action. The miners were also taken on and defeated in a year-long strike, 1984–85. Such measures both created a more flexible labour market and led to the growth of a low-wage and low-skill economy in many sectors.

▶ **Low taxes.** Although Thatcherism failed in its broader goal of reducing the overall level of taxation, it brought about a significant shift in the tax burden from direct taxes (e.g. income tax and corporation tax) to indirect taxes (e.g. VAT). This substantially reduced the progressive nature of the UK tax system and, in the process, widened inequality.

▶ **Deregulation.** In line with free market principles, the Thatcher government removed a wide range of restrictions and controls on the economy. Controls on exchange rates were ended, allowing the pound to 'float'; financial markets were deregulated; and subsidies and supports that had propped up 'failing' industries were scaled down or scrapped.

Weblink ■ www.conwayfor.org.uk

Use the Conservative Way Forward website to find out about current Thatcherite thinking within the Conservative Party.

Minimal state: A state that only maintains domestic order, enforces legal agreements and protects against external attack, leaving other matters in the hands of the individual.

At the heart of the neoliberal 'world view' was a rugged or 'atomistic' individualism, that was best expressed by Thatcher's statement that 'there is no such thing as society only individuals and their families' (suggesting that individuals, like atoms, are separate and independent entities). In many ways, these ideas and policies drew less from traditional conservatism and more from a classical liberal belief in a **minimal state**.

Nevertheless, neoliberalism is only part of the Thatcherite or New Right picture. The other element within Thatcherism, neoconservatism, is clearly rooted within the conservative tradition. Neoconservatism advocated the establishment of a strong state, based on the ideas of **social conservatism**.

Social conservatism: The belief that tradition, order and a common morality provide the basis for a stable and healthy society.

The central themes of 'social Thatcherism' were:

▶ **'Tough' law and order.** Greater emphasis was placed on maintaining public order through a fear of punishment, reflected in the belief that 'prison works'. Custodial sentences were more widely used, prison terms were lengthened and, in some cases, 'tougher' prison regimes were imposed.

Permissiveness: The willingness to allow people to make their own moral choices or to 'do their own thing' because there are no authoritative values.

▶ **Traditional values.** One of the enemies of social Thatcherism was the spread of liberal or **permissive** values, associated in particular with the 1960s. Instead, traditional, 'Christian' or 'family' values were defended.

Differences between . . .
ONE NATION CONSERVATISM AND THATCHERISM

One Nation conservatism	Thatchersim
Paternalism	Self-interest
Tradition	Radicalism
Organic society	Rugged individualism
Social duty	Personal advancement
Pragmatic intervention	Roll back the state
'Middle way' economics	Free-market economics

▶ **National patriotism.** Thatcherites placed a particular stress on strengthening national identity, seen as one of the cornerstones of political strength and social stability. Over time, this came increasingly to be expressed in the form of **Euroscepticism.**

Euroscepticism: Opposition to the process of European integration, based on a defence of national sovereignty and national identity; Eurosceptics are not necessarily anti-European.

Post-Thatcherite consensus

The challenge of Thatcherism had profound effects on the Labour Party. In the early 1980s, it drove Labour to the left, as the party tried to protect its social democratic heritage. This led to the adoption of more radical 'socialist' policies, such as unilateral nuclear disarmament, withdrawal from the European Community, further nationalization and increased investment in the welfare state. Consensus politics gave way to **adversary politics**, as an anti-interventionist Conservative government confronted a clearly pro-interventionist Labour opposition. However, Labour's shift to the left opened up serious ideological divisions within the party, leading to the formation of the breakaway Social Democratic Party (SDP) in 1981. (The SDP later merged with the Liberal Party to create the Liberal Democrats.) Labour's disastrous showing in the 1983 and 1987 general elections nevertheless led to the beginning of the 'modernization' process.

Adversary politics: A form of politics that is characterized by deep ideological conflicts between major parties; the parties offer rival ideological visions.

Under Neil Kinnock, party leader 1987–92, Labour undertook a comprehensive policy review, which abandoned policies such as unilateral nuclear disarmament and the commitment to withdraw from the EC. However, the modernization process was substantially intensified after Tony Blair's appointment as leader in 1994. A key moment in this process came with the adoption, in 1995, of a rewritten Clause Four of the party's constitution, which effectively ditched Labour's commitment to public ownership. To symbolize this ideological shift, Blair started to refer to the party as 'New Labour', thereby distancing it from its old image, ideas and policies.

FOCUS ON . . .
Clause Four, new and old

Clause Four of Labour's 1918 constitution contains a commitment to:

the common ownership of the means of production, distribution and exchange, and the best obtainable system of public administration and control of each industry and service.

Clause Four of Labour's 1995 constitution contains the following commitment:

[We] work for a dynamic economy, serving the public interest in which the enterprise of the market and the rigour of competition are joined with the forces of partnership and co-operation to produce the wealth the nation needs and the opportunity for all to work and prosper, with a thriving private sector and high quality public services.

Third way: The idea of an alternative to both 'top-down' Keynesian social democracy and the free-market policies of Thatcherism.

What became known as 'Blairism', the 'Blair project' or the **'third way'** was a complex and, in many ways, contradictory phenomenon. Seen by some as 'Thatcherism with a human face', it sought to blend a market-orientated economic strategy with continued support for public services. Although it has been argued that there was a shift back to Old Labour priorities after Gordon Brown replaced Blair in June 2007, Blair and Brown were the joint architects of New Labour, and the New Labour project remained in place until 2010 (even though the term New Labour became less and less fashionable).

The chief themes of the New Labour project were as follows:

▶ **Market economics.** As the revised Clause 4 indicated, Labour came to accept that the economy should be regulated by the market and not by the state. Blairism therefore built on Thatcherism and did not try to reverse it. This particularly applied in relation to the core elements of economic Thatcherism – privatization, reduced union power, lower taxes and deregulation. Beyond this, the first Blair government granted semi-independence to the Bank of England in the setting of interest rates. Nevertheless, after 2001 and on the basis of a booming economy, Labour embarked on an expansion of public services, with unprecedented levels of spending on health and education, in particular

▶ **Constitutional reform.** A major distinction between Old Labour and New Labour was the latter's enthusiasm for reforming the constitution. During Blair's first government, 1997–2001, a bold series of constitutional reforms were introduced (see Chapter 6). However, many have argued that Labour's

Differences between . . .
OLD LABOUR AND NEW LABOUR

Old Labour	New Labour
Ideological	Pragmatic
Working class	'Big tent' politics
Managed economy	Market economy
Social justice	Social inclusion
Universal benefits	Targeted benefits
Cradle-to-grave welfare	Welfare-to-work
Traditional constitution	Constitutional reform

conversion to constitutional liberalism was only partial. For example, plans to consider alternatives to the Westminster voting system were quickly dropped and enthusiasm for constitutional reform declined after 2001. After 2007, Brown attempted to revive interest in constitutional reform, taking steps to reduce the prerogative powers of the prime minister and to expand the role of Parliament. But more radical reforms, such as an elected second chamber, a 'written' constitution and an entrenched bill of rights, never progressed beyond the discussion phase.

▶ **'Third way' welfare.** Blair's approach to welfare was different from both the Thatcherite emphasis on 'standing on your own two feet' and the social-democratic belief in 'cradle to grave' support. This was reflected in the wider use of 'targeted' benefits (as opposed to 'universal' benefits), an emphasis on the idea of **'welfare-to-work'** and attempts to reform the public services. Blair's belief in welfare reform was based on what has been called 'social entrepreneurialism', the idea that the public services should be more market-orientated and consumer responsive. Public–private partnerships, such as 'private finance initiatives' (PFIs), were also more widely used, for example, to build schools and hospitals. However, this was the area where differences between Blair and Brown were most acute. As Chancellor, Brown slowed the pace of public sector reform, and after 2007 plans to further reform the welfare state were effectively abandoned.

▶ **Strengthening responsibility.** A key Blairite belief was the idea that rights should always be balanced against responsibilities. In this sense, Blairism was influenced by **communitarianism**. The desire to strengthen social duty and moral responsibilities was reflected in the so-called 'respect agenda', under which new public order laws were introduced (including ASBOs), the prison

Welfare-to-work: Welfare programmes that boost employability skills and provide incentives for people to work.

Communitarianism: The belief that people are happier and more secure if they live within communities that have clear values and a strong culture.

population rose steeply and a series of new anti-terrorism laws were passed. This also led to allegations that New Labour had succumbed to neoconservatism and was endangering a range of vital civil liberties. (These issues are examined more closely in Chapter 9.)

Ideas and policies in the 'age of austerity'

From boom to bust

Party politics in the UK has, since September 2008, lived in the shadow of the dramatic deepening of the global financial crisis and its consequences, namely the longest and deepest recession since the 1930s. These developments opened up new political dividing lines, both between parties and sometimes within parties, that may define UK politics for a generation. David Cameron dubbed the new era the 'age of austerity', while his Chancellor, George Osborne, called it the age of 'no-money politics'. How did the UK go so abruptly from boom to bust? Questions about the origins of the recession are not only linked to debates about how it should be addressed, but also constitute a crucial ideological battleground in its own right.

Leading figures in the Conservative–Liberal Democrat coalition have argued that what they referred to as 'Labour's debt crisis' was a consequence of 'Brown's recession'. In this view, the UK's massive budget deficit (which amounted to 11.5 per cent of GDP in 2008) was essentially a consequence of 'reckless and irresponsible' levels of public spending by Labour governments, particularly since 2001. If the recession and the budget deficit are a consequence of irresponsible spending levels, it is clear that the solution should be to cut spending, and to do so in a swift and robust manner. Labour, by contrast, has tended to explain the budget deficit largely in terms of the impact of a global financial crisis over which it had little control and for which it could not take responsibility. If the UK's swollen budget deficit is blamed on the global financial crisis and the dramatic collapse in government's tax revenues that occurred as the recession deepened (GDP fell by 5 per cent in 2008–09), the solution would appear to be promote growth and avoid any action that might prolong the recession (such as early and severe spending cuts).

Two general points can, nevertheless, perhaps be made. In the first place, the UK's sustained economic boom that started in the 1990s and went on for much of the first decade of the new millennium was based on a combination of factors that were almost certainly unsustainable in the long run. These included low and stable interest rates, low inflation (partly due to the inflow of cheap manufacturing goods from China and other emerging economies), a substantial expansion of the financial sector and a boom in the property market that meant that house prices consistently outstripped inflation. In the case of the UK's growing reliance on the

City and the financial sector generally, this was in part based on financial products and lending strategies that soon proved to be catastrophically unwise and made the UK unusually vulnerable to financial crises that occurred elsewhere (notably in the USA). Second, whatever their cause, the recession and the budget crisis demonstrate that Labour's frequently repeated claim to have brought an 'end to boom and bust' was seriously flawed and misunderstood the nature of the capitalist economy. As Karl Marx (1818–83) noted in the 19th century, capitalist economies always go through cyclical booms and slumps, even though the nature, depth and timing of capitalism's crises may be impossible to predict.

Conservatives under Cameron

The ideas and policies of the Conservative Party since May 2010 have to be understood in the light of the coalition negotiated with the Liberal Democrats. Although the parties had separate and rival manifestos in 2010, within weeks a joint programme for government had been negotiated. This means that, to the extent to which the coalition speaks with one voice rather than two, it has become difficult to identify where Conservative policies start and Liberal Democrat policies finish. Nevertheless, the ideas and policies that have guided the coalition can be traced back to shifts in the Conservative Party, and a revived interest in certain Thatcherite ideas, that can be traced back to the late summer and autumn of 2007. This occurred for three reasons: the need to maintain party unity given that a majority of Conservative MPs continued to hold right-wing or Thatcherite views; the fact that the Conservative's poll lead over Labour reduced the pressure within the party to introduce further 'modernization'; and, probably, the underlying belief of leading modernizers such as Cameron and Osborne that a smaller state remains ideologically desirable. This shift was reflected in greater concern with traditionalist issues such as law and order (highlighted by an attack on Labour's so-called 'broken society'), immigration and the family.

Deficit reduction

Credit crunch: A reduction in the general availability of loans (or credit), usually due to an unwillingness of banks to lend to one another.

The onset of the so-called '**credit crunch**' in 2007, which pre-figured the more severe 2008 crisis, also marked the point at which the leadership's previous emphasis on 'detoxifying' the party's image (by, for example, placing the need for economic stability before either tax cuts or spending cuts) started to be modified. In the period between the crisis of September 2008 and the May 2010 general election, the Conservatives re-engaged more openly with economic Thatcherism. Thus, although all three major parties committed themselves in 2010 to reducing the budget deficit, the Conservatives alone proposed that substantial spending cuts should be introduced in the first year of the new Parliament and that the '**structural**' **deficit** should be entirely removed within the lifetime of the Parliament. The combined impact of the emergency budget in June 2010, which increased VAT (from 17.5 per cent to 20 per cent from January 2011), pushed up

Structural deficit: That part of a budget deficit that stems from a fundamental imbalance between the government's tax revenues and its spending level

Who is ...
David Cameron

David Cameron was born in 1966. He is the son of a stock-broker, whose family has a long history in the world of finance, and is related to the royal family on his mother's side (being a fifth cousin, twice removed, of the Queen). He was educated at Eton, and later read philosophy, politics and economics at Oxford. Cameron worked for the Conservative Research Department between 1988 and 1992, when he was appointed as special advisor, first to the Chancellor of the Exchequer, Norman Lamont, and then to the Home Secretary, Michael Howard. Between 1994 and 2001 he worked as director of corporate affairs at the communications company Carlton. In 2001, Cameron entered Parliament as the MP for Witney in Oxfordshire. He was appointed to the shadow cabinet in June 2003, becoming a party vice chairman when Howard took over the leadership in November of that year. When Howard stood down after the 2005 election defeat, Cameron succeeded him in a vote of all party members. He described himself as a 'compassionate conservative', but he also allegedly called himself the 'heir to Blair', indicating the desire to carry out a kind of Blairite modernization process within the Conservative Party.

Under his leadership, Cameron successfully transformed the party's image, softening its stance in various areas of social policy and extending its appeal beyond its core support. This enabled the Conservatives to achieve a substantial lead in opinion polls over Labour for the first time in a decade and, in May 2010, to become the largest party in the Commons. The formation of a coalition with the Liberal Democrats demonstrated his flexibility and finely-honed political skills, but also his keen instinct for power. The Conservative-led coalition rescued Cameron after an election in which his party had failed to gain a Commons majority.

capital gains tax and introduced a balance sheet levy on banks and building societies, and the £81 billion cuts in government spending announced in the September 2010 spending review, demonstrated that the coalition with the Liberal Democrats had essentially embraced the Conservative commitment to robust deficit reduction. The coalition may, indeed, be looking beyond this to a wholesale restructuring of the state and its role.

However, these developments occurred without a return to the strident neoliberal rhetoric of the 1980s, about the benefits of 'rugged' individualism and free markets. Indeed, the Conservative-led coalition's budget reduction programme has consistently been portrayed as 'necessary' rather than 'desirable'. Stress, in particular, has been placed on the need to restore the fiscal balance in order to prevent the kind of financial crises that brought the Greek, Irish and Portuguese economies close to collapse. In this respect, conservatism under Cameron can be seen to be an example of pragmatism rather than Thatcherite conviction politics. This view has, nevertheless, also been criticized. In a number of respects, the coalition's approach to the deficit and its wider programme of policies bears the hallmark of Thatcherism:

▶ **Political choice.** The coalition's cuts are a political choice, in that they are more severe than those that have been introduced in many other European countries in a similar position and depart from the reflationary policies adopted by most countries after the financial crisis of 2008. Also, economists and other commentators have been divided about the wisdom of swift and severe spending cuts, particularly because of their impact on growth.

▶ **Spending cuts rather than tax rises.** The deficit reduction programme places much greater emphasis on spending cuts than on tax rises (for every £1 raised through higher taxation there will be £4 of public spending cuts). This reflects both a willingness to reduce the size of the state and a Thatcherite desire to keep taxes as low as possible.

▶ **Growth strategy.** The coalition's strategy is largely based on the assumption that, as the public sector of the economy contracts, the private sector will grow. This is based on a faith in the natural vigour of a market economy, and on the Thatcherite theory of '**crowding out**'.

▶ **Privatization.** Plans to cut spending often involve, albeit in different ways, a shift from public provision to private provision, based on the assumption that private businesses are usually more efficient and responsive than public sector bodies.

▶ **Welfare cuts.** The burden of spending cuts affects the welfare state and the benefits system. One of the key features of Thatcherism is that welfare creates a 'culture of dependency' and so hampers the economy.

Crowding out: The theory that an over-large state damages the performance of private businesses by depriving them of necessary resources.

The 'big society'

There are, nevertheless, those who argue that conservatism under Cameron is defined by the distance it has placed between the contemporary party and its Thatcherite past. This may be particularly evident in the emphasis on the so-called 'big society', the central theme developed in the 2010 Conservative manifesto and the nearest thing the coalition government has to an ideological flagship. The notion of the 'big society' is often loose or ill-defined. However, it is most clearly associated with the ideas of so-called 'civic conservatism', which highlights the importance of people's sense of rootedness and belonging to the institutions of civil society, those bodies that stand between the state and the individual. Called by the conservative philosopher, Edmund Burke (1729–97), the 'little platoons', these institutions include family groups, networks, neighbourhoods and locally-based communities. The idea of the 'big society' therefore suggests that people at a local level should take more responsibility and do more to help themselves and their communities, rather than relying on action taken by state institutions and public services.

In this way, the 'big society' helps to replace 'big government', and so helps to mend the UK's supposedly 'broken society'. Such thinking lies behind the notion of 'free schools', attempts to expand the roles of charities and community organizations, and encouragement given to public-sector workers to form cooperatives that would take over the service they deliver. 'Big society' thinking certainly differs from the atomistic individualism of Thatcherism, in that it clearly places an emphasis on cooperation and community action rather than individual self-striving. As Cameron put it, 'there is such a thing as society, it's just not the same as the state'. The significance of the 'big society' may therefore be that it has given the core Thatcherite desire to 'roll back' the state an ideological make-over. Individual responsibility and people 'standing on their own two feet' has perhaps simply been replaced by a call for the regeneration of communities and local activism. Other criticisms of the 'big society' initiative include that it is based on unfounded assumptions about people's interest in engaging in community-based activism; that the withdrawal of state support will harm, rather than help, charities and community groups; and that it will widen inequality because the groups able to take advantage of 'big society' opportunities will tend to be those that possess educational and other advantages.

Weblink ■ http://www.neweconomics.org/sites/neweconomics.org/files/Ten_Big_Questions_about the_Big_Society.pdf

Use this website to gain access to the New Economic Forum's paper *Ten Big Questions about the Big Society*.

In a number of other respects, the Conservative–Liberal Democrat coalition has, nevertheless, departed more clearly from Thatcherite ideas and policies:

▶ **Health spending.** A stronger commitment to public services has been maintained in relation to the NHS, where there has been a promise to increasing health spending in 'real' terms during every year of the 2010–15 Parliament. The major reorganization of the NHS, which started in 2011 and places much more control in the hands of GPs, nevertheless has a Thatcherite character, because it aims to introduce an 'internal market' in health provision.

▶ **Welfare reform.** Although short-term welfare cuts featured prominently in the 2010 spending review, the coalition has a longer-term commitment to creating a unified tax and welfare system that has much in common with 'third way', or Blairite, welfare thinking. This is championed by Iain Duncan-Smith, the work and pensions secretary, who has outlined plans to overhaul the benefits system by introducing a single Universal Credit to replace a complex range of work-related benefits.

▶ **Criminal justice.** After decades in which law and order policies have been dominated by a 'tough', or neoconservative, approach, Kenneth Clarke, the justice secretary, has set about significantly reducing the UK's prison population and placing much greater emphasis on non-custodial sentences. This reflects the end of the assumption that 'prison works' and marks the acceptance of the liberal view that punishment should seek to rehabilitate wrongdoers rather than merely deterring wrongdoing. This trend has, nevertheless, alarmed many Conservative right-wingers.

▶ **Civil liberty.** Whilst in opposition, the Conservatives showed greater sympathy for civil liberties issues and constitutional reform, including supporting a largely elected second chamber, and these commitments have been continued and enlarged under the coalition, doing much to cement the partnership between the Conservatives and the Liberal Democrats.

Weblink ■ Weblink: www.conservatives.com

Use the Conservative Party site to find out about the party's current ideas, policies and campaigns.

Liberal Democrats under Clegg

The Liberal Democratic Party (usually known as the Liberal Democrats) was formed in 1987 through the merger of the Liberal Party and the Social Democratic Party (SDP), which had broken away from the Labour Party in 1981. Between 1983 and 1987, the Liberals and the SDP had worked closely together under the banner of the Alliance, but this constituted little more than an arrangement for fighting general elections. The Liberal Democrats have therefore drawn on a range of ideological traditions. Although they are the party most clearly associated with liberalism, their liberalism encompasses both a classical liberal belief in a minimal state and the free market (reminiscent of economic Thatcherism) and a modern liberal belief in social and economic intervention that sometimes resembles social democracy. Similarly, the merger between the Liberals and the SDP marked an attempt to fuse an ideology orientated around the individual and freedom with one that traditionally favoured equality and social justice.

In electoral terms, the Liberal Democrats set out to 'break the mould of British politics', by which they meant to overthrow the Conservative–Labour two-party system by providing a centrist alternative to the agendas of the left and the right. However, in ideological terms, the Liberal Democrats were generally viewed as a centre-left party, in part as a consequence of attempts dating back to the early twentieth century to encourage the Labour and the Liberal parties to work together in a 'progressive alliance', and perhaps even merge. Such trends were

What is... Liberalism

Liberalism is an ideology that is defined by a commitment to the individual, reflected in the doctrine of 'natural' or human rights (see p. 280).

The core values of liberalism are:

▶ Individualism — the individual is of supreme importance, implying an emphasis on rights or entitlements

▶ Freedom — individuals should enjoy the greatest possible freedom consistent with a like freedom for all

▶ Toleration — people should be willing to accept ideas and practices of which they disapprove, safeguarding diversity and debate.

Liberalism encompasses two contrasting traditions:

▶ *Classical* liberalism believes in a minimal state and free-market capitalism. This views individuals as strongly self-interested and self-reliant creatures.

▶ *Modern* liberalism believes in social welfare and economic intervention. This holds that the state should 'help individuals to help themselves'.

strengthened in the run up to the 1997 general election, as Labour Party modernization narrowed policy differences between the two parties, especially as New Labour showed an increasing interest in constitutional reform, and Blair prepared for a possible Labour–Liberal Democrat coalition. Indeed, after 1997, as Labour in power continued to move to the centre-ground, some in the Liberal Democrats sought to outflank Labour on the left. This was reflected in the commitment to increase income tax by one penny in the pound in order to better fund education and to abolish tuition fees for university students, as well as in opposition to the 2003 Iraq War.

In this light, the advent of a Conservative–Liberal Democrat coalition can be seen to be surprising. Nevertheless, shifts in both parties in the run-up to the 2010 general election arguably provided an ideological basis for the coalition. Cameron had made significant progress in 'detoxifying' the Conservative brand, particularly by emphasizing sympathy for 'green' issues, support for public services and a concern about poverty. Strident economic Thatcherism thus appeared to be modified by an acceptance of aspects of **social liberalism**, linked to social justice and welfare provision. Meanwhile, elements within the Liberal Democrats were shifting in the opposite direction. Associated with the *Orange Book*, published in 2004, which contained significant contributions from Nick Clegg, David Laws, Chris Huhne and Vince Cable, support within the Liberal Democrats grew for a more free-market economic strategy. This aimed to shift the Liberal Democrats

Social liberalism: A commitment to social welfare designed to promote equal opportunities and to help individuals to help themselves.

from the centre-left to the centre-right. After Clegg was elected party leader in 2007, these tendencies became stronger. Nevertheless, apart from dropping the plan to increase income tax, they failed to have much influence on the party's policy programme in the run-up to the 2010 election. During the election campaign, the Liberal Democrats, in common with Labour, advocated a broadly Keynesian approach to the budget deficit, warning that Conservative proposals for early and robust spending cuts risked causing a 'double-dip recession'. The 'hung' Parliament and coalition negotiations with the Conservatives provided Clegg and senior Liberal Democrats the opportunity for a radical reappraisal of their party's economic strategy.

However, although the Conservatives and the Liberal Democrats moved, in a number of ways, closer to one another as the general election approached, they still represent competing political traditions. A variety of 'wedge' issues therefore persist, having the potential to destabilize (and, some have argued, possibly destroy) the coalition. This has applied to issues ranging from university tuition fees and bankers' bonuses to the future of control orders on terrorist suspects. Disagreement also exists on a range of other issues, including education (where many Liberal Democrat councillors are sceptical about the coalition's plan to introduce 'free schools'), Europe, Trident and defence generally, traditional morality, multiculturalism, immigration, NHS reform, nuclear power and civil liberties. 'Wedge' issues that strain the unity of the coalition are also likely to lead to internal divisions within each party, and therefore the growth of factionalism.

Weblink ■ www.libdems.org.uk

Use the Liberal Democrat site to find out about the party's current ideas, policies and campaigns.

Labour under Miliband

The development of Labour's ideas and policies since Ed Miliband became leader in September 2010 has to be understood in the context of the Brown government's response to the dramatic deepening of the global financial crisis in September 2008. There were three strands to this response. First, the Brown government acted quickly to re-capitalize the UK's banking system by pumping £37 billion of taxpayers' money into HBOS, Royal Bank of Scotland and Lloyds TSB, which were each part-nationalized. Second, interest rates were reduced to virtually zero in what came to be called '**monetary stimulus**'. Third, and most controversially, there was a reliance on '**fiscal stimulus**'. This last policy was dictated by Keynesian thinking, according to which the most appropriate response to a recession is for government to 'inject' more money into the economy through public spending than it 'withdraws' through taxation. The

Monetary stimulus: A policy that seeks to stimulate economic growth by reducing interest rates in order to make borrowing easier.

Fiscal stimulus: A policy aimed at promoting economic growth by allowing government spending to exceed tax revenues.

Who is ...
Ed Miliband

Edward Samuel (Ed) Miliband was born in London on Christmas Eve 1969. His parents, Marion Kozak and Ralph Miliband, both had Polish-Jewish backgrounds and had fled the Nazis before the Second World War. Like his brother David, who is four years older, Ed attended Haverstock comprehensive school in north London and later studied philosophy, politics and economics at Oxford. After a brief period as a television researcher, he became a political advisor. Following Labour's 1997 election victory, Miliband became Brown's speech writer and special advisor at the Treasury. In 2005, he was elected MP for Doncaster North. He rose rapidly through the ranks of the Labour government, starting as a parliamentary secretary in 2006 and eventually joining the cabinet in 2008 as the energy and climate change secretary. Miliband was clearly associated with the Brownite wing of the Labour Party and was given the task of writing Labour's 2010 manifesto. After Labour's defeat in 2010 and Brown's resignation, Miliband stood for the leadership of the party against four other candidates, including his brother David, who was viewed by many as the favourite to get the job. However, in September 2010 Ed defeated his brother by just 1.3 per cent of the vote, an outcome that was secured primarily by the strength of his support amongst members of Labour's affiliated trade unions. As leader, Miliband has attempted to balance the pressures generated by a leadership campaign that emphasized the need to move on from the New Labour project and the need to appeal to centrist voters by re-establishing Labour's reputation for economic credibility. These efforts have been hampered by his difficulties in recruiting prominent Blairites into either his inner circle or the shadow cabinet.

resulting budget deficit can be tolerated both because it stimulates demand and so promotes growth, and because it is believed to be self-correcting (increased growth both boosts the tax revenues and reduces the need for public spending, thereby causing the deficit to shrink 'naturally'). This, and the willingness, once again, to use nationalization as a political tool (first applied to the Northern Rock building society in 2007), encouraged some to argue that New Labour was on the wane as Old Labour ideas and policies was returning. However, this interpretation should not be over-stated. It was emphasized that nationalization was, in all cases, being used reluctantly and only as a temporary device, suggesting that it did not herald a return to the mixed economy of old. The Brown government also practised neo-Keynesianism rather than classical Keynesianism, in that it recognized that the budget deficit could not simply be allowed to cure itself. Labour's May 2010 manifesto thus contained proposals for tax increases and spending cuts that were largely intended to start in 2011–12 and aimed to halve the budget deficit by the end of the Parliament. The gulf between Labour and the Conservatives in May 2010 was, though significant, largely about the timing and scale of the deficit reduction programme, rather than whether or not the deficit needed to be addressed.

Ed Miliband's narrow victory in the leadership election over his brother, David Miliband, was widely interpreted as a victory for the Brownite wing of the Labour Party over its Blairite wing. Ed Miliband fostered this view by announcing that 'New Labour is dead', although it was unclear what this meant and it may refer to the years of in-fighting between Blairites and Brownites within the party. The challenge confronting Miliband as party leader was to establish an alternative to the coalition's budget reduction programme without allowing Labour to be attacked as 'deficit deniers', who were edging back towards the failed policies of the past. At the same time, Labour has been as reluctant as previous opposition parties, including the Conservatives under Cameron, to map out 'hard' policy alternatives too early in the Parliament. To do so risks allowing attractive policies to be 'stolen' by the coalition government and may also allow the government to focus criticism on the opposition, rather than the other way round. In this context, Miliband and his shadow chancellor, Ed Balls, have been clear about the need to reduce borrowing from levels that they accept are too high. Labour's position is therefore that the coalition is going too far and too fast in reducing the deficit, broadly keeping faith with the stance the party adopted in 2010. A particular criticism levelled at the coalition has been that its strategy views budget cuts as a panacea in themselves, reviving the Thatcherite belief that public spending merely 'crowds out' private investment. This, Labour argues, amounts to ideological faith rather than an economic strategy. Miliband's alternative to this appears to be an emphasis on restructuring the economy to reduce its dependence on finance and to expand its manufacturing base, although Labour has been reluctant to recognize that the Blair and Brown governments had spurned the opportunity to carry out such a restructuring during the period from 1997 to 2010.

Weblink ■ Weblink: www.labour.org.uk

Use the Labour Party site to find out about the party's policies and current campaigns.

BY COMPARISON . . .

Political parties in the USA

- The USA is the classic example of a two-party system. Its two major parties are the Republicans and the Democrats. These parties have dominated the presidency, usually hold all of the seats in Congress and also control politics at the state level.

- However, in view of the size and diversity of US society, both parties operate as loose coalitions. They are held together by little more than the need to fight presidential elections as national political machines. This results in considerable decentralization. Congressional parties lack the tight party discipline found amongst parliamentary parties in the UK, and state and local party organizations enjoy considerable autonomy.

- Until it began to break apart in the 1960s, Democratic Party support was based on the 'New Deal coalition', composed of blue-collar workers and ethnic minorities in the north together with white southerners. This gave the Democrats a basis for electoral success and inclined the party towards social reform (based on modern liberal thinking, not socialism). The political spectrum in the USA is narrower than in the UK, with no major socialist force ever having developed.

- The Republicans have traditionally been the party of big business, higher income groups and rural interests, encouraging the party to support limited government. Since the 1960s, it has attracted growing support from the white south. From the 1980s onwards, the Republicans have intended to practise a more ideological form of politics, in large part based on the influence of the New Christian Right (the born-again Christian movement) and a greater emphasis on moral and cultural issues, such as abortion, gun control and gay rights.

WHAT YOU SHOULD KNOW

▶▶ A political party is a group of people that is organized for the purpose of winning government power. In a democratic system, parties do this by putting candidates up for election. The main functions of parties are representation, policy formulation, the recruitment of political leaders, the organization of government and the mobilization of the electorate.

▶▶ Power within the main UK political parties has, despite their formal constitutions, usually been concentrated in the hands of their parliamentary leadership. In recent decades, party structures and organization have been affected by factors such as a steady decline in party membership, the introduction of more 'democratic' methods of electing party leaders and the tendency for party strategy and ideological direction to be determined centrally, with leaders playing a major role.

▶▶ The UK has traditionally had a two-party system, with majority Labour and Conservative govern-ments alternating in power. However, two-partyism began to break down in the 1970s under the pressures of class and partisan dealignment. The UK now has multiple or 'overlapping' party systems, due to devolution, the use of PR and the rise of issues that cut across the traditional party-political divide. But two-party politics continues to dominate at Westminster.

▶▶ The early post-war period was dominated by a social-democratic consensus, reflecting support for a broad balance between a capitalist or market economy on the one hand and state interven-tion on the other hand. The social-democratic consensus was associated with a mixed economy, economic management and the idea of 'cradle to grave' welfare.

▶▶ The 'Thatcherite revolution' of the 1980s amounted to a counter-revolution against both the post-war drift towards state intervention and the spread of liberal or progressive social values. 'Economic Thatcherism' was characterized by a belief in individualism and the free market. 'Social Thatcherism' was characterized by the desire to strengthen the state and traditional values.

▶▶ Blairism and New Labour were associated with an acceptance of market economics, support for constitutional reform, a 'third way' approach to welfare, and a desire to strengthen responsibility and social obligations. New Labour set out to build on Thatcherism rather than trying to reverse it. Its supporters have suggested that it is distinct from both Thatcherism and social democracy.

▶▶ Since 2008, the ideas and policies of the UK's major parties have been shaped by the need to respond to the global economic crisis and the resultant recession. In this so-called 'age of austerity', the Conservative–Liberal Democrat coalition has committed itself to removing the budget deficit in a single parliamentary term, whereas Labour claims that the coalition is going too far, too fast.

Test yourself

Short questions:

1 What is a political party?
2 Distinguish between a political party and a faction.
3 What is party government?
4 What is a two-party system?
5 What is a multiparty system?
6 Distinguish between a manifesto and a mandate.
7 Define consensus politics using an example.
8 Define adversary politics using an example.

Medium questions:

9 Explain *three* functions of political parties.
10 How do political parties carry out representation?
11 How do political parties achieve their aims?
12 How do the Labour and Conservative parties elect their leaders?
13 Explain three policies of the Conservative Party.
14 Explain *three* policies of the Labour Party.
15 Explain *three* policy differences between the Labour and Conservative parties.
16 Explain *three* ways in which 'new' Labour differs from 'old' Labour.

Extended questions:

17 How effective are parties in promoting political participation?
18 Discuss the view that the main UK parties are each dominated by their leaders.
19 To what extent does the UK still have a two-party system?
20 To what extent has the Labour Party abandoned traditional socialist policies?
21 To what extent has the Conservative Party abandoned Thatcherism?
22 Why, and to what extent, is there a policy consensus between the major UK parties?
23 To what extent do the Labour and Conservative parties differ on economic issues?
24 How far has coalition government forced the Conservatives and the Liberal Democrats to revise their traditional ideological stances?

Chapter 5 | Pressure Groups

The politics of pressure

PREVIEW

People do not only engage in politics through voting and by joining political parties, they can also become politically active through their membership of groups, organizations and associations of various kinds. This is the world of pressure group politics, sometimes seen as the *informal* face of politics. Indeed, many argue that group politics is in the process of replacing party politics. As fewer people vote and join political parties, the number and size of pressure groups seems to rise and rise. Over 7,000 associations of various shapes and sizes now operate in the UK, half of which have been formed since 1960. What is more, groups have been credited with having developed new styles of political activism, the so-called 'new politics' – popular protests, marches, sit-ins, direct action, and so on – that has proved to be attractive to a growing body of young people disillusioned by 'conventional' politics.

However, the world of pressure politics is a complex and often confusing world. For example, pressure groups differ greatly from one to another, ranging from community groups and local charities to multinational corporations and global lobby groups (such as Greenpeace and Amnesty International). How can pressure groups best be classified? There is also considerable debate about the power of pressure groups. Just how powerful are pressure groups, and which ones are the most influential? Finally, there are questions about the implications of pressure groups for democracy. Do they uphold democracy or undermine it?

KEY ISSUES

■ What functions do pressure groups carry out?

■ What are the different types of pressure group?

■ How do pressure groups exert influence?

■ What determines the success or failure of pressure groups?

■ Do pressure groups help or hinder democracy?

GETTING YOU THINKING

Revolting students?

Before starting the chapter, read this passage and briefly consider the questions on the next page.

During November and early December 2010, the UK experienced a wave of student protests that provoked comparisons with the poll tax riots of 1990 and the anti-Vietnam War demonstrations of the late 1960s. The principal target of student protest was the coalition government's decision to almost triple university tuition fees, allowing them to rise to £9,000 a year. The protests also aimed to highlight issues relevant to young people including access to education, youth unemployment and the coalition's plan to scrap educational maintenance allowances (EMAs), which supported students from poorer families in further education. The campaign of protest involved sit-ins in about 30 universities and culminated on 9 December ('Day X') with tens of thousands of students and education workers demonstrating in central London whilst the Commons debated tuition fees.

What does the revival of student protest tell us about emerging pressure politics in the UK? Some argue that the coalition's programme of spending cuts has radicalized a generation of young people previously only concerned with personal advancement (careers and qualifications). If students are more strident and dedicated than the UK has seen for many years, this creates the possibility that coalition policies may be challenged by an ongoing campaign of direct action (strikes, demonstrations, sit-ins and high-street disruption), especially if students can join forces with the unions. This new-style political activism involves bottom-up, looser organization (resembling anti-globalization or environmental protests) and the widespread use of information technology (iPhones, Google maps, social networking websites and so on). However, others question whether the protests provide evidence that students had become politicized, arguing that, in reality, unlike earlier generations of students, modern students are primarily concerned with self-interest (avoiding increased fees), rather than issues such as justice or fairness. Further concerns have been raised about the link between direct action and violence, as in the attack on a car containing Prince Charles and the Duchess of Cornwall, and about whether such activism may be a threat to democracy.

Damage caused during anti-university fees demonstrations in December 2010 – but is this the real face of protest politics?

What issues do these developments raise?

▶▶▶ What were the aims of the student protests?

▶▶▶ Is popular protest an effective way of influencing government?

▶▶▶ In what sense can direct action be viewed as democratic?

▶▶▶ Why has the use of direct action been criticized?

▶▶▶ Why have protest movements become increasingly common in modern politics?

IN THIS CHAPTER:

The nature of pressure groups • Pressure group power • Pressure groups and democracy

The nature of pressure groups

What are pressure groups? When people are asked to name a pressure group, certain groups – such as Greenpeace, the Countryside Alliance, the Stop the War Coalition and Fathers4Justice – usually come to mind. These are groups that tend to have a high public profile based on their success in grabbing the attention of the media. However, the pressure group universe also includes churches and charities, businesses and trade associations, trade unions and professional associations, **think tanks** of various complexions, and so forth. Although some pressure groups were set up for the specific purpose of influencing government, many pressure groups exist for other purposes and only engage in politics as a secondary or associated activity. For instance, the primary purpose of the AA and RAC is to provide motoring services to their members. Nevertheless, they also lobby government over issues such as motoring taxes and road safety. This also applies to what are undoubtedly the most powerful pressure groups in the UK, major businesses, whose political influence is largely exerted away from the glare of publicity.

Pressure groups are organizations that seek to exert influence on government from outside. They do not therefore put candidates up for election or seek in other ways to 'win' government power. In that sense, they are part of **civil society**. Pressure groups can therefore act as a channel of communication between the people and government. However, their political role is often as 'fuzzy' as their identity.

Think tank: A pressure group specifically formed to develop policy proposals and campaign for their acceptance amongst opinion formers and policy-makers.

Civil society: The sphere of independent bodies, groups and associations that operate outside government control (including families, businesses and pressure groups).

Weblink ■ www.historylearningsite.co.uk/pressure_groups.htm

Use this website to find general information about the nature and types of pressure groups, as well as their links to democracy and pluralism.

Pressure groups and political parties

Pressure groups and political parties have much in common. They are the two main bodies through which the public's views and interests are channelled to government. As such, both of them carry out representation, facilitate political participation and contribute to the policy process. However, on the face of it, groups and parties are very different beasts.

Nevertheless, there is often confusion between pressure groups and political parties, sometimes reflected in disagreement about how a particular body should

What is ... a pressure group

A pressure group is an organized group of people that aims to influence the policies or actions of government.

Pressure groups are defined by three key features:

▶ They seek to exert *influence* from outside, rather than to win or exercise government power. Pressure groups do not make policy decisions, but rather try to influence those who do (the policy-makers). In that sense, they are 'external' to government.

▶ They typically have a *narrow* issue focus. In some cases, they may focus on a single issue (for instance, opposing a planned road development).

▶ Their members are *united* by either a shared belief in a particular cause or a common set of interests. People with different ideological and party preferences may thus work happily together as members of the same pressure group.

be classified. For example, the United Kingdom Independence Party (UKIP) styles itself as a political party and certainly puts up candidates for election, but it has a single-issue orientation (withdrawal from the EU). Similarly, there are significant overlaps in the political and ideological preference of members of the Green Party and members of Greenpeace.

Pressure groups and parties may be confused for a number of reasons:

▶ *Many small political parties resemble pressure groups in that they have a narrow issue focus.* For example, the British National Party (BNP) is primarily concerned with issues of race and immigration. The Green Party, despite developing wide-ranging manifestos, places greatest emphasis on environmental issues such as pollution, economic sustainability and climate change.

▶ *Some pressure groups use elections as a tactical weapon.* Any group that puts candidates up for election is *technically* a party, not a pressure group. But some pressure groups use elections as a means of gaining publicity and attracting media attention, with little or no expectation of winning the elecion, still less of winning government power. For instance, the Legalise Cannabis Alliance contested 21 constituencies in the 2005 general election, gaining, in its strongest constituency, 1.8 per cent of the vote. It has since deregistered as a party.

▶ *Parties and pressure groups may form part of larger social movements.* **Social movements** differ from both parties and pressure groups in that they lack organization and 'card-carrying' members. They are diffuse collections of people defined by a shared sense of political commitment, and thus often encompass both parties and pressure groups. The labour movement incorpo-

Social movement:
A large group of people who are distinguished by common aspirations and a high level of political commitment, but often lacking clear organization.

139

Differences between . . .
PRESSURE GROUPS AND POLITICAL PARTIES

Pressure groups	• • • •	Political parties
Seek to exert influence	• • • •	Seek to win power
Narrow issue focus	• • • •	Broad issue focus
Shared interests/common causes	• • • •	Shared preferences

rates the Labour Party as well as the UK's various trade unions. The green movement, for its part, includes the Green Party and also a wide range of environmental pressure groups.

Weblink ■ www.greenpeace.org

Use the Greenpeace International website to find out about the group's values, organization and current campaigns.

Types of pressure group

As pressure groups appear in such a variety of shapes and sizes, it is often unhelpful to treat them as a 'job lot'. How do pressure groups differ one from another? What categories do pressure groups fall into? Although they can be distinguished in a variety of ways (including local/national/European/transnational groups and temporary/permanent groups) the most common distinctions are between:

▶▶ Sectional and promotional groups
▶▶ Insider and outsider groups.

Interest and cause groups

The interest/cause distinction is based on the *purpose* of the group in question. It therefore reflects the nature of the group's goals, the kinds of people who belong to it, and their motivation for joining. **Sectional groups** (sometimes called 'interest', 'protective' or 'functional' groups) are groups that represent a particular section of society: workers, employers, consumers, an ethnic or religious group, and so on.

Interest groups have the following features:

▶ They are concerned to protect or advance the interests of their members.
▶ Membership is limited to people in a particular occupation, career or economic position.

Sectional group: A pressure group that exists to advance or protect the (usually material) interests of its members.

140

▶ Members are motivated by material self-interest.

Trade unions, business corporations, trade associations and professional bodies are the prime examples of this type of group. They are called 'sectional' groups because they represent a particular section of the population. Specific examples include the British Medical Association (BMA), the Law Society, the National Union of Teachers (NUT) and so-called 'umbrella' or **peak groups** such as the Confederation of British Industry (CBI) and the Trades Union Congress (TUC).

Peak group: A group that coordinates the activities of different pressure groups in the same area of interest; peak groups often work closely with government.

Weblink ■ www.cbi.org.uk

Use the Confederation of British Industry website to find out about its activities and its current policy positions.

Promotional group: A pressure group that exists to advance particular values, ideals and principles.

Promotional groups (sometimes called 'cause', 'attitude' or 'issue' groups) are groups that are based on shared attitudes or values, rather than the common interests of its members. The causes they seek to advance are many and various. They range from charity activities, poverty reduction, education and the environment, to human rights, international development and peace.

Promotional groups have the following features:

▶ They seek to advance particular ideals or principles.
▶ Membership is open to all.
▶ Members are motivated by moral or altruistic concerns (the betterment of others).

Non-governmental organization: A not-for-profit group that draws members from more than one country and is active at an international level.

Specific examples of promotional groups include Friends of the Earth, Amnesty International, Shelter, the Royal Society for the Protection of Birds (RSPB) and the Electoral Reform Society. When involved in international politics, these groups are often called **non-governmental organizations**, or NGOs, examples including the Red Cross, Greenpeace and the Catholic Church.

Differences between . . .
SECTIONAL AND PROMOTIONAL GROUPS

Sectional groups	Promotional groups
Defend interests	Promote causes
Closed membership	Open membership
Material concerns – a group 'of'	Moral concerns – a group 'for'
Benefit members only	Benefit others or wider society

However, the sectional/promotional distinction has been subject to increasing criticism. The distinction may even raise more questions than it answers.

The differences between sectional and promotional groups are blurred in at least three ways:

▶ *Some pressure groups have both sectional and promotional characteristics.* For instance, the UK Coalition of People Living with HIV and AIDS appears to be a sectional group, but also carries out promotional activities linked to public health and education. In a sense, all pressure groups, including charities and churches, have sectional concerns, based on the interests of their professional staff and the property and other capital they own.

▶ *A single pressure group may include members with both sectional and promotional motivations.* This applies to the campaign against a third runway at Heathrow Airport. Protesters have included both local people motivated by sectional concerns about the demolition of homes and a school and the increase in noise pollution, and also people with promotional concerns about climate change and ecological sustainability.

▶ *Some pressure groups try to mask their sectional motivations by adopting the language and arguments of a promotional group.* Moral and altruistic concerns will often carry greater weight with the general public than expressions of naked self-interest. For instance, the BMA exists to advance or protect the interests of doctors, but its spokespeople invariably talk in terms of public health, patients' welfare and the future of the NHS.

Insiders and outsiders

The insider/outsider distinction is based on a group's *relationship to government*. It therefore affects both the strategies adopted by a group and its status – whether or not it is considered 'legitimate' or 'established'. **Insider groups** are groups that are consulted on a regular basis by government. They operate 'inside' the decision-making process, not outside. Their degree, regularity and level of consultation varies, of course. 'Ultra-insider' groups are regularly consulted at ministerial or senior official level within the executive. They may also sit on government policy committees and agencies, and have links to parliamentary select committees. Examples of insider groups include the CBI, National Farmers' Union (NFU), BMA, MENCAP and the Howard League for Penal Reform.

However, not all insider groups are alike. They can be divided into three subcategories (Grant, 1995):

▶ **High-profile insider groups**. These groups straddle the insider/outsider divide by operating both behind the scenes and through mass-media and public-opinion campaigns (e.g. the CBI, NFU and BMA).

Insider group: A pressure group that enjoys regular, privileged and usually institutionalized access to government.

▶ **Low-profile insider groups**. These concentrate on developing contacts with government, and rarely seek to influence the wider public (e.g. the Howard League for Penal Reform).

▶ **Prisoner groups**. These groups are dependent on government, which may fund them or have created them in the first place, as in the case of **quangos** (e.g. the National Consumer Council and the Commission for Equality and Human Rights).

Quango: A quasi-autonomous non-governmental organization: a public body staffed by appointees rather than politicians or civil servants.

On the face of it, insider status is highly desirable. It allows groups to exert direct pressure on the people who matter: those who make policy decisions. Insider status, however, is not always an advantage. As insider groups have to have objectives that are broadly compatible with those of government, as well as a demonstrable capacity to ensure that their members abide by agreed decisions, being an insider can significantly restrict a group's freedom to manoeuvre. In the case of so-called 'prisoner groups', they have no alternative but to be insiders.

Outsider group: A pressure group that is either not consulted by government or consulted only irregularly and not usually at a senior level.

Outsider groups, by contrast, have no special links to government. They are kept, or choose to remain, at arm's length from government. They therefore try to exert influence indirectly via the mass media or through public opinion campaigns. Examples of outsider groups include the Campaign for Nuclear Disarmament (CND), the Animal Liberation Front (ALF) and Fathers4Justice.

However, not all outsider groups are alike. There are three main kinds of outsider group (Grant, 1995):

▶ **Potential insider groups**. Sometimes called 'threshold groups', these aspire to insider status but have yet to achieve it (e.g. the Countryside Alliance).

▶ **Outsider groups by necessity**. These are groups that lack the political knowledge and skills to become insider groups.

▶ **Ideological outsider groups**. These are groups with radical aims that are not compatible with those of government; their members are also often attracted to tactics of mass activism or direct action (see pp. 149–50) (e.g. the Animal Liberation Front, CND and Stop the War Coalition).

Groups may be outsiders for one of two reasons. First, they may be *denied* insider status by government. In this case, outsider status is an indication of weakness. Lacking formal access to government, such groups are forced to 'go public' in the hope of exercising indirect influence on the policy process. Ironically, then, some of the most high profile groups in the country may be amongst the UK's weakest pressure groups. Second, groups may *choose* to operate as outsiders. This reflects the radical nature of a group's goals and a fear of becoming 'domesticated' by being too closely involved with government. Moreover, groups may recognize that outsider strategies, such as petitions, demonstrations and marches, are the most likely way of engaging potential supporters and turning them into activists.

Many outsider groups have therefore been attracted by what is sometimes called the 'new politics', which turns away from 'established' parties, pressure groups and representative processes towards more innovative and theatrical forms of protest politics. This style of politics has been closely associated with the 'new' social movements that emerged in the late 20th and early 21st centuries – the women's movement, the green movement, the peace movement and the anti-capitalist or anti-globalization movement. Protest movements such as the People's Fuel Lobby, the Countryside Alliance, Stop the War Coalition, Make Poverty History, anti-fees demonstrations by students and TUC-backed protests against the coalition's spending cuts have also used such tactics of mass activism.

Weblink ■ www.countryside-alliance.org

Use the Countryside Alliance's website to find out about the group and its current campaigns.

Differences between . . .
INSIDER AND OUTSIDER GROUPS

Insider groups	Outsider groups
Access to policy-makers	No/limited access to policy-makers
(Often) low profile	High profile
Mainstream goals	Radical goals
Strong leadership	Strong grass roots

Although the insider/outsider distinction has become increasingly more widely used, it has its drawbacks. These include the following:

▶ *Many groups employ both insider and outsider tactics.* This certainly applies in the case of high-profile insider groups, which recognize that the ability to mount public-opinion and media campaigns strengthens their hands when it comes to bargaining with government.
▶ *Insider status is more a matter of degree than of simple fact.* Some groups are more 'inside' than others, in terms of the level and regularity of their contacts with government. Even outsider groups, such as Greenpeace and Friends of the Earth, have some degree of insider status.

▶ *Insider/outsider status changes over time.* This happens, most clearly, when new governments are elected with different goals and priorities. For example, the TUC was a high-profile insider until 1979, when it became an ideological outsider during the Thatcher years, returning later to being a kind of semi-insider.

Functions of pressure groups

Pressure groups carry out a range of functions. These include:

▶▶ Representation
▶▶ Political participation
▶▶ Education
▶▶ Policy formulation
▶▶ Policy implementation.

Representation

Pressure groups provide a mouthpiece for groups and interests that are not adequately represented through the electoral process or by political parties. This occurs, in part, because groups are concerned with the specific rather than the general. Whereas parties attempt to broaden their appeal, trying to catch (potentially) all voters, pressure groups can articulate the views or interests of particular groups and focus on specific causes. Some have even argued that pressure groups provide an alternative to the formal representative process through what has been called **functional representation**.

> *However*, questions have also been raised about the capacity of groups to carry out representation:

Functional representation: The representation of groups based on their function within the economy or society; examples include industries, employers, professions, workers, and so on.

▶ Groups have a low level of internal democracy, creating the possibility that they express the views of their leaders and not their members.
▶ The influence of groups on government does not always reflect their membership size or their popular support, as discussed later.

Political participation

Pressure groups have become an increasingly important agent of political participation. Of UK citizens, 40–50 per cent belong to at least one voluntary association, and a large minority (20 per cent) belong to two or more. Moreover, a range of pressure groups, mainly outsider groups, seek to exert influence precisely by mobilizing popular support through activities such as petitions, marches, demonstrations and other forms of political protest. Such forms of political participation have been particularly attractive to young people.

> *However*, the capacity of groups to promote political participation has also been questioned.

Chequebook group:
A pressure group in which
activism is restricted to full-
time professionals, with the
mass membership serving
primarily as a source of
financial support (through
subscriptions and donations).

▶ Group membership does not always involve participation. There is a tendency for modern groups to become '**chequebook groups**'. Examples include some of the UK's largest groups, such as the National Trust and Friends of the Earth.

Education

Much of what the public knows about politics it finds out through pressure groups of one kind or another. Many pressure groups, indeed, operate largely through their ability to communicate with the public and raise political consciousness. Groups therefore often devote significant resources to carrying out research, maintaining websites, commenting on government policy and using high-profile academics, scientists and even celebrities to get their views across. An emphasis is therefore placed on cultivating **expert authority**.

Expert authority:
Respect for people's views
based on their specialist
knowledge; to be 'an'
authority rather than 'in'
authority.

However, the effectiveness of groups in stimulating political education has also been questioned:

▶ Pressure groups are every bit as biased and subjective as political parties, and there are few checks or constraints on what a pressure group spokesperson may say.

Policy formulation

Although pressure groups, by definition, are not policy-makers, this does not prevent many pressure groups from participating in the policy-making process. In particular, pressure groups are a vital source of information and advice to governments. Many groups are therefore regularly consulted in the process of policy formulation, with government policy increasingly being developed through **policy networks**.

Policy network: Links
between government and
non-governmental bodies
(including well-placed
lobbyists, sympathetic
academics, leading
journalists and others)
through which policy
proposals are developed.

However, questions have also been raised about the role of groups in formulating policy:

▶ Only a small body of privileged groups – 'insider' groups, as discussed earlier – are involved in policy formulation.
▶ Many have argued that groups should not influence the policy process because they are not elected and so are not publicly accountable.

Policy implementation

The role of some pressure groups extends beyond trying to shape the content of public policy to playing a role in putting policy into practice. The best example of this is the National Farmers' Union (NFU), which works with the Department for Rural Affairs (Defra) in implementing policies related, for example, to farm subsidies, disease control and animal welfare. Not only do such links further blur the distinction between groups and government, but they also give the groups in question clear leverage when it comes to influencing the content of policy.

However, questions have also been raised about the role of groups in implementing policy:

▶ Some have criticized such groups for being over-close to government, and therefore for endangering their independence.
▶ Others have argued that policy implementation gives groups unfair political leverage in influencing policy decisions.

Pressure group power

How do pressure groups exert influence?

Who do pressure groups seek to influence? What methods do they use? Pressure groups are confronted by a wide range of 'points of access'. Their choice of targets and methods, however, depends on two factors. First, how *effective* is a particular strategy likely to be? Second, given the group's aims and resources, which strategies are *available*?

Pressure groups can exert influence in a variety of ways (the importance of the EU in pressure group politics is discussed in Chapter 10). These include:

▶▶ Ministers and civil servants
▶▶ Parliament
▶▶ Political parties
▶▶ Public opinion
▶▶ Direct action.

Ministers and civil servants

It is easy to understand why pressure groups want to influence ministers and civil servants. They work at the heart of the 'core executive' (see p. 252), the network of bodies headed by the prime minister and cabinet, which develop and make government policy. This is where power lies. Many groups therefore aspire to insider status, and those who have it are reluctant to lose it. But why should government want to consult groups?

Governments consult groups for at least three reasons:

▶ The need for specialized knowledge and *advice* to inform the policy process
▶ The desire to gain the *cooperation* of important groups
▶ The need to gauge the *reaction* of affected groups to proposed policies or government measures.

A very wide range of groups therefore stalk the 'corridors of power'. It is unthinkable that economic, industrial and trade policies would be developed without the consultation of major corporations, trade associations and business groups such as the CBI and Institute of Directors. Groups such as the BMA and the Royal College of Nursing frequently visit the Department of Health, while groups representing teachers, schools, colleges and universities are routinely consulted by the Department for Education and Science. Although such influence may involve formal and informal meetings with ministers, routine behind-the-scenes meetings with civil servants and membership of policy committees may be the most important way of exerting influence.

Parliament

Groups that cannot gain access to the executive may look to exert influence through Parliament. In other cases, groups may use parliamentary lobbying to supplement contacts with ministers and civil servants. Although less can be achieved by influencing Parliament than by influencing the executive, changes can nevertheless be made to the details of legislation or the profile of a political issue. This can happen through influence on, for instance, private members' bills, parliamentary questions (written and oral) and select committee enquiries. The postbags of MPs and peers are full of correspondence from groups of many kinds and concerned with all sorts of issues. Parliamentary lobbying has become increasingly sophisticated with the development, during the 1980s, of a multimillion pound professional consultancy industry. Lobbyists seek to make contact with sympathetic or well-placed MPs and peers, providing them with expensively produced briefing and information packs.

Parliamentary lobbying has grown in importance in recent years for a variety of reasons (discussed more fully in Chapter 7):

▶ More independently minded backbenchers
▶ The introduction of departmental select committees
▶ The growing use of professional lobbyists and political consultants
▶ The fact that the partially reformed House of Lords is more assertive.

Political parties

The motive for groups developing links with political parties is clear. The UK has a system of party government, in that governments are formed from the leading party in the House of Commons. Influencing party policy can therefore lead to influence on government policy. The most obvious way in which groups influence parties is through funding and donations ('he who pays the piper calls the tune'). The best-known example of a link between a pressure group and a political party has traditionally been the relationship between the trade unions and the Labour Party. Affiliated trade unions not only provided the bulk of Labour's funding but also controlled most of the votes at the party's conference. In the last two decades, however, trade union contributions to the Labour Party have declined from three-quarters to under one third of its total funds. The major two parties now both rely on businesses and wealthy individuals for their main source of funding. The Political Parties, Elections and Referendums Act 2000 introduced new rules on party fundraising and spending. Under this, parties now have to reveal where their funding comes from, and some sources of funding (from wealthy foreign individuals, for example) have been banned altogether.

Public opinion

These strategies are adopted by outsider groups, although high-profile insider groups may also engage in public-opinion campaigning. The purpose of such strategies is to influence government *indirectly* by pushing issues up the political agenda, and demonstrating both the strength of commitment and the level of public support for a particular cause. The hope is that government will pay attention for fear of suffering electoral consequences. The classic strategies include public petitions, marches and demonstrations. Such tactics have a long political heritage dating back perhaps to the Chartists in the 1840s and including the Campaign for Nuclear Disarmament's (CND) annual marches, which started in the late 1950s.

However, the tactic has been more widely used in recent years, as was discussed earlier in relation to outsider groups. Public-opinion campaigning is largely geared to attracting media attention and thereby gaining wider influence, as in the case of anti-fees protests by students and anti-cuts demonstrations by trade unions and other groups. Although protests and demonstration seldom have a direct influence on public policy, they can still have a wider imact, not least by damaging the image of a government or prime minister. The outcomes of both the February 1974 and the 1979 general elections were affected by the 1973–4 miners' strike and the 'winter of discontent' (a wave of public sector strikes over the winter of 1978–9), respectively. Similarly, the anti-poll tax protests of 1990 damaged Thatcher's reputation and so contributed to her downfall.

However, pressure groups are not always concerned about wider public opinion and the mass media but, instead, may focus on what has been called 'informed opinion', sometimes called the 'chattering classes'. The purpose of influencing mass public opinion is to alert government to the possibility that its electoral standing could be damaged. However, the purpose of focusing on the 'informed' classes (professional bodies, the specialist media, the 'quality' daily press and magazines) is to exert influence via so-called 'opinion formers'. These are the people best placed to sway the decisions of ministers, civil servants and MPs.

Direct action: Political action that is *direct* in that it imposes sanctions that affect government or the running of the country; direct action is often (but not necessarily) illegal.

Direct action

Direct action as a political strategy overlaps with some forms of public-opinion campaigning. However, whereas most political protests take place within the constitutional and legal framework, being based on established rights of freedom

Civil disobedience:
Law-breaking that is justified
by reference to 'higher' religious, moral or political principles; breaking the law to
'make a point'.

of speech, assembly and movement, direct action aims to cause disruption or inconvenience. Strikes, blockades, boycotts and sit-ins are all examples of direct action. Direct action may be violent or non-violent. Non-violent direct action sometimes takes the form of **civil disobedience**. This applied, for instance, to the Greenham Common Women's Peace Camp in the 1980s and to Brian Haw's five-year anti-war vigil outside Parliament, which was ended by a Law Lords ruling in 2006. Such passive resistance, however, is very different from the tactics that have been employed by some animal rights groups. SHAC (Stop Huntingdon Animal Cruelty) has campaigned from 1999 onwards to stop animal testing at Huntingdon Life Sciences (HLS) in Cambridge. During this period, staff working at HLS have been subject to routine harassment and intimidation, property has been damaged and the company's financial health has been severely weakened by pressure brought to bear on investors.

Which pressure groups are the most powerful?

Some pressure groups are clearly more powerful than others. Some succeed while others fail. But what does 'success' mean? How can we weigh up pressure-group power or influence? These are difficult questions because 'success' may be measured in different ways. Success may mean:

▶ *Affecting* government policy – policy-making power
▶ *Pushing* an issue up the political agenda – agenda-setting power
▶ *Changing* people's values, perceptions and behaviour – ideological power.

Another difficulty in measuring pressure-group power is that there is considerable debate about how power is distributed amongst pressure groups. There is disagreement, in particular, about whether pressure groups tend to *widen* the distribution of power, giving power to the people, or whether they tend to *concentrate* it, strengthening the already powerful. This is often portrayed as a battle between two rival theories of political power, pluralism and **elitism**. The debate has major implications for the relationship between pressure groups and democracy, which is looked at on pp. 158–62.

Elitism: The theory
that political power is
concentrated in the hands
of the few, an elite,
sometimes called a 'power
elite'.

In practice, a variety of factors affect the power of individual groups. These include the following:

▶▶▶ Wealth
▶▶▶ Size
▶▶▶ Organization and leadership
▶▶▶ The government's views
▶▶▶ Popular support
▶▶▶ The effectiveness of opposition.

What is . . . pluralism

Pluralism is a theory of the distribution of political power that holds that power is widely and evenly dispersed in society, rather than concentrated in the hands of an elite or ruling class. In particular, pluralists have a positive view of pressure-group politics, believing that groups promote healthy debate and discussion, and that they strengthen the democratic process (see Pluralist democracy, p. 158).

Pluralism is based on the following assumptions:

▶ Citizens are represented largely through their membership of organized groups
▶ All groups have a measure of political influence
▶ There are many resources and 'levers' available to pressure groups (money, numbers, protests, etc) and these are widely spread
▶ No group can achieve a dominant position, because other groups will always challenge it — there is always a 'countervailing power'

The term pluralism is sometimes used more generally to refer to diversity or multiplicity (the existence of many things). For example:

▶ *Political* pluralism refers to competition for power between a number of parties
▶ *Moral* pluralism refers to the existence of a range of values and ethical beliefs
▶ *Cultural* pluralism refers to the existence of a variety of cultures or ethnic groups within the same society.

Wealth

The most powerful pressure groups in the country are the ones that government must listen to because they have financial and economic power – they are wealthy. This largely explains the power of business groups. Why does government listen to major corporations (such as Shell, BP, Barclays, ICI, Tesco, Sainsbury's, BAE Systems, BT and Vodaphone) and to their peak groups and trade associations?

Business groups have a number of key advantages over other groups:

▶ As the main source of employment and investment in the economy, all governments, regardless of their ideological beliefs, must seek their cooperation and support.
▶ They possess knowledge and expertise that are essential to the formulation of economic, industrial and trade policies.
▶ They possess the financial strength to employ professional lobbyists and public relations consultants, and to make donations to political parties.

▶ They often have high public profiles, have access to the media and can run advertising campaigns.

It is notable, for example, that in the year following the 2010 election about half of all money given to the Conservative Party came from City sources. The reason for this was, presumably, to reduce the likelihood of the coalition taking robust action to tighten financial regulation and reduce banker's bonuses.

Size

Does size matter? Are the largest pressure groups the most powerful? This is one of the assumptions that is made by pluralist theorists, who believe that pressure group power is democratically based. Membership size certainly has advantages:

▶ *Large groups can claim to represent public opinion.* Government listens to them because, at the end of the day, their members can have an electoral impact. Groups such as the RSPB, the Consumers' Association and the National Society for the Prevention of Cruelty to Children (NSPCC) therefore ensure that their membership levels remain above 1 million.

▶ *More members means more subscriptions and donations.* Large groups tend to be wealthy groups. This has led to the growth of so-called 'chequebook' groups (such as WWF, formerly known as the Worldwide Fund for Nature), which aim to achieve mass memberships but leave campaigning in the hands of full-time professionals. About 90 per cent of Greenpeace's total income comes from its members.

▶ *A large membership allows groups to organize political campaigns and protests.* Groups such as trade unions and CND use their members as a key resource. Members are the main people who turn up to marches and demonstrations.

However, it would be a mistake to believe that big groups are always the most powerful groups. For example, membership size cannot usually compensate for a lack of economic power. The CBI is generally more powerful than the TUC, despite the latter representing trade unions with about 7 million members. Similarly, some groups may be small but exert influence through their policy expertise and specialist knowledge. This applies to the Howard League for Penal Reform, which has a membership of only around 3,000. Finally, the density and extent of membership within a particular group of people may be more important than overall size. The BMA's influence stems, in part, from the fact that about 80 per cent of doctors are members, allowing it to claim to speak on behalf of the medical profession generally.

Organization and leadership

Organization helps groups to mobilize their resources effectively and to take concerted action. Some groups are easier to organize than others. For example, producers are easier to organize than consumers; doctors are easier to organize than patients; teachers are easier to organize than students. This also helps to explain why interest groups are often more powerful than cause groups. While interest groups are able to take political action quickly and effectively, the supporters of cause groups are usually scattered, and potential members are difficult to identify and contact. Effective organization also requires financial resources (the best organized groups tend to be the most wealthy) and high quality leadership. Good leaders can bring a number of advantages to groups.

The attributes of an effective leader include:

▶ Acute political skills – they know how the policy process works, who to network with and how to exert pressure.
▶ Good political contacts – they know the 'right' people.
▶ Developed media and presentational skills – they know how to put a case.
▶ A high public profile – they are publicly recognized and maybe even liked.

Examples of high profile pressure-group leaders include Shami Chakrabarti, the director of Liberty, the civil liberties group; and Peter Tatchell, a prominent figure in the gay rights organization OutRage. In other cases, celebrities have been used to heighten the media and public profile of a campaign – Elton John with AIDS awareness, and Bob Geldof and Bono with global poverty and trade reform, and Jamie Oliver with the quality of school meals.

The government's views

Groups are far more likely to succeed when the government is broadly sympathetic towards their aims or goals. When a group's goals clash fundamentally with those of the government, it is consigned to the status of an ideological outsider. Ideological outsiders may be able to bring about long-term changes in political values and attitudes, but they have very little chance of changing government policy in the short term. Traditionally, business groups were more influential under a Conservative government, and the trade unions were more influential under Labour (although this changed in the 1990s as Labour adopted a more clearly pro-business stance). Other examples include the greater influence of groups campaigning against hunting with dogs (such as the RSPCA) and in favour of the right to roam (such as the Ramblers' Association) once a 'sympathetic' Labour government was elected in 1997.

Public support

Pressure groups that enjoy high levels of public support have greater political influence than ones with only minority support. Crudely, governments calculate how much electoral damage may be caused by *not* acceding to a group's demands. The success of the Snowdrop Campaign, in campaigning for a ban on the keeping of handguns, was significantly influenced by the public outrage that had followed the school massacre at Dunblane in 1996. Similarly, the coalition's decision in February 2011 to abandon its plan to privatise England's forests was viewed as a victory for 'people power', the campaigning group, 38 Degrees, having collected half a million signatures on a petition opposing the sale. In other cases, certain groups may enjoy wider public support than others because of the nature of the group itself. Nurses, for example, enjoy wider public respect and support than, say, students. Nevertheless (as nurses would attest), public support is not always reflected in political influence. For instance, massive Stop the War Campaign marches in 2003, and opinion poll opposition, failed to have any impact on the Blair government's decision to participate in the Iraq War.

Weblink ■ www.stopwar.org.uk

Use the Stop the War Coalition website for news and analysis; and for details of the group's current activities.

Effectiveness of opposition

Pressure groups may succeed or fail, less because of their own resources, and more because of the strength or weakness of the forces that oppose them. Groups invariably confront other groups, and interests clash with rival interests. Very few pressure groups have it all their own way. The progress that Action on Smoking and Health (ASH) had in campaigning for measures to discourage smoking was countered through the 1980s and 1990s by a well-funded tobacco lobby that made major donations to the Conservative Party. Trade unions, even during their heyday in the 1970s, suffered from the fact that business groups enjoy a series of structural advantages over them, in particular through their role in the economy. The anti-hunting groups' efforts to persuade the Labour government in 1997 to carry out its commitment to ban hunting with dogs led to resistance through the formation of the Countryside Alliance in 1998. Although the Countryside Alliance failed to prevent a ban being introduced, it nevertheless succeeded in delaying it and in modifying how it has worked in practice.

Are pressure groups becoming more powerful?

Not all debates about pressure group power focus on the power of individual groups. Others address the *overall* power of groups, and whether or not they have generally become more powerful. Commentators increasingly argue, for instance,

BY COMPARISON . . .

Pressure groups in the USA

- It is widely argued that US politics is characterized by particularly intense pressure group influence. This is largely because the fragmented nature of US government provides groups with more 'access points' than in the UK. The two houses of Congress (the Senate and the House of Representatives) are both elected and equally powerful. The Supreme Court has wider powers than UK courts; and the federal system creates an additional layer of government to influence.

- Pressure group influence is particularly intense in Congress because of the USA's relatively weak party system. Members of Congress can therefore develop closer, long-term links with groups than is possible for MPs in the UK. Group influence is also exerted through strong links developed with standing committees. This leads to so-called 'iron triangles', policy networks that involve pressure group leaders and key figures in both standing committees and executive agencies.

- Campaign finance is a particularly important pressure group lever in the USA, a reflection of the ever-increasing cost of usually television-based electoral campaigning. This considerably increases the influence of business groups. Coal, oil, gas, logging, agribusiness and transport companies give huge sums to (usually Republican but also Democrat) federal politicians. This, for example, has affected US policy on environmental issues such as climate change.

- There has been a growth in the number of single-issue groups in recent years, including, for instance, 'pro-life' and 'pro-choice' groups campaigning on abortion. Similarly, organizations claiming to represent the 'public interest' have become more prominent. The best known example is Common Cause, which has tried to counter the influence that 'special interests' have over Washington politics.

that pressure groups have become more influential in recent years, perhaps even more influential than political parties. Have we been witnessing the rise of pressure-group power? Or do pressure groups simply make a lot of noise but have far less impact on policy?

The rise of pressure group power

Those who argue that pressure groups have become more powerful usually draw attention to one of three developments:

▶ **The growth of promotional groups.** Looked at simply in terms of political participation, groups certainly appear to be becoming more important. This is best demonstrated by the growth of promotional or cause groups in particular. Over half the cause groups now in existence have been created since 1960, and the membership of many leading pressure groups dwarfs that of contemporary political parties. The RSPB, with over 1 million members, has a membership larger than the combined memberships of the main three parties. The National Trust is the largest voluntary organization in Europe, with a membership of 3.4 million. Linked to this has been the appeal of the 'new politics', character-ized by greater political activism and the spread of grass-roots participation. 'New' types of political participation include political protest and what has been called **cyberactivism**. Examples of the politics of protest include the activities of left-wing movements such as CND, the 1990 anti-poll tax riots, anti-globalization demonstrations in Seattle (1999), London (2000) and Genoa (2001) and student protest in 2010 against university tuition fees. However, protest politics has also come to be embraced by right-wing move-ments, such as the People's Fuel Lobby and the Countryside Alliance.

Cyberactivism: Political action based on the use of 'new' technology — the Internet, mobile phones, e-petitions, electronic voting, and so on.

▶ **More access points.** A variety of pressure groups have also benefited from the fact that new pressure points have emerged in UK politics:

▷ Devolution has allowed pressure groups to exert influence through the Scottish Parliament, the Welsh Assembly and the Northern Ireland Assembly.

▷ The passage of the Human Rights Act 1998, has substantially increased pressure-group activity focused on the courts. This has especially bene-fited groups that represent the interests of religious or ethnic minorities, and groups that have an interest in civil liberties issues (such as Liberty).

▷ As is discussed in Chapter 10, the process of European integration has encouraged many pressure groups to look to exert influence through EU bodies, especially when they fail to influence the domestic policy process. It has also led to the formation of a range of European-wide pressure groups, examples including the European Small Business

Alliance, European Free Trade Association, Friends of the Earth Europe and the European Association for the Defence of Human Rights.

▸ **Globalization**. Globalization (see p. 22) has strengthened pressure groups in a number of ways. In particular, there is general agreement that business groups have become more powerful in a global age. This is because they are able more easily to relocate production and investment, so exerting greater leverage on national governments. Such trends have strengthened pressures on governments in the UK and elsewhere; for instance, to cut business taxes and reduce corporate regulation. Another feature of globalization has been the emergence of NGOs, such as the World Development Movement and the World Social Forum, as major actors on the global stage. Some 2,400 NGOs, for example, took part in the Earth Summit in Rio de Janeiro in 1992.

The decline of pressure groups

However, not everyone believes that pressure groups have become more important. Some even talk in terms of the decline in pressure-group power in recent years. Such arguments are usually based on one of two developments:

Corporatism: The incorporation of key economic groups into the processes of government, creating a partnership between government, business and labour.

▸ **The end of corporatism**. For some, the high point of pressure-group influence came in the 1970s. This was a period of so-called tripartite government or **corporatism**. A particularly close relationship developed between the government and the leading 'peak' groups, notably the CBI and the TUC. Economic policy was therefore developed through a process of routine consultation and group bargaining. However, corporatism was dismantled in the 1980s and it has never been re-established. The Thatcher government came to power in 1979 with a strong suspicion of the trade unions in particular and of organized interests in general. As a result, it adopted an arm's length approach to group consultation. Although Thatcher's strident anti-corporatism ended with her fall, the free-market ideas that have dominated all subsequent governments have discouraged them from returning to the practice of 'beer and sandwiches at Number 10'.

▸ **A decline in meaningful and active participation**. An alternative explanation of the decline of pressure groups challenges the idea that recent years have witnessed an upsurge in group activity. This suggests that while group membership may have increased, these members have become increasingly passive. This is the phenomenon of 'chequebook participation'. Members of pressure groups (and political parties, for that matter) are happy to pay their subscriptions, but have little interest in wider activism (attending meetings, participating in conferences, sitting on committees, and so forth). This may be a consequence of the decline in 'social capital', as discussed in Chapter 1. Political activism is therefore increasingly confined to a small class of full-time

What is ... pluralist democracy

Pluralist democracy is a form of democracy that operates through the capacity of organized groups and interests to articulate popular demands and ensure government responsiveness. As such, it can be seen as an alternative to parliamentary democracy. The conditions for pluralist democracy include the following:

▶ There is a wide dispersal of power amongst competing groups and, in particular, there are no elite groups
▶ Groups are internally democratic in the sense that leaders are accountable to members
▶ Government is 'neutral' in the sense that it is willing to listen to any group or interest.

professionals. Such trends may also apply to protest politics. Although large numbers of people may, at different times, be attracted to marches and demonstrations, this seldom leads to longer-term political involvement or commitment. It is a form of 'lifestyle' politics, or 'politics lite'.

Pressure groups and democracy

Questions about pressure-group power are closely related to debates about the implications of group politics for democracy. On the one hand, pluralist theorists argue that group politics is the very stuff of democracy, even advancing the idea of pluralist democracy. On the other hand, elitists and others attack pressure groups and claim that they weaken or undermine the democratic process. To examine this debate it is necessary to look at the ways in which pressure groups promote democracy and the ways in which they threaten democracy.

How do pressure groups promote democracy?

Pressure groups promote democracy in a number of ways. They:

▶▶ Supplement electoral democracy
▶▶ Widen political participation
▶▶ Promote education
▶▶ Ensure competition and debate.

Supplementing electoral democracy

Pluralists often highlight the advantages of group representation over representation through elections and political parties. Pressure groups may either supplement electoral democracy (making up for its defects and limitations) or they may have replaced political parties as the main way in which people express their views and interests:

▶ *Pressure groups keep government in touch with public opinion between elections.* One of the weaknesses of elections is that they only take place every few years. By contrast, pressure groups force the government to engage in an ongoing dialogue with the people, in which the interests or views of the various sections of society cannot be ignored.

▶ *Pressure groups give a political voice to minority groups and articulate concerns that are overlooked by political parties.* Elections, at best, determine the general direction of government policy, with parties being anxious to develop policies that appeal to the mass of voters. Pressure groups are therefore often more effective in articulating concerns about issues such as the environment, civil liberties, global poverty, abortion, violence against women and the plight of the elderly.

Participation

The level of political participation is an important indicator of the health of democracy. Democracy, at heart, means government *by* the people. If this is the case, declining electoral turnout and steadily falling party membership highlights a major 'democratic deficit' in UK politics. This, however, is very effectively combated by the growth in the number and size of pressure groups. As discussed earlier, pressure groups have become increasingly effective agents of political participation. Not only has single-issue politics proved to be popular but the grass-roots activism and decentralized organization of many campaigning groups have proved to be attractive to many young people and those who may be disillusioned with conventional politics.

Education

Pressure groups promote political debate, discussion and argument. In so doing, they create a better-informed and more educated electorate. This, in turn, helps to improve the quality of public policy. Without pressure groups, the public and the media would have to rely on a relatively narrow range of political views, those expressed by the government of the day and a small number of major parties. Pressure groups challenge established views and conventional wisdom. They offer alternative viewpoints and widen the information available to the public, especially through their access to the mass media and the use of 'new' communications technology such as the Internet. Pressure groups are therefore prepared to 'speak truth to power'. In many cases, pressure groups raise the quality of political debate by introducing specialist knowledge and greater expertise.

Benefits of competition

Pressure groups help to promote democracy by widening the distribution of political power. They do this, in part, because groups compete against one another. This ensures that no group or interest can remain dominant permanently. As pluralists would argue, there is no such thing as a 'power elite'. Instead, as one group becomes influential, other groups come into existence to combat them and offer rival viewpoints. This is what pluralists call the theory of 'countervailing power'. Trade unions developed in response to the growth of business power. Pro-abortion groups vie against anti-abortion groups. And so on. In this way, public policy is developed through an ongoing debate between rival groups that ensures that political influence is widely and evenly dispersed. Group politics is therefore characterized by a rough balance of power. This is the essence of pluralist democracy.

How do pressure groups threaten democracy?

Pressure groups threaten democracy in a number of ways. They:

▶▶▶   Increase political inequality
▶▶▶   Exercise non-legitimate power
▶▶▶   Exert 'behind the scenes' influence
▶▶▶   Lead to the tyranny of the minority.

Political inequality

A central argument against the pluralist image of group politics is that, far from dispersing power more widely and empowering ordinary citizens, pressure groups tend to empower the already powerful. They therefore increase, rather than reduce, political inequality. Pluralists argue that political inequality is broadly democratic, in that the most successful groups tend to be ones with large membership, and which enjoy wide and possibly intense public support. This is very difficult to sustain. In practice, the most powerful pressure groups tend to be the ones that possess money, expertise, institutional leverage and privileged links to government. What is more, some pressure groups are *much* more powerful than others. For instance, the influence of major corporations cannot, in most cases, be compared with the influence exerted by, say, a trade union, a charity or an environmental group. Pressure groups therefore strengthen the voice of the wealthy and privileged, giving those who have access to financial, educational, organizational and other resources special influence over the government.

By the same token, there are significant, and sometimes large, sections of society that are effectively excluded from the pressure-group universe. This is usually because they are difficult or impossible to organize and so must, at best, rely on others to protect them. Examples of such groups include children, asylum seekers, the homeless, the elderly and the mentally ill.

FOR OR AGAINST?

PRESSURE GROUPS

FOR	AGAINST
Widen power. Pressure groups strengthen representation by articulating interests and advancing views that tend to be ignored by political parties. They also provide a means of influencing government between elections, especially giving a political voice to minority groups that are ignored by political parties.	**Concentrate power**. Groups widen political inequality by strengthening the voice of the wealthy and the privileged: those who have access to financial, educational, organizational or other resources. Other groups are poorly organized, lack resources or are ignored by government.
Promote education. Groups stimulate debate and discussion, helping to create a better-informed and more educated electorate. In particular, they provide citizens with alternative sources of information. In providing government with technical expertise and practical advice, they also improve the quality of public policy.	**Narrow self-interest**. Groups are socially and politically divisive, in that they are concerned with the particular, not the general. In defending minority views or interests, pressure groups may make it more difficult for governments to act in the interest of the larger society.
Extend participation. Groups broaden the scope of political participation. They do this both by providing an alternative to conventional party and electoral politics and by offering opportunities for grass-roots activism. Group participation may be especially attractive to the young and those disillusioned by conventional politics.	**Unaccountable power**. Being non-elected, groups exercise power without responsibility. Unlike politicians, group leaders are not publicly accountable. Pressure groups usually lack internal democracy, meaning that leaders are rarely elected and so are unaccountable to their members.
Limit government. Groups check government power and, in the process, defend rights and freedom. They do this because they are autonomous and independent from government. Groups thus ensure that the state is balanced against a vigorous and healthy civil society.	**Undermine Parliament**. Groups undermine parliamentary democracy by bypassing representative processes. They also make the policy process 'closed' and more secretive by exerting influence through negotiations and deals that are in no way subject to public scrutiny.
Maintain stability. In providing a channel of communication between citizens and government, groups help to uphold political stability by ensuring that government responds to popular demands and concerns. Pressure groups therefore function as a kind of safety valve in the political system.	**Ungovernability**. Groups make societies more difficult to govern, in that they create an array of vested interests that are able to block government initiatives and make policy unworkable. This 'hyperpluralism' can also undermine good economic policy by forcing up public spending and increasing state intervention.

Non-legitimate power

On what basis do pressure groups exert influence? Critics have questioned whether pressure groups exercise rightful or legitimate power in any circumstances. This is because, unlike conventional politicians, pressure-group leaders have not been elected. Pressure groups are therefore not publicly accountable, meaning that the influence they exert is not democratically legitimate. This problem is compounded by the fact that very few pressure groups operate on the basis of internal democracy. Leaders are very rarely elected by their members, and when they are (as in the case of trade unions) this is often on the basis of very low turnouts. Indeed, there has been a growing trend for pressure groups to be dominated by a small number of senior professionals. Some pressure-group leaders may, in fact, be little more than self-appointed political spokespeople.

'Behind the scenes' influence

Regardless of which groups are most powerful, pressure group influence is exerted in a way that is not subject to scrutiny and public accountability. Pressure groups usually exert influence 'behind closed doors'. This particularly applies in the case of insider groups, whose representatives stalk the 'corridors of power' unseen by the public and away from media scrutiny. No one knows (apart from occasional leaks) who said what to whom, or who influenced whom, and how. This is unaccountable power. Not only does this contrast sharply with the workings of representative bodies such as Parliament, but it also diminishes Parliament and undermines parliamentary democracy. Insider links between groups and the executive bypass Parliament, rendering elected MPs impotent as policy is increasingly made through deals between government and influential groups that the House of Commons does not get to discuss.

Tyranny of the minority

Pressure groups, by their very nature, represent minorities rather than majorities. For pluralists, of course, this is one of their strengths. Pressure groups help to prevent a 'tyranny of the majority' that is, perhaps, one of the inevitable features of electoral democracy. However, pressure groups may create the opposite problem. Minority views or 'special' interests may prevail at the expense of the interests of the majority or the larger public. Therefore, as pressure groups become more powerful, elected governments may find it more difficult to serve the public interest and to do what is best for society as a whole. This problem of the 'tyranny of the minority' is most extreme when pressure groups use direct action to achieve their objectives. Through the use of strikes, blockades and even intimidation and violence pressure groups, in effect, 'hold the country to ransom'. Once pressure groups start to operate outside the established legal and constitutional framework they are also operating outside – and arguably *against* – the democratic process.

WHAT YOU SHOULD KNOW

▶▶ A pressure group is an organized group of people that aims to influence the policies or actions of government, typically having a narrow issue focus and being united by either shared interests or a common cause. However, the distinction between pressure groups and political parties is blurred by the fact that many small parties have a norrow issue focus and by the tendency of some pressure groups to use elections as a tactical weapon.

▶▶ Insider pressure groups are groups that exist to advance or protect the (usually material) interests of their members. Promotional groups, by contrast, exist to promote particular values, ideals or principles, and are motivated by the desire to better others or society at large rather than their members. Insider groups are groups that enjoy regular, privileged and (usually) institutional access to government. Outsider groups, by contrast, are either not consulted by government or only consulted irregularly and not usually at a senior level.

▶▶ Pressure groups carry out a range of functions. Amongst others, they provide representation, create opportunities for political participation, educate the electorate, contribute to the formulation of policy and, in some circumstances, help to implement government policy. The effectiveness of pressure groups in these roles has been questioned, however.

▶▶ Pressure groups can exert influence in a variety of ways. Prominent pressure-group methods include contacts with ministers and senior civil servants, lobbying Parliament, developing links with political parties, public-opinion or media campaigns, and the use of direct action.

▶▶ There is no agreement about the distribution of power between and amongst pressure groups. Pluralists believe that political power is widely and evenly divided, while elitists believe that it is concentrated in the hands of the few. The main factors that affect the power of particular groups are wealth, membership size, organizational and leadership strength, the views of government, the level of popular support and the effectiveness of any oppositional forces.

▶▶ Pressure groups may be becoming more powerful in the UK, as is reflected in the growth of promotional groups and protest movements, the widening of access points and the rise of corporate power due to globalization. The end of corporatism and a decline in meaningful and active participation may nevertheless indicate a decline in group power.

▶▶ Some commentators argue that pressure groups promote democracy, mainly by supplementing electoral democracy, increasing levels of political participation, creating a better-informed electorate and distributing power more widely. Others, however, argue that groups threaten democracy by increasing political inequality, exercising non-legitimate power, exerting 'behind the scenes' influence and promoting the tyranny of the minority.

Test yourself

Short questions:

1   What is a pressure group?
2   Outline *two* differences between a political party and a pressure group.
3   Outline, with examples, *two* types of pressure groups.
4   Briefly explain the difference between sectional groups and promotional groups.
5   Outline *two* differences between insider and outsider pressure groups.
6   Outline *two* functions of pressure groups.
7   Distinguish between a pressure group and a social movement.
8   What is pluralism?

Medium questions:

9   Why is it sometimes difficult to distinguish between pressure groups and political parties?
10   Why has the distinction between sectional and promotional pressure groups been criticized?
11   Why may some pressure groups choose to remain as outsider groups?
12   How and why do pressure groups seek to influence Parliament?
13   How do pressure groups use political protests to exert influence?
14   Explain *three* factors that affect the power of pressure groups.
15   Why is it sometimes difficult to assess the power of pressure groups?
16   Explain the growth in the number and size of promotional groups in recent years.

Extended questions:

17   To what extent have pressure groups become more powerful in recent years?
18   Are the largest pressure groups the most powerful groups?
19   Why are some pressure groups more successful than others?
20   To what extent is the UK a pluralist democracy?
21   Have pressure groups replaced political parties as the main vehicle for political participation?
22   Do pressure groups widen the distribution of political power or concentrate it?
23   Assess the view that pressure groups strengthen democracy.

Part 2

Governing the UK

Chapter 6

The Constitution

The purpose of a constitution

On the face of it, the constitution is the least 'sexy' topic in politics. Constitutions appear to be just a collection of rules and, what is more, rules that in the UK are steeped in ancient traditions and customs. Those who are interested in the constitution are people who have a 'legalistic' view of politics, an interest in the theory of politics but not its practice. This image, though, is quite wrong. Constitutions are vital to politics, both to its theory and its practice. Indeed, it may be that there is no more important issue in UK politics than the future of the constitution. Why are constitutions so important?

Constitutions exist for one crucial reason: we cannot trust the government or, for that matter, anyone who has power over us. Constitutions, if you like, are a solution to the problem of power. As power tends to corrupt, we need to be protected from those in government, and this protection is provided by a constitution. Without a constitution, the government could simply do whatever it wanted – and this may mean oppressing minorities, violating freedom or even tyrannizing the mass of the people. This is why questions about the effectiveness of the constitution are so important. In the UK, these questions are particularly pressing because of the unusual, even unique, character of its 'unwritten' constitution. Since the late 1990s, in fact, there has been an upsurge in constitutional reform that is changing forever the way in which the country is governed. How does the UK constitution work? What are its advantages and disadvantages? And how could it work better?

- ■ **What is a constitution, and what forms can it take?**
- ■ **What is the nature of the UK constitution?**
- ■ **What are the strengths and weaknesses of the UK constitution?**
- ■ **Why has constitutional reform become such an important issue?**
- ■ **How should the UK constitution be further reformed?**
- ■ **Should the UK introduce a 'written' constitution?**

GETTING YOU THINKING

The constitution under pressure?

Before starting the chapter, read this passage and briefly consider the questions on the next page.

On the morning of 7 May 2010, the UK awoke to the news that the previous day's general election had resulted in a 'hung' Parliament. This was a highly unusual event. Only one previous general election since 1945 (in February 1974) had failed to give a single party a majority of seats in the House of Commons. When there is a majority party, the outcome of the election is clear and simple: the leader of that party becomes, or remains, the prime minister, and forms a government composed of its members. This also happens swiftly. When there is a change in government, the new prime minister is installed (by the Queen) on the morning after the election. In 2010, however, the Brown Labour government had 'lost' the election (Labour had come second behind the Conservatives) but Cameron and the Conservatives had not 'won' (the Conservative were 19 seats short of a Commons majority). What would happen next?

Such a situation is particularly interesting because, in the UK's uncodified, or 'unwritten', constitution, decisions about the choice of the prime minister are based on conventions. These are rules of conduct or behaviour, which can sometimes amount to little more than informal understandings. How well did the 'unwritten' constitution perform? Five days elapsed between the general election and the formation of a new government. During this period, Brown remained as prime minister, but he nevertheless acknowledged that the Conservatives, as the largest party, should have the first opportunity to form a government. On the day after the election, Cameron made what he called a 'big, open and comprehensive offer' to the Liberal Democrats, and negotiations began on the formation of a coalition. By 12 May, it was clear that these negotiations were heading towards a successful outcome, and hopes for an alternative Labour–Liberal Democrat coalition had evaporated. Brown therefore resigned, allowing for the appointment of Cameron as head of a coalition government. The political uncertainty caused by the election result did not thus lead to a constitutional crisis, and the eventual transition of power was smooth and trouble-free.

William Hague reporting in May 2010 on progress in negotiations on the formation of a coalition – but was the constitution being respected?

What issuess do these developments raise?

▶▶▶   In what sense is the UK constitution 'unwritten'?

▶▶▶   What are the rules about the choice of the prime minister in the UK?

▶▶▶   How did the key players in May 2010 show an understanding of these rules?

▶▶▶   How did the flexible interpretation of these rules help to avoid a constitutional crisis?

▶▶▶   What may be the drawbacks of an 'unwritten' constitution?

IN THIS CHAPTER:

Understanding constitutions • The UK constitution • The changing constitution

Understanding constitutions

A constitution is, most simply, the rules that govern the government. Just as government lays down rules for society at large through the laws it makes, so a constitution establishes a framework of rules which are meant to check or constrain government. A constitution therefore gives practical expression to the principle of **limited government**. Constitutions are a relatively recent development, the 'age of constitutions' having been initiated by the establishment of the first 'written' constitutions: the US constitution in 1787 and the French Declaration of the Rights of Man and the Citizen in 1789. In both these cases, constitutional government was seen as the solution to the rule of absolute monarchs. The same was true in Britain, where the origins of its 'unwritten' constitution can be traced back to the Bill of Rights of 1689 and the Act of Settlement of 1701, both of which helped to transfer power from the king to Parliament in the aftermath of the Glorious Revolution (see p. 12).

Limited government: A form of government in which government power is subject to limitations and checks, providing protection for the individual; the opposite of arbitrary government.

Types of constitution

Constitutions may be classified in three main ways:

▶▶▶ As codified and uncodified constitutions
▶▶▶ As unitary and federal constitutions
▶▶▶ As rigid and flexible constitutions.

Codified and uncodified constitutions

Traditionally, considerable emphasis has been placed on the distinction between 'written' and 'unwritten' constitutions. Written constitutions are, in theory, constitutions that are enshrined in law, while unwritten constitutions are supposedly made up of customs and traditions. The former have been 'created', while the latter have been organic entities that have evolved through history.

However, the written/unwritten distinction has always been misleading:

▶ *No constitution is entirely written.* No constitution is entirely composed of formal rules that are legally enforceable. Even where written documents exist, these do not, and cannot, define all aspects of constitutional practice. This leads to a reliance on unwritten customs and practices.

▶ *No constitution is entirely unwritten.* No constitution consists only of rules of conduct or behaviour. It is a mistake to classify the UK constitution as

What is ... a constitution

A constitution is a set of rules that:

▶ Seek to establish the duties, powers and functions of the various institutions of government
▶ Regulate the relationships between and among the institutions
▶ Define the relationship between the state and the individual; that is, define the extent of civil liberty (see p. 286).

The balance between written (e.g. laws) and unwritten (e.g. customs or conventions) rules varies from system to system, but no constitution is entirely written and none is entirely unwritten. The main types of constitution are codified and uncodified constitutions, unitary and federal constitutions, and rigid and flexible constitutions.

unwritten, as most of its provisions are, in fact, written. As discussed below, statute law is the most significant source of the constitution.

Codified constitution:
A constitution in which key constitutional provisions are collected together within a single legal document, popularly known as a written constitution or the constitution.

More helpful (and more accurate) than the written/unwritten distinction is the contrast between codified and uncodified constitutions. A **codified constitution** is one that is based on the existence of a single authoritative document. This document, the written constitution, lays down (usually in its preamble) the core principles of the system of government. In its main body, it usually outlines the duties, powers and functions of the major institutions of government. It may also include a statement of citizens' rights and freedoms, possibly in the form of a bill of rights (see p. 295). A large proportion of countries, and certainly virtually all liberal democratic states, now possess codified constitutions.

Codified constitutions have three key features (these are illustrated by the US constitution, see p. 173):

▶ In a codified constitution, the document itself is *authoritative*, in the sense that it constitutes 'higher' law – indeed, the highest law of the land. The constitution binds all political institutions, including those that make ordinary law. This gives rise to a two-tier legal system, in which the constitution stands above statute law made by the legislature.
▶ The provisions of the constitution as laid out in the codified document are *entrenched*, in the sense that they are difficult to amend or abolish. The procedure for making and subsequently changing the constitution must therefore be in some way more complex or difficult than the procedure for making ordinary laws.

▶ As the constitution sets out the duties, powers and functions of government institutions in terms of 'higher' law, it is *judiciable*. This means that all political bodies are subject to the authority of the courts, and in particular a supreme or constitutional court.

Uncodified constitution:
A constitution that is made up of rules that are found in a variety of sources, in the absence of a single legal document or written constitution.

Uncodified constitutions have become increasingly rare. Only three liberal democracies (the UK, Israel and New Zealand) continue to have uncodified constitutions, together with a handful of non-democratic states such as Bhutan, Saudi Arabia and Oman. However, the introduction in New Zealand of the Constitution Act 1986 (which consolidated previously scattered laws and principles), and the adoption in 1990 of a bill of rights, has been interpreted by many commentators as indicating that the New Zealand constitution is no longer uncodified.

Uncodified constitutions have three defining features:

▶ The constitution is *not authoritative*. Constitutional laws enjoy the same status as ordinary laws. States that have uncodified constitutions therefore have single-tier legal systems with no form of higher law.
▶ Uncodified constitutions are *not entrenched*. The constitution can be changed through the normal processes for enacting statute law. This is reflected in the UK in the principle of parliamentary sovereignty (see p. 180), through which Parliament can make, unmake and amend any law it wishes, including laws that affect the constitution.
▶ Uncodified constitutions are *not judiciable*. In the absence of higher law, judges simply do not have a legal standard (enshrined in a written constitution) against which they can declare that the actions of other bodies are 'constitutional' or 'unconstitutional'.

Weblink ■ www.constitution.org/cons/natlcons.htm

Use this website for detailed information about constitutions worldwide, including the text of the Magna Carta and the Bill of Rights 1689.

Unitary and federal constitutions

Unitary constitution:
A constitution that concentrates sovereign power in a single body of national government.

Constitutions have also been classified in terms of their content and, specifically, by the institution or structure they underpin. The most widely used such classification is between unitary and federal constitutions. **Unitary constitutions** establish the constitutional supremacy of central government over provincial or local bodies. They do this by vesting sovereignty in the national legislature, meaning that it can create or abolish, strengthen or weaken, all other institutions. In the UK, this is reflected in the fact that Parliament possesses, at least in theory, unri-

BY COMPARISON . . .

The US Constitution

- The US Constitution was the world's first 'written' constitution. It was written by the 'founding fathers' at the Philadelphia Convention in 1787, to provide a system of government for the newly independent USA. The document is only about 7,000 words in length and is largely taken up with a description of the duties, powers and functions of the three branches of federal government: the presidency, Congress and the Supreme Court. The Bill of Rights, consisting of the first ten amendments of the constitution, was introduced in 1789 and ratified in 1791.

- The Constitution is entrenched by the fact that Congress cannot change the Constitution through its normal legislative processes. The amendment process is deliberately complex. Amendments must first be passed by at least two-thirds of the votes in both houses of Congress and then they must be ratified by at least three-quarters of the state legislatures (this currently means 37 states out of 50).

- On the face of it, the US Constitution is highly rigid. A mere 26 constitutional amendments have been passed since 1797, ten of which (the Bill of Rights) were introduced in the first two years of the Constitution's existence. However, although the words of the US Constitution may have changed little, their meaning has been subject to constant revision and updating as judges have interpreted and reinterpreted them. In addition, other aspects of constitutional practice (such as political parties, primary elections and congressional committees) have simply evolved over time.

- The US Constitution is a federal constitution. Although its provisions deal entirely with the institutions of federal government, the Ninth Amendment states that all other powers are reserved to the states and the people. This means that the 50 states (together with the people) are entitled to all the powers not allocated by the constitution.

Federal constitution:
A constitution that is based on the principle of shared sovereignty, in that there are two relatively autonomous levels of government, the national/federal and the regional/state.

valled and unchallengeable legislative authority. Devolved assemblies and local authorities do not, therefore, enjoy a share of sovereignty. By contrast, **federal constitutions** divide sovereignty between two levels of government. Both central government (the federal level) and regional government (the state level) possess a range of powers that the other cannot encroach on. As is discussed in Chapter 10, many argue that devolution has created a 'quasi-federal' structure within UK government.

Rigid and flexible constitutions

An alternative form of classification is based on the ease with which the constitution can be changed. On the face of it, codified constitutions are likely to be relatively inflexible, because their provisions are in some way entrenched in higher law. By the same token, uncodified ones appear to be flexible and adaptable, because laws of constitutional significance can be changed through the ordinary legislative process. However, there is no simple relationship between codified constitutions and rigidity, or uncodified ones and flexibility:

Royal Prerogative: The body of powers, immunities and privileges that are recognized in common law as belonging to the Crown; these powers are now more commonly exercised by ministers than by the monarch.

▶ Codified constitutions can exhibit a surprising degree of flexibility. This does not apply in the formal process of amendment, which is deliberately hard to bring about. However, it may occur through a process of judicial interpretation. For instance, the US Constitution means whatever the justices of the Supreme Court say it means.

▶ Some aspects of the UK's uncodified constitution have remained remarkably resistant to change. These include the principles of parliamentary sovereignty and the constitutional monarchy, both of which date back to the late 17th century, with the formal powers of the monarchy, the **Royal Prerogative**, being much older still.

The UK constitution

Until the 1970s, the UK constitution was widely admired. At home, it tended to be seen as the historical glue that linked the present and the past, and gave the British people their distinctive identity. Schools and colleges did not teach government and politics; instead, students studied what was called 'British Constitution'. Many abroad looked with envy at the UK, seeing its constitution as the key to the country's long period of peaceful political development. However, all of this was to change. A series of events in the 1970s – including the onset of recession, membership of the European Community (EC), clashes between government and the unions, and the rise of Scottish and Welsh nationalism – combined to raise concerns about how the UK was governed, and about the constitution in particular. Was the UK constitution any longer fit for purpose?

In order to review this question, we need to examine three issues:

▶▶ The sources of the constitution
▶▶ The principles of the constitution
▶▶ The strengths and weaknesses of the 'traditional' constitution.

Sources of the constitution

The UK constitution is best thought of as a part-written and uncodified constitution. Indeed, over time it has become an uncodified but *mainly* written constitution. This reflects the fact that, although there is no single, authoritative constitutional document in the UK, most of the rules of the constitution are written down and many of them have a legal status (even though they may not constitute higher law). The rules and principles of the constitution, however, can be found in a variety of places. By contrast with the codified constitution, this makes the UK constitution seem untidy, even confusing.

The most important sources of the UK constitution are:

▶▶ Statute law
▶▶ Common law
▶▶ Conventions
▶▶ Works of constitutional authority
▶▶ European law and treaties.

Statute law

Statute law is law made by Parliament, otherwise known as Acts of Parliament or primary legislation (a statute is a formal, written law). Of course, not all statute laws are of constitutional significance; only the ones that affect the powers and responsibilities of government bodies or the rights and freedoms of citizens are. Statute law, though, is the single most important source of the constitution. This applies because the principle of parliamentary sovereignty (discussed below) implies that statutes outrank all other sources of the constitution (although, as we shall see, EU membership throws this into question). If a statute conflicts with, say, a convention or a common law, the statute will always prevail. In addition, more and more constitutional rules have come to have a statutory basis, both as new constitutional statutes have been enacted and, sometimes, as conventions and common laws are turned into statutes.

Examples of constitutionally significant statute laws include:

▶ Parliament Acts of 1911 and 1949 (limited the powers of the House of Lords)
▶ European Community Act 1972 (authorized the UK's membership of the EC)
▶ Scotland Act 1998 (established the Scottish Parliament)

▶ Government of Wales Act 1998 (established Welsh Assembly)
▶ Human Rights Act 1998 (translated the European Convention on Human Rights into statute law)
▶ House of Lords Act 1999 (excluded all but 92 hereditary peers from sitting in the House of Lords)
▶ Freedom of Information Act 2000 (gave citizens a legal right of access to government information)
▶ Constitutional Reform Act 2005 (provided for a Supreme Court to take over the role of the Law Lords).

Weblink ■ www.cfoi.org.uk

Use the Campaign for Freedom of Information website for information on the issue and on the group's current campaigns.

Common law

Common law refers to a body of laws that are based on tradition, custom and precedent. Although the ultimate source of common law is custom, long-established practices that have come to acquire legal status, the body of common law has largely been created and refined by the courts on a case-by-case basis. This occurs through the use of precedent, where judgements in earlier similar cases are taken to be binding on later cases. Therefore, while statute law is made by politicians, common law is sometimes seen as 'judge-made' law (discussed in Chapter 9).

Constitutional rules that are based on part of common law include:

▶ *Royal Prerogative.* These are the formal powers of the Crown, and they encompass many of the powers of the prime minister and the executive branch of government.
▶ *Traditional rights and freedoms.* Until the passage of the Human Rights Act, the courts recognized what were called 'residual' rights, rights that rested on the common law assumption that 'everything is permitted if it is not prohibited'.

Conventions

Convention: A non-legal rule; a rule of conduct or behaviour.

Conventions are the key unwritten element within the constitution: being non-legal, they often lack clear and unambiguous definition. For example, there is a convention that the government will either resign or call a general election if defeated on a major bill by the House of Commons; but there is debate about what constitutes a 'major' bill. And, anyway, there would be no legal consequences if the government simply ignored this rule. So why are conventions upheld? The answer is that they are upheld by practical political circumstances; in short, they make politics 'workable'. The convention that the **Royal Assent** is always granted is upheld by the monarch's desire not to challenge the 'democratic will' of Parliament, an act that would bring the future of the monarchy into question. Once established, constitutional conventions often assume historical authority, as they come to be based on custom and precedent. That said, conventions can, in effect, be created, as occurred in 2007 when Gordon Brown announced that in future the UK would never declare war without Parliament having debated the issue beforehand.

Examples of major constitutional conventions include:

▶ *The exercise of Crown powers.* The powers of the Royal Prerogative are, in the main, exercised by the prime minister and other ministers, not by the monarch. These powers include the power to appoint, reshuffle and sack ministers, to declare war, to dissolve and recall Parliament, and to ratify international treaties (although, in the future, many of these powers will be subject to parliamentary consultation).

▶ *The appointment of the prime minister.* The monarch appoints as prime minister the leader of the largest party in the House of Commons, or, in the case of a 'hung' Parliament, the politician who is likely to command the confidence of the House of Commons.

▶ *Individual ministerial responsibility* (see p. 244). This broadly defines the relationship between ministers and their departments, and it defines grounds on which ministers should resign.

▶ *Collective ministerial responsibility* (see p. 243). This defines the relationship between ministers and the cabinet, and between the government as a whole and Parliament; it determines, amongst other things, that the government should resign or call a general election if it loses the 'confidence' of the House of Commons.

Works of constitutional authority

One of the peculiarities of the UK constitution is the need to consult works by authors who are considered to be authorities on constitutional issues. These works help to define what is constitutionally 'proper' or 'correct'; although they are certainly written, they are not legally enforceable. Such works are needed for two reasons:

▶ There are many gaps and confusions in the UK's uncodified constitution with, particularly in the case of conventions, uncertainty about how general rules and principles should be applied in practice.

▶ These authoritative works carry out the job of interpretation – saying what the

Royal Assent: The monarch's agreement to legislation passed by the two houses of Parliament; by signing a Bill, it becomes an Act.

constitution *actually* means – that, in a codified constitutional system, would be carried out by senior judges.

Nevertheless, as they lack legal authority, these constitutional works are only consulted, and followed, if they are considered to be relevant and their authors respected. Their status is therefore often subject to debate.

Key works of constitutional authority include:

▶ Walter Bagehot's *The English Constitution* (1963 [1867]). This provides the classic definition of the role of the prime minister (as 'first amongst equals') and of the principle of cabinet government.
▶ A. V. Dicey's *An Introduction to the Study of the Law of the Constitution* (1885). This defines the 'twin pillars' of the constitution: parliamentary sovereignty and the rule of law.
▶ Thomas Erskine May's *Treatise on the Law, Privileges, Proceedings and Usage of Parliament* (usually known as 'Erskine May') (1997 [1844]). This provides the most authoritative account of the practices, procedures and rules of Parliament (Erskine May was the Clerk of the House of Commons 1871–86).

EU laws and treaties

In joining the EC in 1973, the UK became subject to the body of European laws and treaties. The significance of this has grown over time in two ways. First, the process of European integration has continued, if sometimes sporadically. This has meant that European bodies have grown in importance. The European Community, for example, was transformed into the European Union (EU) in 1993. Second, the implications of EC/EU membership have gradually become apparent, as the higher status of European law over UK statute law has gradually been recognized. This has led to a debate (examined below) about the continued significance of parliamentary sovereignty in a context of EU membership. This matter remains unclear, however. This is because not only does the UK not have a codified constitution, but the EU also failed to get its own attempt to create one ratified in 2005, although many of its provisions are included in the Lisbon Treaty.

The most important EU laws and treaties include the following:

▶ *Treaty of Rome 1957*. This was the founding treaty of the then European Economic Community, and all member states, whenever they joined, become subject to it.
▶ *Single European Act 1986*. This was the treaty that established a single market within the EC, ensuring the free movement of goods, services and capital.

▸ *Treaty on European Union (TEU or the Maastricht Treaty) 1993*. This treaty introduced political union in the form of the EU, although the UK negotiated an opt-out on the issue of monetary union (membership of the euro) and, initially, on the Social Charter.

▸ *Treaty of Lisbon 2009*. This was a modified version of the proposed Constitutional Treaty, which would have created an EU Constitution, incorporating and replacing all other treaties. Lisbon, nevertheless, introduced new decision-making arrangements within the Union.

Weblink ■ www.historylearningsite.co.uk/british_constitutionone.htm

Use this website to access general information about the nature and workings of the UK constitution.

Principles of the constitution

Constitutions do not just exist as a collection of simple rules – who can do this, who must do that, and so on. Rather, these rules put into practice a framework of principles which, in a codified constitution, tend to be spelled out in the preamble of the written document. The UK constitution may not have a written document, or a preamble, but it does have a set of core principles. Most important of these are:

▶▶ Parliamentary sovereignty
▶▶ The rule of law
▶▶ Parliamentary government
▶▶ Constitutional monarchy
▶▶ EU membership.

Parliamentary sovereignty

Sovereignty: The principle of absolute and unlimited power, implying either supreme legal authority (legal sovereignty) or unchallengeable political power (political sovereignty) (see p. 180).

Sovereignty is a key concept in all constitutions. This is because it defines the location of supreme constitutional power. If constitutions define the duties, power and functions of the various institutions of government, the sovereign body, or any body that shares sovereignty, has the ability to shape or reshape the constitution itself. In this way, it defines the powers of subordinate bodies. In the UK, sovereignty is located in Parliament or, technically, the 'Crown in Parliament'. Parliamentary sovereignty is strictly a form of *legal* sovereignty: it means that Parliament has the ability to make, unmake or remove any law it wishes. As J. S. Mill (1806–73) put it, 'Parliament can do anything except turn a man into a woman'. Parliamentary sovereignty is, without doubt, the most important principle in the UK constitution, but it is also its most controversial.

However, there are doubts about the accuracy and continuing relevance of parliamentary sovereignty. This is for three reasons:

What is . . . parliamentary sovereignty

Parliamentary sovereignty refers to the absolute and unlimited legal authority of Parliament, reflected in its ability to make, amend or repeal any law it wishes. As the parliamentary authority Blackstone put it, 'what Parliament doth, no power on earth can undo'. Parliamentary sovereignty is usually seen as the central principle of the UK constitution.

Parliamentary sovereignty is based on four conditions:

▶ The absence of a codified constitution — the absence of higher law
▶ The supremacy of statute law over other forms of law — Acts of Parliament outrank common law, case law, and so on
▶ The absence of rival legislatures — no other bodies have independent law-making powers
▶ No Parliament can bind its successors — Parliament cannot make laws that cannot be unmade.

▶ *Parliament is not, and has never been, politically sovereign.* Parliament has the legal *right* to make, amend or unmake any law it wishes, but not always the political *ability* to do so. A simple example would be that Parliament could, in theory, abolish elections, but this would be likely to result in widespread public protests, if not popular rebellion.

The main political constraints on parliamentary sovereignty therefore include the following:

  ▶ Powerful pressure groups, especially major business interests
  ▶ Public opinion, particularly electoral pressures
  ▶ The views of major trading partners, notably the USA and leading EU states
  ▶ The policies of international organizations, such as the EU, the World Trade Organization (WTO) and the UN.

▶ *There has been a shift from parliamentary sovereignty to popular sovereignty.* Evidence of the growth of **popular sovereignty** can be seen, for example, in the wider use of referendums (see p. 45), the establishment of popularly elected devolved assemblies (see Chapter 10) and in more clearly defined citizen's rights, particularly through the Human Rights Act (see pp. 288–90).

▶ *Parliament may no longer be legally sovereign.* This view has developed primarily as a result of EU membership (see pp. 181–2). It is also implied by the idea that devolution has resulted in 'quasi-federalism', reflected in the reluctance of Parliament to challenge decisions made by devolved bodies as discussed in Chapter 10.

Popular sovereignty:
The principle that supreme authority is vested in the people directly, rather than in a representative institution.

The rule of law

Rule of law: The principle that law should 'rule', in the sense that it applies to all conduct or behaviour and covers both private citizens and public officials.

The **rule of law** is the second key principle of the UK constitution. It has traditionally been seen as an alternative to a codified constitution, showing that, even in the absence of higher law, government is still subject to legal checks and constraints. Government, in short, is not 'above' the law. (The rule of law is discussed more fully in Chapter 9.)

Parliamentary government

The UK's constitutional structure is based on a fusion of powers between the executive and Parliament. This is what is meant by parliamentary government (see p. 213). Government and Parliament are therefore overlapping and interlocking institutions. Government, in effect, governs in and through Parliament. (The nature and implications of parliamentary government are discussed more fully in Chapter 7.) However, particular controversy has arisen as a result of the combination of the principle of parliamentary sovereignty and parliamentary government. The close relationship between government and Parliament can lead to a situation in which the executive can use the sovereign power of Parliament for its own ends. This gives rise to the problem of 'elective dictatorship' (see p. 185).

Constitutional monarchy

Although the monarchy lost its absolute power long ago, it remains a constitutionally significant body in the UK. During the 19th century, most of the monarchy's remaining powers were transferred to ministers accountable to Parliament, especially the prime minister. As early as 1867, Walter Bagehot distinguished between the **'dignified' parts** of the constitution (in which he included the monarchy and the House of Lords), from the 'efficient' parts of the constitution (the cabinet and the House of Commons). However, according to Bagehot, 'dignified' institutions still played a vital role even if they did not exercise meaningful political power. The role of the monarchy was thus to promote popular allegiance, to serve as a symbol of political unity above the 'rough and tumble' of conventional party politics.

'Dignified' parts: Long established and widely respected bodies that serve to make the political process intelligible to the mass of people (according to Bagehot).

According to Bagehot (and what he said in the 19th century still holds), the monarch has the right:

▶ To be informed
▶ To be consulted
▶ To warn
▶ To encourage.

EU membership

Membership of the EC/EU has had growing constitutional implications for the UK. These have focused, in particular, on the role and significance of Parliament, and whether Parliament can any longer be viewed as a sovereign legislature. Sovereignty within the UK is now best understood as 'parliamentary sovereignty within the context of EU membership'. (The wider relationship between the UK and the EU is discussed more fully in Chapter 10.)

EU membership encroaches on parliamentary sovereignty in three main ways:

▶ *European law is higher than statute law*. This was established by the *Factortame* case in 1991, when the European Court of Justice, in effect, quashed sections of the Merchant Shipping Act 1988 because they conflicted with the provisions of the Treaty of Rome. Statute law now outranks all other forms of law except key aspects of European law and treaties.

▶ *Some EU bodies, notably the European Commission, have supranational powers.* EU bodies can therefore impose their will on member states regardless of the stance taken by national legislatures. Parliament thus has no power to resist or ignore directives that are issued by the Commission.

▶ *The decline of the 'national veto'.* The national veto served to protect parliamentary sovereignty by allowing any member state to block EC/EU measures that threatened vital national interests. However, a larger proportion of decisions have come to be made by the EU's key decision-making body, the Council of Ministers, by what is called 'qualified majority voting'.

Some people, nevertheless, disagree with this position, arguing that parliamentary sovereignty has largely survived the threats posed to it by EU membership.

Parliamentary sovereignty may remain relevant for one of two reasons:

▶ *In joining the EC in 1973, Parliament did not, and could not, bind its successors.* In other words, the principle of parliamentary sovereignty remains alive and is embodied in Parliament's continuing power to leave the EU. Any loss of Parliament's legislative authority therefore happens because Parliament *tolerates* it. However, although Parliament still enjoys the legal right to leave the EU, the fact that most of the UK's trade is with other member states would make this move economically damaging and perhaps politically impossible.

▶ *European integration has not eroded parliamentary sovereignty so much as 'pooled' it.* This argument reflects the view that member states can achieve more when they work together through the institutions of the EU than they can when they operate as independent nations. The **'pooled' sovereignty** of the EU is therefore greater than the collective national sovereignties of member states.

Pooled sovereignty: The combination of the national sovereignties of member states to enhance their power and influence; the whole is greater than its parts.

Strengths of the UK constitution

The UK constitution has been defended on a number of grounds. These include:

▶▶ Flexibility

▶▶▶ Democratic rule
▶▶▶ Effective government
▶▶▶ History and tradition.

Flexibility

One of the chief strengths of the UK constitution is that it is flexible and easy to change. This occurs in particular because of the importance of statute law. Quite simply, it is easier and quicker to introduce an Act of Parliament than to amend, say, the US Constitution. Flexibility therefore arises from the fact that the UK constitution is not entrenched. The advantage of the UK's 'unfixed' constitution is that it remains relevant and up-to-date. This occurs because it can adapt and respond to changing political and social circumstances. The introduction of devolution was, for instance, a response to rising nationalism in Scotland and Wales.

Democratic rule

The UK's long period of unbroken democratic rule is often seen as evidence of the strength of its constitutional system. The reason why the constitution has a democratic flavour is because of the importance of parliamentary sovereignty. In the UK's uncodified constitution, supreme constitutional authority is vested, ultimately, in the elected House of Commons. Changes to the constitution therefore often come about because of democratic pressure. For instance, social and economic changes in the 19th century led to the extension of the franchise through a series of reform acts. Similarly, the powers of the House of Lords were reduced through the Parliament Acts, because of a growing belief that an unelected second chamber should no longer have the right to block the policies of elected governments. The democratic character of the UK constitution is also maintained by the fact that the influence of unelected judges is kept to a minimum. In the USA, the constitution effectively means what the judges of the Supreme Court say it means, and these judges are in no way publicly accountable.

Effective government

Supporters of the UK constitution often argue that it helps to make UK governments stronger and more effective. This occurs for two reasons:

▶ Given the absence of a 'written' constitution, government decisions that are backed by Parliament cannot be overturned by the judiciary.
▶ The UK's system of parliamentary government, based on the Westminster model (see p. 23), usually means that governments get their way in Parliament.

This concentration of power in the hands of the executive within the parliamentary system allows UK governments to take strong and decisive action. This is best reflected in radical, reforming governments such as the Attlee governments of

1945–51, which, amongst other things, set up the NHS, introduced comprehensive national insurance and nationalized a wide range of industries; and in the Thatcher governments of 1979–90, which introduced privatization, deregulated the economy and started to reform the welfare state.

History and tradition

This is an argument most commonly associated with conservative thinkers. In their view, a key strength of the constitution is that, being based on tradition and custom, it links present generations to past generations. Because of the role of common law and conventions in particular, the UK constitution has developed and grown over time, giving it an 'organic' character (the constitution is like a living thing). This contrasts starkly with codified constitutions, which, by definition, have been 'created'. The benefit of an organic constitution that is based on custom and tradition is that it has historical authority. Constitutional rules and principles have been 'tested by time' and therefore been shown to work. This can be seen most clearly in relation to the 'dignified' aspects of the constitution, such as the monarchy and the House of Lords.

Criticisms of the UK constitution

The UK constitution has nevertheless been subject to growing criticism. These criticisms have been levelled especially at the 'traditional' constitution, the constitution that existed before the Blair government's reforms started in 1997 (discussed below), but many commentators argue that they remain relevant to the contemporary, 'reformed' constitution.

The most important of these are:

▶▶ Uncertainty
▶▶ Elective dictatorship
▶▶ Centralization
▶▶ Weak protection of rights.

Uncertainty

Critics of the UK constitution point out that it is sometimes difficult to know what the constitution *says*. Confusion surrounds many constitutional rules because, quite simply, they are not hard and fast. This applies particularly to the constitution's unwritten elements. For instance, the convention of individual ministerial responsibility requires that ministers are responsible for blunders made by their departments. But does this mean that they should resign when civil servants make mistakes or only when mistakes are made by the minister? Further, does 'responsibility' imply that anyone has to resign, or just that the minister must provide answers and promise to put mistakes right? It is difficult, in such cases, to escape the conclusion that the constitution is made up as we go along.

What is . . . elective dictatorship

Elective dictatorship is a constitutional imbalance in which executive power is checked only by the need of governments to win elections. In the UK, it is reflected in the ability of a government to act in any way it pleases as long as it maintains control of the House of Commons.

Elective dictatorship occurs for a number of reasons:

▶ The absence of a codified constitution means that Parliament has sovereign power
▶ The subordinate status of the House of Lords means that the sovereign power of Parliament is, in practice, exercised by the House of Commons
▶ The 'first-past-the-post' voting system (see p. 71) means that the House of Commons is (usually) dominated by a single majority party
▶ Tight party discipline means that government has majority control over the Commons, and so can use parliamentary sovereignty for its own ends.

Elective dictatorship

The most serious and challenging criticism of the UK constitution is that, in practice, it gives rise to the problem of 'elective dictatorship'. This term was coined in 1976 by Lord Hailsham, a former Conservative minister and later a Lord Chancellor under Thatcher. It draws attention to the simple fact that, once elected, UK governments can more or less act as they please (that is, act as dictators) until they come up for re-election. This occurs through a combination of two factors:

▶ Sovereign power is vested in the hands of Parliament.
▶ Parliament is routinely controlled, even dominated, by the government of the day.

The problem of elective dictatorship is that, in concentrating power in the hands of the executive, it allows the government of the day to shape and reshape the constitution however it wishes. This creates the impression that, in effect, the UK does not have a constitution. As John Griffiths (1997) put it, the constitution in the UK is 'what happens'. The other concern is that, in widening the powers of government, it creates the possibility that government may become oppressive and tyrannical.

Centralization

A further target of criticism has been that the UK has an overcentralized system of government with weak or ineffective checks and balances. One of the key features of liberal democracy is that government power is limited through internal tensions between and amongst government bodies. However, UK government is

FOCUS ON . . .
Checks and balances

The idea of checks and balances stems from the basic liberal fear that government is always likely to become a tyranny against the individual ('power tends to corrupt'). Government power must therefore be limited or constrained. This can be done by creating institutional tensions within the system of government by fragmenting government power. As the political philosopher Thomas Hobbes (1588–1679) put it, 'liberty is power cut into pieces'. A network of checks and balances therefore ensures that government is at war with itself, limiting its ability to wage war against its citizens.

The checks and balances that are commonly found in liberal democracies include:

▶ The separation of powers (see p. 277)
▶ Bicameralism (see p. 230)
▶ Parliamentary government
▶ Cabinet government (see p. 247)
▶ Judicial independence
▶ Federalism or devolution.

characterized more by the concentration of power than its fragmentation. This can be seen in many ways:

▶ The prime minister tends to dominate the cabinet.
▶ The House of Commons is more powerful than the House of Lords.
▶ The executive usually controls Parliament.
▶ Central government controls local government.

The constitutional reforms that have been introduced since 1997 have certainly tried to address this problem, particularly through devolution and the early stages of Lords reform. Although these reforms have been widely credited with having dispersed government power, many argue that they have not gone far enough. This will be looked at later in relation to the Blair government's reforms.

Weak protection of rights

The final criticism is that the UK constitution provides weak protection for individual rights and civil liberties. In part, this is a consequence of elective dictatorship and the fact that, except for elections, there is nothing that forces the government to respect individual freedom and basic rights. Elections, indeed, can only do this inadequately as they tend to empower majorities rather than minorities or individuals. However, this concern also arises from a traditional unwillingness to write down individual rights and freedoms, to give them legal substance.

As discussed earlier, individual freedom in the UK traditionally rested on 'residual' rights that were supposed to be part of common law. The passage of the Human Rights Act 1998 has certainly changed this, by both defining rights more clearly and making it easier for them to be defended in the courts. However, it stops well short of being an entrenched bill of rights as its provisions could be set aside by Parliament, as has occurred, for instance, over terrorism legislation. (This issue is examined more closely in Chapter 9.)

The changing constitution

Constitutional reform has been a prominent issue in the UK since the late 1990s. Having been dismissed for many years as being almost un-British, questions about reshaping, and even replacing, the UK constitution have attracted wider political attention. Most importantly, interest in constitutional reform has extended beyond long-term advocates, such as the Liberal Democrats, and now encompasses both the Labour and Conservative parties.

This has (apparently) overcome the core problem of constitutional reform in the UK – how could the traditional parties of government be persuaded to support measures that would only tie their own hands if they are in power? In that sense, the UK's 'unwritten' constitution, with its bias in favour of elective dictatorship, was self-perpetuating. It was easy to see why 'third' parties would be enthusiastic for constitutional reform: these reforms would limit the power of *other* parties, not themselves. But it has been less easy to see why the larger parties would take up an issue that, on the face of it, conflicted with their interests. And if they did take up the issue, how far would they be prepared to take it?

This section examines the following themes:

▸▸ The constitution under Blair and Brown, 1997–2010
▸▸ The constitution under Cameron and Clegg, since 2010
▸▸ Other possible reforms, especially the possibility of introducing a codified constitution.

Weblink ■ www.ucl.ac.uk/constitution-unit

Use the Constitution Unit of University College London for research and analysis on constitutional change in its various forms.

The constitution under Blair and Brown

The Labour Party had traditionally been little more interested in changing the constitution than was the Conservative Party. This even applied in relation to the then Conservative-dominated House of Lords. A commitment to abolish and replace the Lords in the 1960s was quickly abandoned as too divisive and too difficult. In 1978, and again in 1979, the Callaghan Labour government tried, under pressure from the Scottish and Welsh nationalists, to introduce devolution; but this was defeated by opposition within its own ranks and the issue was then ignored for over a decade. How, then, was New Labour converted to a radical programme of constitutional reform during the 1990s?

Two factors explain this important shift:

▶ Eighteen years in opposition (1979–97) had gradually encouraged the Labour Party to think like a 'third' party. Constitutional reform proved attractive as it promised to shackle a likely Conservative government.

▶ Many in the Labour Party had come to believe that the party was most likely to return to power through a coalition with the Liberal Democrats. This required that Labour showed greater sympathy for constitutional reform.

What reforms did the Blair government introduce after 1997? How effective were they – how radically was the UK constitution changed? Labour's 1997 manifesto committed the party to a bold and far-reaching programme of constitutional reform. This programme was motivated by a combination of principled beliefs and party-political advantage. The reforms were influenced by a desire to strengthen checks and balances after the radical reforms of the Thatcher period (see Chapter 4). The other consideration, though, was to bolster Labour's position in Scotland (against the threat from the Scottish National Party) through granting devolution and to end Conservative control of the House of Lords.

The Blair government was, without doubt, the most radical reforming government on constitutional matters of any elected in the 20th century. Blair's programme was bold and far-reaching, with a slate of major constitutional bills dominating the legislative agenda in its early years.

These reforms included the following:

▶ A Scottish Parliament and a Welsh Assembly were established in 1999.
▶ A Northern Ireland Assembly was created in 1998, as part of the larger Good Friday Agreement.
▶ A Greater London Authority, consisting of a London mayor and the Greater London Assembly, was set up in 2000.
▶ Referendums were held to approve the creation of each of the new government bodies.
▶ PR electoral systems were used for each of the newly established bodies (see Chapter 3).
▶ The Human Rights Act (HRA) was passed in 1998.
▶ 'Stage one' of the reform of the House of Lords was carried out in 2000, with the removal of all, apart from 92, hereditary peers.

What is more, these reforms were not an end in themselves. Instead, they created momentum for further, and perhaps more radical, constitutional change. For example, once devolved assemblies are established, especially with the democratic legitimacy that comes from a successful referendum, an appetite for greater independence is created. This was reflected in growing demands in Wales for their Assembly to be granted the same powers as enjoyed by the Scottish Parliament. Similarly, the HRA is no ordinary Act of Parliament. It has a 'semi-entrenched' status, in that, although its provisions can be set aside by Parliament, this can only be done through a special parliamentary procedure. 'Stage one' of the reform of the House of Lords also invited speculation about the possible nature of 'stage two', the replacement of the House of Lords by an alternative (and possibly elected) second chamber.

Nevertheless, aside from problems related to individual measures, this phase of Labour's constitutional reforms was also criticized:

▶ *Enthusiasm for constitutional reform quickly started to fade.* This was, perhaps, a simple consequence of the fact that, having won a 'surprise' landslide victory in 1997, Labour ministers and MPs quickly lost their enthusiasm for throwing away power. Certain commitments were therefore abandoned. This was seen in the failure to hold the promised referendum on an alternative to the Westminster voting system (even though the Jenkins Commission had proposed an alternative in the form of 'AV plus'). 'Stage two' of Lords reform also appeared to have been shelved. Constitutional reform was therefore very much a passion of the first Blair government, 1997–2001. The only major constitutional reform subsequently introduced, the Constitutional Reform Act 2005, was part of a separate agenda, linked to the reform of the judiciary (as discussed in Chapter 9).

▶ *The reforms were piecemeal.* There was no 'constitutional blueprint' that informed Blair's reforms, which may have given the programme greater coherence and clearer goals. Instead, the reforms were individual solutions to particular problems.

▶ *The reforms reshaped existing constitutional arrangements but did not address deeper problems.* In particular, the reforms failed to provide a solution for the problem of elective dictatorship, arguably the central weakness of the UK's constitutional system. The major 'hole' in the Blair reforms was the lack of substantive parliamentary reform. It was notable that the government retreated on the issues that could have brought this about – electoral reform at Westminster, and an elected and more powerful second chamber. Also, no mention was made of the possibility of a codified constitution or an entrenched bill of rights.

The transition from Blair to Brown in 2007 appeared to lead to renewed interest in constitutional issues. This occurred because in the light of Labour's declining electoral support, Brown was eager to signal that 'things had changed' – that there had been a change of government and not merely a change of prime minister. Brown's proposals for a 'citizens' state' included both short-term measures to surrender or limit the powers of the prime minister and the executive, and long-term proposals to review more far-reaching changes. His main object of criticism was the huge concentration of power in the hands of the prime minister that occurs through the use of the Royal Prerogative without any need to consult Parliament or any other body. Through a combination of new conventions and a Constitution Act, a wide range of powers would, in future, only be exercised through consultation with, and the approval of, Parliament.

These include the power to:

▶ Declare war
▶ Request a dissolution of Parliament (call a general election)
▶ Recall Parliament
▶ Ratify international treaties
▶ Make top public appointments without scrutiny
▶ Restrict parliamentary oversight of the intelligence services
▶ Choose bishops
▶ Appoint senior judges
▶ Direct prosecutors in particular cases
▶ Set rules governing the civil service
▶ Set rules for entitlements to passports and pardons.

How radical are these proposals? On the one hand, they go a long way towards completing the process of transferring power from the monarchy to Parliament that began with the Glorious Revolution in the 17th century. However, on the other hand, these changes do not, in themselves, bring about a major shift in the relationship between the executive and Parliament. So long as the government of the day controls Parliament through majority control of the House of Commons, it has little to fear from being forced to consult Parliament or gain parliamentary approval for its actions. More radically, Brown committed himself to promoting political debate and public consultation about longer-term proposal, including the possible introduction of a codified constitution and an entrenched bill of rights. Nevertheless, lack of progress on these and other issues, such as 'stage two' Lords reform, shows how high rhetoric on constitutional reform is often not translated into either serious debate or policy change.

The constitution under Cameron and Clegg

The formation of the Conservative–Liberal Democrat coalition in 2010 had mixed implications for the constitution. In many ways, the smooth, if protracted, transition of power following the election (as five days of coalition negotiations took

Who is...
Gordon Brown

Gordon Brown was born on 20 February 1951 in Glasgow, Scotland. He grew up in the town of Kirkcaldy, Fife, the son of a Presbyterian minister, and was accepted to read history at the University of Edinburgh at the age of only 16, achieving an undergraduate degree (1972) and a doctorate (1982). Brown was elected to Parliament on his second attempt as the MP for Dunfermline East in 1983 and quickly achieved prominence as the leading figure within the younger generation of Labour Party 'modernizers'. Following Labour's landslide 1997 general election victory, Brown became Chancellor of the Exchequer, a post that he held for over ten years, making him the longest-serving Chancellor in modern history. During this time, he built massive power in the Treasury, effectively establishing a 'dual monarchy' with Tony Blair. Having decided not to stand for the Party leadership in 1994 on the death of John Smith, Brown's uneasy relationship with Blair became increasingly strained, particularly after the 2005 election. Brown eventually achieved his long-standing ambition to become prime minister in June 2007, when Blair stepped down. As prime minister, Brown was disadvantaged by his poor communications skills, awkward personal style and seeming lack of public empathy, all highlighted by an unsympathetic media. He was, nevertheless, most impressive at the moment of greatest crisis, when his bold and swift decision to recapitalize the banking system in September 2008 helped to avert a possibly much more serious financial crisis in the UK.

place before the resignation of Brown and the appointment of Cameron as prime minister) highlighted the benefits of the flexible, uncodified constitution, as discussed earlier in the chapter. The scope that the constitution affords for the exercise of executive power was nevertheless also evident. This was most clearly apparent in the proposal to introduce the '55 per cent rule'. The coalition's acceptance of the principle of fixed-term Parliaments was accompanied by the idea that, in future, governments could only be forced to resign if they were defeated on a vote of confidence that had been supported by at least 55 per cent of MPs. The purpose of this proposal was to consolidate the coalition by 'locking in' both parties, making it more difficult for either of them to precipitate a general election without the agreement of the other. However, the '55 per cent rule' would have, in effect, re-written the convention of collective ministerial responsibility, under which any defeat of the government on a vote of confidence is meant to precipitate a general election. The 'rule' threatened, thereby, to reduce the power of Parliament in general and of backbenchers in particular. In the end, the proposal was withdrawn due to opposition from Conservative backbenchers.

A further example of executive power was the decision to make Parliament's new fixed term five years in length. Although five years had been the previous *maximum* term, parliamentary terms in the UK had customarily been shorter (between 1945 and 2010, the average Parliament lasted just over three years and nine months). Extending the period between general elections, as this measure effectively did, can be viewed as a way of safeguarding the government of the day from popular pressures, even though it could also be viewed as a reduction of prime ministerial power (as the prime minister has lost the capacity to decide the date of the next election).

However, in other respects, the formation of a coalition government also gave renewed impetus to the issues of constitutional and political reform. This was largely due to the Liberal Democrats' long-standing commitments in the area, which reflect both its status as a 'third' party (wishing to constrain larger, 'governing' parties) and its typically liberal concern about the corrupting nature of political power and the need to protect individual freedom. Any chance of a Conservative–Liberal Democrat coalition therefore depended on agreement on a bold agenda of constitutional reform, especially as the Liberal Democrats had essentially accepted the Conservative approach to economic policy. Such agreement was, nevertheless, easier to bring about because of the fact that, whilst in opposition, the Conservatives had shown greater sympathy for constitutional change, not least by supporting the idea of a largely elected second chamber. The importance that the coalition attached to constitutional and political reform was evident in the decision to give Nick Clegg, the Liberal Democrat leader and deputy prime minister, personal responsibility for constitutional issues.

The prospect of meaningful constitutional change under the coalition, after a decade of faltering progress under Labour, is underpinned by the need to ensure that the Liberal Democrats can claim to have some achievements as a result of their participation in the coalition. Nevertheless, like Labour in 1997, the coalition has no grand plan or overall vision for constitutional reform, meaning that the previous tendency towards piecemeal reform is almost certain to persist. Although the gap on constitutional issues between the Conservatives and the Liberal Democrats may have narrowed, it has by no means disappeared, as a significant proportion of Conservatives continue to favour the traditional constitution. The key areas of constitutional reform that have been mapped out for action under Cameron and Clegg are as follows:

▶ *Electoral reform.* The Liberal Democrats' chief constitutional demand in forming the coalition was electoral reform for the House of Commons. The party had long favoured proportional representation, ideally using the STV

Who is...
Nick Clegg

Nick Clegg was born in Chalfont St Giles, Buckinghamshire, in 1967. He was the third of four children born to a Dutch mother and a half-Russian father. Educated at Westminster School, he studied social anthropology at Cambridge, later attending the University of Minnesota and the College of Europe in Bruges. After a spell working in New York as a trainee journalist, Clegg worked at the European Commission in Brussels and, in 1999, was elected to the European Parliament as MEP for the East Midlands, stepping down from this post in 1999. He became MP for Sheffield Hallam in 2005, and was quickly appointed the Liberal Democrats' spokesman on Europe, later taking over the home affairs portfolio. On the resignation of Sir Menzies Campbell in 2007, Clegg stood for the leadership of the party, eventually beating his rival Chris Huhne by just 1.2 per cent of the vote. Gordon Brown's decision to introduce televised leaders' debates in the run up to the May 2010 election gave Clegg an opportunity to enjoy equal stature with Brown and Cameron. He capitalized on this opportunity with a particularly strong showing in the first debate, which gave the Liberal Democrats a substantial, if temporary, boost in the polls, and led to talk of 'Cleggmania' gripping the country. Although the Liberal Democrats eventually lost five seats in May 2010, the 'hung' parliament that emerged gave Clegg and his party a historic opportunity to participate in government for the first time since 1945. The decision to form a coalition with the Conservatives, taking the post of deputy prime minister, was almost certainly the most significant decision of Clegg's political career.

system, while the Conservative manifesto stated a firm commitment to maintain 'first-past-the-post'. Ironically, the compromise of holding a referendum on the introduction of the majoritarian AV system was an option that had only been outlined in 2010 in Labour's manifesto. (See Chapter 3 for a fuller discussion of the AV referendum and its implications.)

▶ *Lords reform.* On this issue the Conservative and Liberal Democrat 2010 manifestos coincided: both parties were committed to a largely or entirely elected second chamber. This, nevertheless, concealed the fact that many Conservative MPs have little sympathy for an elected second chamber, both because of the benefits that are allegedly associated with nomination and because an elected second chamber may become a rival to the Commons. The fact that it took until May 2011 for Clegg to bring forward proposals for Lords reform (six months later than initially intended), helps to illustrate how difficult progress in this area tends to be, both because of the divergence of views on the issue and the range of interests that need to be taken into account. (See Chapter 7 for a more detailed discussion of Lords reform and other aspects of parliamentary reform.)

▶ *Bills of rights and the judiciary.* On this issue, the preferences of the Conservatives and the Liberal Democrats diverge significantly. The Conservatives are committed to replacing the Human Rights Act with a 'British Bill of Rights', which would neither enjoy the quasi-entrenched status of the HRA nor a direct association with the European Convention on Human Rights. The Liberal Democrats, by contrast, also support the idea of a bill of rights, but, for them, this bill of rights would be fully entrenched and so serve to constrain Parliament. An independent commission has therefore been set up to examine this issue (which is discussed further in Chapter 9).

▶ *Europe.* The UK's relationship with the EU is a key policy area where the Conservatives won concessions from the Liberal Democrats. Although the coalition's policy of requiring that a referendum be held before any future transfer of powers to Brussels can be accepted as a principled position by most Liberal Democrats, its political implications are essentially Eurosceptical. This is because the 'referendum lock' serves as an obstacle to further European integration. In addition, membership of the euro has been ruled out for the current Parliament. (See Chapter 10 for a discussion of the relationship between the UK and the EU.)

▶ *Devolution.* The Conservative Party's abandonment of its hostility towards devolution in the early 2000s significantly diminished the scope for disagreement with the Liberal Democrats on this issue. The coalition's commitment to hold a referendum on further Welsh devolution marks an acceptance by Conservatives of the fact that Scottish-style devolution, involving the devolution of law-making power, is not necessarily a threat to the unity of the UK, especially as this does not go as far federalism, which is supported by many Liberal Democrats. At the same time, the establishment of a commission to examine the 'West Lothian question' is a concession to usually right-wing Conservatives, who are concerned about the imbalances that have been generated by Scottish devolution in particular, without committing the coalition to take action on this issue. (See Chapter 10 for a further discussion of devolution.)

A codified constitution?

The idea of a written constitution has long been debated by students of politics. However, that is exactly what this issue was: an academic debate, a debate between those who *study* politics, not between those who *practise* politics. This has now changed. The Liberal Democrats have long supported the introduction of a codified constitution and a bill of rights. They were joined in the 1980s by newly formed pressure groups, such as Charter 88. Labour's interest in the subject was demonstrated but its willingness to give the Human Rights Act (1998) a semi-entrenched status, and by the acknowledgement by Brown when he became prime minister in 2007 that the issue should be considered.

Two major *practical* obstacles nevertheless stand in the way of the introduction of a 'written' constitution:

▶ *There is no process through which a written constitution could be introduced.* Opponents of a codified constitution have often dismissed the idea as simply unachievable. This is because there is no mechanism within the UK's political and legal system to establish higher law. Indeed, this appears to be impossible, as the sovereign legislature, Parliament, cannot bind itself. The only solution to this problem is that a mechanism would have to be 'invented', and the most likely mechanism would be some kind of cross-party constitutional convention to draw up the provisions of the codified document followed by a referendum to give it popular authority.

▶ *The major parties disagree about the nature and the content of the constitution.* Without at least a broad consensus on constitutional issues among the major parties, a codified constitution would simply be impossible. They would need to agree to both the principle of codification and the detailed provisions of the constitution itself. Agreement on the former is difficult because so long as parties believe they have the prospect of winning parliamentary majorities (especially the Labour and Conservative parties), they have reason to be suspicious about the implications of a codified constitution. Agreement on the latter (detailed provisions) may be even more difficult, as protracted debate about the nature of the second chamber has shown.

And then there are questions about the desirability of codification. No possible constitutional reform would have more profound implications. A codified constitution would significantly affect:

▶ The power of government
▶ The relationship between the executive and Parliament
▶ The relationship between central government and devolved and local bodies
▶ The relationship between judges and politicians
▶ Individual rights and freedoms.

Supporters of codification argue that only a written constitution is a proper constitution. As the central purpose of a constitution is to limit government power, the constitution must be independent from the government itself. How can we trust a government that can enlarge its own powers at will? This is the

A CODIFIED CONSTITUTION

FOR	AGAINST
Clear rules. As key constitutional rules are collected together in a single document, they are more clearly defined than in an 'unwritten' constitution. This creates less confusion about the meaning of constitutional rules and greater certainty that they can be enforced.	**Rigidity**. Codified constitutions tend to be more rigid than uncodified ones because higher law is more difficult to change than statute law. The constitution could therefore easily become outdated and fail to respond to an ever-changing political environment.
Limited government. A codified constitution would cut government down to size. It would provide a solution to the problem of elective dictatorship by ending parliamentary sovereignty. Higher law would also safeguard the constitution from interference by the government of the day.	**Judicial tyranny**. Judges are not the best people to police the constitution because they are unelected and socially unrepresentative. A codified constitution would be interpreted in a way that is not subject to public accountability. It may also reflect the preferences and values of senior judges.
Neutral interpretation. A codified constitution would be 'policed' by senior judges. This would ensure that the provisions of the constitution are properly upheld by other public bodies. Also, as judges are 'above' politics, they would act as neutral and impartial constitutional arbiters.	**Legalistic**. Codified constitutions are legalistic documents, created by people at one point in time. They are often dry and only properly understood by lawyers and judges. Unwritten constitutions, on the other hand, have been endorsed by history and so have an organic character.
Protecting rights. Individual liberty would be more securely protected by a codified constitution because it would define the relationship between the state and the citizens, possibly through a bill of rights. Rights would therefore be more clearly defined and they would be easier to enforce.	**Political bias**. Constitutional documents, including 'written' constitutions, are inevitably biased because they enforce one set of values or principles in preference to others. Codified constitutions can never be 'above' politics. They may therefore precipitate more conflict than they resolve.
Education and citizenship. A written constitution has educational value, in that it highlights the central values and overall goals of the political system. This would strengthen citizenship (see p. 54) by creating a clearer sense of political identity, which may be particularly important in an increasingly multicultural society.	**Unnecessary**. Codified constitutions may not be the most effective way of limiting government power. Improving democracy or strengthening checks and balances may be better ways of preventing over-mighty government, making a written constitution unnecessary.

central defect of the uncodified constitution, and its roots lie in the principle of parliamentary sovereignty. The only way of overthrowing parliamentary sovereignty is through the creation of an entrenched and judiciable constitution. Not only would this put the powers of government bodies and the relationship between the state and its citizens beyond the control of the government of the day, but it would also allow judges, who are 'above' politics, to become the guardians of the constitution.

Opponents of codification tend to advance one of two broad arguments. In the first place, they dismiss a written constitution in principle, usually warning that it is an artificial, legalistic device that would, anyway, lead to the tyranny of judges over democratic politicians. Second, they argue that the goal of limited government can be achieved through other means. Such a view places more faith in the fragmentation of power and the strengthening of checks and balances than in the establishment of higher law. From this perspective, the approach to constitutional reform that has been adopted by Blair and Brown is the right way for the UK to go. In other words, constitutional reform should continue to run with the grain of the 'unwritten' or 'unfixed' constitution, rather than embrace an entirely different constitutional framework.

WHAT YOU SHOULD KNOW

▸▸ A constitution is a set of rules that seek to establish the duties, powers and functions of the various institutions of government, and define the relationship between the state and the individual. In codified constitutions, key provisions are collected together within a single legal document, popularly known as a 'written' constitution. Uncodified constitutions are made up of rules that are found in a variety of sources.

▸▸ The UK has a part-written but uncodified constitution. Its key sources are statute law (law made by Parliament), common law (based on custom and tradition), conventions (non-legal rules), works of constitutional authority and, since 1973, European law and treaties.

▸▸ The main principle of the UK constitution is parliamentary sovereignty, reflected in Parliament's ability to make, amend or repeal any law it wishes. The other important principles of the UK constitution are the rule of law, parliamentary government, the constitutional monarchy and EU membership. The nature and status of parliamentary sovereignty has been threatened by a variety of developments, not least the higher status of EU law.

▸▸ The UK constitution has been defended on a number of grounds. These include that it is flexible and adapts to changing political and social circumstances; that it is democratic, in that supreme constitutional authority is (in practice) vested in the elected House of Commons; that it promotes strong and stable government; and that it is rooted in history and tradition.

▸▸ The criticisms of the UK constitution include that there is uncertainty about the meaning of constitutional rules; that it leads to elective dictatorship (resulting from a combination of parliamentary sovereignty and executive domination of Parliament); that checks and balances are weak; and that individual rights have traditionally been poorly protected.

▸▸ The UK constitution has changed significantly in recent years. The Blair reforms saw the introduction of devolution, the beginning of Lords reform, the introduction of the Human Rights Act and the wider use of referendums and PR electoral systems. Under the Conservative–Liberal Democrat coalition, constitutional issues have once again become prominent, largely because progress with constitutional change was one of the key objectives the Liberal Democrats sought to achieve through participation in the coalition.

▸▸ The issue of a codified constitution is the subject of intense debate. A codified constitution would significantly affect the power of government, the relationship between the executive and Parliament, the relationship between central government and devolved and local bodies, the relationship between judges and politicians, as well as the rights of the individual. Supporters view it as an essential device of limited government; opponents dismiss it either as a recipe for judicial tyranny or as unnecessary.

Test yourself

Short questions:

1 What is a constitution?
2 Outline *two* features of a codified constitution.
3 What is an uncodified constitution?
4 Distinguish between a federal constitution and a unitary constitution.
5 In what sense is the UK constitution 'unwritten'?
6 What is a constitutional convention?
7 Distinguish between statute law and common law, as sources of the UK constitution.
8 What is 'elective dictatorship'?

Medium questions:

9 Explain the main features of the UK constitution.
10 Explain, using examples, the sources of the UK constitution.
11 Explain *three* principles of the UK constitution.
12 Where, in the UK constitutional system, is sovereignty located?
13 What criticisms have been made of the UK constitution?
14 What are the main strengths of the UK constitution?
15 What difficulties have been generated by constitutional reform since 1997?
16 How might a codified constitution act as a check on government?

Extended questions:

17 Assess the strengths of the UK constitution.
18 Why has the UK constitution been criticized?
19 Should the UK remain uncodified?
20 How significant have been the constitutional reforms introduced by the coalition government since 2010?
21 Assess the benefits of the constitutional changes that have been introduced since 1997?
22 How and why has pressure for constitutional reform grown in recent years?
23 'Recent constitutional reforms in the UK have removed the need for a codified constitution.' Discuss.

Chapter 7

Parliament

The importance of Parliament

The term 'parliament' comes from the French *parler*, meaning 'to speak'. Parliament is therefore basically a debating chamber. Some even refer to it as the 'debating chamber of the nation'. But Parliament is much more than a place where people talk. It is also the place where laws are made and where the government (or the executive) confronts the opposition. Parliament is the UK's supreme law-making body, and it is the key institution within its 'parliamentary' system of government. This means that the government does not operate separately from Parliament, but rather it governs *in* and *through* Parliament.

And yet, the decline of Parliament has been a recurrent theme in the UK, dating back to the 19th century. Parliament, it seems, has lost power to many bodies – disciplined political parties, the executive, lobbyists and pressure groups of various kinds, the mass media, a 'federal' EU, and so on. For some, Parliament has simply become an irrelevance, a sideshow to the real business of running the country. But this image is an unbalanced one. Parliament does make a difference, even though it attracts less and less press coverage. The question is: does it make *enough* difference? A weak Parliament has implications for the effectiveness of democracy, the accountability of government, the quality of public policy – the list goes on. Although Parliament has changed significantly in recent years, there is continued and growing pressure for more radical change. How effective is Parliament? And how could it be made more effective?

- ■ **What are the powers and composition of the House of Commons and the House of Lords?**
- ■ **In what sense does the UK have 'parliamentary government'?**
- ■ **What are the functions of Parliament?**
- ■ **How powerful is Parliament? What difference does it make?**
- ■ **How could the House of Commons be strengthened?**
- ■ **How should the House of Lords be reformed?**

GETTING YOU THINKING

An elected second chamber?

Before starting the chapter, read this passage and briefly consider the questions on the next page.

On 17 May 2011, Nick Clegg set out the coalition governments options for replacing the House of Lords. The new second chamber would consist of 300 members, 80 per cent of whom would be elected using the single transferable vote system and who would serve for a single 15-year term. The first elections for the chamber were scheduled to take place in 2015. These were historic proposals, which aimed to sweep away 1,000 years of parliamentary history. While the Commons has long been the democratic voice of Parliament, the Lords has traditionally represented upper-class interests and professions – bishops, judges, the aristocracy and the like. Indeed, until 2000, the vast majority of peers sat in the House of Lords on the basis of nothing other than the accident of birth. They inherited their seats along with their noble titles (they were barons, earls, viscounts, and so on).

However, is a largely elected second chamber such a good idea? Some have argued, for instance, that there is little point in having *two* elected chambers, as this will only create confusion about which one of them speaks 'for' the people. Will two elected chambers simply be a recipe for institutional rivalry within Parliament? Others warn that the specialist knowledge and expertise that has been built up in the House of Lords over the years will be squandered. There are, moreover, concerns about whether these reforms will ever be enacted. After all, they are at best a compromise between the Liberal Democrats' long-standing commitment to establishing a fully elected second chamber and a more traditionalist desire to retain at least some of the features of the existing Lords. Moreover, many MPs can be expected to be reluctant to create a democratic rival to the House of Commons. Problems such as these perhaps help to explain why debate about the make-up and the future of the second chamber has gone unresolved for over 100 years.

The traditional House of Lords, convened for the 2007 Queen's Speech – but for how long will it survive?

What issues do these developments raise?

▶▶▶   **What was the traditional composition of the House of Lords?**

▶▶▶   **How was the composition of the Lords altered by the 2000 reform?**

▶▶▶   **What are the problems of a non-elected second chamber?**

▶▶▶   **What problems may a largely elected second chamber cause?**

▶▶▶   **Do you think the second chamber should be fully elected?**

The role of Parliament

The make-up of Parliament

Although Parliament is often treated as a single institution, it is in fact composed of three parts:

▶▶▶   The House of Commons
▶▶▶   The House of Lords
▶▶▶   The monarchy (or, in legal terms, the 'Crown in Parliament').

The House of Commons

Composition

The composition of the House of Commons is easy to describe as there is only one basis for membership: all Members of Parliament (MPs) win their seats in the same way. The composition of the House of Commons is as follows:

▶   The House of Commons consists of 650 MPs (this number is not fixed but varies each time changes are made to parliamentary constituencies. The size of the Commons is due to be reduced to 600 in 2015.)
▶   Each MP is elected by a single-member parliamentary constituency using the 'first-past-the-post' voting system (see p. 71).
▶   MPs are (almost always) representatives of a party and are subject to a system of party discipline.
▶   Most MPs are categorized as **backbenchers**, while a minority are categorized as **frontbenchers**.

Powers

The House of Commons is politically and legally the dominant chamber of Parliament. This applies to such an extent that the Commons is sometimes taken to be identical with Parliament itself. However, a distinction should be made between the formal powers of the House, enshrined in law and constitutional theory, and its political significance (discussed later).

The two key powers of the House of Commons are:

▶   *The House of Commons has supreme legislative power.* In theory, the Commons can make, unmake and amend any law it wishes, with the Lords only being able to delay these laws. The legal sovereignty of Parliament is thus exercised in

Backbencher: An MP who does not hold a ministerial or 'shadow' ministerial post; so-called because they tend to sit on the back benches.

Frontbencher: An MP who holds a ministerial or 'shadow' ministerial post, and who usually sits on the front benches.

practice by the Commons (subject only to the higher authority of EU laws and treaties).

▶ *The House of Commons alone can remove the government of the day.* This power is based on the convention of collective ministerial responsibility (see p. 243). A government that is defeated in the Commons on a major issue or a matter of confidence is obliged to resign or to call a general election.

House of Lords

Composition

The composition of the House of Lords is both complex and controversial. It is *complex* because there are three distinct bases for membership of the House, meaning that there are four kinds of peers. It is *controversial* because none of these peers is elected. The current membership stems from the House of Lords Act 1999, which removed most (but not all) of the previously dominant hereditary peers, and from the 2005 Constitutional Reform Act, which removed the Law Lords from the House of Lords and set up a Supreme Court and which came into existence in 2009.

The House of Lords consists of the following:

▶ **Life peers.** Life peers (as the title implies) are peers who are entitled to sit in the Lords for their own lifetimes. They are appointed under the Life Peerages Act 1958. Life peers are appointed by the prime minister, with recommendations also being made by opposition leaders. Since 2000, a number of so-called 'people's peers' have been appointed on the basis of individual recommendations made to the House of Lords Appointments Commission. Life peers now dominate the work of the Lords. They account for the overwhelming majority of peers, (678 out of a total of 792 peers in April 2011, not counting 39 who were on leave of absense or were otherwise disqualified from voting).

▶ **Hereditary peers.** These are peers who hold inherited titles which also carry the right to sit in the House of Lords. In descending order of rank, they are dukes, marquises, earls, viscounts and barons, and their female equivalents. Once there were over 700 hereditary peers, but since 1999 only 92 are permitted to sit. These 92 were elected by all the hereditary peers in the 'unreformed' House of Lords.

▶ **'Lords Spiritual'.** These are the bishops and archbishops of the Church of England. They are collectively referred to as the 'Lords Spiritual' (as opposed to all other peers, the 'Lords Temporal'). They are 26 in number, and they have traditionally been appointed by the prime minister on the basis of recommendations made by the Church of England. However, under the coalition government's proposals for Lords reform their number would be reduced to 12.

Powers

The House of Lords' legislative powers are set out in the Parliament Acts of 1911 and 1949. The Lords has the following powers:

Money bill: A bill that contains significant financial measures, as determined by the Speaker of the House of Commons.

▶ *The Lords can delay bills passed by the House of Commons for up to one year.* However, the Lords cannot delay '**money bills**' and, by the so-called Salisbury convention, the Lords cannot defeat measures that are outlined in the government's election manifesto.

▶ *The Lords possess some veto powers.* These are powers that cannot be overridden by the Commons. They include:

  ▶ The extension to the life of Parliament – delays to general elections
  ▶ The sacking of senior judges, which can only be done with the consent of both Houses of Parliament
  ▶ The introduction of secondary, or delegated legislation.

Weblink ■ www.parliament.uk

Use the Parliament website for a host of information about how Parliament works, its composition and activities.

The monarchy

The monarchy is often the 'ignored' part of Parliament. This is understandable because the role of the Queen is normally entirely ceremonial and symbolic. As a non-executive **head of state**, the monarch symbolizes the authority of the Crown.

The monarch is associated with Parliament in a number of ways:

Head of state: The leading representative of a state, who personally embodies the state's power and authority; a title of essentially symbolic significance, as opposed to the head of government.

▶ *Appointing a government.* The Queen chooses the prime minister who, in turn, appoints other members of the government. In practice, the Queen usually has little choice over this matter, as the leader of the largest party in the House of Commons is the only person who can command the confidence of Parliament.

▶ *Opening and dismissing Parliament.* The Queen opens Parliament through the State Opening at the beginning of the parliamentary year, usually in late October/early November. At the request of the prime minister, she dismisses (or 'dissolves') Parliament in order to allow for a general election to be held.

▶ *The Queen's speech.* This is a speech that is delivered at the beginning of each parliamentary session, which informs Parliament of the government's legislative programme. The speech (known as the 'gracious address') is written by the prime minister. In July 2007, Gordon Brown initiated the practice of the prime minister himself pre-announcing draft proposals for the Queen's Speech at the end of the previous parliamentary session.

▶ *The Royal Assent.* This is the final stage of the legislative process, when the Queen (or her representative) signs a bill to make it an Act. This, however, is a mere formality as, by convention, monarchs never refuse to grant the Royal Assent. In Walter Bagehot's formulation, the monarchy is a 'dignified' rather than 'effective' institution.

Functions of Parliament

Parliament is sometimes classified as an 'assembly', a 'legislature' or a 'deliberative body'. The truth is: it is all these things. Parliament has many functions within the political system. The key functions of Parliament are:

⏩ Legislation
⏩ Representation
⏩ Scrutiny and oversight
⏩ Recruitment and training of ministers
⏩ Legitimacy.

Legislation

Legislature: The branch of government that has the power to make laws through the formal enactment of legislation (statutes).

Parliament makes laws. This is why it is classified as a **legislature**. Indeed, Parliament is the supreme legislature in the UK, in that it can make and unmake any law it wishes (subject to the higher authority of EU law), as expressed in the principle of parliamentary sovereignty (see p. 180). Parliament is not restricted by a codified constitution, and no other law-making body can challenge Parliament's authority. Devolved assemblies, local authorities and ministers can only make laws because Parliament *allows* them to.

However, Parliament's effectiveness as a legislature has also been questioned:

Private member's bill: A bill that is proposed by an MP who is not a member of the government, usually through an annual ballot.

▶ The bulk of Parliament's time is spent considering the government's legislative programme. Only a small number of bills, **private member's bills**, are initiated by backbenchers, and these are only successful if they have government support.
▶ Party control of the House of Commons means that government bills are rarely defeated, and most amendments affect the details of legislation, not its major principles. It is more accurate to say that legislation is passed *through* Parliament rather than *by* Parliament.
▶ The Lords play a subordinate role in the legislative process. It is essentially a 'revising chamber'; most of its time is spent 'cleaning up' bills not adequately scrutinized in the Commons.

Weblink ■ www.polis.parliament.uk

Use the Parliamentary Online Indexing Service for access to resources on Parliament and very useful fact sheets about Parliament's working, history and membership.

FOCUS ON . . .
How laws are passed

A government bill has to go through the following parliamentary stages:

▶ **Preparatory stages.** Before bills are passed, their provisions may have been outlined in a **White Paper** or a **Green Paper**. Since 2002, most government bills have been published in draft for what is called preleg-islative scrutiny, which is carried out by select committees (see p. 210).

▶ **First reading.** The bill is introduced to Parliament through the formal reading of its title and (usually) the setting of a date for its second reading. There is no debate or vote at this stage.

▶ **Second reading.** This is the first substantive stage. It involves a full debate that considers the principles (rather than the details) of the bill. It is the first stage at which the bill can be defeated.

▶ **Committee stage.** This is when the details of the bill are considered line by line. It is carried out by a public bill committee (formerly known as a standing committee),

consisting of about 18 MPs, but it may be considered by a **Committee of the Whole House**. Most amendments are made at this stage, and new provisions can be included.

▶ **Report stage.** This is when the committee reports back to the full House of Commons on any changes made during the committee stage. The Commons may amend or reverse changes at the report stage.

▶ **Third reading.** This replicates the second reading in that it is a debate of the full chamber, enabling the House to take an overview of the bill in its amended state. No amendments may be made at this stage, and it is very unusual for bills to be defeated at the third reading.

▶ **The 'other place'.** Major bills are considered first by the Commons, but other bills may start in the Lords. Once passed by one chamber, the bill goes through essentially the same process in what is referred to as the 'other place', before finally going to the monarch for the Royal Assent.

White Paper:
A statement of policy by the government outlined in terms of legislative proposals.

Green Paper:
A consultative document that usually outlines a range of legislative options.

Representation

Parliament is the key link between government and the people, reflected in the fact that the UK has a system of parliamentary democracy (see p. 43). The representative function of Parliament is carried out by the elected House of Commons and operates through the relationship between MPs and their constituents. Nevertheless, as discussed in Chapter 3, there is considerable debate about how this representation happens in practice. The traditional, Burkean view of representation suggests that MPs use their own judgement in acting on behalf of their constituents. The doctrine of the mandate, by contrast, suggests that MPs serve their constituents by 'toeing a party line'.

However, the effectiveness of parliamentary representation has also been criticized:

FOCUS ON . . .

The social background of MPs

▶ **Social class**. MPs are predominantly middle class. Over four-fifths have a professional or business background, with the main professions being law, management, education, the civil service and local government. The manual working class is significantly under-represented, even in the Labour party (10 per cent).

▶ **Gender**. Women continue to be substantially under-represented in the Commons, but they have made substantial progress since the 1980s, when their numbers stood at only just over 3 per cent of MPs. The 2010 election saw the largest ever number of women MPs at 139 (21 per cent of the total). This increase largely occurred because of deliberate steps taken by the Labour Party to increase the proportion of its women candidates.

▶ **Ethnicity**. Ethnic minorities are under-represented. In 2010 only 27 black/Asian MPs were elected, 4 per cent of the whole and less than half the proportion of black/Asian citizens in larger society.

▶ **Age**. MPs are predominantly middle-aged: 70 per cent of them are between 40 and 59, with the average age being 50.

▶ **Education**. MPs are better educated than most UK citizens. Over two-thirds are graduates. Also, more of them have attended independent (or 'public') schools, especially Conservative MPs (two-thirds of them).

▶ **Sexual orientation**. There are 11 openly gay MPs, mostly Labour. However, this is likely to be an underestimate of the total number.

Committee of the Whole House: A meeting of the full chamber of the House of Commons to consider the committee stage of a government bill.

▶ As the House of Lords is unelected, it carries out no representative role and undermines the democratic responsiveness of Parliament (see For and against an elected second chamber, p. 231).

▶ The 'first-past-the-post' voting system undermines the effectiveness of representation in the House of Commons (see Chapter 3).

▶ MPs and peers are socially unrepresentative of larger society.

Scrutiny and oversight

Scrutiny: Examining something in a close or detailed way.

Responsible government: A government that is answerable or accountable to an elected assembly and, through it, to the people.

Parliament does not govern, but its role is to check or constrain the government of the day. Many therefore argue that Parliament's most important function is to 'call the government to account', forcing ministers to explain their actions and justify their policies. It does this through **scrutinizing** and overseeing what government does. This is the key to ensuring **responsible government**. In this role, Parliament acts as a 'watchdog', exposing any blunders or mistakes the government may make. Parliamentary oversight is underpinned by the conventions of individual responsibility (see p. 244) and collective responsibility.

However, the effectiveness of Parliament in carrying out the scrutiny of government has also been questioned:

▶ As the majority of MPs in the House of Commons (normally) belong to the governing party, their primary role is to support the government of the day, not to criticize and embarrass it.

▶ Question Time is often weak and ineffective. Oral questions seldom produce detailed responses, and are used more to embarrass ministers than to subject them to careful scrutiny. Prime minister's questions, in particular, often

FOCUS ON . . .
How Parliament calls ministers to account

▶ **Question Time.** The best known aspect of Question Time is Prime Minister's Questions (PMQs), which takes place each Wednesday from 12.00 to 12.30. MPs ask one notified question of the prime minister and one (unscripted) supplementary question. PMQs are dominated by clashes between the prime minister and the leader of the opposition, who is able to ask four or five 'supplementaries'. Question Time also extends to other ministers, forcing them to answer oral questions from MPs. Each department features in a four-week cycle.

▶ **Select committees.** Select committees scrutinize government policy (as opposed to public bill committees, which examine government legislation). There are 19 departmental select committees (DSCs), which shadow the work of each of the major government departments. They carry out inquiries and write reports, being able also to carry out question-and-answer sessions with ministers, civil servants and other witnesses, and to ask to see government papers.

▶ **Debates and ministerial statements.** Government policy can be examined through *legislative debates* and through *emergency debates* that are held at the discretion of the Speaker. *Adjournment debates* allow backbenchers to initiate debates at the end of the parliamentary day. Ministers are also required to make formal statements to Parliament on major policy issues.

▶ **The opposition.** The second largest party in the House of Commons is designated as 'Her Majesty's loyal opposition'. It is given privileges in debates, at Question Time and in the management of parliamentary business to help it carry out its role of opposing the government of the day. On 'opposition days' (sometimes called 'supply days'), opposition parties choose the subject for debate and use these days as opportunities either to criticize government policy or to highlight alternative policies.

▶ **Written questions and letters.** Much information is provided to MPs and peers in answers to written questions (as opposed to oral questions in Question Time), and ministers must respond to letters they receive from MPs and peers.

degenerates into a party-political battle between the prime minister and the leader of the opposition that generates more heat than light.

▶ Although select committees are widely seen as more effective than Question Time, they also have their disadvantages. These include that:

  ▶ The government has a majority on each of these committees (the committees reflect the composition of the House of Commons).

  ▶ Individual committee appointments are influenced by the whips, who ensure that loyal backbenchers sit on key committees, although committee chairs have been elected by the Commons since June 2010.

  ▶ Select committees have no executive power. At best, they can criticize government; they cannot change government policy.

Recruitment and training of ministers

Parliament acts as a major channel of political recruitment. In the UK, all ministers, from the prime minister downwards, must be either MPs or peers. Before they become frontbenchers, they 'cut their teeth' on the back benches. The advantage of this is that by participating in debates, asking parliamentary questions and sitting on committees, the ministers of the future learn their political trade. They gain an understanding of how government works and of how policy is developed.

However, the effectiveness of this recruitment and training role has also been questioned:

▶ Ministers are recruited from a limited pool of talent: mainly the MPs of the largest party in the House of Commons.

▶ Parliamentarians may acquire speechmaking skills and learn how to deliver sound bites, but they do not gain the bureaucratic or management skills to run a government department.

▶ Fewer and fewer ministers have experience of careers outside of politics.

Legitimacy

The final function of Parliament is to promote legitimacy. When governments govern through Parliament, their actions are more likely to be seen as 'rightful' and therefore to be obeyed. This occurs for two reasons:

▶ Parliament, in a sense, 'stands for' the public, being a representative assembly. When it approves a measure, this makes it feel as though the public has approved it.

▶ Parliamentary approval is based on the assumption that the government's actions have been properly debated and scrutinized, with any weaknesses or problems being properly exposed.

However, Parliament's ability to ensure legitimacy has also been criticized:

▶ Being non-elected, the House of Lords has no democratic legitimacy.
▶ Respect for Parliament has been undermined by scandals involving, for example, 'cash for questions' (MPs being paid for asking parliamentary questions) and 'cash for peerages'.

Parliamentary government

Not only does Parliament carry out a number of major functions within UK government, but it is also the lynchpin of the political system itself. The UK has a *parliamentary* system of government. This is why the UK system is often said to be based on a 'Westminster model' (see p. 23). But in what sense is the UK system of government 'parliamentary'? And what does this imply about the role and significance of Parliament?

In a parliamentary system, government and Parliament form an interlocking whole, based on a 'fusion' of power between the executive and the legislative branches of government (see Figure 7.1). Government is 'parliamentary' in the sense that it is drawn from, and accountable to, Parliament. This implies that Parliament (or, in practice, the House of Commons) has the power to bring the government down. In theory, this should make Parliament the dominant institution – governments should only be able to act as Parliament allows. This, indeed, did briefly happen in the UK during Parliament's so-called 'golden age' in the 1840s. During this period, Parliament regularly defeated the government, meaning that policy was genuinely determined by the views of MPs. However, the development of modern, disciplined political parties changed all this. The majority of MPs in the House of Commons came to see their role not as criticizing the government but as defending it. The primary function of Parliament therefore shifted from making government accountable to maintaining it in power. This is why parliamentary government is often associated with the problem of executive domination, or what Lord Hailsham called 'elective dictatorship' (see p. 185).

Presidential systems, on the other hand, may produce more powerful and independent legislatures or parliaments. This is because the doctrine of the separation of powers (see Figure 7.2 and p. 277) ensures that the government and Parliament are formally independent from one another and separately elected. In the USA, for instance, this gives Congress a degree of independence from the presidency that makes it probably the most powerful legislature in the modern world (see The US Congress, p. 225).

What is . . . parliamentary government

A parliamentary system of government is one in which government governs in and through Parliament. It is based on a 'fusion' between the legislative and executive branches of government. Parliament and government are therefore overlapping and interlocking institutions. This violates the doctrine of the separation of powers in a crucial way.

The chief features of parliamentary government are as follows:

▶ Governments are formed as a result of parliamentary elections, based on the strength of party representation in the Commons

▶ The personnel of government are drawn from Parliament, usually from the leaders of the largest party in the House of Commons

▶ Government is responsible to Parliament, in the sense that it rests on the confidence of the House of Commons and can be removed through defeat on a 'vote of confidence'

▶ Government can 'dissolve' Parliament, meaning that electoral terms are flexible within a five-year limit (although this has been restricted by the introduction of fixed-term Parliaments)

▶ Government has a collective 'face', in that it is based on the principle of cabinet government (see p. 247) rather than personal leadership (as in a presidency)

▶ As a parliamentary officer, the prime minister is the head of government but not the head of state; these two roles are strictly separate.

Figure 7.1 **Parliamentary government**

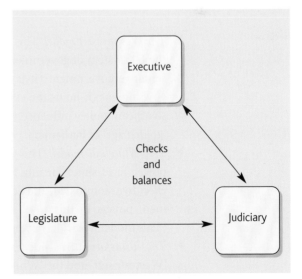

Figure 7.2 **The separation of powers**

Differences between . . .
PARLIAMENTARY AND PRESIDENTIAL GOVERNMENT

Parliamentary government	● ●●	Presidential government
Fusion of powers	● ●●	Separation of powers
Governments are formed through parliamentary elections	● ●●	Governments are separately elected
Overlap of personnel	● ●●	Separation of personnel
Government removable by legislature	● ●●	Legislature cannot remove government
Flexible-term elections (usually)	● ●●	Fixed-term elections
Cabinet government	●● ●●	Presidentialism
Separate head of government and head of state	●● ●●	Presidents are both head of government and head of state

The effectiveness of Parliament

Theories of parliamentary power

Parliamentary power has been interpreted in three different ways:

▶ *The Westminster model.* This is the classic view of Parliament as the lynchpin of the UK system of government. It implies that Parliament delivers both representative government (it is the mouthpiece of the people) and responsible government (it holds the executive to account). In this view, Parliament has significant policy influence. (This model was perhaps only realistic during the 'golden age' of Parliament.)

▶ *The Whitehall model.* This model suggests that political and constitutional power have shifted firmly from Parliament to the executive. Parliament is executive-dominated, and acts as little more than a 'rubber stamp' for government policy. In this view, Parliament has no meaningful policy influence. (This model was widely accepted until the 1980s.)

▶ *The transformative model.* This model provides an alternative to the 'Westminster' and the 'Whitehall' models of parliamentary power. It accepts that Parliament is no longer a policy-making body, but neither is it a simple irrelevance. In this view, Parliament can transform policy but only by reacting to executive initiatives. (This model has been generally accepted in recent years, not least because of recent changes within the parliamentary system.)

Weblink ■ www.hansardsociety.org.uk

Use the Hansard Society website for information on ways of strengthening Parliament and of promoting democracy.

Parliament and government

How effective is Parliament in practice? There is no *fixed* relationship between Parliament and government. The principles of parliamentary government establish a framework within which both Parliament and government work, but, as was pointed out earlier, this does not determine the distribution of power between them. Parliament has huge *potential* power, but its *actual* ability to influence policy and constrain government may be very limited.

Four main factors affect Parliament's relationship to government:

▶▶ Extent of party unity
▶▶ Size of majority
▶▶ Advent of coalition government
▶▶ Impact of the Lords.

Party unity and its decline

Party unity is the key to understanding the relationship between Parliament and government. It is the main lever that the executive uses to control Parliament in general and the House of Commons in particular. The decline of Parliament stems from the growth of party unity in the final decades of the 19th century. By 1900, 90 per cent of votes in the Commons were party votes (that is, votes in which at least 90 per cent of MPs voted with their party). This was a direct consequence of the extension of the franchise and the recognition by MPs that they needed the support of a party machine in order to win elections. During much of the 20th century, MPs appeared to be mere **'lobby fodder'**. This created the impression that government had nothing to fear from Parliament. The government could always rely on its loyal troops in the House of Commons to approve its legislative programme and to maintain it in power, creating an 'elective dictatorship'.

However, this image of mindless party discipline is now outdated. Party unity reached its peak in the 1950s and early 1960s when **backbench revolts** all but died out. Since then, backbench power has been on the rise as party discipline has relaxed.

Lobby fodder: MPs who speak and vote (in the lobbies) as their parties dictate without thinking for themselves.

Backbench revolt: Disunity by backbench MPs, who vote against their party on a 'whipped' vote.

FOCUS ON . . .
How party unity is maintained

▶ **The whipping system**. The whips are often seen as 'the stick' that maintains party discipline. The job of the whips is to make sure that MPs know how their parties want them to vote, indicated by debates being underlined once, twice or three times (obedience is essential in the case of a 'three-line' whip). The whips:

- Advise the leadership about party morale
- Reward loyalty by, for example, advising on promotions
- Punish disloyalty, ultimately by 'withdrawing' the whip (suspending membership of the parliamentary party).

▶ **The 'payroll' vote**. Ministers and shadow ministers *must* support government policy because of the convention of collective responsibility. This ensures the loyalty of between 100 and 110 frontbench government MPs.

▶ **Promotion prospects**. This is the 'carrot' of party unity. Most backbench MPs wish to become ministers, and loyalty is the best way of advancing their careers because it gains them the support of ministers and the whips.

▶ **Ideological unity**. Most MPs, on most occasions, do not need to be *forced* to 'toe a party line'. As long-standing party members and political activists, they 'believe' in their party or government.

Notable examples of party disunity include:

▶ *Labour governments of Harold Wilson and James Callaghan, 1974–79*. During this period, 45 per cent of Labour MPs voted against the government at some stage, with 40 of them doing so on more than 50 occasions. Amongst the policies defeated were devolution to Scotland and Wales in 1978.

▶ *Conservative government under John Major, 1992–97*. This period was characterized by dramatic clashes between the Major government and a small but determined group of Eurosceptic backbenchers. The withdrawal of the whip from 8 Eurosceptic rebels in November 1994 (another resigned the whip in sympathy) merely underlined the party's divisions. Major was forced to push through European votes by calling them votes of confidence.

▶ *Labour government under Tony Blair, 2001–07*. During Blair's second and third terms, Labour backbenchers rebelled against the government on over 20 per cent of all divisions. Some of these rebellions were very large. On 64 occasions, 40 or more Labour MPs voted against the government, including major rebellions on high-profile issues, such as foundation hospitals (involving 65 MPs), university 'top-up' fees (72), the Iraq War (139) and the replacement of Trident nuclear submarines (94).

Why has party unity declined? There are long-term and short-term answers to this question. The long-term answers are:

▶ MPs are generally better educated than they were in the 1950s and 1960s, coming overwhelmingly from professional middle-class backgrounds. This has made them more critical and independently minded.

▶ More MPs are now 'career politicians'. As politics is their only career, they have the time and resources to take political issues more seriously. Many MPs used to have 'second' jobs, usually in business or as lawyers.

The short-term factors include the public standing of the government and the likelihood of it winning re-election, the personal authority of the prime minister and the radicalism of the government's legislative programme. This helps to explain, for example, the difference between Blair's first government (1997–2001) and his second and third governments (2001–07). In the latter period, Blair's personal standing had dropped as a result of the Iraq War, the government's majority and its poll ratings had fallen, and divisive issues such as anti-terror legislation, welfare reform and university 'top-up' fees had become more prominent.

Weblink ■ www.revolts.co.uk

Use this website for an authoritative and entertaining analysis of backbench behaviour in the UK, run by Philip Cowley at the University of Nottingham.

Size of majority

If the party system is the single most important factor affecting the performance of Parliament, the second is that the governing party usually has a majority control of the Commons. This occurs not because of voting patterns (no party has won a majority of *votes* in a general election since 1935), but because of the tendency of the 'first-past-the-post' voting system to over-represent large parties (see Chapter 3). This happens very reliably: for example, only one general election since 1945 (February 1974) has failed to produce a single-party majority government.

However, the size of a government's majority is also crucial. The larger the government's majority, the weaker backbenchers will usually be. For instance, with a majority of 178 after the 1997 election it would have taken 90 Labour MPs to defeat the Blair government (assuming that all opposition MPs voted against the government). Once Blair's majority had fallen to 65 after the 2005 election, this could be done by just 34 Labour MPs. The contrast between small and large majorities can be stark. The 1974–79 Labour government, which had at best a majority of 4 and was for some time a **minority government**, was defeated in the

Minority government: A government that does not have overall majority support in the assembly or parliament; minority governments are usually formed by single parties that are unable, or unwilling, to form coalitions.

House of Commons on no fewer than 41 occasions. However, with landslide majorities in 1997 (178) and in 2001 (167), the Blair government suffered no defeats in the House of Commons in its first two terms.

Advent of coalition government

The first – and, almost certainly, the most significant – implication of the Conservative–Liberal Democrat coalition, formed in 2010, was that it led to the creation of a majority government despite the election of a 'hung' Parliament. The coalition's 'official' majority of 77 seats amounted, in practice, to an effective majority of 83, due to the fact that some Northern Ireland MPs never take up their seats. Once the idea of a possible Labour–Liberal Democrat coalition had been abandoned as unfeasible (as it would still have produced a minority government), the only realistic alternative to a Conservative–Liberal Democrat coalition was a minority Conservative government. As the Conservatives were 19 seats short of a Commons majority, such a government would have been vulnerable to pressure in Parliament, both from other parties and, almost as important, from its own backbenchers. Previous minority governments in the UK, such as the minority Labour administrations elected in 1924, 1929 and October 1974, have been weak and short-lived. Not only did the formation of a coalition created the possibility of an effective government, able to resist parliamentary pressures, but the government also speedily committed itself to the introduction of fixed-term Parliaments, demonstrating the coalition's determination to serve out a full five-year term.

However, there is also a general expectation that coalition government will rejuvenate Parliament. This is based on the belief that a coalition will radically alter the dynamics of executive–Parliament relations in the UK. Single-party majority governments (the norm in the UK since 1945) are able to control the Commons so long as they maintain party unity and, if their majorities are substantial, even backbench revolts may have marginal significance. By contrast, coalitions are forced to manage the Commons not simply by maintaining unity in a single party, but by establishing and maintaining unity across two or more parties. The process of inter-party debate, negotiation and conciliation that this inevitably involves is widely believed to make the legislature an important focus of policy debate. In short, coalition government means that the support of back-bench MPs for government policy cannot simply be taken for granted. The key factor here is the degree of unity and cohesion amongst the coalition partners in Parliament, and the Conservative–Liberal Democrat coalition inevitably lacks the ideological and tribal unity that is normally associated with a single-party government. Particular concern has focused on Liberal Democrat MPs, whose support may be difficult to maintain because, being the smaller party, they have the least to gain and, perhaps, the most to lose from the coalition. Experience across continental Europe suggests that smaller coalition parties tend to suffer from a loss of political identity, straining the loyalty of their supporters both in the legislature and beyond. The strains that this may generate could be evident in a growing pattern of Liberal Democrat backbench disloyalty. This was evident in December 2010, when a majority of Liberal Democrat MPs either voted against the government or abstained on the issue of increasing university tuition fees, despite the fact that the policy had been proposed by a Liberal Democrat minister, Vince Cable. Misgivings amongst Liberal Democrat MPs over the pace and shape of NHS reforms also contributed in April 2011 to the announcement of a period of further review and consultation.

Alternatively, the Liberal Democrats may exploit their position as a pivotal party (a party that is capable, potentially, of entering a coalition with either major party) to exert disproportional influence within the coalition. This would occur if Cameron and the Conservative leadership become increasingly anxious about 'keeping the Liberal Democrats on board'. In these circumstances, Liberal Democrat assertiveness may stimulate disaffection, and possibly disloyalty, from the ranks of the Conservative right. This would be particularly destabilizing given the ideological divide between many left-leaning Liberal Democrats and right-wing Conservatives.

In other respects, coalition government may be a recipe for a weak Parliament. As we have already seen, the coalition's majority means that, in practice, 42 Liberal Democrat or Conservative MPs would have to vote against the government in order to threaten it with defeat. Even in the case of university tuition fees, when 21 Liberal Democrats and 6 Conservatives voted against the government, the policy still passed the Commons with a majority of 21. It is also significant that the process of inter-party consultation and negotiation that coalition government involves is more likely to take place within the executive itself, and often at its highest levels, rather than within Parliament. In fact, most coalitions involve the centralization, not the decentralization, of decision-making processes (as discussed in Chapter 8). There are also a number of reasons for believing that the coalition will be able to maintain its unity in the Commons, or at least keep levels of disunity relatively small:

▶ In rapidly producing a detailed programme for government before the end of May 2010, which was presented to both parliamentary parties for debate and approval, the coalition resolved many of the policy issues that may otherwise have dogged the government and, perhaps, even threatened its existence.

▶ Where policy differences have not been resolved, the coalition has made extensive use of independent commissions and forums, allowing sensitive issues to be effectively 'buried' or to be resolved through a 'neutral' process.

▶ The support of Liberal Democrat MPs for the coalition tends to be upheld by their prominent representation in government. Most importantly, the Liberal Democrat leader, Nick Clegg, is deputy prime minister, and he serves alongside four other Liberal Democrats in the cabinet. The Liberal Democrats are also marginally 'over-represented' in government – the balance between

Conservatives and Liberal Democrat in the government is 5:1, compared with 6:1 amongst MPs.

▶ Ideological shifts in both coalition parties (as discussed in Chapter 4) in the years leading up to 2010 mean that the range of policy differences between the Conservatives and the Liberal Democrats has been significantly reduced, especially amongst party leaders and MPs.

▶ Having entered into a coalition, there may be a significant electoral cost for any party that pulls out, or for both parties should the coalition be seen to fail. In that sense, the coalition may be a one-way street, in that MPs from both the Conservative Party and the Liberal Democrats may believe that they have no realistic option other than to make the coalition work.

Impact of the Lords

Although the House of Lords is clearly the subordinate chamber of Parliament in terms of its formal powers, it is often a more effective check on the executive than the Commons. Executive control of the Commons is normally secured through a combination of the voting system (creating a single-party majority) and the party system. By contrast, in the Lords:

▶ *Party unity is more relaxed.* This occurs because, being non-elected, peers do not need a party machine to remain in post. Once appointed, peers are there for life. This robs the government of its ability to discipline peers and so 'enforce' the whip.

▶ *There was no guarantee of majority control.* In fact, until 2000, the dominance of hereditary peers meant that the Conservatives effectively enjoyed an in-built majority in the Lords. Labour governments, on the other hand, confronted a consistently hostile second chamber. The House of Lords' checking power was therefore used in a highly partisan way.

These factors were dramatically demonstrated by the fact that, while the Blair government suffered no defeats in the Commons during its first two terms in office, it was defeated in the Lords on no fewer than 353 occasions. By contrast, the average number of Lords' defeats per session during the Conservative governments of 1979–97 was just over 13. However, the level of opposition that the Blair government encountered in the House of Lords was untypical, even by the standards of previous Labour governments. It involved fierce clashes over terrorism legislation, with a range of other measures being either amended or delayed as a result of Lords' pressure, including the outlawing of hunting with dogs, the introduction of foundation hospitals, restrictions on jury trial and changes to pension regulations. The 'partially reformed' House of Lords appears to have become a more significant check on the government than the 'traditional' House of Lords had been. Why has this happened?

The greater impact of the Lords can be explained in a number of ways:

▶ *No majority party in the Lords.* In the 'partially reformed' Lords, there is a balance between Conservative and Labour representation, each party having about 29 per cent support. All parties (including any future Conservative government) have to seek support from other parties and from crossbenchers in order to get legislation passed.

▶ *More assertive Lords.* The removal of most of the hereditary peers has encouraged the members of the House of Lords to believe that they have a right to assert their authority. As peers now feel that the Lords is more properly constituted, they are more willing to challenge the government, especially over controversial proposals and legislation.

▶ *Landslide majorities in the Commons.* Some peers argued that they had a duty to check the government of the day because the Commons had become so ineffective in this respect due to landslide majorities (as in 1997 and 2001).

▶ *The politics of the Parliament Acts.* Although the Parliament Acts allow the Commons to overrule the Lords, their use is very time-consuming as it means that bills get regularly passed back and forth between the two Houses of Parliament (a process called 'parliamentary ping-pong'). Governments are therefore often more anxious to reach a compromise with the Lords than to 'steamroller' a bill through using the 1949 Parliament Act. (This Act has, in fact, only been invoked on four occasions.)

Although the Conservative–Liberal Democrat coalition has longer-term plans to reform the second chamber, its more immediate actions threatened to strengthen executive control over the House of Lords, rather than to weaken it. In particular, it has appointed a substantial number of new peers (117 were appointed in the period between May 2010 and January 2011 alone), and the majority of these were Conservatives and Liberal Democrats. With other appointments due to be made, the size of the Lords will exceed 800. These actions have been taken in line with the coalition's stated aim of ensuring that the representation of the major parties in the Lords reflects their popular vote at the previous general election. Such a policy would greatly strengthen support for the government in the House of Lords, particularly as the combined popular vote for the Conservatives and the Liberal Democrats in 2010 was 59 per cent. The coalition's strategy in the appointment of new peers thus threatens to reverse the situation established by the removal of the bulk of hereditary peers in 1999, which deprived any government of majority control of the Lords. Nevertheless, looser party unity in the Lords compared with the Commons continues to impose a major constraint on the executive. By mid-May 2011, the coalition had been defeated in the House of Lords on sixteen occasions, while it had suffered no such reverses in the House of Commons.

Reforming Parliament

Debate about the reform of Parliament has been going on for well over 100 years. This debate has been fuelled, most of all, by anxiety about the growth of executive power and Parliament's declining ability effectively to check the government of the day. However, support for parliamentary reform has by no means been universal. Some argue that the present arrangements have the advantage that they guarantee **strong government**, sometimes seen as one of the key advantages of the Westminster model. Nevertheless, as with the larger issue of constitutional reform (discussed in Chapter 6), there has been growing pressure in recent years to reform and strengthen Parliament. The following sections examine the reforms that have taken place in recent years in the House of Commons and the House of Lords. They also consider how each of these chambers could be further strengthened.

Strong government:
A situation in which government can govern, in the sense of translating its legislative programme into public policy.

Reforming the House of Commons
Commons reform under Blair

The main reforms of Parliament introduced under Blair, between 1997 and 2007, concern the Lords rather than the Commons. However, a number of changes did take place in the Commons, although their net impact was modest, especially in view of the government's large majorities in 1997 and 2001, and its emphasis on tight party discipline, particularly in its early years (seen as 'control freakery'). The main changes were:

▶ **Once-a-week Prime Minister's Questions.** Introduced in 1997, this shift halved the number of occasions that the prime minister stood before the Commons, even though the total time remained the same (30 minutes). Critics have seen this as an attempt to reduce the prime minister's exposure to Parliament.

▶ **Liaison Committee scrutiny.** Introduced in 2002, this allows for twice-yearly appearances of the prime minister before the Liaison Committee of the House of Commons, which is mainly composed of the chairs of the departmental select committees (DSCs).The prime minister is thus subject to scrutiny by some of the most senior, experienced and expert backbenchers in the House of Commons. On the other hand, most of these chairs are from the majority party.

Open government:
A free flow of information from government to representative bodies, the mass media and the electorate, based on the public's 'right to know'.

▶ **Freedom of Information Act 2000.** Freedom of information was not a parliamentary reform as such. Rather, it was an attempt to widen the public's access to information that is held by a wide range of public bodies, helping in particular to ensure **open government**. Nevertheless, the Act, which came into full

Who is...
Tony Blair

Tony Blair was born in Edinburgh, Scotland on 6 May 1953, the son a law lecturer. He was educated at Fettes College, a prominent independent school in Edinburgh, and later went on to study jurisprudence at St John's College, Oxford. Blair joined the Labour Party in 1975 and in 1983, he was selected to fight the safe Labour seat of Sedgefield in Durham, close to where he had grown up. Following Labour's fourth successive election defeat in 1992, Blair was appointed shadow home secretary under the new leader, John Smith. His phrase, coined by Gordon Brown, that Labour would be 'tough on crime, tough on the causes of crime' reflected an important shift away from traditional social democracy and provided the foundations for a 'third way' approach to criminal justice. John Smith's sudden death in 1994 provided Blair with an opportunity to fight for and win the party leadership. As leader, Blair substantially accelerated the 'modernization' process in the party (sometimes seen as the 'Blair project'), radically reshaping the party's image and ideological orientation, and using the term 'New Labour' to distinguish the party from its past. In 1995, Clause Four of the Labour's constitution was re-written (see p. 115). New Labour's landslide election victory in 1997 made Blair, at 42, the youngest UK prime minister since Lord Liverpool in 1812. Blair surpassed the record of all previous Labour leaders in achieving three successive election victories (the first two with landslide victories) and serving as prime minister for ten years. In the early period, he achieved remarkable levels of personal popularity, adopting a 'presidential' style of leadership that downgraded the cabinet and marginalized Parliament and the party. However, growing unpopularity, linked to the Iraq War of 2003, gradually undermined his authority, leading to his promise, in October 2004, that the following election would be his last one. Blair finally handed over the party leadership to Gordon Brown on 24 June 2007, resigning as prime minister on 27 June.

effect in 2005, has strengthened parliamentary scrutiny by giving MPs and peers easier access to government information. However, the Act was also used to bring to light details of the expenses of MPs and peers, helping to precipitate the 2009 expenses scandal that did so much to undermine the reputation of Parliament.

▶ **Wider constitutional reforms.** These, once again, are not reforms *of* Parliament, but they are reforms that have important implications *for* Parliament. The most significant ones in this respect were devolution, the introduction of the Human

Rights Act (HRA) and the wider use of referendums. Devolution has meant that responsibility for domestic legislation in Scotland, Wales and Northern Ireland is now in the hands of devolved bodies, as opposed to Parliament (see Chapter 10). The HRA has helped to transfer responsibility for protecting individual rights from Parliament to the courts, as these rights now, in a sense, 'belong' to citizens (see Chapter 9). Referendums have given the people, rather than Parliament, final control over a range of constitutional reforms (see Chapter 2). The net impact of wider constitutional changesunder Blair was therefore to marginalize Parliament, rather than strengthen it.

Commons reform under Brown

On taking over as prime minister, Gordon Brown moved quickly to give up or modify a number of powers that used to belong exclusively to the prime minister or the executive. In the main, this involved strengthening Parliament by improving the government's need to consult with, or gain approval from, the House of Commons. Such moves bring Parliament more closely into line with the oversight and confirmation powers of the US Congress.

Parliament, and more specifically the Commons, must now be consulted on the exercise of a variety of powers. These include the power to:

▶ Declare war
▶ Dissolve Parliament
▶ Recall of Parliament
▶ Ratify treaties
▶ Choose bishops and appoint judges.

This amounts to a major extension of Parliament's ability to oversee the exercise of power under the Royal Prerogative. Previously, the exercise of Crown powers was only subject to parliamentary scrutiny if, and when, the executive chose. However, as with the reforms under Blair, they did not bring about a major change in the relationship between Parliament and the executive. Quite simply, so long as the reins of party discipline remain tight, and governments can expect to enjoy majority control of the Commons, increased consultation and approval powers are unlikely to be used by Parliament to block major government initiatives.

Important developments nevertheless took place in relation to select committees. The introduction of the system of departmental select committees in 1979 was heralded as the most significant reform of the Commons in the 20th century. However, they have failed to bring about a significant shift of power from the executive to Parliament. The select committees were neutered by the intrusion of the party system into their work. This occurred through the influence of the whips on select-committee appointments, a matter that was made worse by Brown's decision in 2007 to allow parliamentary private secretaries (effectively, unpaid government ministers) to sit on these committees.

BY COMPARISON . . .
The US Congress

The US Congress is a bicameral legislature, composed of the 435-member House of Representatives (lower chamber) and the 100-member Senate (higher or second chamber). Unlike Parliament, the chambers have equal legislative powers and both are elected (see Elections in the USA, p. 86). Congress is widely seen as the most powerful legislature in the world. It genuinely makes policy, whereas Parliament is a reactive and policy-influencing body. That said, most policy is initiated by the executive, so in the USA it is true to say that 'the president proposes and Congress disposes'.

Congress is powerful for three main reasons:

● The US Constitution allocates Congress an impressive range of formal powers. These include the power to declare war, the ability to override a presidential veto on legislation and the power to impeach the president. The Senate has a range of further powers, notably to confirm presidential appointments (e.g. cabinet members and Supreme Court judges) and to ratify treaties.

● The president cannot count on controlling Congress through party unity because the two are separately elected. This means both that the opposition party may control one or both chambers of Congress, and that party unity is weaker than in Parliament. The primary loyalty of Congressmen and women and of Senators is to the 'folks back home' (their voters), rather than to their party.

● Congress has a powerful system of standing committees, which exert significant influence over US government departments and their budgets. These are the 'powerhouse' of Congress. The system of departmental select committees (DSCs) in the UK is largely modelled on congressional standing committees, but they are significantly weaker in practice.

These concerns led to the establishment of the House of Commons Reform Committee. Under its influential chair, Tony Wright, the Committee proposed in November 2009 that chairs of departmental and other select committees should in future be directly elected by a secret ballot of MPs, using the AV voting system. In the case of individual members of these committees, the Committee recommended that they be elected from within party groups by secret ballot. These proposals would go a long way to freeing the select committee system from the control of the whips and, in particular, from manipulation by the government of the day (which has a majority of chairs and of committee members. In March 2010, the Commons agreed that the chairs of select committees should be elected by MPs, but this reform was not extended to committee members. The coalition government elected in May 2010 has, nevertheless, committed itself to bringing forward the proposals of the Wright Committee in full.

Commons reform under Cameron and Clegg

The formation of the Conservative–Liberal Democrat coalition led to the emergence of a bold and extensive programme of parliamentary reform. This was largely a consequence of the participation of the Liberal Democrats, the major party most deeply and consistently committed to political and constitutional reform. The coalition's programme of reform nevertheless also takes account of Conservative concerns about weakening government by creating an 'over-strong' Parliament. In general, the proposed Commons reforms seek either to strengthen government's accountability to Parliament or to expand popular participation in the workings of Parliament. These reforms include the following:

▸ **Fixed-term Parliaments**. By preventing prime ministers from calling general elections at a time most favourable to their party, fixed-term Parliaments should generally both reduce the size of government majorities and make changes in government more frequent. Both tendencies are likely to enhance the influence of Parliament. However, the impact of fixed-term Parliaments is hotly debated (see p. 267).
▸ **Referendum on AV**. Although rejected in 2011, AV was likely to have boosted representation for 'third' parties such as the Liberal Democrats, and could have been expected to lead to more 'hung' Parliaments. It is widely believed that the greater likelihood of minority or coalition government would have forced the executive to be more accountable to Parliament.
▸ **Recall of MPs**. MPs are to be subject to the power of recall, allowing voters to force a by-election where an MP is found to have engaged in serious wrongdoing and having had a petition calling for a by-election signed by 10 per cent of his or her constituents. This is intended to strengthen the representative function of the House of Commons.

▶ **Public initiated bills**. The public is to be given the ability to suggest topics for debate in Parliament through petitions that secure at least 100,000 signatures, the petition with the most signatures being eligible to be voted on in Parliament.

▶ **Public reading stage**. A 'public reading stage' is to be introduced for bills, giving the public an opportunity to comment on proposed legislation online. A dedicated 'public reading day' within a bill's committee stage, where public comments can be debated by the committee scrutinizing the bill, has also been proposed.

▶ **House business committee**. The coalition proposes to establish a House of Commons business committee by 2013, which would give backbenchers greater influence over the management of their affairs, although it is unclear what this will involve.

However, it is by no means clear that such a reform programme would lead to a meaningful shift in the balance of power between Parliament and the executive. For example, in making general elections less frequent, five-year, fixed-term Parliaments may erode, rather than strengthen, the democratic legitimacy of Parliament, weakening its capacity to 'speak for the nation'. As for the possible use of AV as an alternative to FPTP for Westminster elections, this would only have marginally reduced the likelihood of single-party majority government, and the proposal was, anyway, rejected in a referendum in May 2011. Similarly, the opportunities these proposals create for private citizens to initiate bills, or to comment on bills, will not change the fact that Parliament primarily exists to consider the government's legislative programme and that this is a process essentially controlled by the government itself. It is therefore notable that these and earlier reform programmes have ignored the two reforms that would substantially enhance the role of the Commons: a thorough going and radical reform of the select committee system and the introduction of a genuinely proportional system for Westminster elections.

Reforming the Lords

The greatest attention in recent years in reforming Parliament has fallen on the Lords rather than the Commons. This is because the defects of the 'unreformed' Lords were so serious and so pressing. The most obvious of these were that:

▶ The majority of peers (if not of working peers) sat in the House of Lords on the basis of heredity.

▶ The Lords exhibited a strong and consistent bias in favour of the Conservative Party.

The fact that, despite this, major reform has been so long delayed is evidence of how difficult it is to reform the Lords. The major obstacles to reform have traditionally been the Conservative Party (concerned to introduce reform only to prevent more radical reform, as in the case of the Life Peerages Act 1958) and the Lords itself. Any attempt to abolish or reform the Lords would be likely to stimulate such a battle with the Commons that the government's entire legislative programme would be put at threat. Moreover, Labour was often divided over the issue. Whereas some Labour MPs wished to abolish the Lords altogether, others favoured its replacement by a fully elected second chamber, with others even being happy with the status quo for fear of creating a stronger check on any future Labour government. Nevertheless, the Blair government began a phased process of reform in 1999.

Stage one reform of the Lords

In planning to reform the House of Lords, the Blair government learned the lessons of previous, unsuccessful attempts at reform. In particular, it recognized that, while there was general agreement about the central weaknesses of the Lords, there was substantial disagreement about what should replace it. Should the Lords be reformed or abolished? Should a reformed second chamber be wholly appointed, wholly elected or a mixture of the two? If the composition of the second chamber were to be altered, should its powers also change, and if so how? The solution was to introduce reform in two stages:

▶ *Stage one.* This would involve the removal of hereditary peers, without any further changes to the composition and powers of the chamber.
▶ *Stage two.* This would involve the replacement of the House of Lords by a revised second chamber.

The advantage of this approach was that difficult and divisive questions about the composition and powers of the second chamber could be put to one side while reforming energies focused on the 'easier' problem: ending the hereditary principle. Reform was duly brought about through the House of Lords Act 1999. To ease the passage of this bill, the government agreed to a compromise whereby a proportion of hereditary peers survived until stage-two reform took place. The number of hereditary peers was thus reduced from 777 to 92.

However, stage two has proved far more difficult. In the first place, this reflected a declining appetite within the Labour government to press ahead with further reform. The removal of most of the hereditary peers and the appointment of a large number of new Labour life peers had quickly put an end to Conservative dominance in the Lords. Furthermore, the new spirit of assertiveness in the partially reformed Lords made some ministers anxious about the prospect of a partially or wholly elected second chamber. Second, disagreement about the nature of any replacement chamber has continued.

The steps taken to develop stage two proposals have included the following:

- ▶ The Wakeham Commission (chaired by Lord Wakeham, a former Conservative minister) was set up by the Blair government to outline proposals for stage-two reform. It reported in 2000, recommending a largely appointed second chamber, with only a minority of peers elected. There would be no radical change in the role and powers of the second chamber, with a clear determination to ensure that the Commons remained the dominant body. However, these proposals met with wide-ranging opposition, with even the Conservatives, who had defended the hereditary principle in 1999, backing the idea of an 80 per cent elected chamber.

- ▶ The task of developing proposals was then passed to a Joint Committee of both Houses. This reported in December 2002, presenting seven options, ranging from a wholly appointed to a wholly elected chamber. However, when these proposals were placed before the House of Commons, each of the seven options was defeated, throwing the reform process into turmoil.

- ▶ Jack Straw, the Leader of the Commons, placed nine proposals for reform before the House of Commons in March 2007. The proposals that gained approval were: for the retention of a bicameral parliament (backed by a majority of 253); for an 80 per cent elected element (38 majority) for a fully-elected Lords (113 majority); and for the removal of the remaining hereditary peers (280 majority). However, no legislation subsequently emerged, and it was believed that some Conservatives had backed the most radical proposal, for a fully-elected Lords, in the hope of preventing any reform being carried out.

- ▶ One of the key agreements under which the Conservative–Liberal Democrat coalition was formed in 2010 was to bring forward proposals for a wholly or mainly elected second chamber on the basis of proportional representation. The cross-party committee set up for this purpose was chaired by Nick Clegg and was charged with developing a draft bill by December 2010. The fact that the draft bill did not emerge until May 2011 is a further indication of the difficulty of making progress on this issue. The key features of the proposals are that the new chamber will have 300 members, 80 per cent of whom will be elected using the single transferable vote system and who will serve for a single 15-year term. A joint committee comprising MPs and peers has nevertheless been set up to decide the final composition of the chamber. The proposals do not recommend changes to the powers of the second chamber, but broadly focus on trying to make the chamber more effective and responsive in carrying out its traditional role.

What is ... bicameralism

Bicameralism is the theory or practice of breaking up legislative power through the creation of two chambers. However, a distinction can be drawn between partial bicameralism and full bicameralism

- ▶ *Partial* bicameralism is when the legislature has two chambers but these are clearly unequal, either because the second chamber has restricted popular authority or because it has reduced legislative power. The UK Parliament is a good example of partial (or deformed) bicameralism.
- ▶ *Full* bicameralism exists when there are two co-equal legislative chambers, each able to check the other. The US Congress is a good (if rare) example of full bicameralism.

The future second chamber?

The historic vote in March 2007 suggested that the long-awaited consensus on the shape of the future second chamber may at last have emerged. Certainly, it demonstrated that support for bicameralism was greater than support for unicameralism – support for simple abolition leading to a one-chamber Parliament (once favoured by Labour) had fallen to such a point that this option could be discarded. It thus provided the basis for the 2011 Clegg proposals. However, significant debate continues to take place over the desirable nature of the future second chamber. This issue, as ever, is complex. Much of the debate is about composition, with support being expressed for three different options: an appointed second chamber, an elected second chamber or some combination of the two. Nevertheless, the question of composition cannot be considered separately from the issue of powers. The restricted powers of the current House of Lords have usually been explained in terms of its non-elected status. Any largely or wholly elected second chamber could reasonable demand, and expect to be given, wider power if not equality with the first chamber.

Supporters of an elected second chamber tend to emphasize two key benefits. First, they stress the benefits of democracy, arguing that the only legitimate basis for exercising political power is success in free and fair elections. Second, they emphasize the benefits of full bicameralism, viewing a more powerful second chamber with popular authority as a way to combat 'elective dictatorship'. By contrast, supporters of an appointed or nominated second chamber tend to stress the following two benefits. The first is that an appointed chamber could (rather like the present House of Lords) have greater expertise and specialist knowledge than the first chamber. The second is that partial bicameralism has undoubted benefits, in that it makes clashes between the two chambers less likely and does not lead to confusion about the location of popular authority. Those who back a

AN ELECTED SECOND CHAMBER

FOR

Democratic legitimacy. A second chamber, like all policy-making institutions, must be based on popular consent delivered through competitive elections. In a democracy, this is the only basis for legitimate rule. Appointed members simply do not have democratic legitimacy.

Wider representation. Two elected chambers would widen the basis for representation. This could happen through the use of different electoral systems, different electoral terms and dates, and through different constituencies. This would significantly strengthen the democratic process.

Better legislation. The non-elected basis of the House of Lords restricts its role to that of a 'revising chamber', concerned mainly with 'cleaning up' bills. Popular authority would encourage the second chamber to exercise greater powers of legislative oversight and scrutiny.

Checking the Commons. Only an elected chamber can properly check another elected chamber. While the House of Commons alone has popular authority, the second chamber will also defer to the first chamber. Full bicameralism requires two co-equal chambers.

Ending executive tyranny. The executive dominates Parliament largely through its majority control of the Commons. While this persists, the only way of properly checking government power is through a democratic or more powerful second chamber, preferably elected by PR.

AGAINST

Specialist knowledge. The advantage of an appointed second chamber is that its members, like life peers, can be chosen on the basis of their experience, expertise and specialist knowledge. Elected politicians may be experts only in the arts of public speaking and campaigning.

Gridlocked government. Two co-equal chambers would be a recipe for government paralysis through institutionalized rivalry both between the chambers and between the executive and Parliament. This is most likely to occur if the two chambers are elected at different times or on the basis of different electoral systems.

Complementary chambers. The advantage of having two chambers is that they can carry out different roles and functions. This can be seen in the benefits of the Lords' role as a revising chamber, complementing the House of Commons. Only one chamber needs to express popular authority.

Dangers of partisanship. Any elected chamber is going to be dominated, like the House of Commons, by party 'hacks', who rely on a party to get elected and to be re-elected. An appointed second chamber would, by contrast, have reduced partisanship, allowing peers to think for themselves.

Descriptive representation. Elected peers may have popular authority but it is very difficult to make sure that they resemble the larger society, as the make-up of the Commons demonstrates. This can better be done through a structured process of appointment that takes account of group representation.

mixture of elected and appointed members tend to suggest that such a solution offers the best of both worlds – a measure of democratic legitimacy but also expertise and specialist knowledge. However, any such solution can also be criticized for containing the worst of both worlds as well as for leading to confusion through creating two (or possibly more) classes of peer.

Weblink ■ www.electthelords.org.uk

Use the Elect the Lords website for information and arguments in favour of a democratic second chamber.

WHAT YOU SHOULD KNOW

▶▶ Parliament is composed of the House of Commons, the House of Lords and the monarchy. The House of Commons is the politically and legally dominant chamber, having supreme legislative power and being the only chamber that can remove the government of the day. The House of Lords is composed of life peers, hereditary peers, the Lords Spiritual and the Law Lords. It can delay non-financial bills passed by the House of Commons for up to one year.

▶▶ Parliament is the supreme legislature in the UK. It carries out representation, scrutinizes the activities of government, recruits and trains ministers, and confers legitimacy on the general activities of government.

▶▶ The UK has a system of parliamentary government, in that government governs in and through Parliament, based on a 'fusion' between the legislature and the executive. This distinguishes the UK's system from the USA, which has a presidential system of government based on a separation of powers between Congress and the presidency.

▶▶ The key factors that affect Parliament's relationship to government are the extent of party unity, the size of the government's majority and the impact of the House of Lords. The 'revival' of Parliament since the 1970s has occurred through a decline in party unity and the greater assertiveness of the partially reformed Lords.

▶▶ The performance of the Commons was affected under Blair and Brown by reforms such as the introduction of Liaison Committee scrutiny of the prime minister, the Freedom of Information Act, by the requirement that Parliament must be consulted on the exercise of a variety of powers, including the declaration of war and the dissolution and recall of Parliament. Since 2010, the coalition has sought to promote a wide range of parliamentary reform, but it is questionable its proposals will fundamentally aler the balance between Parliament and the executive.

▶▶ 'Stage one' reform of the House of Lords took place in 1999 with the removal of all but 92 hereditary peers. This created a more assertive partially reformed second chamber. However, debate continued on 'stage two' of the reform process, the replacement of the House of Lords by a revised second chamber. There has been growing support for a largely or wholly elected second chamber. This provided the basis for the coalition's 2011 proposal for the establishment of a slimmed down and largely elected chamber.

▶▶ The benefits of an elected second chamber may include greater democratic legitimacy, wider representation, improved legislation and more effective checks on both the Commons and the executive. Its drawbacks may be a loss of specialist knowledge, gridlocked government, confusion about the location of democratic authority and less independently-minded peers.

Test yourself

Short questions:

1   What are the powers of the House of Commons?
2   What are the powers of the House of Lords?
3   Outline *two* functions of Parliament.
4   Outline the functions of the House of Commons.
5   Outline the functions of the House of Lords.
6   Briefly explain *two* features of parliamentary government.
7   Briefly explain *two* features of presidential government.
8   Define the principle of parliamentary sovereignty.

Medium questions:

9   In which ways does the composition of the House of Commons differ from that of the House of Lords?
10   What are the main functions of Parliament?
11   In which ways is Parliament representative?
12   Why has the UK system of government been considered to be parliamentary?
13   In which ways is Parliament sovereign?
14   How does parliamentary government differ from presidential government?
15   Explain *three* ways in which Parliament carries out its scrutinizing role.
16   Why has it proved difficult to reform the House of Lords?

Extended questions:

17   To what extent does the House of Commons have greater power and influence than the House of Lords.
18   How effective is Parliament in carrying out its representative role?
19   How effective is Parliament in checking executive power?
20   How well does Parliament carry out its functions?
21   Has the UK Parliament become an irrelevant institution?
22   How, and to what extent, has the influence of the House of Commons changed in recent years?
23   Should the UK have a fully elected second chamber?
24   To what extent has coalition government altered the relationship between Parliament and the executive?

Chapter **8** **Prime Minister, Cabinet and Executive**

Role of the executive

PREVIEW

What is the executive, and why is it important? The executive is the powerhouse of government. It is the part of government that provides political leadership, the part that makes decisions and enforces them. This is why so much attention in politics focuses on ways of ensuring that executive power is checked or constrained, making the executive accountable for its actions. Without these, government might become a tyranny against the people. However, attention also falls on who has power *within* the executive. Who wields executive power? Most people's answer to this is: the prime minister. But just how powerful are prime ministers?

Prime ministers are certainly the best-known figures in politics. When we vote, our main thought is generally who will be the prime minister. When major events happen, it is the prime minister who speaks for the government or on behalf of the nation. The impression is that the prime minister, in effect, 'runs the country'. Nevertheless, the prime minister does not govern alone. In fact, at least in theory, the UK executive is collective rather than personal. Government policy is meant to made by the cabinet, a collection of senior ministers, not by the prime minister acting alone. Does collective cabinet government still operate in the UK; and if not, why not?

Beyond the cabinet, there is an extensive collection of departments, executive agencies and other bodies. Some argue that real power lies with the so-called 'core' executive, a network of institutions and groups that includes ministers, senior civil servants and political advisors of various kinds. How important is this 'core' executive?

KEY ISSUES

- ■ **Who is who in the UK executive?**
- ■ **What is the role of the prime minister?**
- ■ **What is the role of the cabinet?**
- ■ **Where does power lie within the executive?**
- ■ **What are the powers of, and constraints on, the prime minister?**
- ■ **How far does personality and leadership style affect executive power?**

GETTING YOU THINKING

A dual premiership?

Before starting the chapter, read this passage and briefly consider the questions on the next page.

On 12 May 2010, the Conservative–Liberal Democrat coalition held its first press conference. It was a remarkable affair: one hundred red velvet chairs had been set up on the lawn of the Downing Street garden, creating the impression more of a wedding than a press conference. Out strode David Cameron and Nick Clegg talking and animated with laughter, stride matching stride. During a good-humoured press conference, the chemistry between the two men was very evident. But what was most striking was their seemingly equal billing, which appeared to redefine Clegg's role as 'merely' deputy prime minister. This reflected the novel political realities of coalition government. Clegg was essential to the formation of the coalition government and he remains crucial to its survival. Without Clegg, Cameron would have had to form a minority government, which would have left him vulnerable to pressure from both opposition parties and his own backbenchers.

However, such an image may overstate Clegg's position in a number of ways. In the first place, it is by no means clear that Clegg is inclined to operate as a counterweight to Cameron. Although he has considerable *potential* power as deputy prime minister and leader of the coalition's junior party, there are few political or ideological divisions between Cameron and Clegg. As important is the fact that Clegg's personal future is inextricably linked to the success of the coalition. If it fails, it is difficult to see how he can survive as the Liberal Democrat leader. Moreover, he is keenly aware that highlighting divisions between the Liberal Democrats and the Conservatives will only damage the coalition's reputation for unity and stability, putting at risk its possible re-election. Initially, at least, Clegg's real role within the coalition may have been to act more as an agent of Cameron helping to 'deliver' Liberal Democrat support, rather than as a counterweight. Indeed, if the coalition fails, Clegg and the other pro-coalition senior Liberal Democrats may find that they have no other home than the Conservative Party.

Cameron and Clegg enter No 10 for the first time together in May 2010 — but are they set to continue to walk stride by stride?

What issues do these developments raise?

▶▶▶ How can Clegg's strength in the Cameron cabinet be explained?

▶▶▶ What are the limitations on Clegg's position within the government?

▶▶▶ Is the relationship between Cameron and Clegg based on personal or political factors?

▶▶▶ In practice, does Clegg act as a counterweight to Cameron, or as his agent?

▶▶▶ Would a 'dual premiership' be a good thing?

IN THIS CHAPTER:

Prime minister, cabinet and ministers   •   Who has power in the executive?

Prime minister, cabinet and ministers

Executive: The branch of government that is responsible for the implementation of laws and policies made by Parliament.

Prime minister: The head of government and chair of the cabinet.

The **executive** is, technically, responsible for executing or implementing government policy. As such, it is the 'sharp end' of government, the bit that impacts on the public. However, its role is much wider and more significant. It is the chief source of political leadership, and controls, most importantly, the policy process. In short, the executive 'governs'.

The executive branch extends from the **prime minister** to members of the enforcement agencies such as the police and the military, and includes both ministers and civil servants. There are two parts to the executive:

▶ The *political* executive (roughly equivalent to 'the government of the day'). This is composed of ministers and its job is to take overall responsibility for the direction and co-ordination of government policy.

Bureaucracy: The administrative machinery of government; literally it means 'rule by officials'.

▶ The *official* executive, or **bureaucracy**. This is composed of civil servants and its job is to provide policy advice and to implement government policy.

Prime minister

The prime minister is, without doubt, the single most important figure in the UK political system. He or she is the UK's chief executive. But what this means in practice is the subject of considerable debate and argument. Until the 1980s, the post of prime minister had little official recognition. The person who held the post was technically known as the First Lord of the Treasury (the title that still appears on the door of 10 Downing Street). However, the power attached to the office has grown enormously. Some even highlight the trend towards **presidentialism**. Who becomes the prime minister, and what role does the prime minister play?

Presidentialism: The tendency for political leaders to act increasingly like executive presidents, through the rise of personalized leadership.

To become the prime minister, a politician must fulfil three qualifications:

▶ *Prime ministers must be MPs.* By convention, all prime ministers sit in the House of Commons. No Lord has been appointed as prime minister since Lord Salisbury in 1895.

▶ *They must be a party leader.* Many prime ministers are appointed as a result of being elected as leader of their parties (James Callaghan in 1976, John Major in 1992 and Gordon Brown (see p. 191) in 2007); others are removed when they lose the leadership (Margaret Thatcher (see p. 250) in 1990, Tony Blair (see p.

223) in 2007). In a very unusual step, Major resigned as the Conservative leader in June 1995 in order to precipitate a leadership election, without standing down as prime minister.

▸ *His or her party usually has majority control of the House of Commons.* Most prime ministers come to power as a result of general election victories (Wilson in 1974, Thatcher in 1979, Blair in 1997), and most leave office as a result of election defeats (Callaghan in 1979, Major in 1997). However, there is possible confusion in the event of a 'hung' Parliament. In May 2010, the Queen asked David Cameron (see p. 123), the leader of the largest party in the House of Commons, to form a government, despite the fact that the Conservatives were 19 seats short of an overall majority. This occurred on the basis of a deal with the Liberal Democrats to form a coalition government (see p. 79).

Role of the prime minister

The role of a prime minister is, in the UK's uncodified constitution, a matter that has developed over time and been shaped more by practical circumstances than the allocation of formal responsibilities. The traditional view of the role of the prime minister was summed up by Walter Bagehot (1963 [1867]). According to Bagehot, the prime minister is '*primus inter pares*', or 'first among equals'. This view implied that prime ministers were:

▸ 'First' in the sense that they are the primary representatives of government, both in relation to the monarch and through the right to be consulted about all significant policy issues.

Cabinet: The committee of leading ministers which is empowered to make official government policy.

▸ 'Among equals' in the sense that all members of the **cabinet** had an equal influence over decisions.

However, this traditional formulation has long since ceased to be accurate. It fails to capture the full range and significance of the role of the modern prime minister. The key aspects of the modern role of the prime minister are:

▸ **Making governments**. Although the prime minister is formally appointed by the Queen, it is he or she who then appoints all other members of the government. This power to 'hire and fire' extends to the cabinet and to other ministers, and it gives the prime minister substantial control over the careers of his or her party's MPs and peers.

Core executive: An informal network of bodies and actors that play a key role in the policy process (see p. 252).

▸ **Directing government policy**. As the central figure in the so-called **core executive**, the prime minister sets the overall direction of government policy and defines its strategic goals. In so doing, he or she can interfere in any aspect of policy, although economic policy and foreign policy tend to be the major concerns of most prime ministers.

▶ **Managing the cabinet system**. The prime minister chairs cabinet meetings, determines their number and their length, and also sets up and staffs cabinet committees (see p. 256). As discussed later, the relationship between the prime minister and the cabinet is a major determinant of prime ministerial power.

▶ **Organizing government**. Prime ministers are responsible for the structure and organization of government. This involves setting up, reorganizing and abolishing government departments, as well as being responsible for the civil service.

▶ **Controlling Parliament**. As leader of the largest party in the House of Commons, the prime minister effectively controls the lower chamber and, through it, Parliament itself. This control may, nevertheless, be limited in the event of a 'hung' Parliament.

▶ **Providing national leadership**. The prime minister's authority is largely based on being elected by the people, and the link between the prime minister and the people has been strengthened by the media's relentless focus on the office. National leadership is most important at times of national crisis, war or in response to major events.

Weblink ■ www.number10.gov.uk

Use the Number 10 Downing Street website as a wide-ranging source of information about the prime minister and related bodies, including the cabinet. This site can be used to send emails to the Prime Minister.

The cabinet

The cabinet is a committee of the leading members of the government. It comprises usually 20–23 members, most of whom are secretaries of state responsible for running Whitehall departments. Within the cabinet there is a pecking order, with the posts of Chancellor of the Exchequer, foreign secretary, home secretary and, if apponted, **deputy prime minister** being regarded as the 'plum' jobs. This may also mean that such ministers (and others) form an inner circle of ministers who are consulted more frequently by the prime minister, sometimes in the form of a **kitchen cabinet**. Since the time of Thatcher, the cabinet has met once a week, on Wednesday morning (it previously met twice a week, on Tuesdays and Thursdays), although it may be convened at other times as the prime minister chooses.

Role of the cabinet

There is a major gulf between the role of the cabinet in theory and in practice. In constitutional theory, the cabinet is the top body in the UK executive, the highest decision-making forum. The UK therefore has a system of cabinet government

Deputy prime minister: A senior cabinet minister who acts for the PM in his or her absence; this position in the UK is neither official nor permanent and does not have set responsibilities.

Kitchen cabinet: A loose and informal group of policy advisors consulted by the prime minister outside the formal cabinet, including senior ministers, officials and special advisors.

Table 8.1 David Cameron's cabinet

Name	Office
David Cameron (Con)	Prime Minister
Nick Clegg (LD)	Deputy Prime Minister
George Osborne (Con)	Chancellor of the Exchequer
William Hague (Con)	Foreign Secretary
Theresa May (Con)	Home Secretary
Kenneth Clarke (Con)	Justice Secretary and Lord Chancellor
Andrew Lansley (Con)	Health Secretary
Liam Fox (Con)	Defence Secretary
Baroness Warsi (Con)	Conservative Party Chairman
Vince Cable (LD)	Business Secretary
Michael Gove (Con)	Education Secretary
Andrew Mitchell (Con)	International Development Secretary
Caroline Spelman (Con)	Environment Secretary
Chris Huhne (LD)	Energy and Climate Change Secretary
Iain Duncan Smith (Con)	Work and Pensions Secretary
Philip Hammond (Con)	Transport Secretary
Eric Pickles (Con)	Secretary for Communities and Local Government
Jeremy Hunt (Con)	Culture, Media and Sport Secretary
Danny Alexander (LD)	Chief Secretary to the Treasury
Michael Moore (LD)	Secretary of State for Scotland
Owen Paterson (Con)	Secretary of State for Northern Ireland
Cheryl Gillon (Con)	Secretary of State for Wales
Lord Strathclyde (Con)	Leader of the House of Lords

Weblink ■ www.number10.gov.uk

Use this website to get an up-to-date list of cabinet members and other ministers, including their biographical background.

(see p. 247) based on the convention of collective ministerial responsibility (see p. 243). However, it is widely accepted that over a long period, and possibly accelerating in recent years, the cabinet has lost out to the prime minister. The idea, anyway, that all major government decisions can be discussed and decided in once-a-week meetings rarely lasting over two hours (and under Blair, sometimes as little as 30 minutes) is simply absurd. It is now widely accepted that meaningful policy debate is, in most cases, conducted elsewhere. Nevertheless, the cabinet continues to play a significant (if often overlooked) role. In short, cabinet meetings still have a purpose.

The main aspects of the role of the cabinet are:

▶ **Formal policy approval**. Even though meaningful debate and the formulation of policy decisions effectively takes place elsewhere, these must be approved by the cabinet in order to become *official* government policy. However, there is no guarantee that major policy decisions will not be made by the prime minister, sometimes without consulting the cabinet. (For example, Blair's decision in May 1997 to grant the Bank of England semi-independence in setting interest rates was made through consultation only with the Chancellor, Gordon Brown.)

▶ **Policy coordination**. This is the key role of the modern cabinet. The cabinet serves to ensure that ministers know what is going on in other departments and also helps to reconcile the responsibilities of ministers for their individual departments with their responsibilities to the government as a whole. It therefore helps to 'join up' government at its most senior level.

▶ **Resolve disputes**. Most differences between ministers and between departments are resolved at a lower level. However, the cabinet can at times serve as a final court of appeal for disagreements that cannot be resolved elsewhere.

▶ **Forum for debate**. The cabinet can be used by the prime minister and other ministers as a sounding board to raise issues and to stimulate discussion. Nevertheless, the time available for this is very limited as cabinet agendas are full and usually dominated by government business.

▶ **Party management**. In considering policy, the cabinet also takes account of the views and morale of the parliamentary party. This is why the chief whip attends cabinet meetings and is usually a full cabinet member.

▶ **Symbol of collective government**. Regular cabinet meetings to which the prime minister reports and at which major policies are approved maintain the collective 'face' of UK government. This is underpinned by the convention of collective ministerial responsibility.

Ministers and civil servants

The two main groups within the executive are ministers and civil servants. But how do they differ? Traditionally, a very clear distinction existed between the roles and responsibilities of ministers and civil servants. This was based on the convention of individual ministerial responsibility (see p. 244). Ministers are expected to run government departments in the sense that they make policy and oversee the work of civil servants. They are appointed by the prime minister, usually from the ranks of the majority party in the House of Commons (although, as Gordon Brown's 'government of all the talents' has demonstrated, ministers can also be appointed from other parties or have no party affiliation). However, all ministers must be MPs or peers, emphasizing that the UK executive is a 'parliamentary'

What is . . . collective ministerial responsibility

Collective responsibility is a convention that defines the relationships between the executive and Parliament and between ministers and the cabinet. It has two main features:

▶ It implies that the government is collectively responsible to Parliament, in the sense that it rests on the confidence of the House of Commons. Therefore, if a government is defeated on a **vote of confidence** in the Commons, it is obliged to resign or call a general election. In this circumstance, all the ministers resign.

▶ It implies that all ministers are obliged to support official government policy in public and in Parliament (based on the assumption that these policies have been agreed by a collective cabinet). All ministers, junior and cabinet ministers, should therefore 'sing the same song'. Failure to do so means that a minister should resign or face being sacked by the prime minister. This also implies cabinet secrecy: cabinet discussions, and disagreements, must not be made public.

Vote of confidence: A vote on the life of the government itself; if defeated, the government is obliged to call a general election.

executive. There is, nevertheless, a hierarchy of ministers, creating a ministerial ladder. The main rungs on this ladder are:

▶ *Secretaries of state.* These are cabinet ministers in charge of a government department (although HM Treasury is headed by the Chancellor of the Exchequer).

▶ *Ministers of state.* These are junior to secretaries of state but senior to other ministers and PPSs; they are not usually in the cabinet, a common exception being the chief secretary to the Treasury.

▶ *Parliamentary under-secretaries of state.* These are junior to ministers of state and not members of the cabinet, although they may serve on cabinet committees.

▶ *Parliamentary private secretaries (PPSs).* These are the unpaid 'eyes and ears' for senior ministers; officially they are not members of the government.

Civil servants, by contrast, are appointed government officials. Their two key roles are to provide ministers with policy advice and to implement government policy. In so doing, they are meant to abide by the following three traditional principles, which date back to the Northcote-Trevelyan reforms of the mid-to-late 19th century. These principles are:

▶ *Permanence*: civil servants remain in post as ministers and governments come and go.

▶ *Neutrality*: civil servants are expected to be loyal and supportive of any minister and any government, whatever its political views.

What is . . . individual ministerial responsibility

Individual responsibility is the convention that defines the relationship between ministers and their departments. It has two main features:

▶ It implies that ministers are responsible to Parliament for the policies and actions of their departments. This is reflected in an obligation to inform and explain (via Question Time or select committees), but it may extend to resignation in the event of blunders or policy failures. In theory, individual responsibility implies that ministers take responsibility for the mistakes of their civil servants, but in practice they now only resign as a result of blunders that they have made personally (see Why ministers resign, p. 263). (The conduct expected of ministers is set out in more detail in Questions on Procedure for Ministers (1992), The Ministerial Code (1999) and the Cabinet Manual (2011).

▶ It implies that civil servants are responsible to their ministers. This suggests that civil servants should be loyal and supportive of whatever minister or government is in office, although if they have ethical concerns about a minister's conduct they should refer these to the cabinet secretary.

▶ *Anonymity*: civil servants are 'nameless' in the sense that they are not public figures.

The purpose of these principles was to improve the efficiency of government and the effectiveness of policy-making. Permanent civil servants who did not come and go as governments changed could accumulate expertise and specialist knowledge. Moreover, neutral policy advice would be more worthwhile than politically biased advice; it would make government policy more 'workable'.

However, these apparently clear-cut distinctions between ministers and civil servants was always more blurred in practice:

▶ *Ministers could not make all policy decisions.* In practice, they therefore made only 'major' decisions; that is, those that had a significant impact on the public, were politically controversial or involved substantial public spending.

▶ *Ministers' policy decisions were largely based on the advice they received from civil servants.* In that sense, a minister's formal responsibility for policy-making may have been misleading.

▶ *Civil servants controlled the flow of information to ministers.* Ministers knew what civil servants told them.

▶ *Civil servants may have been politically biased.* This view was traditionally advanced by Labour left-wingers, who believed that senior civil servants were a 'conservative veto group', influenced by their educational and social backgrounds. Under Thatcher, civil servants were thought to be concerned with

Differences between . . .
MINISTERS AND CIVIL SERVANTS

Ministers	• • •	Civil servants
Elected politicians (mainly)	• • •	Appointed officials
Party members	• • •	Politically neutral
Temporary	• • •	Permanent
Public figures	• • •	Anonymous
Run departments	• • •	Work in departments
Make policy	• • •	Advise on policy
Responsible to Parliament	• • •	Responsible to ministers

career self-interest, and therefore to be unsympathetic to attempts to 'roll back' the state.

In the light of such concerns, major changes have been introduced in the civil service since the 1980s, especially by the Thatcher and Blair governments. The net impact of these changes has been to reduce the traditional reliance that ministers had on civil servants by providing alternative sources of advice (from political advisors, think-tanks and the like) and ensuring that senior civil servants are 'one of us', as Thatcher put it. These changes have been upheld by all subsequent governments and have led some to conclude that the civil service now has too little power, rather than too much power.

Weblink ■ www.civilservice.gov.uk

Use the Civil Service website for general information about the civil service and for related news stories.

Who has power in the executive?

Theories of executive power

Debate about the location of executive power has been one of the recurrent themes of UK politics. Different views have been fashionable at different times, but the question has remained the same – who runs the country? It would be a mistake, however, to treat these contrasting models of executive power as simply 'right' or 'wrong'. So complex and ever-fluctuating is executive power that none

FOCUS ON . . .

How the civil service has changed

The Thatcher and Blair governments have introduced a range of changes that have changed the civil service in important ways. These changes have been motivated: (1) by a desire to strengthen the commitment to government policy, and (2) by a wish to improve efficiency and cut costs. Some claim that these changes have eroded the principles of permanence, neutrality and anonymity.

The main changes include the following:

▶ An insistence on a 'can do' culture, in which promotion is linked to positive support for government priorities and goals

▶ A split between Whitehall-based policy advisors and a growing number of executive agencies responsible for implementing policy

▶ A wider role for politically appointed special advisors to work alongside both ministers and civil servants

▶ The appointment of 'outsiders' to senior posts, now accounting for some 20 per cent of such appointments

▶ Increased 'contracting out' of government work to private businesses

▶ Wider use of think-tanks and other bodies as sources of policy advice, breaking the monopoly of the civil service.

of these models fully explains who has power in all cases and in all circumstances. Each of these models, nevertheless, captures some 'truth' about this thorny issue. The main theories of executive power are:

▶▶ Cabinet government
▶▶ Prime-ministerial government
▶▶ Presidentialism
▶▶ Core executive model

Cabinet government

This 'traditional' view of the UK executive emphasizes that power is collective and not personal. It is located in the cabinet rather than the prime minister. Moreover, within the cabinet, all ministers are equal. Each of them has the capacity to influence government policy and shape the direction in which the government is going. Such a view has clear implications for the prime minister, who is regarded as 'first' in name only. In other words, the prime minister has no more power than any other member of the cabinet. The theory of cabinet government is underpinned by the convention of collective responsibility, in which all ministers are expected to support publicly decisions made by the cabinet, or resign from the government. This helps to ensure **cabinet collegiality**, in the sense that disagree-

Cabinet collegiality: A sense of solidarity among cabinet members borne out of loyalty to the government and an awareness that they stand or fall together.

What is... cabinet government

Cabinet government is one of the key constitutional principles within the UK political system. It developed in the 19th century alongside the convention of collective responsibility. Cabinet government has three central features:

▶ The cabinet 'fuses' the executive and legislative branches of government, as its members head government departments but are also drawn from and accountable to Parliament. Bagehot (1963 [1867]) therefore described the cabinet as the 'hyphen that joins and the buckle that links' government to Parliament.

▶ The cabinet is the senior executive organ. It controls the policy-making process and makes all major government decisions.

▶ Within the cabinet, policy is made democratically with each member's views carrying equal weight. The prime minister is therefore merely 'first among equals'.

ment or dissent is only ever expressed within the secrecy of the cabinet room and never in public.

However, collective cabinet government in its formal sense is clearly outdated. It goes back to a period before the development of disciplined political parties in the House of Commons. In such circumstances, a minister's threat of resignation could, potentially, threaten the life of the government itself. All ministers therefore had to be kept on board. However, as parties became unified, this threat diminished. The primary loyalty of MPs shifted from individual cabinet members – patrons or friends – to their party. Cabinet government and collective responsibility therefore diminished in significance.

What does the cabinet government model tell us about executive power?

▶ It provides a reminder that, despite the growth in prime ministerial power, no prime minister can survive if he or she loses the support of the cabinet.

▶ It is kept alive by the fact that the prime minister's authority is linked to the backing he or she receives from the 'big beasts' of the cabinet, some of whom may enjoy such widespread support within the government and party that they are effectively 'unsackable'.

Prime-ministerial government

As the 20th century progressed, increasing concerns were expressed about the traditional theory of cabinet government. These were invariably fuelled by an awareness of the growing power of the prime minister. In many ways, this process can be traced back to the 19th century and the development of disciplined political parties, enabling the prime minister to use the leverage of party leadership. How could the prime minister any longer be dismissed as 'first amongst equals' if the focus of party loyalty focused on him as opposed to his 'equals'? This led to the belief that cabinet government had been replaced by prime-ministerial government, an assertion first made by Richard Crossman (1963) in a new introduction to Bagehot's *English Constitution*. The core feature of this view is that it is the prime minister, and not the cabinet, who dominates both the executive and Parliament. This happens because the prime minister is both head of the civil service and the leader of the largest party in the Commons.

What does the prime ministerial government model tell us about executive power?

▶ It highlights the undoubted growth in prime-ministerial power, particularly since 1945.
▶ It acknowledges that the cabinet is no longer the key policy-making body.

Presidentialism

Since the 1990s, some commentators have drawn attention to what they have seen as the growth of presidentialism in the UK (Foley, 1993, 2000). This suggests that UK prime ministers increasingly resemble presidents, with prime ministers such as Wilson, Thatcher and Blair usually being seen as key examples. To a large extent, this view overlaps with the prime-ministerial government model. Most importantly, both views emphasize the dominance of the prime minister over the cabinet. For instance, in no sense do US presidents share executive power with their cabinets (as occurs, at least in theory, in the UK). Rather, the US cabinet is a strictly subordinate body, a mere 'sounding board' and a source of advice for the president.

However, the process of 'presidentialization' has allegedly altered the role and influence of the prime minister and affected the working of UK government in broader ways. Evidence of growing presidentialism in UK politics includes the following:

▶ *Growth of 'spatial leadership'*. This is the tendency of prime ministers to distance themselves (giving them 'space') from their parties and governments by presenting themselves as 'outsiders' or developing a personal ideological stance (for example, 'Thatcherism' or 'Blairism').
▶ *Tendency towards 'populist outreach'*. This is the tendency of prime ministers to try to 'reach out' directly to the public by claiming to articulate their deepest hopes and fears. It is evident in the growing tendency of the prime minister to speak *for* the nation over major events, political crises or simply high-profile news stories. It is also reflected in the 'cult of the outsider', the attempt by prime ministers to present themselves as non-establishment figures on the side of the ordinary citizen.

What is ... prime-ministerial government

Prime-ministerial government is usually seen as the principal alternative to the theory of cabinet government. Crudely, it suggests that the prime minister has displaced the cabinet as the apex of the executive. The prime-ministerial thesis has three features:

▶ The prime minister 'fuses' the legislative and executive branches of government, in that he or she is drawn from and accountable to Parliament and also, as chief executive, controls the administrative machinery of government.

▶ The prime minister dominates the policy-making process. He or she makes major government decisions and exerts influence (potentially) over all policy areas.

▶ The cabinet is a subordinate body. It is no longer a meaningful policy-making organ but, rather, a source of advice and support for the prime minister.

▶ *Personalized election campaigns.* The mass media increasingly portrays elections as personalized battles between the prime minister and the leader of the opposition. Party leaders thus become the 'brand image' of their parties or government, meaning that personality and image have become major determinants of political success or failure.

▶ *Personal mandates.* This is the trend for prime ministers to claim popular authority on the basis of *their* electoral success. Prime ministers have therefore become the ideological consciences of their party or government, their chief source of conviction and policy direction.

▶ *Wider use of special advisors.* Prime ministers increasingly rely on hand-picked political advisors rather than on cabinets, ministers and senior civil servants. These advisors often have a personal loyalty to the prime minister rather than to the party or government.

▶ *Strengthened Cabinet Office.* The size and administrative resources available to the **Cabinet Office** have grown, turning it (perhaps) into a small-scale prime minister's department responsible for coordinating the rest of Whitehall.

Cabinet Office: The body that services the cabinet system, through the cabinet secretariat, and is responsible for co-ordinating policy across Whitehall departments and ensuring effective policy delivery; the nerve centre of government.

Weblink ■ www.cabinetoffice.gov.uk

Use the Cabinet Office website as a source of information about the activities of this key coordinating body.

Nevertheless, such trends suggest that UK prime ministers increasingly *resemble* presidents, not that they have become presidents. Quite simply, prime ministers cannot become presidents because the UK has a system of parliamentary government rather than presidential government (see p. 214). For instance, the UK does not have a constitutional separation of powers between the legislature and executive, as characterizes the US system. Similarly, despite the growth of personalized election campaigning in the UK, prime ministers continue to be appointed as a result of parliamentary elections, not by a separate electoral process, as occurs in the USA.

What does the presidentialization thesis tell us about executive power?

▶ It stresses the growth of personalized leadership and draws attention to the importance of the *direct* relationship between the prime minister and the people.

▶ It highlights the growing political significance of the mass media in affecting power balances within the executive and within the larger political system.

Who is . . .
Margaret Thatcher

Margaret Thatcher was born in 1925, the daughter of a shopkeeper and mayor of Grantham, Lincolnshire. She was educated at the local grammar school and studied chemistry at Oxford, where she became involved with Conservative politics. Elected as MP for Finchley in 1959, she was appointed Education Secretary in 1970 by Edward Heath. It was whilst serving in the Heath government (1970–74) that she was converted to a radical right-wing agenda that later became known as 'Thatcherism'. In 1975 she challenged, and defeated, Heath for the party leadership, and in 1979 she went on to win the general election, becoming the UK's first female prime minister. Thatcher dominated UK politics in the 1980s, gaining landslide election victories in 1983 and 1987. She earned (from the Russians initially) the nickname, 'The Iron Lady', for her robust and often abrasive style of leadership, demonstrated by her approach to the Falklands War of 1982 and her determination to follow a radical programme of privatization and deregulation, the reform of the trade unions, tax cuts and market reforms in health and education. Her downfall came in December 1990 when, weakened by her stance on Europe and the unpopularity of the Poll Tax, she was challenged for the party leadership by Michael Heseltine. Her successor, John Major, made her a life peer in 1992, Baroness Thatcher. Thatcher had the longest continuous period in office since Lord Liverpool, who was prime minister in the early 19th century.

Weblink ■ www.margaretthatcher.org

Use the Margaret Thatcher Foundation website as a source of information about Thatcher, her life and ideas.

Differences between . . .

PRIME MINISTERS AND PRESIDENTS

Prime ministers ●··●	Presidents
Head of government ●··●	Head of government and head of state
Elected via parliamentary elections ●··●	Separately elected
Control of legislature ●··●	Independent legislature
Collective cabinet ●··●	'Sounding-board' cabinet
No department ●··●	Personal department

Core executive model

An alternative way of understanding where power lies is to go beyond the simplistic 'cabinet versus prime minister' debate and to recognize that both the prime minister and cabinet operate within the context of the 'core executive' (Smith, 1999). This models suggests that:

▶ Neither the prime minister nor the cabinet is an independent actor.

▶ Each of them exercises influence in and through a network of relationships, formal and informal. This brings a range of other actors and institutions into the picture.

▶ The balance of power within the core executive is affected by the resources available to its various actors.

▶ Wider factors, such as economic and diplomatic developments, influence the workings of the core executive.

What does the core-executive model tell us about executive power?

▶ It emphasizes that prime ministerial power is not only constrained by cabinet collegiality, but also by the need to operate within a complex of organizations and procedures. Power is never monocratic (concentrated in the hands of a single person or body).

▶ It highlights that power within the executive is more about building relationships with key bodies and actors than simply being a matter of 'command and control'.

Understanding prime ministerial power

The formal powers of the prime minister are relatively modest, certainly by comparison with an executive president. They are derived from the Royal Prerogative, which is now, in the main, exercised by the prime minister (and other ministers) and not by the Queen. These include the powers to:

FOCUS ON . . .
The core executive

The core executive is an informal network of bodies and actors at the apex of government which play key roles in the formulation of policy and the direction of government (see Figure 8.1). The main bodies and actors within the core executive are:

▶ The prime minister, leading members of the **Prime Minister's Office** and other close advisors and confidantes
▶ The cabinet (or at least its 'big beasts'), the main cabinet committees and leading figures within the Cabinet Office

▶ Senior officials in the Treasury and other major government departments, and in other bodies including the Bank of England and the security and intelligence services
▶ Individuals and outside organizations (including think-tanks) that the prime minister or leading cabinet members may look to for policy advice
▶ Key MPs and peers, especially government whips and possibly chairs of important select committees.

Prime Minister's Office: A collection of senior officials and political advisors (numbering over 100) who advise the prime minister about policy and implementation, communications, party management and government relations.

▶ Appoint ministers and other senior figures (including top judges and senior bishops of the Church of England)
▶ Dissolve and recall Parliament (although this has greatly been reduced by the introduction of fixed-term Parliaments)
▶ Sign treaties
▶ Grant honours.

However, this list of formal powers does not capture the full significance of the post of the prime minister. Prime ministers are much more important than their 'constitutional' role suggests. But their power is largely informal rather than formal. It is based more on the ability to persuade and influence than to dictate. Prime ministers are powerful basically because they stand at the apex of three crucial sets of relationships. These relationships explain how prime ministers exert influence across the system of government; but they also explain why that influence is always conditional and subject (at least potentially) to constraints.

The key relationships of the prime minister are with:

▶ The cabinet, individual ministers and government departments
▶ His or her party and, through it, with Parliament
▶ The people, often through the mass media.

Nevertheless, it is always dangerous to generalize about prime ministerial power. The extent of this power fluctuates not only from prime minister to prime

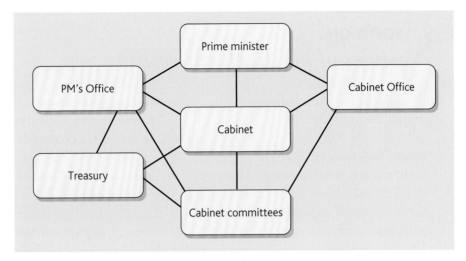

Figure 8.1 **Relationships within the core executive**

minister but also at different times within the same premiership. As H. H. Asquith (prime minister, 1908–16) put it, 'the post of the prime minister is whatever its holder chooses and is able to make of it'. What the prime minister 'chooses' to make of his or her office highlights the importance of personality and the prime minister's **leadership style**. Quite simply, prime ministers are not all alike; they bring different motivations, personal qualities and attributes to their office. On the other hand, what the prime minister is 'able' to make of his or her office depends on:

Leadership style: The strategies and patterns of behaviour through which a leader seeks to achieve his or her goals.

▶▶ The powers of the prime minister
▶▶ The constraints on the prime minister
▶▶ The existence of single-party government or coalition government.

Powers of the prime minister

The key levers and resources available to the prime minister are:

▶▶ The power to hire and fire
▶▶ The ability to manage the cabinet
▶▶ Leadership of the party
▶▶ Institutional supports
▶▶ Access to the media.

Hiring and firing

Patronage: The granting of favours or privileges; patronage usually involves control over jobs and appointments.

The key power of the prime minister is the power of **patronage**, the ability to appoint and sack, promote and demote all ministers in the government, including the cabinet. This strengthens the prime minister in two key ways:

FOCUS ON . . .
Styles of political leadership

Three distinctive styles of leadership can be identified (Burns, 1978):

▶ **Laissez-faire leaders**. These are leaders who are reluctant to interfere in matters outside their personal responsibility. They tend to have a 'hands-off' approach to cabinet, government and party management (e.g. Alec Douglas Home).

▶ **Transactional leaders**. These are leaders who act as 'brokers', concerned to uphold the collective face of government by negoti- ating compromises and balancing rival individuals, factions and interests against one another (e.g. Edward Heath and John Major).

▶ **Transformational leaders**. These are leaders who inspire or are visionaries. They tend to be motivated not only by strong ideological convictions, but they also have the personal resolution and **political will** to put them into practice (e.g. Margaret Thatcher and Tony Blair).

Political will: A determination to achieve desired outcomes based on an assured understanding of the means of achieving them.

▶ The prime minister can ensure the appointment and promotion of loyal supporters and especially of politicians who share his or her political or ideological preferences. By the same token, rivals, critics or ideological opponents can either be kept out of the government or be restricted to junior positions.

▶ The fact that the prime minister controls their political careers ensures that both ministers and the majority of backbenchers (would-be ministers) remain loyal and supportive. They understand that they serve *under* the prime minister.

Thatcher therefore consolidated her position between 1979 and 1983 by transforming her cabinet from one dominated by 'wets' (One Nation conservatives) to one in which all the key economic posts were in the hand of 'drys' (Thatcherites). Similarly, only half of Blair's first cabinet of 1997 remained in post after the 2001 election, four years later. On becoming prime minister in June 2007, Gordon Brown carried out the largest cabinet reshuffle for over 100 years in order to put his personal stamp on the government and to indicate that, in effect, a change of prime minister meant a change of government. Eleven members of the old cabinet either stood down or were sacked, and nine new people entered the cabinet, including seven who had never previously held a cabinet post. The defence secretary, Des Browne, was the only minister to remain in the same post he had previously held.

However, the power of patronage has its limits. In hiring and firing ministers, prime ministers must take account of the following considerations:

- All ministers must be MPs or peers.
- All (or at least the vast majority) of ministers must come from the majority party.
- Party unity requires an ideological and political balance within the cabinet.
- Particular groups should be represented for instance, women.
- Opponents may be less dangerous inside government (where they are subject to collective responsibility) than outside.
- The advent of coalition government means that the hiring and firing of ministers must take account of the need to maintain the coalition, significantly expanding the influence of Nick Clegg as the deputy prime minister (as discussed below).

Cabinet management

Cabinet system: The cabinet and the network of bodies linked to it, notably committees, sub-committees and the Cabinet Secretariat.

Prime ministers have considerable scope for managing and controlling the cabinet and the larger **cabinet system**. This enables prime ministers to harness the decision-making authority of the cabinet to their own ends. It also means that the prime minister can effectively determine the role and significance of the cabinet. How is this done? Amongst other things, prime ministers:

- Chair cabinet meetings, manage their agendas and discussions, and sum up decisions (votes are rarely held in cabinet).
- Convene cabinet meetings and decide how often they will be called and how long they will last.
- Decide the number and nature of cabinet committees, sub-committees and ministerial groups, and appoint their members and chairs (the prime minister will usually chair the most important cabinet committees).

Since the 1950s, the number and duration of cabinet meetings has steadily declined, from about 100 a year to about 40. Under Blair, they rarely lasted more than one hour, although they lengthened under Brown. Cabinet meetings are generally used simply to address formal business, with wider discussion not encouraged and dissent not tolerated. Thatcher and Blair, in particular, made greater use of committees and sub-committees. Blair tended to adopt a more informal style of decision-making, sometimes called 'sofa government'. This involved operating through 'bilaterals', meetings between Blair and individual ministers, which either bypassed the cabinet system or effectively made policy before it was ratified by the full cabinet.

However, the prime minister's ability to manage and control the cabinet has its limits:

- The cabinet's support for the prime minister is conditional on the prime minister being popular and successful.

FOCUS ON . . .
How cabinet committees work

Cabinet committees are sub-committees of the full cabinet, which consider particular aspects of government policy. They have been used in greater numbers since 1945, their benefit being that the cabinet works more quickly and efficiently in smaller groups composed of relevant ministers. Senior officials and junior ministers may also be members of cabinet committees, which have, over time, spawned a range of sub-committees and more informal ministerial groups.

Cameron set up nine full cabinet committees in May 2010. Perhaps the most important of these is the Coalition Committee, whose role is to manage the coalition by providing a forum for reviewing and resolving disputes between its partners. The committee is composed of five Conservatives and five Liberal Democrats, and is co-chaired by Cameron and Clegg. In addition, each cabinet committee has a chair from one of the parties and a deputy chair from the other party.

Finally, the cabinet committee system provides Clegg with an important power base, as he chairs or co-chairs five of the nine full committees, including the one on political and constitutional reform, which has a wide-ranging remit.

▶ Cabinet resignations, particularly the resignation of senior figures, can damage political support for, and the public standing of, the prime minister. (These issues are looked at on pp. 259–60.)
▶ Coalition government under Cameron since 2010 means that the process of cabinet management has become entangled in the larger process of coalition management (as discussed below).

Party leadership

Party leadership underpins all other aspects of prime ministerial power. It sets the prime minister apart from all other ministers and gives him or her leverage across the wider governmental system. This happens in at least three ways:

▶ Party leadership increases the prime minister's authority within the cabinet and government, as other ministers recognize that party loyalty focuses on the person of the prime minister and not on any other minister.
▶ It allows the prime minister to control Parliament through commanding a disciplined majority in the House of Commons.
▶ More widely, party members recognize that the party's fortunes are closely linked to the prime minister's personal standing. This tends to discourage party splits and public criticism of the prime minister.

However, the benefits that flow from party leadership are limited:

▶ As the party leader, the prime minister is meant to deliver electoral success. If the government becomes unpopular, and especially if the prime minister is viewed as an electoral liability, party loyalty can evaporate quickly.

▶ As will be discussed later, no prime minister can survive without the support of his or her party.

Institutional supports

Since 1945, prime ministerial power has grown significantly as a result of the build-up of bodies and advisors who support the prime minister. This has helped to compensate for a traditional weakness of the prime minister. Whereas other members of the cabinet are supported by government departments composed of thousands of expert and experienced civil servants, the prime minister does not have a department.

The two most important bodies serving the prime minister are:

▶ The Prime Minister's Office, which since 2002 has also included the Policy Unit

▶ The Cabinet Office, which has developed into the coordinating hub of the UK executive, helping to 'join up' the work of the Whitehall government departments.

The role and influence of the Cabinet Office was significantly extended under Blair, who created new special offices and units, such as the Delivery Unit (to monitor and improve policy delivery), the Social Exclusion Unit, the Performance and Innovation Unit, the Women's Unit and the UK Anti-Drugs Co-ordination Unit. In addition, the number and significance of special advisors, who are responsible directly to the prime minister, has increased markedly. Whereas Major had eight special advisors, Blair eventually had 50. Blair also became the first prime minister to give senior special advisors formal control over civil servants. Although David Cameron has continued this policy, the Conservative-led coalition is committed to reducing the number of political advisors.

However, the benefit of these institutional supports is limited:

▶ They are meagre by comparison with the institutional supports available to a US president (see US presidency, p. 261).

▶ Even the expanded Cabinet Office does not amount to a prime minister's department.

Access to the media

The growing influence of the mass media, and particularly of radio and television, has been a major factor in altering the power of the prime minister since 1945. The expansion of the 'broadcast' media, and increasingly the 'new' media (cable and satellite television, the Internet, and so on), has not only increased the flow of political information to the public, but also reordered power relationships within the political executive. The mass media, for example, is a key factor in explaining the growth of presidentialism.

The mass media strengthens prime ministerial power in three main ways:

▶ The growth of 'political celebrity' gives prime ministers and other party leaders the ability to appeal 'over the heads' of their senior colleagues, parties and government institutions, directly to the public. This is reflected in the phenomenon of spatial leadership.

▶ The media's obsession with personality and image guarantees that media attention focuses primarily on political leaders, and especially on the prime minister. The public profile of the prime minister therefore eclipses that of other politicians, including senior cabinet colleagues.

▶ Control over government communications means that prime ministers have been able to structure the flow of information to the public. This was particularly evident in the Thatcher period, through the work of her press secretary, Bernard Ingham; during the Blair era, through the influence of Alistair Campbell; and under Cameron, through the role played until January 2011 by the former editor of the *News of the World*, Andy Coulson. It gave rise to an emphasis on '**spin**' and so-called 'news management'. Examples have included:

> ▷ The use of 'leaks', or unattributable briefings
> ▷ The careful 'vetting' of information and arguments before release to the media
> ▷ Feeding of stories only to sympathetic media sources
> ▷ Releasing of information close to media deadlines to prevent checking or the identification of counter-arguments
> ▷ The release of 'bad' news at times when other, more important, events dominate the news agenda
> ▷ The backing of key newspapers can bolster the image of the prime minister and ensure that any criticism is muted. Political bias within the UK's print media means that this normally benefits Conservative prime ministers, although Blair succeeded in gaining the support of the Murdoch newspapers (*The Sun*, the *Times* Group, the *News of the World* and so on. The fact that Cameron's popularity held up well during his first year in office, despite his controversial policy agenda, can partly be explained by the support of nine of the UK's national dailies for one or other of the coalition parties (only the *Mirror* supported Labour).

However, media attention does not always work to the benefit of the prime minister:

Spin: The biased or distorted presentation of information so as to gain a desired response; being 'economical with the truth'.

▶ 'Bad news' stories (such as policy blunders and ministerial resignations) are often 'hyped' by the media, turning a problem into a crisis.

▶ The emphasis on 'spin' and 'news management' may prove (as Blair discovered) to be counter-productive, as it undermines trust in government and the credibility of the prime minister.

Constraints on the prime minister

The main constraints on the prime minister are:

⏩ The cabinet
⏩ The party
⏩ The electorate
⏩ The media
⏩ The pressure of events.

The cabinet

Although the full cabinet is often now dismissed as a merely 'dignified' institution, in particular circumstances it can still act as a major constraint on the prime minister. The influence of the cabinet is most clearly reflected in the power that can be wielded by leading individual ministers, the 'big beasts'.

The political 'weight' of a cabinet minister is determined by three factors:

▶ The seniority of his or her office
▶ His or her standing within the party
▶ His or her public profile.

Prime ministers may either have to conciliate key cabinet colleagues, or accept the damage that their resignations may cause. This can be seen, for example, in the weakening of Thatcher's authority in the late 1980s, which was affected by growing disunity within her cabinet. In particular, her public image and standing within the party were damaged by the resignations of three senior ministers:

▶ Michael Heseltine (defence secretary) in 1986
▶ Nigel Lawson (Chancellor of the Exchequer) in 1989
▶ Geoffrey Howe (deputy prime minister) in 1990.

Although Thatcher survived each of these resignations, they provided the context for her eventual downfall in December 1990. A leadership election was precipitated by Heseltine's challenge, with Lawson and Howe giving Heseltine's bid strong public support.

The clearest example of a prime minister being forced to conciliate a powerful cabinet colleague was Tony Blair in relation to Gordon Brown, his Chancellor of the Exchequer, 1997–2007. Because of Brown's high standing in the party, his prominence in the process of Labour Party 'modernization', and (perhaps) agreements that were made in 1994 when Brown decided not to stand against Blair for the vacant Labour leadership, Blair granted Brown and the Treasury unprecedented power after 1997. This created a kind of 'dual monarchy' within the Blair government. Brown was able to use his powerbase within the Treasury to exert influence over all aspects of domestic policy, controlling not only the flow of money, but also policy developments, such as the pace and nature of welfare reform. The clearest evidence of Brown's power was his ability effectively to veto the UK's entry into the European single currency, by the establishment of five economic tests that had to be passed before euro membership could go ahead.

Examples of cabinets taking collective action against the prime minister are extremely rare, however. This is because the fate of the prime minister and of the government are so closely entwined. However, in her memoirs, Thatcher (1993) claimed that she had been ousted by a cabinet coup through the withdrawal of ministerial support once she had failed to secure re-election as party leader on the first ballot. As we shall see, though, Thatcher only lost the support of her cabinet once she had lost the support of her parliamentary party. Her cabinet may have precipitated her resignation, but it did not *cause* her downfall.

The party

Prime ministers can, in most cases, count on the support of their party, both inside Parliament and beyond. However, this support is conditional. Party leadership is a responsibility as well as a source of power. In particular, parties look to prime ministers to provide leadership that will help to maintain party unity and ensure the party's electoral success. The failure to do so can bring a heavy price. The most dramatic example of this was the fall of Thatcher. The key factor in the removal of Thatcher was her failure to win sufficient support from MPs in the leadership election. She fell four votes short of being 15 per cent ahead of her nearest challenger (even though she secured an overall majority), as the then party rules required.

Backbench support for Thatcher had been undermined by growing divisions over Europe, precipitated by her increasingly strident opposition to further European integration and by the stark unpopularity of the poll tax (a flat-rate local government tax on individuals which replaced the rates). The poll tax had been introduced in Scotland in 1989, and was introduced in England and Wales in 1990. In particular, Thatcher had come to be viewed by many Conservative MPs as an electoral liability. In these circumstances, they acted to save themselves and their party, rather than the prime minister.

John Major's premiership was blighted by deepening tensions within the Conservative Party over Europe. Having tried to place the UK 'at the heart of Europe', he faced growing hostility from a small but highly determined group of

BY COMPARISON . . .
The US presidency

- The president is elected (together with a 'running mate', who becomes the vice president) through fixed-term presidential elections that occur every four years. Under the twenty-second amendment of the US Constitution, presidents can only serve for two full terms in office. The president appoints a cabinet, but this is merely an advisory group that aids the president in making decisions.

- The US president is the chief executive (head of government) and head of state (equivalent to the Queen). The president exercises a broad array of powers, some provided by the US Constitution, some based on custom and tradition, and some delegated by Congress. The president's roles include commander-in-chief of the armed forces, chief diplomat, chief legislator and head of party.

- The main institutional support available to the president is provided by the Executive Office of the President (EOP), which serves as his or her personal bureaucracy. The EOP employs a staff of about 1,500, and includes the National Security Council and the Council of Economic Advisers. The USA also operates a 'spoils system', which allows in-coming presidents to make, directly or indirectly, about 4,000 appointments at senior and middle-ranking levels of their administrations.

- Most commentators have agreed that presidential power has increased since the 19th century. This has been the result of two main developments. First, especially since F. D. Roosevelt, 1933–45, presidents have been expected to develop legislative programmes. This means that Congress is largely engaged with examining bills that come from the White House. Second, especially since 1945, presidents have assumed greater prominence in foreign affairs, in keeping with their role as world leaders. This gave rise to the idea of the 'imperial presidency'.

Eurosceptic MPs. Open criticism and escalating backbench revolts finally persuaded Major to take the 'nuclear option' of resigning as party leader in June 1995 to precipitate a leadership election in which he hoped to defeat his critics. Although he emerged as the victor, the tactic, if anything, further damaged his authority and failed to resolve the party's ideological disputes. A record of almost unremitting party division after 1992, and Major's declining authority over his party, undoubtedly contributed to the disastrous Conservative defeat of 1997.

Weblink ■ www.johnmajor.co.uk

Use this website for information about John Major and the 1990–97 Conservative government.

Although much less dramatic, Blair's authority over the Labour Party declined significantly after the outbreak of the Iraq War in 2003. This stimulated the largest backbench rebellion against any government for over 100 years, and led to a mood of restiveness and unease amongst a growing proportion of Labour backbenchers that lasted for the rest of his premiership. The renewed power of backbenchers was also demonstrated once Brown became party leader and prime minister in June 2007. In his first month as prime minister, Brown suffered eight backbench rebellions (even though none led to a government defeat), more than the total number of revolts against all incoming prime ministers in their first month since 1945.

The electorate

The prime minister's increasingly direct relationship with the public is usually a major strength, but it can also be a source of vulnerability. In a sense, the state of public opinion underpins all the other constraints on the prime minister. When prime ministers are popular and their governments are riding high in the polls, their authority over the cabinet and the party is assured. However, when the government's popularity dips, and its chances of winning the next election are thrown into doubt, life becomes much more difficult for the prime minister.

For example, Thatcher's vulnerability in the late 1980s coincided with declining poll ratings and early signs of improved support for the Labour Party. Major's control of his party was damaged by a succession of by-election defeats and defeats in local and European Parliament elections. Blair's authority over his party and his government was weakened by Labour's reduced majority in 2005 and improved poll ratings for the Conservative Party. Blair's declining personal popularity leading up to the 2005 general election, in fact, persuaded him to pre-announce his resignation. This left him as a 'lame duck' prime minister for the rest of his term in office. In the case of Brown, his stature as prime minister was badly damaged in October 2007 by confused messages over the likely timing of the next general election (the 'election that never was'). This squandered the brief poll lead

FOCUS ON . . .
Why ministers resign

The three most common grounds on which ministers resign are:

▶ **Policy disagreements.** Linked to collective responsibility, ministers may resign if they feel unable to support government policy, as occurred with Robin Cook and Clare Short in 2003 over the Iraq war, and Nigel Griffiths (deputy leader of the Commons) over the renewal of Trident in March 2007. However, such resignations are rare, as dissenting ministers are usually willing to keep their policy reservations to themselves.

▶ **Ministerial blunders.** Individual responsibility has been narrowed in the sense that ministers are now only prepared to resign in the event of blunders for which they are personally responsible, and not to take responsibility for mistakes by their civil servants. Examples include Lord Carrington in 1982 over the failure to predict the Argentine invasion of the Falklands, Edwina Currie in 1988 over fears about salmonella in eggs, and Beverley Hughes in 2004 over immigration checks. In many other cases, ministers have been able to 'ride out' such crises.

▶ **Personal scandals.** The most common ground for ministerial resignations is revelations about the personal behaviour or conduct of a minister, particularly when these attract negative media coverage and threaten to destabilize the workings of government. Examples include Peter Mandelson in 1998 over a house loan from a fellow minister, and again in 2001 over allegations about the granting of a passport; David Blunkett in 2004 over the fast-tracking of a passport application for his ex-lover's au pair, and in 2005 over business dealings; and Peter Hain in 2008 over donations to his deputy leadership campaign.

Weblink ■ http://news.bbc.co.uk

Use this website for further details about, and analysis of, these and other ministerial resignations.

---

over the Conservatives he had established in the early months of his premiership. Brown's standing was further damaged by the deepening of the global financial crisis in September 2008 and by the subsequent sharp recession, both of which undermined his reputation for economic competence.

The mass media

However, the prime minister's relationship with the public is, in fact, rarely direct. Instead, his or her image is presented to the public through the 'prism' of the mass media. While prime ministers have tried to exploit their access to the media for personal benefit, there are also indications that the media is becoming more critical of politicians generally and more difficult to manage. This was evident in battles between the Blair government and the BBC over allegations that, in the run-up to the Iraq War, the government had 'sexed up' a dossier emphasizing the military threat posed by Iraq to the UK. The relationship between the prime minister and the media nevertheless reached a particular low under Brown. It was widely argued that Brown lacked the communication and presentational skills to be a successful modern leader. It is also clear that the media plays a major role in bringing about ministerial resignations, in that perhaps the most important decision the prime minister has to make in these circumstances is the balance between the damage done to his or her image and to the government generally by continuing negative media coverage, and the damage that would be caused by a ministerial resignation.

The media's coverage of politics has become more difficult for prime ministers to manage for the following reasons:

▶ *A tendency to 'hype'.* Increasingly intense commercial pressures force the media to make their coverage of politics 'sexy' and attention grabbing. A 'crisis' is more interesting than a 'problem'; a 'split' is more interesting than a 'division'; and a 'bitter attack' is more interesting than 'criticism'.

▶ *The blurring of facts and interpretation.* The coverage of news and current affairs has changed in recent years. Whereas once television news, and the broadsheet press in particular, tried to distinguish clearly between news and comment, the difference between 'what happened' and 'what it means' is increasingly blurred by an attempt to define 'the story'.

▶ *Television increasingly follows the print media in its style of political and current affairs coverage.* This means not only that television stories are picked up from newspaper headlines, but that this has also affected the style of current affairs coverage on television.

The pressure of events

When Harold Macmillan was prime minister in 1957–63 somebody asked him what worried him most. Famously, he replied: 'Events, dear boy, events'. In other words, Macmillan was highlighting the limited control that prime ministers have over 'what happens'. In theory, prime ministers 'run the country', but in practice surprises come along that demonstrate how little control they actually have. For instance, Thatcher 'initiated' the Falklands War of 1992, and considerably benefited from the victory; but, had the outcome been different (as it very nearly was), her premiership may have been destroyed.

John Major was less fortunate over 'Black Wednesday', 16 September 1992, when intensifying currency speculation finally forced the UK to leave the Exchange Rate Mechanism (ERM) (an arrangement which linked the value of the pound to that of other EC currencies). The ERM crisis had a profound effect on the rest of Major's premiership, because it destroyed the government's reputation for economic competence. The Major government consistently lagged behind Labour in the polls from 'Black Wednesday' until its eventual defeat in 1997.

In the case of Blair, his public reputation was badly damaged by the suicide of David Kelly, a biological war expert who had contributed to the development of the government's Iraq military dossier in July 2003. Kelly's death substantially intensified media and political speculation about the basis on which the decision to go to war was made and about the honesty and trustworthiness of the prime minister. In the case of Brown, his reputation for effective leadership and economic competence was destroyed by the recession that started in 2008, despite his robust response to the global financial crisis that had precipitated it.

In many ways, the problem of 'events' is a structural one and not merely a question of random surprises. This occurs in three main ways:

▶ *Prime ministers only control top-level decisions.* The implementation of decisions is in the hands of bodies and actors over whom prime ministers have very little direct control. For example, the effectiveness of welfare reforms is affected by decisions taken by people such as hospital managers, doctors, head teachers, college principals, lecturers, and so forth.

▶ *The growth of presidentialism has over-stretched the prime minister's breadth of interests.* Prime ministers are now expected to speak out on *all* important questions, domestic and international, and they are also held responsible for blunders and mistakes wherever they may occur. Rising crime levels, bad weather and flooding, war casualties, economic figures, splits within the EU, and so forth therefore present prime ministers with a seemingly endless range of 'events' to respond to.

▶ *Prime ministerial power may be counter-productive.* The ability of prime ministers to react appropriately to political events may be impaired by their increasing reliance on close confidantes and hand-picked advisors. They are told what their advisors think they want to hear, meaning that they may not be exposed to a sufficiently wide range of views. Prime ministers may, as a result, lose their political 'touch'. Examples of this may include miscalculations such as Thatcher's introduction of the poll tax and Blair's stubborn determination to support the USA in Iraq.

The prime minister and coalition government

Conventional accounts of prime ministerial power are based on the assumption of single-party majority rule. The prime minister, indeed, is often simply viewed as the leader of the majority party in the Commons. When there is a majority party, the prime minister's power is largely determined by his or her party's unity, both within the cabinet and government and within Parliament. A Commons majority and a unified party are the two key requirements for effective prime ministerial power. A 'hung' Parliament changes this because, in minority or coalition governments, prime ministers are much more vulnerable to pressures exerted by another party or other parties. In view of the formation of the Conservative–Liberal Democrat coalition in 2010, David Cameron's power as prime minister must be understood in the light of the new and dynamic framework that coalition government establishes. Although this subjects the prime minister to a range of challenges, it may also bring opportunities. How does coalition government affect prime ministerial power?

The first development that had implications for the prime minister was the speedy commitment in May 2010 to the idea of fixed-term Parliaments, a reform long-backed by the Liberal Democrats. Under this, the next UK general election will take place on 7 May 2015 (although the prime minister has the ability to alter the date by up to two months). An election could still be triggered before the end of the five-year term either if a motion of confidence is passed and no alternative government is found, or if a motion for an early general election is agreed either by at least two-thirds of the Commons or without a division. These arrangements replaced the so-called '55 per cent rule', which would have required that motions of no confidence had to gain the support of 55 per cent of MPs in order for a government to fall, but this was withdrawn after opposition from Conservative backbenchers. The introduction of fixed-term Parliaments is significant because it means that the prime minister has effectively surrendered a key power, the ability to dissolve Parliament and to call a general election. This is one of the prerogative powers that the prime minister, by convention, exercises on behalf of the Crown. The voluntary abandonment of this power by Cameron has widely been welcomed, but the introduction of fixed-term Parliaments has also stimulated criticism (see p. 267).

One of the key implications of coalition government is that it adds an important new constraint on the prime minister's power of patronage. The appointment of a cabinet in the first place, and subsequent reshuffles, promotions and demotions, have to take account of their impact on the cohesion of the coalition itself. In May 2010, it was important for Cameron to bind the whole cabinet, its Conservative and Liberal Democrat members alike, into the coalition, especially in view of the unpopular nature of some of the policies he was committed to (public spending cuts, tax increases, the tripling of university tuition fees and so on). With this in mind, Liberal Democrats were given prominent roles in the Cameron government. Nick Clegg, the Liberal Democrat leader, was appointed deputy prime minister, and four other Liberal Democrats were appointed to the cabinet. The appointments of Vince Cable (business secretary), and David Laws (chief secretary to the Treasury) were particularly significant, as, through them, Cameron also ensured that Liberal Democrats were closely involved in coalition's economic strategy. Indeed, as Treasury secretary, Laws was responsible for

FOR OR AGAINST?

FIXED-TERM PARLIAMENTS

FOR	AGAINST
Electoral fairness. The major criticism of the traditional system of flexible-term elections is that they gave the prime minister, and therefore the governing party, a significant and unfair advantage at election time. In particular, prime ministers can use their power to dissolve Parliament to call an election at a time that is most favourable to their own party, as indicated by polling trends. This creates a bias in favour of the government's re-election and puts opposition parties at a further disadvantage, in that they are forced to plan their election strategies by trying to second-guess the prime minister. Fixed-term Parliaments are therefore as a way of ensuring electoral fairness.	**Benefits to the government of the day**. Regardless of fixed-term Parliaments, electoral unfairness will persist because governments can still structure their policy programme to ensure that, at the end of their term in office, circumstances are as favourable as possible to their re-election. Unpopular and 'tough' policies can therefore be rolled out at the beginning of a Parliament, in the knowledge that the government will not have to face the verdict of the electorate until its full term has elapsed. Similarly, prime ministers and governments may well benefit from not being drawn into playing games with the opposition about the date of the next election (as Brown found in 2007).
Avoiding needless speculation. Flexible-term Parliaments, in which prime ministers can call 'snap' elections, create ongoing and unhelpful speculation about the date of the next election. Political debate therefore focuses, unhelpfully and unnecessarily, on the government of the day's strategy for re-election, rather than on the strengths and weaknesses of its policy programme. The introduction of fixed-term Parliaments would, at a stroke, reduce distractions and trivial speculation.	**Longer campaigns**. One of the advantages of flexible-term Parliaments is that a lack of knowledge about the date of the next election means that electoral campaigns are relatively short, usually three to four weeks in length. Knowing the date of the next election many years in advance may simply mean, as in the USA, that election campaigns start earlier, possibly a year before the election itself. The final period of a fixed-term Parliament may therefore, effectively, be devoted to electioneering.
Greater stability. Uncertainty about the date of the next election creates an unstable political and economic environment. Governments that know that they are going to serve a full term in office have the time to develop policies carefully and implement them fully, without their policy programme being interrupted by a surprise election. Similarly, business is able to plan for the longer term in the knowledge that possible changes in government, and therefore changes in government policy, can only occur at set and predictable intervals.	**Over-long terms**. A particular criticism of the coalition's proposal for fixed-term Parliaments in the UK is the decision to institute five-yearly terms, which are longer than those instituted elsewhere (Australia and New Zealand have three-year terms, and the Canadian Federal Legislature has a four-year term). Although Parliament used to have a five-year maximum term, in practice Parliaments were much shorter (on average, just over three years and nine months between 1945 and 2010). Longer Parliaments mean that government is less responsive to the electorate.

FOCUS ON . . .

Coalition fault-lines and tensions

The dynamics of coalition government differ from those of single-party governments. In particular, a number of additional fault-lines or tensions can assert themselves, as follows:

▶ *Unity and distinctiveness?* Coalition governments are drawn in two quite different directions. On the one hand, in order to govern effectively, coalitions must remain unified: they must speak with a single voice, not a number of voices. The failure to do so risks both making the coalition appear incoherent and unstable, and exposing fault-lines that can only widen as they attract media attention. On the other hand, coalitions are composed of separate parties, and these parties must preserve their distinctive identities in order to satisfy internal factions and party supporters. Stressing unity and blurring distinctiveness therefore risks opening up divisions between a party's parliamentary leaders and its grass-roots members.

▶ *Ideological and policy gaps.* Coalitions lack the tribal and ideological cohesion that bind a single-party government together. Instead, compromises have to be forged between parties with different ideological and policy preferences, and the scale and scope of these differences does much to determine the coalition's success or failure.

▶ *Balance between influence and blame.* An important possible source of tension within a coalition arises from the relative influence of the coalition partners. Smaller parties may become frustrated because they have marginal influence, or, if they exploit their pivotal power, they can become over-strong, leading to disaffection within the larger party. Similarly, blame may be disproportionately shared. In continental Europe, where coalitions are the norm, small parties usually have little policy influence, but shoulder more than their fair share of blame when things go wrong.

negotiating the programme of spending cuts with each government department. According to the Coalition Agreement for Stability and Reform (2010):

▶ The initial allocation of cabinet and other posts was agreed between the prime minister and the deputy prime minister.
▶ Future allocations will be approximately in proportion to the parliamentary strength of the two parties.
▶ The prime minister, in consultation with the deputy prime minister, will make nominations for the appointment of ministers.
▶ The prime minister will nominate Conservative ministers and the deputy prime minister will nominate Liberal Democrat ministers.
▶ No Liberal Democrat minister or whip may be removed on the recommendation of the prime minister without full consultation with the deputy prime minister.

The constraints that coalition government imposes on the prime minister's powers of patronage were quickly illustrated at the end of May 2010, when Laws resigned over controversy regarding his parliamentary expenses. The decision to replace him as Treasury secretary with another Liberal Democrat, Danny Alexander was in line with a like-for-like arrangement that maintained the party balance in the cabinet. At the same time, the failure to sack Vince Cable in December 2010, over remarks he voiced opposing to Rupert Murdoch's proposed take-over of BSkyB (a matter over which he should have been politically neutral), may also be instructive. Cameron and Clegg's reluctance to lose Cable reflected the important role that Cable plays in maintaining the coalition. Not only is Cable's business portfolio politically prominent, but he also enjoys significant support amongst grass-roots Liberal Democrats. His continued presence in the cabinet therefore tends to strengthen Liberal Democrat support for the coalition and keep disaffection within the party over the coalition under control. In any case, the treatment of Cable contrasted sharply with that of the coalition's enterprise tsar, the former Conservative cabinet minister Lord Young, who was sacked in November 2010 for suggesting that most British people had 'never had it so good' during the 'so-called recession'.

Nevertheless, the constraints that coalition government imposes on the prime minister do not stop with the exercise of prerogative powers. Rather, they extend across all the decision-making processes of government, inhibiting the prime minister's capacity to exert policy leadership. This occurs because, unlike single-party governments, coalitions involve an ongoing and complex process of negotiation, conciliation and conflict resolution between coalition partners. In the case of the Conservative–Liberal Democrat coalition, Cameron's policy influence has been limited in a number of ways:

▶ In relation to the significant range of topics over which there is deep disagreement between the Conservatives and the Liberal Democrats, independent commissions or policy reviews have been set up to develop compromise proposals. By January 2011, no fewer than 90 such commissions or reviews were in existence, considering topics ranging from the proposal for a British bill of rights and the replacement of the Trident nuclear system to the future of control orders on terrorist suspects. Such devices may help to keep the peace between coalition partners, but they also prevent the prime minister, or indeed any other senior minister, from taking personal control over controversial issues.

▶ One of the important features of coalition government is the greater need for formalized decision-making to maintain trust and transparency between coalition partners. This has occurred, among other things, through the development of the Cabinet Manual, published in 2011, which provides guidance about the conduct and relationships between government ministers. The greater emphasis on formal rules and official guidance makes a return to Blair-style 'sofa government' much more difficult, greatly restricting the prime minister's ability to influence departmental agendas through bilateral meetings with key ministers.

▶ In the case of higher level strategic and policy differences between the coalition partners, Cameron has used what is sometimes called 'the quad' – meetings between Cameron, Clegg and their two closest senior cabinet colleagues, the Chancellor George Osborne, and Danny Alexander. Such arrangements to ensure unity between the coalition partners are also evident in the fact that there is a Liberal Democrat presence in every government department and in the coalitions use of cabinet committees (see p. 256).

▶ Undoubtedly, the most important relationship within the coalition is between Cameron and Clegg, who quickly developed a close working relationship and meet on a regular basis. Some have argued that Clegg's 'deputy' role within this relationship is misleading as, to keep the coalition on track, the two must function as equals. This is especially the case, as Clegg's support was both crucial to the formation of the coalition in the first place and remains vital to its continued existence. The question is, then, how far is Clegg prepared to go in using his potential leverage?

However, it is by no means clear that the coalition always constrains Cameron's freedom of manoeuvre as prime minister. For example, during his first year in office, Cameron suffered no serious policy reverses due to opposition from within the cabinet or government. This was particularly remarkable in view of the controversial nature of many of the policies that the coalition was unveiling. One of the reasons for this may have been the prominence that senior Liberal Democrats have enjoyed within the coalition government's decision-making processes. As figures such as Clegg, Alexander and Cable have very clearly been 'insiders' rather than 'outsiders', this has made it more difficult for them to become a focus of disaffection. Clegg, the cabinet minister with the greatest capacity to constrain Cameron, operated, in the early period at least, less as a counterweight to the prime minister and more as his agent within the government and the wider coalition. This was in part, a reflection of the relatively narrow ideological and policy gap between Cameron and Clegg, and between leading Conservative 'modernizers' and senior Liberal Democrats. Indeed, in some ways, Cameron may enjoy much greater freedom of manoeuvre to pursue his favoured policy agenda within a coalition with the Liberal Democrats than he would have done leading a single-party Conservative government, especially one that either lacked a majority or had a slim majority. However, the defeat of AV and poor local election results in May 2011 may encourage Clegg personally and the Liberal Democrats generally to become more assertive in their dealings with Cameron and the Conservatives.

WHAT YOU SHOULD KNOW

▶▶ The executive is the branch of government that is responsible for the implementation of laws and policies made by Parliament. It comprises the political executive (roughly equivalent to the 'government of the day') and the official executive, the civil service.

▶▶ The prime minister is the single-most important figure in the UK political system. Traditionally, prime ministers were seen as 'first amongst equals', but this is now seriously outdated. The key aspects of the modern role of the prime minister are to make governments, direct government policy, manage the cabinet system, organize government, control Parliament and provide national leadership.

▶▶ The cabinet's role is to provide formal approval to government policy, help to coordinate policy and the workings of government, resolve high-level disputes that cannot be resolved elsewhere, act as a forum for debate, help to manage the majority party and maintain collective government.

▶▶ Ministers are departmental bosses, entrusted (in theory) with the making of policy. Civil servants provide policy advice and carry out government policy; they are meant to be permanent, neutral and anonymous. Recent changes have blurred the distinction between the two.

▶▶ The major theories of executive power are cabinet government, prime ministerial government, presidentialism and the core executive model. None of these models is 'true', but each contributes to our general understanding of the workings of executive power.

▶▶ Prime ministers are much more important than their 'constitutional' role suggests. Their key sources of power lie in their ability to hire and fire, to manage the cabinet, their leadership of the party, the institutional supports now available to them and their direct access to the media.

▶▶ The extent of prime ministerial power depends on three important sets of relationships. These are with the cabinet, individual ministers and government departments; with his or her party and, through it, with Parliament; and with the people, often through the media. The main constraints on a prime minister are the cabinet, the party (which can ultimately remove him or her), public opinion and the electorate, the media and the pressure of events.

▶▶ Coalition government generally constrains the prime minister, as coalition management dictates that the junior partner and factions within both coalition parties must be conciliated. But, if senior relationships are strong, coalitions may also benefit the prime minister. However, the implications of coalition government for the prime minister are certain to be fluid, affected as they will be by the changing balance between unity and distinctiveness within the coalition itself.

Test yourself

Short questions:

1 Outline *two* functions of the prime minister.
2 Outline *two* functions of the cabinet.
3 What is cabinet government?
4 What is prime ministerial government?
5 Outline the role of a minister.
6 How do ministers differ from civil servants?
7 What is the core executive?
8 Outline *two* powers of the prime minister.

Medium questions:

9 Distinguish between the conventions of collective responsibility and individual responsibility.
10 How do prime ministers control the cabinet?
11 What are the main sources of prime ministerial power?
12 In what circumstances do ministers resign?
13 Explain *three* factors that may affect the appointment of ministers.
14 Explain *three* factors that limit the power of the prime minister.
15 Distinguish between the role of a prime minister and the role of a president.
16 Explain the main relationships within the core executive.

Extended questions:

17 To what extent does the prime minister control the cabinet?
18 Have prime ministers become more powerful, or less powerful, in recent years?
19 To what extent have UK prime ministers become more like presidents?
20 Discuss the view that all of the prime minister's powers are limited.
21 Assess the limitations on the prime minister.
22 To what extent does the UK still have collective cabinet government?
23 How, and to what extent, does coalition government affect the power of the prime minister?
24 To what extent do prime ministers' personalities and leadership styles affect their power?
25 'Prime ministers are only as powerful as their parties allow them to be.' Discuss.

Chapter 9

Judges and Civil Liberties

Is the law political?

Law and politics are supposed to be different things. Law is a form of social control; it defines what *can* and what *cannot* be done. When judges administer the law, by presiding over court proceedings, they are meant to act in a strictly non-political way. Being neutral and independent from the other institutions of government, judges (and therefore law itself) are 'above' politics. How accurate is this image of non-political judges and a non-political court system?

In practice, law and politics are closely related to one another. The laws that judges administer are made by politicians, and so reflect particular moral, social and political values. Furthermore, the law does not speak for itself; it is interpreted by judges who may be influenced by their own beliefs and prejudices. Can judges (or, for that matter, any of us) be strictly impartial? Political pressures also come from outside. Ministers, MPs, the tabloid press and lobby groups of various kinds are increasingly willing to express views about judicial decisions, especially in high-profile cases to do with terrorism and rape, for instance. Indeed, especially under New Labour, civil liberties became a major battleground between judges and ministers. Finally, recent years have seen major changes within the judiciary. The introduction in 2009 of a Supreme Court tends to strengthen the tendency for senior judges in the UK to act as policy-makers, threatening to give them a role similar to that of US judges.

- **What is the role of the judiciary?**
- **How independent are judges?**
- **Can judges be morally and politically neutral?**
- **What are civil liberties, and how are they protected in the UK?**
- **How and why have judges and ministers clashed in recent years?**
- **How can the judiciary best be reformed?**

GETTING YOU THINKING

Rights in conflict?

Before starting the chapter, read this passage and briefly consider the questions on the next page.

On 18 May 2010, two Pakistani students, Abid Nasser and Ahmad Faraz Khan, won their appeals against deportation after a hearing by the Special Immigration Appeals Commission (SIAC). The two men were among 11 who had been arrested in April 2009 amid fears that they were planning a bomb attack on targets in Manchester. The ruling occurred despite the SIAC being satisfied that Nasser was an al-Qaeda operative who posed a serious threat to the national security of the UK. The ruling was criticized by the home secretary, Theresa May, and effectively scuppered the government's attempts to dispose of the much criticised control orders of its Labour predecessor and centre its counter-terrorism strategy, on removing foreign terrorist suspects to their country of origin. May's criticism stressed the need for a balance between respect for individual rights and civil liberties, on the one hand, and the need to protect the public, on the other. However, others believe that the courts in this and other cases are playing a crucial role in preventing a slide towards authoritarianism, which would allow the government to abuse rights and basic freedoms almost at will.

The ruling in this cased was based on Article 3 of the European Convention on Human Rights, incorporated into UK law by the Human Rights Act of 1998, which states that 'No one shall be subject to torture or inhuman or degrading treatment or behaviour.' In this case, the SIAC accepted evidence that 'there is a long and well-documented history of disappearances, illegal detention and torture' in Pakistan. From the human rights perspective, the right not to be tortured is a fundamental and universal right. It is a right that belongs to all people regardless of nationality, and it should not be set aside for reasons of political inconvenience. Supporters of this view therefore reject the very idea of a 'balance' between liberty and public safety.

Counter-terrorism officers showing their presence at a London mainline station – but is the protection of the public putting basic freedoms at risk?

What issues do these developments raise?

▶▶▶ On what grounds were the two Pakistani men allowed to remain in the UK?

▶▶▶ Why has the ruling been criticized?

▶▶▶ Should human rights be treated as fundamental and universal?

▶▶▶ Who should make decisions about the extent of civil liberty in the UK: judges or politicians?

▶▶▶ Where should the balance lie between upholding rights and protecting the public?

IN THIS CHAPTER:

The role of judges   •   Judges and civil liberties   •   Reform of the judiciary

The role of judges

Judiciary: The branch of government that is responsible for deciding legal disputes and which presides over the court system.

The chief role of the **judiciary** is to define the meaning of law. In this sense, judges interpret or 'construct' law. This is in line with the principle of the separation of powers, which establishes a three fold distinction between the various functions of government and the institutions that exist to carry out those functions. In this view, judges do not 'make' law, they only apply the law as laid down by Parliament. However, in practice, the role of judges is more complex than the principle of the separation of powers implies. Not only is it difficult to determine where *interpreting* law ends and *making* law begins, but judges are often drawn into wider, non-judicial activities that may overlap with the functions of other branches of government.

What do judges do?

Judges carry out a variety of roles, judicial and non-judicial. Judges:

▶ **Preside over court proceedings.** In this role, judges make sure that the rules of court procedure are properly followed by both sides in a case. A judge acts rather like an umpire or referee in a sporting competition. Their job is to ensure a 'fair trial'. In carrying out this role, judges also serve as a source of specialist knowledge, providing, for example, advice to juries in criminal cases on points of law and, possibly, directing a verdict.

▶ **Interpret and apply the law.** This, in most cases, means that they interpret statutes laid down by Parliament. Although, in theory, judges apply 'the letter of the law', they are able to exercise a measure of discretion in the way that they interpret statutes. However, this can lead to conflicting interpretations by judges and by ministers.

▶ **'Make' law, in certain cases.** In a sense, all law is 'judge-made' law. This is because laws ultimately mean what judges say they mean. But some laws are more 'judge-made' than others. Whereas judges can only *interpret* Acts of Parliament, they effectively *determine* the nature of **common law**. Common law, which is particularly important in the English legal tradition, is built up on the basis of judicial precedent. This happens as judges in one case accept judgements in earlier similar cases as binding, through what is known as 'case law'. Such law is therefore, in effect, made up of a collection of decisions made by judges.

Common law: Law that is based on long-standing customs and traditions; common law is used mainly in the UK and its former colonies.

What is ... the separation of powers

Proposed by the French political philosopher, Montesquieu (1689–1755), the doctrine of the separation of powers proposes that each of the three key functions of government should be carried out by separate and independent branches of government. These functions and branches are:

Function	Branch
make law	Legislature
implement/execute law	Executive
interpret law	Judiciary

The separation of powers aims to fragment government power in the hope of preventing tyranny and protecting freedom. Its purpose is to ensure that 'power is a checked power'. Most rigorously applied in the USA, but found to some degree in all liberal democracies, it implies that the three branches of government should be both *independent* from one another (with no overlaps of personnel) and *interdependent* (giving rise to checks and balances (see p. 186) between and amongst the branches).

Mandatory sentences: Sentences that are laid down in legislation, and so remove discretion over sentences from judges.

▶ **Decide sentencing in criminal cases.** This is a further important area of discretion, as judges have traditionally had a free hand in deciding what sentences to hand out. Nevertheless, this role has been reduced in recent years, as a result of the wider use of minimum or **mandatory sentences**. Some judges have argued, in turn, that mandatory sentences allow politicians to encroach on the role of the judiciary.

▶ **Chair public inquiries and commissions.** Judges are used for this purpose because of their reputation for being independent and impartial. Public enquiries are also run like court proceedings, and may even have a quasi-judicial character. Such a role has also led to criticism, however. In chairing inquiries, judges inevitably come into close contact with ministers and senior officials, and this may compromise their independence and tend to give them a pro-government bias.

Examples of prominent public inquiries chaired by judges include:

▶ Lord Nolan's inquiry into standards in public life (1995)
▶ Lord Scott's inquiry into the sale of arms to Iraq (1996)
▶ Sir William MacPherson's inquiry into the killing of the black teenager, Stephen Lawrence (1999)
▶ Lord Hutton's inquiry into the circumstances of the death of the weapons expert, David Kelly (2003)

▶ Lord Saville's inquiry into the Bloody Sunday massacre in 1972 in Northern Ireland (reported in 2010).

Weblink ■ www.hmcourts-service.gov.uk

Use the government's Court Service website to find more information about the court system and related matters.

The rule of law

Rule of law: The principle that law should 'rule', in the sense that it applies to all conduct or behaviour and covers both private citizens and public officials.

The **rule of law** is one of the fundamental principles of the UK's 'unwritten' or uncodified constitution. The key idea of the rule of law is that the law should apply equally to all, rulers and ruled alike. This, in the words of the 19th-century constitutional expert A. V. Dicey, ensures a 'government of laws' and not a 'government of men'. The alternative to the rule of law is therefore arbitrary government. In this way, the rule of law establishes the relationship between government and the people. As John Locke (1632–1704) put it, 'Wherever law ends, tyranny begins'.

However, the rule of law is a complex principle, and it is best explained as a collection of sub-principles. There has been, moreover, significant debate about how far the law 'rules' the UK. Harden and Lewis (1988) even described the rule of law as the 'noble lie' of the British constitution. The most important sub-principles are:

▶ **No one is 'above' the law.** This implies that everyone is bound by the law. The law applies to ministers and public officials as well as to other members of

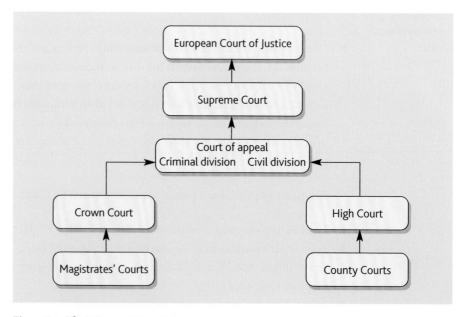

Figure 9.1 **The UK court structure**

Administrative law: The body of law that governs the exercise of powers and duties by public authorities.

society. This is supposed to ensure that public officials use their power reasonably and do not exceed the limits placed on its use. This aspect of the rule of law is upheld through **administrative law** and by the practice of judicial review (see pp. 287–8).

However, concerns have been expressed about the extent to which this principle applies in the UK:

- Many of the powers of the prime minister and other ministers are based on the Royal Prerogative, which is not subject to judicial oversight.
- As Parliament is sovereign, it can make, unmake and amend any law it wishes and so, in that sense, it is 'above' the law.
- The principle of **parliamentary privilege** means that MPs and peers are not subject to legal restrictions on what they can say in Parliament.
- The Queen, as head of the legal system, is not properly subject to the law.

Parliamentary privilege: A set of legal privileges intended to safeguard MPs and peers from outside interference, notably the right to absolute freedom of speech within Parliament.

- **Equality before the law.** The law is meant to treat all citizens alike; it is no respecter of persons. All people should therefore have the same legal rights and have the same access to the legal system. Considerations of race, colour, creed, religion, wealth, social status and official position must be irrelevant to how people are treated by the court system.

  However, concerns have been expressed about the extent to which this principle applies in the UK:

  - Legal disputes may be prohibitively costly for many, and only the wealthy can afford to be represented by top lawyers.
  - Access to legal aid is not always easy and may exclude people from middle-income groups.
  - Judges may be biased against, for instance, women, ethnic minorities and the poor because they tend to come from narrow and privileged social and educational backgrounds (as discussed below).

- **The law is always applied.** Disputes must be resolved by the application of the law rather than by other means. This means that there must be a certainty of punishment for breaches of law – law cannot apply in certain circumstances but not in others. By the same token, there should be punishment *only* for breaches of law – people should not be penalized except through the **due process** of law.

Due process: The proper conduct of legal proceedings, involving, in particular, respect for an individual's legal rights.

  However, concerns have been expressed about the extent to which this principle applies in the UK:

  - Not all crimes are reported and therefore legally addressed (this applies, for instance, in the case of most rapes).

What is ... human rights

Human rights are rights to which people are entitled by virtue of being human. They are a modern and secular version of what used to be called 'natural' rights, which were believed to be God-given. Human rights are:

▶ *Universal* in that they belong to all humans everywhere, regardless of nationality, ethnic or racial origin, social background, and so on
▶ *Fundamental* in that they are inalienable — a human being's entitlement to them cannot be removed
▶ *Absolute* in that, as the basic grounds for living a genuinely human life, they cannot be qualified (they must be fully upheld in all circumstances).

Although human rights are moral assertions, they have increasingly formed part of international law. The best examples of this are the UN Declaration of Human Rights (1948) and the European Convention of Human Rights and Fundamental Freedoms (1953).

> ▶ As police resources are limited, many crimes are not detected (for example, speeding offences).
> ▶ 'Trial by the media' means that people may be 'punished' without legal proceedings having taken place, or, perhaps, despite being acquitted.

▶ **Legal redress is available through the courts.** If people's rights have been infringed (whether by other citizens, organizations or the state), they should be able to protect themselves through the law. For many legal experts and a growing body of senior judges, this implies that the law should defend fundamental human rights. This is the aspect of the rule of law that safeguards the individual from the state.

However, concerns have been expressed about the extent to which this principle applies in the UK:

> ▶ There is no entrenched bill of rights (see p. 295) to protect fundamental human rights.
> ▶ The Human Rights Act can be set aside, if Parliament wishes.
> ▶ Access to the European Court of Human Rights is expensive and time-consuming.

Judges and politics

One crucial aspect of the role of the judiciary is that judges are meant to be strictly impartial and non-political. This is one of the basic differences between liberal democracies and authoritarian regimes. In the latter, the courts simply become instruments of the state. In the Soviet Union, for example, judges applied what was called 'socialist legality' and, during the 1930s in particular, 'show trials' were used to expose and punish opponents of the regime. By contrast, in liberal democracies, the authority of law is linked to the fact that it is supposed to be non-political. This, in turn, is based on the assumption that the law is interpreted by judges who are independent and impartial.

Judges may be 'political' in two senses: they may be subject to external bias or to internal bias:

▶ *External* bias comes from the influence that other political bodies, particularly the executive and Parliament, are able to exert on the judiciary.
▶ *Internal* bias stems from the prejudices and sympathies of judges themselves, particularly when these influence the decisions they make.

These two forms of bias are meant to be kept at bay through the principles of judicial independence and judicial neutrality.

Are judges independent?

Judicial independence:
The principle that the actions and decisions of judges should not be influenced by pressure from other branches of government.

The principle of **judicial independence** is one of the key parts of the constitution. Based on the separation of powers, it holds that there should be a strict separation between the judiciary and other branches of government. Judges can therefore apply the law as their own experience and legal training dictates, rather than as ministers, civil servants or parliamentarians would wish. As such, judicial independence is a vital guarantee of the rule of law. Law cannot act as a constraint on government if the executive and Parliament can influence judges in how they interpret and apply the law. How is judicial independence maintained? And how far is it upheld in practice?

The independence of the judiciary is maintained in a number of ways:

▶ **Appointment process.** The process through which judges are appointed is meant to involve little political interference; otherwise, judges may be selected on the basis of their sympathy for the government of the day. When judges were appointed by the prime minister and the Lord Chancellor, it was very difficult to rule out the influence of political considerations. However, the establishment of the Judicial Appointments Commission has introduced greater independence into this process (see How judges are appointed, p. 282).

▶ **Security of tenure.** Security of tenure means that once they are appointed, judges cannot be sacked. They remain in office until their retirement age of 70. The possibility of removal or demotion cannot therefore be used to affect their

FOCUS ON . . .
How judges are appointed

- The process for making senior judicial appointments has changed significantly in recent years. Traditionally, Law Lords and Appeal Court judges were appointed by the prime minister on the advice of the Lord Chancellor, while High Court judges and more junior judges were appointed by the Lord Chancellor. To be eligible for judicial appointment, candidates had to have a minimum of 20 years' experience as a barrister or, since 1990, as a solicitor with substantial experience as an advocate.

- The Constitutional Reform Act led to the creation of a Judicial Appointments Commision (JAC), launched in April 2006. The JAC now has the job of selecting candi-dates for appointment to judicial office in England and Wales. Formal selection continues to be made by the Lord Chancellor. The Lord Chancellor may reject the first candidate proposed by the JAC, but not the second. Both the JAC and the Lord Chancellor are both required to appoint judges strictly on the basis of merit. The Commission has 15 members including six lay people and five judges.

- Members of the Supreme Court are appointed by a selection commission composed of the President and Deputy President of the Supreme Court and a member of the judicial appointment bodies for England and Wales, Scotland and Northern Ireland.

Weblink ■ www.supremecourt.gov.uk

Use the Supreme Court website for information about the composition and workings of the Court, and its recent judgements.

---

decision-making. Senior judges can only be removed by an address of both houses of Parliament, something that has not happened since 1830. Junior judges enjoy security of tenure during 'good behaviour' and can be removed by the Lord Chancellor if, for instance, they are found guilty of a criminal offence.

- **Pay.** The pay and rewards of judges are safeguarded from political influence. Judges are paid out of the Consolidated Fund, which is not subject to annual review by the House of Commons, and their salaries and other forms of remuneration are decided by an independent pay review body.

- **Freedom from criticism.** There are constitutional conventions that forbid MPs and peers – and therefore also ministers – from putting pressure on judges by criticizing court rulings and judicial decisions in Parliament (although, as will be seen later, these are often breached in practice). These conventions are meant to apply to ministers as well. The '*sub judice*' rule forbids people, including politicians, from commenting on cases that are currently being considered.

▶ **Independent legal profession.** Judges are appointed from the ranks of lawyers who belong to an autonomous legal profession. Standards within the profession are regulated by the Law Society, not by government. Lawyers and judges are therefore not trained by the state, as in some other European countries.

▶ **Role of the Lord Chancellor.** The Lord Chancellor was once a major threat to judicial independence, being both the head of the judiciary and a member of the cabinet. Since 2006, the former role has been transferred to the Lord Chief Justice, and the Lord Chancellor's influence over judicial appointments has been much reduced. Under the Constitutional Reform Act (CRA) 2005, the Lord Chancellor has to swear an oath to defend the independence of the judiciary.

▶ **Creation of the Supreme Court.** The CRA also provided for the replacement of the House of Lords as the highest court of appeal in the UK by the Supreme Court, which was established in 2009. The Supreme Court significantly strengthens judicial independence as it breaks the link between the courts and Parliament. The Law Lords of old used to sit in the House of Lords, constituting its appellate committee.

In view of the potential political significance of judicial decisions, the independence of judges is always a principle under pressure. Traditionally, the main concern about the effectiveness of judicial independence focused on the appointment process. While this was controlled by the prime minister and the Lord Chancellor, and so long as the Lord Chancellor's office 'fused' the roles of head of the judiciary and cabinet minister, judicial independence always appeared to be a constitutional fiction. This concern has substantially been addressed though the establishment of the Judicial Appointments Commission.

A second concern about judicial independence stems from a growing willingness of ministers publicly to criticize the courts. This has particularly applied in the case of successive home secretaries. Examples of this include:

▶ In 2003, David Blunkett condemned the release of the nine Afghan hijackers.
▶ In 2005, Charles Clarke criticized the release of terrorist suspects from Belmarsh Prison.
▶ In 2007, John Reid attacked the decision not to deport the murderer of the London headmaster, Philip Lawrence, when he is released.

▶ In 2010, Theresa May criticized the refusal to deport two terrorist suspects to Pakistan, despite it having been acknowledged that they had links to al-Qaeda.

In being increasingly willing to make public statements about how the courts should address issues related to public order and civil liberties, and in expressing disappointment at the stance that judges have taken, the principle of judicial independence has been tested to its limits. On the other hand, there is little evidence that judges have been cowed by this public criticism. If anything, evidence of greater **judicial activism** in recent years suggests a determination on the part of judges to develop their own view of the 'proper' application of law. Increasingly common public clashes between ministers and judges therefore provide evidence of the health of judicial independence. After all, beyond public criticism, ministers have few other ways in which they can influence judicial decision-making except through the introduction of new Acts of Parliament.

Judicial activism: The willingness of judges to arbitrate in political disputes, as opposed to merely declaring the 'letter of the law'.

Are judges neutral?

Neutrality: The absence of any form of partisanship or commitment; a refusal to 'take sides'.

The other way in which judges may be political is through their own biases or prejudices; in other words, they may lack **neutrality**. Judicial neutrality implies, strictly speaking, that judges have no political sympathies or ideological leanings. Neutral judges are therefore political eunuchs. In practice, however, neutrality in this sense is perhaps impossible to achieve – all people have their own views and opinions; no one is capable of being completely impartial and objective. As a result, like other public officials (such as civil servants, the police and the military) judges are meant to be neutral in the sense that they are able to ensure that their own views and beliefs do not *affect* their professional behaviour. Personal preferences and beliefs must, if you like, be left at the court door. If internal bias does not intrude, judges will be able to act on the basis of legal considerations alone. How is judicial neutrality maintained? And how effective is it in practice?

Judicial neutrality is maintained in a number of ways:

▶ **Political restrictions.** Judges are not supposed to engage in open political activity. Although magistrates may be members of political parties, this would not be acceptable for judges. Similarly, judges are expected not to express open support for pressure groups or protest movements.

▶ **Legal training.** The extensive process of legal training (senior judges have usually worked as barristers or junior judges for between 20 and 30 years) is designed to enable judges to focus entirely on legal considerations. Their ability to act impartially and objectively is strengthened by the requirement that court proceedings are conducted fairly and that judgements are based on evidence.

▶ **Accountability.** A further factor that strengthens objectivity is that senior judges must explain their rulings, highlighting, in the process, the points of law that have affected them. Accountability is also upheld by the existence of appeals and, therefore, by the knowledge that cases can be reheard by higher courts.

▶ **Not public figures.** Judges have traditionally been discouraged from speaking out on political matters and from becoming involved in public controversy. The so-called 'Kilmuir rules', issued in the mid-1950s, forbade judges from participating in public debates about policy matters in order to preserve their neutrality. However, as will be seen, these restrictions have been relaxed since the late 1980s.

The main attacks on judicial neutrality have traditionally come from the political left. In his classic study of the politics of the judiciary, Griffiths (1997) argued that a conservative bias tends to operate within the senior judiciary, which stems from the fact that judges are overwhelmingly male, white, upper-middle-class and public-school and 'Oxbridge' educated. Similar arguments have been used to suggest that judges are biased against women, ethnic minorities and, indeed, any group poorly represented within the ranks of the senior judiciary. Such concerns were particularly prominent during the 1980s, linked to the rulings made by Lord Denning and Lord Donaldson, who was a former Conservative councillor and public critic of trade union power. Although the views and preferences of senior UK judges have become both more diverse and more liberal in recent years, this has yet to be reflected in a diversity of backgrounds. For example, in 2007:

▶ Of 639 Circuit judges, only 73 were female.
▶ Of 108 High Court judges, only one was from an ethnic minority.
▶ Regarding education, 70 per cent of judges were privately educated and 78 per cent went to Oxford or Cambridge.

Other concerns about judicial neutrality have arisen from a growing trend for senior judges in the UK to take a public stand on policy issues. This has occurred, in part, because of the removal in the late 1980s of restrictions on judges engaging in public debate, in the belief that their expertise and experience would assist the policy process. By writing articles and delivering speeches, and sometimes through their written judgements, senior judges in recent years have demon-strated growing support for human rights and **civil liberties**. This could be seen in the 1998 Law Lords' ruling that the former Chilean dictator, General Pinochet, should be extradited to Spain to face charges of murder, torture and genocide. It was later revealed that one of the Law Lords, Lord Hoffman, had failed to disclose his links to the human rights group Amnesty International, and the ruling was

Civil liberties: A range of rights and freedoms that belong to the citizen and mark out a 'private' realm which government should leave alone (see p. 286).

What is ... civil liberty

Civil liberty marks out a 'private' sphere of existence that belongs to the citizen, not the state. Civil liberties therefore encompass a range of rights and freedoms that are 'negative' in the sense that they demand non-interference on the part of government. Civil liberties often overlap with, and may be based on, human rights; but the two ideas are different. Whereas civil liberties are rights that are based on citizenship and are therefore specific to particular states, human rights, by definition, belong to all people in all societies. The classic civil liberties are usually thought to include:

▶ Freedom of speech
▶ Freedom of the press
▶ Freedom of religion
▶ Freedom of association.

Civil liberties are often confused with civil rights. The former are freedoms *from* government; the latter are generally 'positive' rights, rights of participation and access to power. Civil rights campaigns typically call for a widening of voting and political rights, and for an end to discrimination, as in the case of the US civil rights movement in the 1960s.

subsequently overturned. Recent Lord Chief Justices have also, at times, launched outspoken attacks on government policy:

International law:
The rules that define the behaviour of, and relationship between, states; the UN is the main source of international law.

▶ Lord Bingham, Lord Chief Justice 1996–2000, called for the rule of law to be understood to include protection for fundamental human rights and to require that states comply with their obligations under **international law**.
▶ Lord Woolf, Lord Chief Justice 2000–05, spoke out against some of the provisions of the Constitutional Reform Act and severely criticized the government's handling of the constitutional reform process.
▶ Lord Phillips, Lord Chief Justice 2005–08 (and the first to be head of the English and Welsh judiciary), criticized the wider use of mandatory sentences and, in 2007, strongly condemned proposals for the creation of a Ministry of Justice.

Although such interventions demonstrate the robust independence of the senior judiciary in the UK, they also highlight the extent to which judges have become public figures whose views can no longer be said to be 'above' politics.

Weblink ■ www.justice.gov.uk

Use the website of the Ministry of Justice to find out more about the administration of justice in England and Wales. The Ministry of Justice is responsible for the courts, prisons, probation, criminal law and sentencing.

Judges and civil liberties

Protecting civil liberties

The maintenance of civil liberties is generally seen as a defining feature of a liberal democracy. This is because civil liberties establish the relationship between the state and the individual. In doing this, they provide citizens with protection from government interference. The UK's commitment to civil liberties has traditionally been weak by comparison with countries such as the USA and France, where they are formally enshrined in constitutional documents. The US Declaration of Independence (1776) expressed a commitment to the 'unalienable rights' of life, liberty and the pursuit of happiness. The first ten amendments of the US Constitution, ratified in 1791, constitute the 'Bill of Rights', and are largely made up of civil liberties, including the right to freedom of religion, speech, the press, and assembly (The First Amendment), the right to keep and bear arms (The Second Amendment), and so on. The French Revolution led to the establishment of the Declaration of the Rights of Man and the Citizen (1789).

By contrast, the UK has traditionally been reluctant to give basic rights and freedoms explicit legal expression. Instead, it relied on the freedoms that were supposed to be embodied in the common law belief that 'everything is permitted that is not prohibited'. In other words, UK citizens had 'residual' rights; they had the right to do anything that the law did not forbid. As these 'residual' rights were never clearly spelled out, they were very difficult to uphold in law. Furthermore, if UK citizens thought that their rights and freedoms were under threat, they had only a limited range of ways in which to seek redress. These included contacting an MP or local councillor, appealing to an administrative tribunal, or complaining to an **ombudsman**. However, in recent years, the protection of civil liberties has increasingly fallen to the courts. This has happened for two reasons:

▶ The wider use of the power of judicial review
▶ The introduction of the Human Rights Act.

Judicial review

Judicial review is an important way in which judges can check the powers of other public bodies. In the USA, judges have very far-reaching powers of judicial review because of the existence of a codified constitution. As the US Constitution lays down the powers of other branches of government, judges can declare their actions to be 'unconstitutional' if they conflict with the provisions of the constitution. In the UK, in the absence of a codified constitution, judicial review is not so far-reaching. In particular, judges cannot overturn Acts of Parliament because of the principle of parliamentary sovereignty. Nevertheless, they can determine the lawfulness of actions that are carried out on the basis of **delegated legislation**.

Ombudsman: A public officer appointed to safeguard citizens' rights and investigate allegations of maladministration; the Parliamentary Commissioner for Administration, set up in 1967, acts as the 'parliamentary ombudsman'.

Judicial review: The power of the judiciary to 'review' and possibly overturn laws, decrees and actions of other branches of government and public bodies.

Delegated legislation: Laws that allow other bodies to act with Parliament's legal authority; secondary or enabling legislation.

Ultra vires: Literally, 'beyond the power'; this applies when public servants have acted illegally because their actions have no statutory authority.

This is done by using the doctrine of **ultra vires**. Judges can decide, quite simply, that other political actors are acting beyond their proper powers. In recent years, judges have been increasingly willing to use this power, particularly in relation to ministers.

Judges have traditionally been reluctant to use their powers of judicial review. However, the growth in judicial activism since the 1980s has seen a steep rise in its use. In 1980, there were only 533 applications for judicial review, but by 1999 this had risen to over 4,500. In many cases, judicial review has been applied to administrative tribunals dealing with subjects such as finance and tax, pensions appeals, and the provision of social security and child support. In other cases, ministers have been in the firing line. Between 1992 and 1996, the then home secretary, Michael Howard, was defeated by the courts on no fewer than ten occasions. More recent examples include the 2011 High Court ruling that the education secretary Michael Gove had abused his power in failing properly to consult six councils over plans to scrap their school building programmes.

However, the use of judicial review has proved to be controversial. On the one hand, it has proved to be an important way in which judges can protect civil liberties and ensure that ministers do not act in ways that are illegal, improper, irrational or simply disproportional. On the other hand, the growth of judicial activism has been criticized because it allows judges, in effect, to make policy and, in the process, to challenge the authority of elected governments.

The Human Rights Act 1998

The Human Rights Act (HRA), which came into effect in 2000, incorporated the European Convention on Human Rights (ECHR) into UK law. (The ECHR is not related to the EU.) The Act was a major constitutional reform in that it marked a shift in the UK in favour of an explicit and codified legal definition of individual rights. In doing so, it substantially widened the capacity of the judiciary to protect civil liberties and check the exercise of executive power and, in certain respects, legislative power. However, the HRA did not introduce any new rights. Its main provision is that courts should interpret all legislation (statutes and delegated legislation) in such a way as to be compatible with the European Convention. The UK ratified the European Convention in 1951 (it came into force in 1953) and British citizens have had the right of access to the European Court of Human Rights in Strasbourg since 1966. The main impact of the HRA has therefore been that it has made the European Convention substantially more accessible to UK citizens. Access to the Strasbourg court was very costly and extremely time-consuming. However, the HRA has brought the European Convention to the forefront of UK politics, influencing both judicial decision-making and affecting the behaviour of all public bodies.

The European Convention establishes a wide range of rights, including the following:

- ▶ Right to life
- ▶ Freedom from torture
- ▶ Freedom from slavery or forced labour
- ▶ Right to liberty and security
- ▶ Right to a fair trial
- ▶ No punishment without trial
- ▶ Right to respect for private and family life
- ▶ Freedom of thought, conscience and religion
- ▶ Freedom of expression
- ▶ Freedom of assembly and association (including the right to join a trade union)
- ▶ Right to marry
- ▶ Freedom from discrimination (sex, race, colour, language, religion, and so on)
- ▶ Right to education
- ▶ Right to free elections with a secret ballot.

The HRA is, nevertheless, a statute of a very particular kind. It does not constitute an entrenched bill of rights, and it cannot be used to overturn Acts of Parliament. It does not, therefore, invest the judiciary with the powers of constitutional judicial review. Nevertheless, when a court believes that legislation cannot be reconciled with Convention rights, it issues a 'declaration of incompatibility'. This forces Parliament (or, in practice, the executive) either to revise the legislation in question and bring it into line with the Convention, or to set aside certain of its provisions through the process of 'derogation' (meaning the repeal or modification of a law). The UK, for instance, derogated from Article 5 of the European Convention, during 2001–05, in order to pass 'tougher' anti-terrorism legislation. As the HRA is not binding on Parliament, it may not be considered as 'higher' law. Rather, it hovers somewhere between an ordinary statute law and an entrenched bill of rights.

Cases in which the HRA or the ECHR have been used to protect or extend individual rights include the following:

- ▶ The rights of 'spouses' to succeed to a tenancy in the event of a tenant's death was extended to homosexual couples (2004).
- ▶ Nine terrorist suspects held without trial in Belmarsh Prison were released on the grounds that the law on which their detention was based discriminated illegally between foreign nationals and UK subjects (2004).
- ▶ The decision not to deport the murderer of Philip Lawrence when his sentence is completed to his country of origin, Italy (2007).
- ▶ The Court of Appeal blocked the deportation to Jordan of Abu Qatada, believed to be a senior figure in al-Qaeda (2008).
- ▶ In a ruling linked to the HRA, the Supreme Court declared that measures to freeze the assets of terrorist suspects were unlawful (2010).

▶ An immigration tribunal prevented the deportation to Pakistan of two terrorist suspects associated with al-Qaeda (2010).

The HRA, and the rulings that have been made under it, have led to considerable controversy. Supporters of the HRA argue that it has significantly strengthened the ability of judges to apply the rule of law and uphold individual rights, including the rights of unpopular minorities. This will, over time, force ministers and other public bodies to be more sensitive to civil liberties issues, thereby promoting greater accountability and improving trust in government. This also extends to the wider public, for whom the HRA has had educational benefits. It has made citizens more aware of their rights and encouraged them to be more assertive in protecting them. In this way, the HRA helps to fulfil one of the functions that, in other systems, is performed by a 'written' constitution. The HRA may, indeed, be a particularly good example of the benefits of the UK's flexible and pragmatic constitution. It provides more effective protection for civil liberties but stops short of allowing judges to strike down Acts of Parliament.

Criticisms of the HRA have come from various directions, though. First, it is commonly argued that the Act allows judges to overstep their traditional role. Through their interpretation of the HRA, judges are, effectively, able to 'rewrite' legislation. This, arguably, makes judges too strong, in that they are able to act more like judges in the USA, who are able to encroach on the policy-making role of politicians. How appropriate is it for the courts to have 'quasi-legislative' powers under which unelected and socially unrepresentative judges can alter the law on policy matters, like access to social security and the right to a tenancy? Second, Conservatives in particular have called either for the amendment or the removal of the HRA, on the grounds that it constitutes an abstract set of principles which, once applied, lead to confusion and bad decisions. (This view, nevertheless, fails to take account of the fact that there is nothing new about HRA rights, the European Convention having been accepted by Labour and Conservative governments in the UK since the early 1950s.) Third, the HRA – or, more commonly, judges' interpretation of the Act – has been criticized for applying an unbalanced view of individual rights that fails to take sufficient account of civic responsibilities or the need to protect the larger society. This has lead to a battle over how civil liberties should be understood between judges and politicians.

Civil liberties under threat?

Conflict in recent years between senior judges and the executive has been the result of at least three factors:

▶ The growth of a human rights culture amongst the senior judiciary, which has been reflected in a greater *willingness* of judges to challenge ministers

▶ The impact of the Human Rights Act, which has widened the *ability* of judges to intervene in politics

▶ A (perceived or actual) trend for governments to expand their own powers, often at the expense of civil liberties and individual rights.

Authoritarianism: The practice of rule 'from above'; government that is imposed on citizens regardless of their consent.

The third of these developments has led to allegations about the growth of **authoritarianism** in the UK. The 2007 film, *Taking Liberties*, which examined the Blair government's record on civil liberties, even warned about the emergence in the UK of a 'police state'. Have civil liberties been under threat? If so, why has this happened?

The Labour government's record on civil liberties between 1997 and 2010 was a mixed one. In the first place, this period witnessed major advances in individual rights, widely welcomed by groups campaigning on civil liberties issues, such as Charter 88, Liberty, and Freedom and Law. The Human Rights Act was the most significant example of this, but others included the Freedom of Information Act 2000, which marked a major advance in open government and helped to establish a public right to know. Other examples of a strengthening of rights include the establishment of the right to roam through the Countryside and Rights of Way Act 2000. This was a culmination of many generations of campaigning by ramblers and civil liberties groups.

On the other hand, Labour's critics drew attention to its civil liberties 'blind spot', reflected in the growth of legislation that expands the power of the state and weakens or removes civil liberties or individual rights. Various measures have contributed to this 'drift towards authoritarianism'. For example:

▶ The right to a jury trial was restricted in 1999 by new rules that made it more difficult for people accused of theft, burglary and assault from opting to be tried by a Crown Court (where juries sit), rather than by a magistrate.

▶ Detention was introduced for asylum seekers whose claims have been refused, and access to the benefits system was replaced by shopping vouchers for refugees.

▶ Public order legislation led to restrictions being imposed on the right to protest.

▶ Anti-social behaviour orders (ASBOs), first introduced in 1999, imposed a range of restrictions on (usually young) 'offenders', often on the basis of hearsay evidence and in the absence of a jury.

▶ The Identity Card Act 2006 provided for identity cards to be phased-in on a voluntary basis from 2009 (although these plans were abandoned after Labour's 2010 defeat).

However, the government's most controversial measures were its anti-terrorism legislation, passed in the aftermath of 9/11 (the 2001 terrorist attack on New York and Washington) and 7/7 (the coordinated 2005 terrorist attacks on London).

These laws were controversial because they have, in various ways, allowed the government to detain people without trial. The right to a fair trial is sometimes seen as the core civil liberty, because, without it, the government would be able to punish citizens without having to prove that they have broken the law.

Three major pieces of anti-terrorism legislation have been significant:

▶ *The Anti-terrorism, Crime and Security Act 2001*. This introduced detention without trial of foreign nationals suspected of involvement in terrorism, and gave the police more powers to hold and question suspects. (In December 2004, the Law Lords, sitting, exceptionally, with nine members rather than the usual five, ordered the release of nine terrorist suspects from Belmarsh Prison on the (technical) grounds that this law discriminated unlawfully against foreign nationals.)

▶ *The Prevention of Terrorism Act 2005*. This introduced a process of 'control orders', which allowed the secretary of state to impose various restrictions on the liberty of individuals who could not be deported. (In effect, this amounted to the government's response to the December 2004 Law Lords' ruling by removing discriminatory references to non-British citizens. The majority of the Belmarsh detainees who had been released then became subject to control orders.)

▶ *The Terrorism Act 2006*. This heightened the government's powers to deport people from the UK who were considered to be promoting terrorism. It also introduced a new offence of 'glorifying, exalting or celebrating' terrorism. However, the House of Commons rejected the proposed extension of detention without trial for 90 days in favour of a lower period of 28 days.

▶ *Counter-terrorism Bill 2008*. This sought to extend the period of pre-charge detention from 28 days to 42 days, although the measure was defeated in the House of Lords.

The election of the Conservative–Liberal Democrat coalition in 2010 nevertheless created the prospect that tension between the executive and the judiciary over civil liberties may significantly reduce. This was because, albeit to different degrees, both the Liberal Democrats and the Conservatives had criticized what some had viewed as 'Labour's attack on civil liberties'. The coalition quickly acted to abandon proposals for the introduction of identity cards and indicated that the use of ASBOs was to be ended. Similarly, in 2011 the 28-day limit on detaining terrorist suspects without charge was about to lapse, with a preference being expressed for this to revert to 14 days. The issue of control orders, introduced in 2005, nevertheless highlighted differences within the coalition over the balance between public safety and civil liberties. Although the Liberal Democrats had been committed to scrapping control orders, in the end, resistance within the Conservative Party meant that control orders were reformed rather than abolished, important aspects of them surviving in the form of 'terrorism prevention and investigation measures'.

Weblink ■ www.liberty-human-rights.org.uk

Use this website for news and comment about civil liberties issues. Liberty (formally known as the National Council on Civil Liberties) is a prominent campaigning organization on the issues of individual rights and personal freedom.

Conflicting views of civil liberties

However, it is misleading to view tensions between the judiciary and the executive as a simple battle between freedom and authority, or between the individual and the state. Rather, it is a conflict between competing views of civil liberty and contrasting ideas about which rights should be protected. For instance, when governments have been accused of 'threatening' civil liberties they have invariably defended themselves on the grounds that they are protecting other, *different* rights and freedoms. At the heart of this conflict are the rival ideas of 'constitutional democracy' and 'majoritarian democracy' (see p. 48), discussed in Chapter 2. But what is the basis for these conflicting views?

Critics of strong government – including not merely senior judges, but also many peers in the House of Lords, the Liberal Democrats and groups such as Liberty – have understood civil liberties as being closely related to human rights. Civil liberties, in this view, 'belong' to the citizen, and so should not, in any circumstances, be weakened or ignored by government. This presents civil liberties as *absolute* entitlements. They serve as the basis for democracy because they provide the ultimate guarantee that citizens can think and act for themselves. The right to liberty, reflected, in particular, in freedom from detention without trial, is therefore a basic feature of liberal-democratic government. Such thinking, for instance, influenced the Law Lords' decision to release the Belmarsh terrorist suspects in December 2004. In explaining their ruling, Lord Nicholls argued that the 2001 anti-terrorism legislation was incompatible with the rule of law. Lord Hoffmann stated this case still more boldly in declaring that 'The real threat to the life of the nation comes *not from terrorism but from laws such as these*' (italics added).

Ministers have nevertheless sometimes taken a quite different position, arguing that they are defending, not attacking, basic rights and freedoms. In this view, rights are always *relative* because the rights of one person have to be set against the rights of other people, and also because civil liberties must be balanced against civil duties or obligations. In particular, the rights of terrorist suspects – and, for that matter, the rights of other potential or actual wrong-doers – must be set against the larger rights of society, especially the right to life and freedom from fear, intimidation and violence. From this perspective, the right to life is the most important of civil liberties. This implies that the rights of potential victims (ordinary citizens going about their business) may have to be weighed more seriously than the rights of terrorist suspects. What is more, the

BY COMPARISON . . .

Judges in the USA

● US judges have much greater political significance than do UK judges because of the existence of a codified constitution. As the 'guardian of the constitution', the Supreme Court has the power of constitutional judicial review. It can therefore determine the powers and responsibilities of the presidency and Congress, as well as the balance between federal and state government. This makes the Court a clearly political institution, not just a legal one.

● The Justices of the Supreme Court are nominated by the president and confirmed by the Senate in a process that is often strongly influenced by political factors. Presidents seek to alter the ideological balance of the Court through their nominations. However, as Supreme Court judges enjoy security of tenure and have no compulsory retirement age, they cannot control justices once they are appointed. Presidents may also be lucky or unlucky in the number of appointments they are able to make.

● During the 1950s and 1960s, the Supreme Court (under Chief Justice Warren) had a liberal impact on US politics. It ended racial segregation in American schools, extended voting rights to blacks in many Southern states and upheld the right to abortion. Since the 1970s, a series of Republican presidents have succeeded in making the Supreme Court a more conservative body, helping, amongst other things, to see a restoration of capital punishment and restrictions imposed on access to abortions.

right 'balance' between civil liberties and public safety is a matter that should be decided by Parliament, acting in the interests of the mass of citizens, rather than by unelected judges.

Weblink ■ www.justice.org.uk

Use this website for critical analysis and comment on civil liberties in the UK. Justice is one of the country's leading legal and human rights organizations.

Reform of the judiciary

The Supreme Court

The Constitutional Reform Act 2005 introduced a series of reforms that have, and will continue to have, major constitutional and judicial significance. At the heart of these reforms is the creation of a new UK Supreme Court. The Court opened in October 2009 at the former Middlesex Guildhall Crown Court building in Parliament Square. The 12-strong Court replaced the Law Lords. It initially consisted of existing Law Lords but, as justices of the Supreme Court, they cease to be members of the House of Lords. The Court:

▶ Hears appeals on arguable points of law of general public importance
▶ Acts as the final court of appeal in England, Wales and Northern Ireland
▶ Hears appeals from civil cases in England, Wales, Northern Ireland and Scotland and criminal cases in England, Wales and Northern Ireland
▶ Has assumed the devolution jurisdiction of the Judicial Committee of the Privy Council (this makes the Court genuinely the 'Supreme Court of the United Kingdom')

The Constitutional Reform Act (CRA) and the new Supreme Court have a number of advantages:

▶ They substantially strengthen the separation of powers. This is done by tackling two anomalies. The first anomaly was that the highest court of appeal in the UK, the Law Lords, sat in the House of Lords, creating a fusion between the judiciary and the legislature. The second anomaly arose from the office of Lord Chancellor which, uniquely, fused judicial (head of the judiciary), legislative (presiding officer of the House of Lords) and executive (cabinet minister)

What is ... a bill of rights

A bill of rights is a document that specifies the rights and freedoms of the individual, and so defines the legal extent of civil liberty. Entrenched bills of rights can be distinguished from statutory ones:

▶ An *entrenched* bill of rights is enshrined in 'higher' law and therefore provides the basis for constitutional judicial review.
▶ A *statutory* bill of rights (sometimes called a statute of rights) can be amended or repealed through the same processes as other statute laws. (The Human Rights Act 1998 is a statute of rights, even though it can be used to call other statutes into question.)

FOR OR AGAINST?

A BILL OF RIGHTS

FOR	AGAINST
Accountable government. An entrenched bill of rights, like a written constitution, is a way of ensuring that government is based on laws, not on the arbitrary wishes of ministers. The establishment of higher law is the only way in which the rule of law can be properly upheld. This, in turn, will improve trust and confidence in government.	**Rule by judges**. A bill of rights would, as in the USA, turn judges into policy-makers. This would lead to 'judicial tyranny', as judges would be able both to make laws and to interpret them. Vital checks and balances in the political system would therefore be undermined. An expanded role for the judiciary is particularly undesirable because judges are unelected and also socially unrepresentative.
Liberty protected. A bill of rights would provide a clear and final definition of the proper relationship between the individual and the state. Civil liberties and individual rights would no longer be determined by battles between rival branches of government, over which rights are most important. Civil liberty would stand above both the executive and Parliament.	**Politicization**. As judges become more powerful, the political pressures on them will inevitably increase. Systems in which judges apply higher law usually struggle to maintain judicial independence. Similarly, judges find it difficult, and maybe impossible, to stand outside the political arena when their rulings have far-reaching policy implications.
Educational benefits. A bill of rights would strengthen the awareness of rights and individual freedoms throughout the political system. Citizens would have a better understanding of rights that 'belong' to them in a constitutional sense. Politicians and public officials would be constantly reminded of the need to act in accord with individual rights.	**A 'rights culture'**. A bill of rights would merely strengthen tendencies already fostered by the HRA. Citizens would become increasingly aware of their rights whilst ignoring their civic duties and broader responsibilities. Individual and minority rights would therefore be emphasized at the expense of the wider needs of the community, including the maintenance of public order and social cohesion.
Consensus on rights. The foundations for a bill of rights already exist in the UK, in the form of the European Convention and, more recently, the HRA. There is, therefore, a broad consensus about the liberties any bill of rights should protect. This would make its introduction easier and less controversial.	**Artificial rights**. Bills of rights are created by legal and constitutional experts, based on abstract principles such as human rights. They do not benefit from the wisdom of history and tradition, unlike the rights that are enshrined in common law. Once applied, artificial rights often have implications quite different from the expectations of their creators.

roles. The post of Lord Chancellor has been merged with that of Secretary of State for Constitutional Affairs. The Lord Chief Justice has become the head of the judiciary, and a separate Lords Speaker has been appointed.

▶ The CRA addressed long-term concerns about the independence of the judiciary that arose from the control that ministers exercised over the process of judicial appointments by creating the Judicial Appointments Commission.

▶ Attempts have been made to make the senior judiciary more diverse and socially representative. This has happened through the make-up of the Judicial Appointments Commission, six of whose members, including its first Chair (Baroness Usha Prashar), are laypeople.

Although the Supreme Court helps to address a number of long-standing constitutional problems, its creation divided the judiciary and provoked a number of concerns. While some argue that the Supreme Court reflects a trend towards UK judges becoming policy-makers like their US counterparts, others point out that the UK Supreme Court does not come close to resembling the US Supreme Court. Not only does the UK Supreme Court operate within an uncodified constitution in which its powers are largely confined to judging whether or not ministers and officials have taken decisions that lie within their competences as set out by Act of Parliament, but it is hardly 'supreme' in that appeals can be made to the European Court of Justice and the (non EU) European Court of Human Rights. A further concern is that progress in making the senior judiciary more socially representative is likely to be slow. This is in view of the statutory requirement on the JAC to make appointments on the basis of merit, expertise and experience, and because senior judges will continue to be appointed mainly from the ranks of long-standing barristers. Finally, the Supreme Court has been seen as a 'missed opportunity' by those who favour more radical reform, particularly by those who call for an entrenched bill of rights.

A UK bill of rights?

The UK Supreme Court differs significantly from the US Supreme Court. In the USA, the Supreme Court operates within a codified constitutional system, which invests the senior judiciary with the power of constitutional judicial review. The US Supreme Court can therefore strike down Acts of Congress. In the absence of a codified constitution, the UK Supreme Court is subject to the principle of parliamentary sovereignty (see p. 180). It cannot act as the guardian of the constitution. That role will continue to be reserved for Parliament, subject to the 'higher' authority of EU law. The only court that could challenge the authority of Parliament is therefore the European Court of Justice, which interprets and applies EU law and treaties, and is quite separate from the European Court of Human Rights.

The idea of a UK bill of rights has caused some confusion, however. For example, when leading Conservatives have called for the replacement of the Human Rights Act by a 'British bill of rights' they have been arguing for a revised, and perhaps weakened, version of the HRA. It would be *revised* in that it would no longer simply be based on the provisions of the European Convention, and it may be *weakened* in the sense that it may no longer be used to call other legislation into question. However, when the Brown government raised the idea of a UK 'bill of rights and responsibilities', its purpose was to enhance the Human Rights Act, rather than replace it. This later view is one that is supported by many Liberal Democrats.

Many advocates of a UK bill of rights thus support the introduction of an entrenched bill of rights that serves as higher law. This would bring the UK into line with states such as New Zealand, which have an entrenched bill of rights without having a fully written constitution. Such a development would have profound implications for civil liberties, the judiciary and the larger political system.

As far as civil liberties are concerned, an entrenched bill of rights would bring an end to the current battles between judges and ministers over which rights should be upheld and in what circumstances. Entrenchment would give designated individual rights unchallengeable legal authority. From the perspective of the judiciary, such a bill of rights would, for better or worse, substantially widen its role and increase its political significance. Whereas, at present, governments (supported by Parliament) can overturn the judiciary's interpretation of the Human Rights Act, judges' interpretation of an entrenched bill of rights would be final. From the perspective of the political system, an entrenched bill of rights would alter not only the balance of power between and amongst the branches of government, but it would also alter the political culture by creating a greater awareness of individual rights and freedoms.

WHAT YOU SHOULD KNOW

▶▶ The judiciary is the branch of government that is responsible for deciding legal disputes and which presides over the court system. The chief role of the judiciary is to define the meaning of law. In this sense, judges interpret or 'construct' law.

▶▶ The rule of law is the principle that the law should 'rule' in the sense that it applies to all conduct and behaviour, and covers both private citizens and public officials. The most important sub-principles of the rule of law are that no one is above the law, that there is equality for all before the law, that the law is always applied and that legal redress is available through the courts.

▶▶ Judges are meant to be independent and politically neutral. The independence of the judiciary is maintained through the appointment process, security of tenure, arrangements for their pay, freedom from criticism and the independence of the legal profession. Judicial neutrality is maintained by political restrictions on judges, their legal training and expertise, their accountability through the appeals system and the fact that judges are not meant to be public figures.

▶▶ The judiciary has become more politically significant in recent years through clashes between judges and ministers over civil liberties. The key civil liberties are freedom of speech, freedom of the press, freedom of religion and freedom of association. The main ways in which the judiciary can protect civil liberty are through judicial review and via the Human Rights Act 1998.

▶▶ The Human Rights Act incorporated the European Convention on Human Rights into UK law. Although it is not 'higher' law, it can be used to call other laws into question. It therefore hovers somewhere between an ordinary statute law and an entrenched bill of rights.

▶▶ Conflict in recent years between senior judges and the executive has been the result of several factors. These include the growth of a human rights culture amongst the senior judiciary, the wider powers the judiciary has gained through the Human Rights Act and the (perceived or actual) trend for governments to have become more authoritarian, expanding their own powers often at the expense of civil liberties.

▶▶ The Constitutional Reform Act 2005 has strengthened the independence of the judiciary. It also provided for the replacement of the House of Lords by the Supreme Court. The reform process and debate initiated by the Human Rights Act has created the possibility of the introduction in the UK of a bill of rights. An entrenched bill of rights is a controversial issue, largely because it would significantly enlarge the political role of judges, for better or worse.

Test yourself

Short questions:

1   What is the judiciary?
2   Outline the role of the judiciary.
3   Describe *two* functions of judges.
4   Define judicial independence.
5   Define judicial neutrality.
6   What is the rule of law?
7   What is civil liberty?
8   Outline *three* civil liberties.
9   Distinguish between civil liberties and human rights.
10 Distinguish between law and politics.

Medium questions:

11 Explain *three* ways in which judicial independence is maintained.
12 Explain *three* ways in which judicial neutrality is maintained.
13 What implications does the separation of powers have for the judiciary?
14 Why is judicial independence important?
15 In what ways is the rule of law undermined in the UK?
16 How do judges protect civil liberties?
17 What implications does judicial review have for the relationship between judges and ministers?
18 What are the features of the Human Rights Act?

Extended questions:

19 To what extent is the rule of law upheld in the UK?
20 To what extent are judges politically neutral and impartial?
21 To what extent has the creation of the Supreme Court enhanced the power and influence of judges in the UK?
22 Why, and to what extent, have judges come into conflict with judges in recent years?
23 How effective are judges in protecting civil liberty?
24 How could civil liberties be better protected in the UK?
25 To what extent have civil liberties been under threat in recent years?
26 Assess the significance of the Human Rights Act on political processes in the UK.
27 Should the UK introduce an entrenched bill of rights?

Chapter 10

The EU and Multilevel Governance

Multiple levels of government

The study of government has traditionally meant the study of *central* government at a *national* level. The study of UK government therefore focused primarily on bodies such as the Westminster Parliament, the prime minister and the cabinet, with only a little attention being given to local authorities. This was never the whole story, but in recent times the picture has changed considerably. Instead of all the main decisions in politics being made at the centre (in Westminster and Whitehall), they are increasingly made at a number of levels. Government, in this sense, has been 'stretched'. How has this happened? And what are the implications of having more levels of government?

In the UK, this process has happened in two ways. The first is through the introduction of devolution. The creation, since 1997, of a Scottish Parliament, a Welsh Assembly and a Northern Ireland Assembly has drawn power 'downwards' in important ways. To a greater or lesser degree, domestic affairs in Scotland, Wales and Northern Ireland are now decided by devolved bodies, rather than by 'London'. But this development has also stimulated controversy. How far should devolution go, and may it eventually lead to the break-up of the UK? The second development is the process of European integration. This has sucked power 'upwards', as decisions and responsibilities that once belonged to UK central government are now made at the EU level. But has the EU developed into a European 'superstate'? And has EU membership benefited the UK, or damaged it?

- ■ **How important is local government?**
- ■ **What are the powers and responsibilities of the Scottish Parliament, the Welsh Assembly and the Northern Ireland Assembly?**
- ■ **What are the implications of devolution for the UK?**
- ■ **Where does power lie within the EU?**
- ■ **What impact does EU membership have on UK politics?**

Independence for Scotland

Before starting the chapter, read this passage and briefly consider the questions on the next page.

On 5 May 2011, the Scottish National Party (SNP) claimed a historic victory in the Scottish Parliament elections. In winning 69 seats out of the 129 being contested, the SNP formed the first single-party majority government since the Parliament was set up in 1999. Scotland had therefore elected a government that was committed to the break-up of the UK. Not only had the SNP been set up to fight for Scottish independence, but it stood in the 2011 elections on a clear commitment to hold a referendum on the issue within the lifetime of the Parliament. How had the UK got to this point? And is the momentum in favour of Scottish independence now unstoppable?

For some, these developments were simply the inevitable consequence of a process that had been initiated by the 'yes' vote in the 1997 devolution referendum. A Scottish Parliament would 'bring politics home', shifting attention away from London and focusing it increasingly on Edinburgh. Scottish nationalism would therefore grow and, with it, the appetite for full independence. This is what the SNP had hoped for, and what opponents of devolution had feared. However, many Labour politicians had calculated quite differently. They had anticipated that devolution would stem, not increase, the tide of Scottish nationalism. Having their own Parliament to deal with domestic affairs, the Scottish people would be happy to remain within the UK. Critics of the SNP government go further and warn against the danger of Scotland being 'railroaded' into independence. Not only did the SNP not gain an electoral majority (45 per cent of electors voted SNP in 2011), but opinion polls continue to show that about two-thirds of Scottish people have serious doubts about independence. While growing support for the SNP may reflect a desire to strengthen devolution and expand Scottish self-rule, it is questionable whether it reflects a genuine wish for independence.

A jubilant Alex Salmond, the SNP leader, celebrating the party's 2011 election success – but did this success reflect a genuine appetite for independence in Scotland?

What issues do these events raise?

▶▶▶   Why was the SNP victory a 'historic' event?

▶▶▶   What do you understand by 'devolution'?

▶▶▶   How and why may devolution have strengthened nationalism in Scotland?

▶▶▶   Why have some hoped that devolution would weaken Scottish nationalism?

▶▶▶   Would an independent Scotland be good (a) for Scotland and (b) for the rest of the UK?

Towards multilevel governance

State: A political association that establishes sovereign control within defined territorial borders.

England became a unified **state** at the end of the War of the Roses (1455–85), which had witnessed a series of civil wars fought between the House of Lancaster and the House of York. Thereafter, centralized government operated throughout England, characterized by the establishment of sovereignty. However, the English state was, over time, to develop into a '**union state**', eventually becoming the United Kingdom. The main stages in this process were as follows:

Union state: A state made up of regions that retain their own distinctive cultural (and possibly national) traditions and identities.

▶ Between 1536 and 1542, Wales became part of England, having previously only been subject to indirect control. After 1542, English law applied also in Wales, and English was established as the only permissible language for official purposes. Wales, in turn, gained representation in the Westminster Parliament.

▶ The Act of Union of 1707 formally united England and Scotland, creating the Kingdom of Great Britain. Under this, the English and Scottish Parliaments were both abolished and replaced by a new Parliament at Westminster.

▶ Under the Act of Union of 1800, the Kingdom of Great Britain merged with the Kingdom of Ireland to form the United Kingdom of Great Britain and Ireland. When the Irish Free State was established in 1922 (later to become the Republic of Ireland), the UK became the United Kingdom of Great Britain and Northern Ireland.

Unitary state: A state in which sovereignty is concentrated in a single institution of central government; the centre therefore determines the powers and responsibilities of lower levels of government.

The unity of the UK is embodied in the principle of parliamentary sovereignty (see p. 180). This makes the UK a **unitary state**. The Westminster Parliament is able to make, unmake and amend any law it wishes, having supreme legal authority within the borders of the UK. However, trends in recent years have made government more complex and multifaceted. In the first place, there has been a shift from government to what is called 'governance'. But what is governance? Whereas government is a *thing*, a set of institutions with formal powers, governance refers to an *activity*. It is the ways in which social life is organized or coordinated. As such, it takes account of the fact that government works increasingly closely with businesses and other private bodies.

Multilevel governance: A complex policy process in which political authority is distributed horizontally and vertically between subnational, national and supranational levels of government.

The second trend is that government now operates on more levels. This has giving rise to the idea of **multilevel governance**. Multilevel governance (see Figure 10.1) has placed the UK state and the principle of parliamentary sovereignty under growing pressure. Much of this pressure stems from the

What is ... sovereignty

Sovereignty, in its simplest sense, is the principle of absolute and unlimited power. As such, sovereignty is the defining feature of a state, emphasizing the state's supreme authority over its internal affairs (sometimes called 'internal sovereignty'). The location of internal sovereignty largely determines the constitutional make-up of a state. In the UK, sovereignty formally resides with Parliament.

However, a distinction is commonly made between legal and political sovereignty:

▶ *Legal* sovereignty refers to supreme legal authority: that is, an unchallengeable 'right' to establish any law one wishes. (Parliament is sovereign in a strictly legal sense.)
▶ *Political* sovereignty refers to absolute political power: that is, an unrestricted 'ability' to act however one wishes. (Only an absolute dictator would have full political sovereignty.)

growing importance of the European Union and its impact on almost every aspect of UK politics. As discussed in Chapter 6, membership of the EU is now one of the key principles of the UK constitution, perhaps also implying that the traditional idea of parliamentary sovereignty needs to be rethought. Devolution (see p. 310) has had no less of an impact. As we shall see, the creation of devolved assemblies in Scotland, Wales and Northern Ireland does not technically alter the unitary character of the UK state. Nevertheless, the fact that these bodies are all elected, and were created through successful referendums, can invest them with a significant measure of popular authority and may even allow them to challenge the Westminster Parliament itself. Some argue that devolution has already created a form of 'quasi-federalism' (as discussed later in the chapter) and may possibly lead to the break-up of the UK.

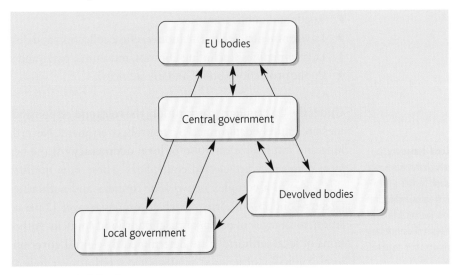

Figure 10.1 **Multilevel governance**

Nation: A group of people who share a common language, religion, traditions and culture, and regard themselves as a natural political community.

Nation-state: A state in which the population have a shared national identity, based (usually) on the same language, religion, traditions and history.

However, the issue of multilevel governance goes well beyond questions about sovereignty and the growing complexity of government. It is also closely linked to national identity and the politics of allegiance. In other words, it affects how people *feel* about who they are, and about the communities they identify with. Since the early 19th century, political allegiances have been shaped above all by nationalism (see p. 311) and the idea that people somehow 'belong' to a **nation**. Most states in the modern world are therefore '**nation-states**'. Ultimately, the United Kingdom may therefore only survive so long as a unifying sense of 'Britishness' persists. Many believe that this sense of British national identity has been undermined by both Europe and devolution. The transfer of policy-making authority from UK institutions to EU bodies has, arguably, not only eroded sovereignty but also diluted our sense of Britishness. Devolution, for its part, has encouraged people in Scotland and Wales to become more aware of their distinctive national identities and, perhaps, weakened their allegiance to the UK.

Local and devolved government

Local government

The lowest level within the UK's system of multilevel governance is local government. This consists of the coordination and provision of a wide range of public services by local authorities. These services include those that impact most significantly on citizens' lives:

- Schools
- Social services
- Planning and land use
- Roads and public transport
- Environmental health (including refuse collection and disposal)
- Local amenities (including libraries, museums, parks and sports facilities)
- Public protection (police and fire services).

Local democracy: The principle that local decisions should be made in line with local wishes, implying both local elections and a measure of local autonomy (freedom from the centre).

Under the UK's unitary constitution, the roles and responsibilities of local authorities are entirely determined by central government. Nevertheless, the UK has a long and impressive tradition of **local democracy**. At the heart of this system of local democracy are elected councillors. These now number over 100,000, and they serve in a complex network of councils and authorities, ranging from the Greater London Authority, which encompasses over 12 per cent of the UK population, to an array of parish or neighbourhood councils. Although the broad functions of local authorities are determined by central government, until the 1980s local councillors exercised significant discretion over how these functions were carried out. This degree of local autonomy was upheld by the fact that about 40

Rates: A property-based local government tax that was linked to the notional rental value of residential and business properties.

per cent of local spending was raised locally by the '**rates**'. Such a balance between central control and local autonomy was seen to have a variety of advantages.

The benefits of local democracy included that it:

▶ Widened opportunities for popular participation, in giving many more citizens a chance of standing for or holding public office
▶ Allowed authorities to take account of local needs and interests
▶ Ensured a dispersal of power, as local government could act as a check on central government.

However, the 1980s witnessed a series of clashes between central government and local government. These clashes stemmed from the election in 1979 of the Thatcher government, which was committed to 'rolling back' the frontiers of the state. As roughly one-third of public money was spent at a local level, the overall level of public spending would only come down if local authorities spent less. When authorities such as the Greater London Council (GLC) attempted to maintain (or even increase) their spending levels, the Thatcher government acted to reduce their power and independence. This led to a significant increase in central control over local government, threatening the very basis of local democracy, and also, in some ways, even altered the role of local government. However, recent years have seen evidence of a revival or renewal of local government.

The decline of local democracy

Local democracy has declined in a number of ways:

▶ **Defects of local democracy.** When the Thatcher government set about altering local–central relations during the 1980s, it met little resistance because of the moribund state of local democracy. Local democracy is defective in a number of ways:

  ▹ Electoral turnouts of often 30–40 per cent are lower than for any other public bodies, and are amongst the lowest for any modern democracy.
  ▹ Local elections tend to be dominated by national issues, and are commonly interpreted as opinion polls on the popularity of government of the day.
  ▹ The use of the FPTP voting system (see p. 71) in England and Wales has meant that many councils are permanently controlled by a single party, with power being concentrated in the hands of a small group.
  ▹ Councillors tend to be unrepresentative of their local populations (for example, their average age is 58, and 39 per cent of them are retired).

▶ **Loss of financial control.** Major changes have taken place in local government finances. In 1989 in Scotland and in 1990 in England and Wales, the rating

Poll tax: A flat-rate tax on individuals (a 'head tax').

Council tax: A revised version of the rating system in which property is taxed according to eight bands (A to H), with a 25 per cent discount for single occupants.

system was replaced by the 'poll tax'. The poll tax was introduced in the hope that it would encourage voters to support low-spending, not high-spending, parties. However, its unpopularity (which contributed to the downfall of Margaret Thatcher; see p. 250) led, in 1993, to the introduction of the 'council tax'. More significantly, during the Thatcher–Major years, central government gained an unprecedented level of control over local spending. This system has remained substantially in place under Labour since 1997. There are now three main sources of local finance:

▷ Central government grants provide roughly half of all local revenue.
▷ The 'uniform business rate', which is a tax on business property and is effectively set by central government, provides about a quarter of local revenue.
▷ The council tax provides just over one-fifth of revenue. It is the only source of funding that is locally controlled, but central government has the power to 'cap' the council tax by imposing a legal maximum on tax levels.

▶ **The rise of 'enabling' councils.** Local government was important largely because it provided a wide range of public services. However, from the 1980s onwards, in a drive for cost-cutting and greater efficiency, local authorities have been forced to place the provision of services increasingly in the hands of private bodies. This has turned councils from being 'providers' into being 'enablers'. Services such as refuse collection, school meals and park maintenance have commonly been handed over to private businesses, whereas housing associations have taken control of most of the UK's public housing stock. In many cases, the role of local authorities has been reduced to setting standards and negotiating contracts for services that others deliver.

Local government renewed?

Local government has nevertheless been reinvigorated in a number of ways:

▶ **The Greater London Authority.** The abolition of the left-wing controlled Greater London Council (GLC) in 1986 symbolized central government's assault on local democracy during that period. The creation, in 2000, of the Greater London Authority (GLA), comprising a directly-elected London mayor and a 25-member Greater London Assembly, therefore marked a significant revival of local democracy. However, the GLA is a much weaker body than the GLC of old. It has strategic, but not operational, responsibilities for transport, fire and emergency services, and economic development and planning, and enjoys little financial independence from central government.

▶ **Source of experimentation and innovation.** Some of the most interesting developments in UK politics have, in recent years, stemmed from local government. The idea of elected mayors, established by the GLA, is widely seen as an important way of reviving local democracy. Elected mayors both raise the profile of local government and encourage the adoption of bolder and more popular policy initiatives. An example of this is London's experiment in road pricing through the 'congestion charge', introduced in 2003, which is increasingly being looked to as a model by other cities in the UK and elsewhere. Other political innovations include the use of postal voting and of electronic voting (see For and against digital democracy, p. 58). Since 2000, local authorities have also acquired new roles in economic development and regeneration, encouraging them to develop strategies to attract inward investment and to improve the local infrastructure.

▶ **Multilevel governance.** Local government has been able, to an extent, to counter stronger central control by developing links with other levels of government, notably devolved bodies and EU institutions. In Scotland, Wales and Northern Ireland, local authorities now come within the responsibility of devolved assemblies. This has led, for instance, to the introduction of the proportional STV voting system (see p. 77) for Scottish local elections. Links between local government and the EU have also become more prominent. The EU has become an important additional source of funding, mainly through the European Regional Development Fund and the Social Fund. Virtually every local council in the UK also has a lobbying presence in Brussels. In the case of the GLA, this is done through 'London House' in Brussels. Smaller local authorities often achieve representation within the EU through the Local Government International Bureau (LGIB).

Weblink ■ www.lga.gov.uk

Use the local government association website to find out more about the work and activities of English and Welsh local authorities.

Devolution: a disunited UK?

Devolution has been the most significant change to the UK's constitutional arrangements since 1997. The first elections for the Scottish Parliament and the National Assembly for Wales (usually known as the Welsh Assembly) were held in May 1999, following successful referendums in 1997. The Northern Ireland Assembly came into existence in 1998, as a consequence of the Belfast Agreement (also known as the Good Friday Agreement). Although highly controversial in its initial stage – the Conservatives strongly opposed Scottish and Welsh devolution, and the Welsh devolution referendum was won by a margin of less than 1 per cent of the vote – devolution has quickly become a popular and established feature of UK politics. The proportion of voters in Scotland, Wales and Northern Ireland

What is ... devolution

Devolution is the transfer of power from central government to subordinate regional institutions (to 'devolve' means to pass powers or duties down from a higher authority to a lower one). Devolved bodies therefore constitute an intermediate tier of government between central and local government (see Figure 10.2). Devolution differs from federalism (see p. 314) in that, although their territorial jurisdictions may be similar, devolved bodies have no share in sovereignty. Their responsibilities and powers are determined by the centre, which can, in theory at least, abolish them.

Devolution nevertheless comes in different forms:

▶ *Administrative* devolution allows regional institutions to implement policies decided elsewhere
▶ *Legislative* devolution (sometimes called 'home rule') operates through elected regional assemblies that are invested with policy-making responsibilities and, usually, have some tax raising powers.

who want to return to direct rule from Westminster has consistently fallen, and all major UK parties now support devolution. Nevertheless, many questions persist. What has been the impact of devolution in Scotland, Wales and Northern Ireland? How has devolution affected England? Has devolution benefited the UK political system, or damaged it?

Devolution and nationalism

Devolution in the UK has largely been a response to the emergence of Scottish and Welsh nationalism. Although Plaid Cymru (in English, the 'party of Wales') was formed in 1925 and the Scottish National Party (SNP) was formed in 1934, these

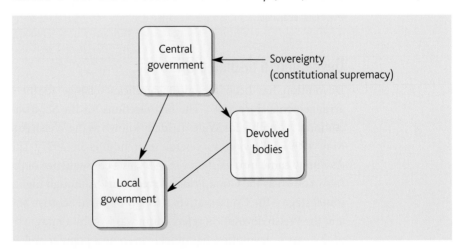

Figure 10.2 **The structure of devolution**

What is . . . nationalism

Nationalism is, broadly, the belief that the nation is the central principle of political organization. As such, it is based on two core assumptions: (1) that humankind is naturally divided into distinct nations, and (2) that the nation is the only legitimate unit of political rule. However, nationalism has taken a variety of political forms, ranging from a desire to establish independent statehood (national self-determination) to the urge to conquer other nations in the cause of national greatness.

Political nationalism is often distinguished from cultural nationalism:

▶ *Political* nationalism, in its 'classical' form, is the belief that all nations have a right to independence and self-government, achieved by becoming a nation-state
▶ *Cultural* nationalism is the regeneration of the nation as a distinctive civilization; this stresses the need to defend or strengthen a national language, religion or way of life, rather than achieve overtly political ends.

parties did not win seats at Westminster until the 1960s. They grew in significance during the 1970s due to a combination of growing electoral support (the SNP won 11 seats in October 1974, and Plaid Cymru won 3 seats) and the weakness of the 1974–79 Labour government. After it had lost its majority in 1976, Labour looked to the nationalist parties for support, and did so by backing plans for devolution. Two unsuccessful attempts were made to introduce assemblies in Scotland and Wales. In 1978, the government was defeated by its own backbenchers and, in 1979, referendums in Scotland and Wales failed to support the proposals (Scotland voted 'yes' but a low turnout meant that the required 40 per cent of the electorate did not back the proposal).

In the light of these referendum setbacks, nationalism waned in the 1980s. However, it was revived during the 1990s due both to growing resentment against rule by a London-based Conservative government that, for a time, had no representation in either Scotland and Wales, and to growing economic self-confidence in Scotland linked to North Sea oil. This was complemented by renewed interest in devolution within the Labour Party, sparked by John Smith's election as party leader in 1992. Using the Scottish Constitutional Convention (SCC), Labour worked with the Liberal Democrats, a number of small Scottish parties (but only briefly with the SNP), churches and other civic groups to develop a framework for Scottish devolution. Plans for Welsh devolution were largely drawn up to complement Scottish proposals. Labour's election in 1997 provided the basis for these plans to be implemented.

However, the link between devolution and nationalism is complex. Although all agree that devolution has been a *consequence* of nationalism, it is less clear whether it has been a *cause*. Does devolution fuel nationalism, or weaken it? Many in the Labour Party hoped that devolution would help to stem the tide of Scottish and Welsh nationalism. In their view, growing nationalism was largely a consequence of frustration at being ruled from London by an English-dominated Parliament. By giving Scotland and Wales greater control over domestic affairs, devolution should therefore weaken separatist nationalism and, in the process, strengthen the UK. Such hopes seemed to be borne out by declining support for both the SNP and Plaid Cymru in the second round of devolution elections in 2003.

The nationalist parties nevertheless had a quite different view of the implications of devolution. Although the goal of the SNP and Plaid Cymru was (and remains) the break-up of the UK brought about by the achievement of Scottish and Welsh independence, they saw devolution as a step on this road. In this view, devolution is likely to strengthen nationalism as it would help to give Scotland and Wales clearer political identities, providing the foundation for more radical demands. This scenario appeared to be borne out by the defeat of the Labour–Liberal Democrat coalition in the 2007 Scottish Parliament elections and the formation of a minority SNP administration. Nevertheless, opinion polls in Scotland continue to show that there is only minority support for independence. While this persists, it is unlikely that the SNP will press ahead with their promised referendum on the issue.

In the case of Northern Ireland, devolution has had contrasting implications for nationalism. On the one hand, it has led to a polarization of views, as support has grown for 'extreme' **Unionist** and **Republican** parties (the Democratic Unionist Party (DUP) and Sinn Fein) at the expense of 'moderate' ones (the Ulster Unionist Party (UUP) and the Social Democratic and Labour Party (SDLP)). On the other hand, the prospect of participating in government has encouraged the DUP and Sinn Fein to work together within a power-sharing executive, which was formed in May 2007. This perhaps illustrates the emergence in Northern Ireland of more flexible and pragmatic forms of Unionism and Republicanism.

Unionism: A form of Northern Ireland nationalism that seeks to uphold the union between Great Britain and Northern Ireland; the dominant political tradition of Ulster Protestants.

Republicanism: A form of Northern Ireland nationalism that is committed to creating a united Ireland through the incorporation of Northern Ireland into the Republic of Ireland; the dominant political position of Ulster Catholics.

Asymmetrical devolution: A form of devolution that operates differently in different regions, with no common pattern of devolved powers and responsibilities within the state.

Weblink ■ www.devolution.info

Use the DevWeb site to gain access to a wealth of information about the nature and workings of devolution across the UK.

Devolution: how does it work?

The UK has a novel form of devolution, in that it operates in quite different ways in different parts of the UK. This is what is called **asymmetrical devolution**. Scotland, Wales and Northern Ireland therefore each have different systems of devolution:

Primary legislative power: The ability to make law on matters which have been devolved from Westminster.

Secondary legislative power: The ability to vary some laws passed by the Houses of Parliament, creating dependency on Westminster legislation.

▶ **The Scottish Parliament.** The Scottish Parliament is an example of legislative devolution. It has **primary legislative powers** on most fields of domestic policy and limited tax-varying powers (the ability to raise or lower income tax by 3 pence in the pound).

▶ **Welsh Assembly.** The Welsh Assembly was, in origin, an example of administrative devolution, in that it had no control over taxation and only **secondary legislative powers**. However, following an affirmative referendum in March 2011, the Welsh Assembly gained primary legislative powers in all 20 areas for which it is responsible.

▶ **Northern Ireland Assembly.** The Northern Ireland Assembly has some primary legislative power but no control over taxation, although its powers can be expanded in line with the principle of 'rolling' devolution if power-sharing proves to be successful.

Central government continues to retain control of overall economic policy, defence policy and foreign affairs (apart from the Northern Ireland Assembly's role in facilitating cross-border cooperation with the Republic of Ireland). Funding for the devolved bodies is allocated by the UK Treasury as a 'block', although the devolved institutions can spend their blocks as they wish within the framework of their powers. The devolved bodies nevertheless have broad responsibilities, including:

▶ Agriculture, forestry, fisheries and food
▶ Culture, media and sport
▶ Economic development
▶ Education and training
▶ Environment
▶ Health
▶ Home affairs (except Wales)
▶ Legal system (only in Scotland)
▶ Local government and housing
▶ Social services
▶ Trade and industry (very limited in Wales)
▶ Transport.

Has devolution made a difference? To what extent has public policy in Scotland, Wales and Northern Ireland diverged from the rest of the UK as a result of devolution? Some significant changes have undoubtedly taken place in Scotland. These include the abolition of upfront tuition fees for university students, the reintroduction of free long-term care for the elderly and higher teachers' pay. Local government elections have also been changed with the introduction of the proportional single transferable vote (STV) voting system. The Welsh Assembly has pioneered new initiatives in childcare and early years policies, and has abolished prescription charges. It has also reorganized the NHS to bring it in line with local government boundaries in Wales. The impact of devolution in Northern Ireland was limited by the suspension of the Northern Ireland Assembly between 2002 and 2007 (following a number of earlier, shorter suspensions between 1999 and 2002). However, the restoration of power-sharing between the DUP and Sinn Fein is likely to provide the basis for the development, over time, of a distinctive approach to domestic policy.

Weblink ■ www.devolution.ac.uk

Use this website, which is part of the Economic and Social Research Council research programme, to gain access to a wide range of reports about devolution and constitutional change.

Quasi-federalism?

Devolution is commonly described as a 'process' rather than an event. This implies that the establishment of devolved bodies in Scotland, Wales and Northern Ireland was not an end in itself. Rather, it was a prelude to further, and probably more radical, changes. Indeed, many commentators already describe devolution arrangements in the UK as a form of '**quasi-federalism**'. Quasi-federalism implies that devolution has already gone beyond the simple handing down of power by a sovereign Westminster Parliament and has come, in some ways, to resemble federalism. Why has quasi-federalism come about?

The devolution process has been strengthened in the UK by a number of factors:

Quasi-federalism:
A division of powers between central and regional government that has some of the features of federalism without possessing a formal federal structure.

▶ **Democratic legitimacy**. A major factor in determining the success of devolution in the UK was the decision to hold devolution referendums in 1997. These ensured that newly created devolved bodies began life with a measure of democratic legitimacy. Subsequent elections in 1999, 2003, 2007 and 2011 have bolstered the democratic credentials of the devolved institutions and, in the

What is... federalism

Federalism refers to legal and political structures that distribute power territorially within a state. It requires the existence of two distinct levels of government, each of which has a measure of constitutional autonomy (see Figure 10.3). Its central feature is the notion of shared sovereignty. Federalism therefore contrasts with devolution in which sovereign power continues to be located within central government. Classical federations are few in number: the USA, Switzerland, Belgium, India, Canada and Australia. However, many more states have federal-type features.

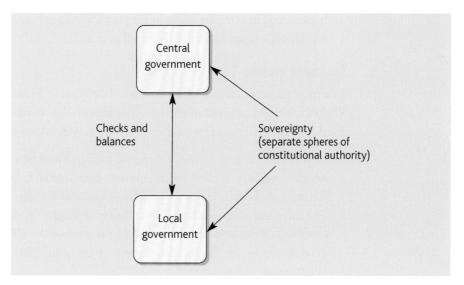

Figure 10.3 **Federalism**

process, helped to strengthen the sense of separate Scottish, Welsh and Northern Irish political identities.

▶ **Asymmetrical devolution.** The uneven nature of devolution tends to strengthen centrifugal forces within the UK. This is because where devolution was initially weaker, as in Wales, the existence of stronger versions of devolution serve to fuel demands for greater decentralization. This has been evident in growing calls in Wales for full legislative devolution. Moreover, any increase in the powers of weaker devolved bodies will, almost inevitably, encourage stronger bodies (such as the Scottish Parliament) to demand greater autonomy.

▶ **Party control.** The full significance of devolution was disguised by the fact that, in its early years, Labour ruled in Westminster and in Edinburgh and Cardiff (albeit within a coalition or as a minority administration). Policy differences and political disagreements between the two levels were therefore likely to be relatively modest. However, a change in government at either level, as would sooner or later inevitably happen, would create greater political distance between central government and the devolved bodies. The election of a majority SNP administration in Scotland in 2011 thus raises the prospect of further devolution and possibly even Scottish independence.

▶ **Realignment of pressure group politics.** Devolution has significantly altered patterns of pressure group politics within the UK. Businesses, trade unions and promotional groups of various kinds increasingly look to influence policy through devolved bodies. As these groups establish closer links with devolved bodies they, in turn, are likely to support growing demands for further decentralization and strengthened devolved powers.

The English question

The most glaring example of asymmetrical devolution in the UK is the fact that England, with 84 per cent of the UK's population, has remained entirely outside the devolution process. This has happened for very good reasons:

▶ Devolution has largely been a response to the growth of sub-UK nationalisms which have been fuelled by resentment that Scotland, Wales and Northern Ireland have been ruled by an English-dominated Parliament.

▶ The sheer size of England makes the idea of an English Parliament highly problematical. If the domestic affairs of 84 per cent of the UK's population were determined by an English Parliament, what would be the purpose of the Westminster Parliament?

Nevertheless, the absence of English devolution has been a cause of constitutional and political difficulties. The key constitutional difficulty is what has been called the 'West Lothian question'. The political difficulties that this has generated have been reflected in growing resentment in England that it is the only part of the UK that lacks a discrete political voice. The Conservative-led coalition set up an independent commision in 2010 to consider ways in which the West Lothian question could be resolved. Furthermore, English taxpayers have been funding policy innovations and improved services in Scotland and Wales that have not benefited England. Although the so-called '**Barnett formula**' aims eventually to bring about

Barnett formula: The formula (devised by the then Treasury secretary, Joel, later Lord, Barnett) for determining the level of funding from UK taxes of expenditure in Scotland, Wales and Northern Ireland.

FOCUS ON . . .
The West Lothian question

▶ The West Lothian question is a constitutional anomaly that has resulted from the introduction of devolution in Scotland, Wales and Northern Ireland, but not in England. (It is named after Tam Dalyell, the MP for West Lothian, who first raised the issue in 1979.)

▶ The West Lothian question asks whether it is right that Scottish MPs should be able to vote at Westminster on English domestic matters, when English MPs are unable to vote on Scottish domestic matters because these are controlled by the Scottish Parliament.

▶ This constitutional imbalance has been used either to criticize devolution as being unfair and undesirable, or to call for English devolution. It has also led to calls for 'English votes on English laws' at Westminster (the idea that only English MPs should be able to vote on matters that only affect English citizens).

BY COMPARISON . . .

Federalism in the USA

- US government is divided into federal and state levels. Federal government, located in Washington DC, consists of Congress, the presidency and the Supreme Court. There are 50 states, each possessing a state legislature, a governor and a state supreme court.

- The constitutional basis for US federalism is based on the Tenth Amendment of the Constitution, which guarantees that powers not delegated to the federal government are 'reserved to the states respectively, or to the people'. The support of three-quarters of state legislatures is also needed for constitutional amendments to be ratified.

- The creation of a federal system, rather than a unitary one, was largely a consequence of historical factors. The 13 original states had each been British colonies, which were keen to preserve their distinctive political identities and traditions. Federalism also suits the geographical size and social diversity of the USA, as Washington DC is both politically and geographically remote from many sections of the American population.

- The balance within the US federal system has changed significantly over time. Initially, federal and state governments operated quite separately. However, from the late 19th century onwards, the states became increasingly dependent on the flow of federal funds through 'grants in aid'. This increased with the advent of so-called 'big' government in the 20th century. However, since the 1980s, this trend has been reversed. Under the slogan of 'new federalism', the Reagan and Bush Jr administrations in particular attempted to transfer welfare responsibilities from federal government to the less prosperous state governments.

a convergence in per capita spending, block funding continues to advantage Scotland, Wales and Northern Ireland at the expense of England.

A possible solution to these problems would be the introduction of a system of regional government in England that would complement the devolved assemblies elsewhere. In 1998, the Blair government therefore set up nine Regional Development Agencies (RDAs), with the possibility that these could, in due course, be transformed into elected regional assemblies. However, a strong 'no' vote in the 2004 referendum on the establishment of an assembly for the North East of England has effectively blocked any further progress in this direction by demonstrating little public support for English regional government. In June 2010, the newly-formed Conservative-led coalition announced its intention to abolish RDAs, further undermining the prospects for English regionalism.

The UK and the EU

The development of the EU

In the aftermath of the Second World War, a set of powerful, and possibly irresistible, historical circumstances came together to support the process of European integration. The most significant of these were:

▶ The need for economic reconstruction in war-torn Europe through cooperation and the creation of a larger market
▶ The desire to preserve peace between France and Germany, whose antagonisms had contributed to the outbreak of both the First World War and the Second World War
▶ The need to incorporate Germany more effectively into a wider Europe in order to prevent further bouts of expansionism
▶ The desire to safeguard Western Europe from the threat of the Soviet Union, which had emerged as a superpower in the post-1945 period and had extended its control throughout Eastern Europe
▶ The wish of the USA to establish a prosperous and united Europe, both as a market for US goods and as a bulwark against the spread of communism.

The earliest form of integration was the European Coal and Steel Community (ECSC), which was formed in 1952 by France, Germany, Italy, the Netherlands, Belgium and Luxemburg (the 'Six'). The same countries formed the European Economic Community (EEC), established by the Treaty of Rome, which they signed in 1957. The EEC was committed to the establishment of a common European market and the broader goal of an 'ever closer union among the peoples of Europe'. Although many of the early supporters of European integration favoured a 'federal' Europe, in which the sovereignty of the European nations would be 'pooled', the more powerful tendency turned out to be a 'functionalist' one, based on incremental steps towards integration, particularly in the area of economic cooperation.

However, the UK refused to participate in these developments, despite being invited. This occurred for a number of reasons:

▶ Having fought alongside the USA and the Soviet Union and having emerged victorious in the Second World War, the UK saw itself as one of the 'big three', not as a minor power.

▶ Many in the UK felt culturally and historically distinct from 'Europe' having, for example, more in common with the Commonwealth and with the USA.

▶ The UK was more concerned with preserving its 'special relationship' with the USA than with forming alliances with 'Europe'.

▶ Not having been defeated or invaded, the UK was less affected than many continental European powers by the Second World War.

Weblink ■ www.civitas.org.uk/eurofacts

Use this Civitas website to access a helpful series of EU fact sheets (Civitas is the Institute for the Study of Civil Society).

Nevertheless, attitudes to what in the UK was called the 'Common Market' gradually changed, at least amongst leading politicians. This was largely due to growing anxiety about the UK's loss of great power status (caused, amongst other things, by the end of empire and events such as the 1956 Suez crisis) and concern about the UK's economic decline relative to EEC states. Harold Macmillan's Conservative government was the first to apply to join the 'Common Market' in 1961, followed by Harold Wilson's Labour government in 1967. Both attempts were rejected by President de Gaulle of France, who feared that the UK was still too closely aligned with the USA, and that the UK would, anyway, threaten the Franco-German alliance that had come to dominate the EEC. Edward Heath's Conservative government finally succeeded in joining (along with Ireland and Denmark) in 1973.

The EEC formally merged with the ECSC and Euratom in 1967, forming what became known as the European Community (EC). However, through the 1960s and 1970s the EEC/EC remained what it had in origin been: an organization to facilitate economic cooperation amongst member states. The integration process was relaunched as a result of the signing in 1986 of the Single European Act (SEA), which envisaged an unrestricted flow of goods, services and people throughout Europe (a 'single market'), to be introduced by 1993. The Treaty on European Union (TEU) (or the Maastricht treaty), which was negotiated in 1991,

Table 10.1   Key events in EC/EU history, including the UK's involvement

1952	European Coal and Steel Community (ECSC) set up
1957	Treaty of Rome signed
1958	European Economic Community (EEC) and Euratom established
1961	UK's first application to join EEC (rejected in 1963)
1967	UK's second attempt to join EEC (rejected)
1967	EC formed through the merger of EEC, ECSC and Euratom
1973	The UK, Ireland and Denmark join the EC
1975	UK referendum supports continued membership of the EC
1979	First direct elections for European Parliament
1981	Greece joins the EC
1986	Spain and Portugal join the EC; Single European Act signed
1993	Treaty on European Union (Maastricht Treaty) ratified, creating the EU
1995	Austria, Finland and Sweden join the EU
1999	The euro is launched in 11 of the 15 member states
2004	Ten more states join the EU, bringing its size to 25
2007	Bulgaria and Rumania join the EU. The reform treaty (Lisbon Treaty) is signed
2009	Treaty of Lisbon ratified

Political union: The establishment of common citizenship rights within the EU and a strengthening of EU institutions to ensure common policies in designated areas.

Monetary union: The establishment of a single European currency, the euro, regulated by the European Central Bank.

ratified in 1992 and took effect in 1993, led to the creation of the European Union (EU). This committed the EU's 15 members (Greece, Portugal, Spain, Austria, Finland and Sweden having joined) to both **political union** and **monetary union**. The centrepiece of this proposal was the establishment of a single European currency, the euro, which took place in 1999 with notes and coins being introduced in 2002 (although four states, including the UK, remained outside the 'eurozone').

In 2004, the EU began its most radical phase of enlargement as ten countries of central and eastern Europe and the Mediterranean joined, bringing about the reunification of Europe after decades of division by the Iron Curtain. Bulgaria and Rumania subsequently joined in 2007, bringing the total number of EU states to 27. However, the enlargement project ran counter to the desire for further integration in important ways. In particular, a larger number of member states made it more difficult, and sometimes impossible, for EU bodies, and especially the Council of Ministers, to make decisions. This led to moves to establish a constitution for the EU. The first attempt to do this, the constitution treaty, was abandoned after the defeat of referendums in 2005 in France and the Netherlands. Many of the features of the constitution treaty nevertheless resurfaced in the Treaty of Lisbon, which was ratified in 2009.

The workings of the EU

The EU is a very difficult political organization to categorize. It is no longer a confederation of independent states operating on the basis of **intergovernmentalism** (as the EEC and EC were when they were created). The sovereignty of member states was enshrined in the so-called 'Luxembourg compromise' of 1966. This accepted the practice of unanimous voting in the Council of Ministers, granting each member state a **national veto**. However, as a result of the SEA, the TEU and other treaties, the practice of **qualified majority voting** has been applied to a wider range of policy areas. This narrows the scope of the national veto and allows even the largest state to be outvoted. This trend has been compounded by the fact that EU law is binding on all member states and that the power of certain EU bodies has expanded at the expense of national governments. The EU, therefore, hovers somewhere between intergovernmentalism and **supranationalism** (see How the EU works, p. 322). The EU may not yet have created a federal Europe, but because of the superiority of European law over the national law of member states, it is perhaps accurate to talk of a 'federalizing' Europe.

Weblink ■ www.europa.eu.int/index_en.htm

Use the EU official website to find links to EU bodies such as the European Parliament, the Council of Ministers and the European Commission.

As an economic, monetary and, to a significant extent, political union brought about through voluntary cooperation amongst states, the EU is a unique political body. The transition from Community to Union, achieved via the TEU, not only extended intergovernmental cooperation into areas such as foreign and security policy, home affairs and justice, and immigration and policing, but also established the notion of EU citizenship (members of the EU states can live, work and be politically active in any other member state). In the UK in particular, such developments have been highly controversial. Often dubbed Europe's 'awkward partner', the UK has struggled to come to terms with its European identity. '**Euroscepticism**' has remained strong, especially in the Conservative Party, fuelled by the fear of a European 'superstate' that would threaten both national sovereignty and national identity.

Nevertheless, although the EU has done much to realize the Treaty of Rome's goal of establishing 'an ever closer union', it stops far short of realizing the early federalists' dream of establishing a 'United States of Europe'. This has been ensured partly by respect for the principle of **subsidiarity**, which, in the TEU, expresses the idea that EU bodies should only act when matters cannot sufficiently be achieved by member states. Decision-making within the New Europe is increasingly made on the basis of multilevel governance, involving subnational,

Intergovernmentalism: A form of interaction between states that takes place on the basis of sovereign independence, meaning that states cannot be forced to act against their will.

National veto: The power of member states to block Council of Ministers' decisions on matters that threaten vital national interests.

Qualified majority voting: A system of voting within an EU Council of Ministers in which different majorities are needed on different issues, with states' votes weighed (roughly) according to size.

Supranationalism: The existence of a supranational body that is higher than the nation-state and capable of imposing its will on it.

Euroscepticism: Opposition to the process of European integration, based on a defence of national sovereignty and national identity; Eurosceptics are not necessarily anti-European.

Subsidiarity: The principle that, within a federal-type system, decisions should be made at the lowest possible level.

FOCUS ON . . .

How the European Union works

▶ **European Commission.** This is the executive-bureaucratic arm of the EU. It is headed by 27 commissioners (one from each of the member states) and a president (since 2004, José Manuel Barroso). It proposes legislation, is a watchdog that ensures that EU treaties are respected, and is broadly responsible for policy implementation.

▶ **The Council.** Formerly called the Council of Ministers, this is the decision-making branch of the EU and comprises ministers from the 27 states who are accountable to their own assemblies and governments. The presidency of the Council rotates amongst member states every six months. Important decisions are made by unanimous agreement, and others are reached through qualified majority voting or a simple majority.

▶ **The European Council.** Informally called the European Summit, this is a senior forum in which heads of government, accompanied by foreign ministers and two

commissioners, discuss the overall direction of the Union's work. A President of the European Council was appointed in 2009 (Herman Van Rompuy).

▶ **European Parliament.** The EP is composed of 736 Members of the European Parliament (MEPs) (72 from the UK), who are directly elected every five years. The European Parliament is more a scrutinizing assembly than a full legislature. Its major powers (to reject the EU's budget and dismiss the European Commission) are too far-reaching to be exercised on a regular basis.

▶ **European Court of Justice.** The ECJ interprets, and adjudicates on, European Union law. There are 27 judges, one from each member state, and eight advocates general, who advise the Court. As EU law has primacy over the national law of member states, the court can 'disapply' domestic laws. A Court of First Instance handles certain cases brought by individuals and companies.

national, intergovernmental and supranational levels, with the balance between them shifting in relation to different issues and policy areas. This image of complex policy-making is more helpful than the sometimes sterile notion of a battle between national sovereignty and EU domination.

The impact of the EU on the UK

It is often said that the UK is *in* Europe but not *of* Europe. Although the UK's relationship with the EU may be characterized by continuing 'awkwardness', it has not been able to escape a process of 'Europeanization'. How, and to what extent, has EU membership affected UK politics? The implications of EU membership for

FOCUS ON . . .
The EU's 'democratic deficit'

The idea of a 'democratic deficit' has been used to explain how EU membership has undermined democracy in the UK. The idea of a 'democratic deficit' is based on the following logic:

▶ More and more policies are being made at EU level rather than by elected UK governments
▶ EU bodies are not properly democratic: the only directly elected EU body, the European Parliament, is weak and has little influence over policy
▶ European integration therefore runs hand-in-hand with the erosion of democracy and public accountability.

On the other hand, pro-Europeans often argue that fears about the 'democratic deficit' are exaggerated. They point out that:

▶ Major EU decisions are made either in the Council of Ministers or the European Council by national leaders who are directly accountable to their electorates
▶ Member states are responsible for ratifying key EU treaties (usually done by a parliamentary vote or a referendum)
▶ The European Parliament is gradually becoming more powerful, and this trend is likely to continue.

the constitution and parliamentary sovereignty have been examined in Chapter 6. Other important areas affected by EU membership include:

▶▶ Public policy
▶▶ Political parties
▶▶ Pressure groups
▶▶ Public opinion.

Public policy

This is an area of considerable debate. Every year the EU issues more than 12,000 regulations, directives, decisions and recommendations which have an impact on the UK and other member states. This has led some to highlight a growing 'democratic deficit' as decision-making authority is transferred from Parliament to non-elected EU bodies. However, the EU's policy influence is very different in different areas. For example, health, education, social security and social services have been little affected by membership of the EU. The UK's opt-out on the single currency also helps to preserve the UK's economic sovereignty, although it has no choice about conforming to rules about the free movement of goods, services and capital throughout the EU. Similarly, the UK's decision not to participate in the Schengen Agreement (which provides for the free movement of people within the EU) has allowed the UK to retain border and immigration controls. On the other hand, agriculture and fisheries policies are now dominated by the EU through the Common Agricultural Policy (CAP) and the Common Fisheries Policy. While British farmers have benefited substantially from the CAP, the country as a whole pays more than it gets back because of the UK's relatively small agricultural sector.

Regional aid has been an important area of EU policy-making. This is provided through grants from the European Regional Development Fund, which helps small businesses and supports economic regeneration, particularly in Wales, Scotland, Northern Ireland and the north of England. The EU is also closely involved in setting and monitoring standards in environmental policy and consumer affairs. This ranges from regulating the quality of bathing beaches and the effectiveness of pollution controls to the ways in which products such as ice cream, sausages and beer can be sold. The impact of the EU on social policy in the UK was restricted by the opt-out, negotiated in 1991, from the Social Chapter of the TEU. The incoming Labour government in 1997, however, relinquished the opt-out. The UK therefore became subject to a wide range of regulations about matters such as working hours and the rights of part-time workers. Progress towards establishing common foreign and defence policies within the EU, while still limited, has developed considerably in recent years with the intergovernmental Common Foreign and Security Policy (CFSP) and European Security and Defence Policy (ESDP). However, while the EU has taken an increasingly larger role in representing member states on bodies such as the World Trade Organization and the International Monetary Fund, national governments, not least the UK, have been less willing to limit their independence in relation to military matters.

Political parties

Membership of the EU has affected UK parties in two main ways. In the first place, Europe has been a cross-cutting issue that has tended to divide both the Labour and Conservative parties. Divisions within the Labour Party, for instance, led Wilson to renegotiate EC membership in 1974 and to call the 1975 referendum on continued membership. During 1981–87, Labour supported withdrawal from the EU. Euroscepticism grew within the Conservative Party from the late 1980s onwards, leading to divisions that threatened the survival of the Major government and contributed to its landslide defeat in 1997. Second, the European issue has given rise to new political parties. The single-issue Referendum Party contested the 1997 general election, while the UK Independence Party (UKIP) won three seats in the European Parliament elections of 1999 and, more dramatically, secured 12 seats in 2003.

Weblink ■ www.politics.guardian.co.uk/eu

Use this website to access the Guardian's special reports on the UK and the EU.

EUROPEAN INTEGRATION

FOR	AGAINST
Maintains peace. By promoting economic, monetary and political union, the EU has created a level of interdependence amongst states that makes war or major conflict in Europe unthinkable. In particular, it has ensured peace between France and Germany, and prevented German expansion by incorporating it into the wider Europe. Since 2004, it has helped reunite eastern and western Europe.	**Doomed to failure**. Many view the 'European project' as inherently unstable. This is because national, language and cultural differences make it impossible for EU bodies to establish genuine political allegiances. These tensions have become greater as a result of the competing pressures generated by EU expansion and EU integration. Integration seeks to impose union on increasingly dissimilar peoples.
Economic benefits. The establishment of a continent-wide market underpins prosperity and economic growth. This has been achieved, since 1993, by the establishment of a single market which promotes competition and efficiency and, since 1999, by a single currency that further removes obstacles to trade. The EU also gives Europe security within the global economy.	**Weaker national identity**. As power is transferred from national governments to EU bodies, historically embedded national identities are weakened. This may make the peoples of Europe feel rootless and insecure. It may also give rise to a nationalist backlash in which anti-Europeanism is linked to opposition to immigration and hostility to minority groups.
Greater influence. European states, which would be minor powers if they acted independently, gain greater influence on the world stage when they 'pool' sovereignty through the EU. The global influence of the EU, and therefore of member states, is greater the more powerful EU bodies become. Europeanization is therefore a response to globalization.	**Threatens democracy**. EU integration has been driven largely by political elites and business interests, which have attempted to manipulate European populations into supporting the New Europe. Further, the 'democratic deficit' can never be overcome because of the distance between EU institutions and European populations. EU bodies will therefore never be properly democratically accountable.
Wider opportunities. The establishment of EU citizenship offers individuals a wider and, sometimes, stronger set of rights, freedoms and opportunities. European citizens can live and work anywhere in the EU. Moreover, the growth of a European identity helps people to escape from narrow and insular nationalism, recognizing what unites them rather than what divides them.	**Unbalanced influence**. The EU has always benefited a limited number of large states, often at the expense of other states and groups. For instance, the wasteful and inefficient CAP was largely constructed to protect French farmers and to consolidate an alliance between the two dominant powers, France and Germany. EU integration primarily benefits economically powerful states and may eventually lead to a German-dominated

Pressure groups

The process of European integration has had a major impact on patterns of pressure group activity in the UK. This has occurred as pressure groups have responded to the transfer of policy-making responsibilities from national governments to EU bodies. Most of this lobbying focuses on the European Commission, the main source of EU regulations and directives. Many major pressure groups have therefore set up offices in Brussels as well as in London. The growing influence of the European Parliament has also led to more intensive lobbying at Strasbourg. One of the most prominent consequences of this process has been the growing number of European-wide pressure groups, which help national groups to pool their resources and to achieve a higher public profile. Over 700 such groups have come into existence, mainly representing business interests. Examples of such European-wide groups include the Committee of Professional Agricultural Organisations (COPA), which provides a European voice for the National Farmers' Union and the European Trade Union Confederation (ETUC), through which the Trades Union Congress (TUC) operates.

Public opinion

How has EU membership affected public attitudes within the UK? The evidence here is that relatively little has changed. The UK's failure to adopt a more clearly European identity, and to participate more fully in EU initiatives, is underpinned by continuing public scepticism about the benefits of EU membership. Before the 1975 referendum, roughly two-thirds of people polled claimed to oppose continued EC membership. Although this was turned into an almost two-thirds victory for the 'yes campaign', Euroscepticism soon reasserted itself. Opinion surveys across the EU have consistently demonstrated that knowledge of, interest in and support for the 'European project' is lower in the UK than in any other member state. For example, in a December 2007 Eurobarometer opinion poll, conducted by the European Commission, only 37 per cent of UK citizens said they had benefited from EU membership, against an EU average of 58 per cent.

Some have explained these trends in terms of the continued impact of the historical and cultural factors that encouraged the UK to refuse the invitation to join the EEC in 1957. Others, however, point to the increasingly strident anti-Europeanism of the UK tabloid press since the early 1980s, especially those owned by Rupert Murdoch's News Corporation. An additional factor is that, since the Heath government 1970–74, no UK government (Labour or Conservative) has made the case for a positive engagement with 'Europe' by clearly emphasizing the benefits of EC/EU membership. Why should the British people show enthusiasm for the 'European project' when its governments have been consistently so lukewarm about it?

WHAT YOU SHOULD KNOW

▶ Modern government has become increasingly complex and multifaceted through moves towards multilevel governance in recent years. This has happened largely through devolution and the process of European integration. Both developments have had implications for sovereignty and national identity.

▶ Local government in the UK has come under growing pressure since the 1980s. Central control has been extended over local finance, narrowing the scope for local autonomy. Local councils have also changed from being 'providers' to 'enablers'. Nevertheless, there is evidence of local renewal in, for instance, the creation of the Greater London Authority.

▶ Devolution is the transfer of power from central government to subordinate regional institutions that have no share in sovereignty. Devolution in the UK has largely been a response to the growth of Scottish and Welsh nationalism. However, there is considerable debate about the impact of devolution on nationalism especially after the election of a majority SNP administration in Scotland in 2011.

▶ The UK has a system of asymmetrical devolution. The Scottish Parliament has primary legislative powers on most fields of domestic policy and limited tax-varying powers. The Welsh Assembly initially had no control over taxation and only secondary legislative powers. The Northern Ireland Assembly has some primary legislative power but no control over taxation.

▶ The EU is a very difficult political organization to categorize. It is no longer a confederation of independent states operating on the basis of intergovernmentalism. However, it has yet to become a fully supranational body. The shift from the national veto to qualified majority voting in the Council of Ministers and the superiority of European law over the national law of member states means that it is accurate to talk of a 'federalizing' Europe.

▶ The European Commission (the executive-bureaucratic arm of the EU) proposes legislation, is a watchdog that ensures that EU treaties are respected, and is broadly responsible for policy implementation. In the Council and the European Council, national ministers make major strategic decisions about the EU. The European Parliament is more a scrutinizing assembly than a legislature. The European Court of Justice interprets EU laws and treaties.

▶ EU membership has affected a growing body of public policy in the UK, especially in areas such as agriculture, fisheries and regional aid. Political parties have been affected through divisions within established parties and the growth of anti-European parties. UK pressure groups have increasingly focused attention on EU bodies. EU membership has had little impact in terms of building support in the UK for the 'European project'.

Test yourself

Short questions:

1 What is multilevel governance?
2 Define 'local democracy'.
3 Distinguish between devolution and federalism.
4 Outline *two* differences between legislative devolution and administrative devolution.
5 In what sense is devolution in the UK 'asymmetrical'?
6 Define 'European federalism'.
7 How do intergovernmentalism and supranationalism differ?

Medium questions:

8 How does central government control local government in the UK?
9 What are the implications of devolution for sovereignty?
10 In what ways has devolution in the UK created a 'quasi-federal' system?
11 How do the powers and responsibilities of the Scottish Parliament differ from those of the Welsh Assembly?
12 What factors have prevented the extension of devolution to England?
13 What may be the solutions to the 'West Lothian question'?
14 How important is the European Commission within the EU?
15 In what ways does the EU impose its will on member states?
16 How has EU membership affected pressure group politics in the UK?

Extended questions:

17 Discuss the view that the UK has effectively abandoned local democracy.
18 How successful has devolution been in the UK?
19 Has 'asymmetrical devolution' led to instability and unfairness?
20 Why, and to what extent, has the UK remained an 'awkward partner' within the EU?
21 Assess the advantages of EU integration.
22 Discuss the view that the EU has developed into a 'superstate'.
23 Why, and to what extent, is there conflict between EU integration and EU expansion?
24 Should the UK withdraw from the EU?

Further reading

Chapter 1 Introducing politics and government

Crick, B. *In Defence of Politics* (Harmondsworth and New York: Penguin, 2000).

Hay, C. *Why We Hate Politics* (Cambridge: Polity, 2007).

Heffernan, R., Cowley, P. and Hay, C. *Developments in British Politics 8* (Basingstoke: Palgrave Macmillan, 2011).

McCormick, J. *Contemporary Britain* (Basingstoke: Palgrave Macmillan, 2007).

Richards, D. 'Challenges to the Westminster model', *Politics Review*, vol. 17, no. 3, 2008.

Stoker, G. *Why Politics Matters: Making Democracy Work* (Basingstoke: Palgrave Macmillan, 2006).

Wright, T. *British Politics: A Very Short Introduction* (Oxford: Oxford University Press, 2003).

Chapter 2 Democracy and participation

Beetham, D. *Democracy: A Beginner's Guide* (Oxford: Oneworld Publications, 2005). A stimulating and wide-ranging introduction to the subject.

Beetham, D. and Boyle, K. *Introducing Democracy: 80 Questions and Answers* (Cambridge: Polity Press, 1995).

Beetham, D., Byrne, I. Ngan, P. and Weir, S. *Democracy Under Blair: A Democratic Audit of the UK* (London: Politicos, 2002).

Cole, M. *Democracy in Britain* (Edinburgh: Edinburgh University Press, 2006). An accessible account of both the theory of democracy and democratic practice in the UK.

Crick, B. *Democracy: A Very Short Introduction* (Oxford: Oxford University Press, 2002). An authoritative introduction to democracy from a key campaigner for citizenship education and democratic reform.

Holden, B. *Understanding Liberal Democracy* (London: Harvester Wheatsheaf, 1993). A helpful analysis of the sometimes complex theory and practice of liberal democracy.

Chapter 3 Elections and voting

Cowley, P. and Kavanagh, D. *The British General Election of 2010* (Basingstoke: Palgrave Macmillan, 2010).

Denver, D. *Elections and Voters in Britain* (Basingstoke: Palgrave Macmillan, 2007).

Farrell, D. *Electoral Systems: A Comparative Introduction* 2nd edn. (Basingstoke: Palgrave Macmillan, 2011).

Leonard, D. and Mortimore, R. *Elections in Britain: A Voter's Guide* (Basingstoke: Palgrave Macmillan, 2005).

Norris, P. and C. Wlezien (eds) *Britain Votes 2005* (Oxford: Oxford University Press, 2005).

Chapter 4   Political parties

Fielding, S. *The Labour Party: Continuity and Change in the Making of 'New' Labour* (Basingstoke: Palgrave Macmillan, 2003).

Heywood, A. *Political Ideologies: An Introduction* 4th edn (Basingstoke: Palgrave Macmillan, 2007).

Ingle, S. *The British Party System* (London: Pinter, 2000).

Kelly, R. 'Conservatism under Cameron: The New Third Way', *Politics Review*, vol. 17, no. 3, 2008.

Leach, R. *Political Ideology in Britain* 2nd edn (Basingstoke: Palgrave Macmillan, 2009).

Lee, S. and Beech, M. *The Cameron–Clegg Government – Coalition Politics in an Age of Austerity* (Basingstoke: Palgrave Macmillan, 2011).

O'Hara, K. *After Blair: David Cameron and the Conservative Tradition* (Cambridge: Icon Books, 2007).

Chapter 5   Pressure groups

Baggot, R. *Pressure Groups Today* (Manchester: Manchester University Press, 1995).

Byrne, P. *Social Movements in Britain* (London: Routledge, 1997).

Coxall, B. *Pressure Groups in British Politics* (Harlow: Pearson Longman, 2001).

Grant, W. *Pressure Groups and British Politics* (Basingstoke: Palgrave Macmillan, 1999).

Jordon, G. and Maloney, W. *The Protest Business* (Manchester: Manchester University Press, 1997).

Jordon, G. and Maloney, W. *Interest Groups and Democracy* (Basingstoke, Palgrave Macmillan, 2007).

Maloney, W. 'Interest groups in Britain', *Politics Review*, vol. 16, no. 4, 2007.

Chapter 6   The constitution

Barnett, H. *Britain Unwrapped: Government and Constitution Explained* (London: Penguin, 2002).

Bogdanor, V. (ed.) *The British Constitution in the Twentieth Century* (Oxford: Clarendon, 2003).

Brazier, R. *Constitutional Practice: The Foundations of British Government* (Oxford: Oxford University Press, 1999).

Foley, M. *The Politics of the British Constitution* (Manchester: Manchester University Press, 1999).

Hazell, R. (ed.) *Constitutional Futures: A History of the Next Ten Years* (Oxford: Oxford University Press, 1999).

King, A. *Does the United Kingdom Still Have a Constitution?* (London: Sweet and Maxwell, 2001).

Norton, P. 'The Constitution under Gordon Brown', *Politics Review*, vol.17, no. 3, 2008.

Chapter 7   Parliament

Cowley, P. *The Rebels: How Blair Mislaid His Majority* (London: Politicos, 2005).

Hansard Society Commission Report *The Challenge for Parliament: Making Government Accountable* (London: Hansard Society, 2001).

Norton, P. *Parliament in British Politics* (Basingstoke: Palgrave Macmillan, 2005).

Riddell, P. *Parliament Under Blair* (London: Politicos, 2002).

Rogers, R. and Walters, R. *How Parliament Works* (London: Pearson Longman, 2004).

Rush, M. *Parliament Today* (Manchester: Manchester University Press, 2005).

Russell, M. 'The House of Lords: Reform Past and Future', *Politics Review*, vol. 17, no. 1, 2007.

Chapter 8   Prime Minister, cabinet and executive

Buckley, S. *The Prime Minister and Cabinet* (Manchester: The Politics Association, 2006).

Foley, M. *The British Presidency* (Manchester: Manchester University Press, 2000).

Heffernan, R. 'Prime-Ministerial Predominance', *Politics Review*, vol. 17, no. 3, 2008.

Hennessy, P. *The Prime Minister: The Office and its Holders since 1945* (London: Penguin, 2000).

Seldon, A. and Kavanagh, D. (eds) *The Blair Effect 2001–5* (Cambridge: Cambridge University Press, 2005).

Smith, M. J. *The Core Executive in Britain* (Basingstoke: Macmillan, 1999).

Rhodes, R. and Dunleavy, P. (eds) *Prime Minister, Cabinet and Core Executive* (London: Macmillan, 1995).

Chapter 9   Judges and civil liberties

Griffiths, J. A. G. *The Politics of the Judiciary* (London: Fontana, 1997).

Kennedy, H. *Just Law: The Changing Face of Justice and Why it Matters to Us All* (London: Vintage, 2005).

Madgwick, P. and Woodhouse, P. *The Law and Politics of the Constitution* (Hemel Hempstead: Harvester Wheatsheaf, 1995).

Rosenberg, J. *Trial of Strength: The Battle Between Ministers and Judges Over Who Makes the Law* (London: Richard Cohen Books, 1997).

Stevens, R. *The Independence of the Judiciary* (Oxford: Oxford University Press, 1993).

10 The EU and multilevel governance

Bogdanor, V. *Devolution in the UK* (Oxford: Oxford University Press, 2001).

Geddes, A. *The European Union and British Politics* (Basingstoke: Palgrave Macmillan, 2004).

Mather, J. *The European Union and British Democracy* (Basingstoke: Palgrave Macmillan, 2000).

McCormick, J. *Understanding the European Union*, 5th edn (Basingstoke: Palgrave Macmillan, 2011).

O'Neill, M. (ed.) *Devolution in British Politics* (London: Longman, 2004).

Watts, D. and Pilkington, C. *Britain in the European Union Today* (Manchester: Manchester University Press, 2005).

Wilson, D. and Game, C. *Local Government in the United Kingdom*, 5th edn (Basingstoke: Palgrave Macmillan, 2011).

Bibliography

Bagehot, W. (1963 [1867]) *The English Constitution*. London: Fontana.

Baggot, R. (1995) *Pressure Groups Today*. Manchester: Manchester University Press.

Barnett, H. (2002) *Britain Unwrapped: Government and Constitution Explained*. London: Penguin.

Barnett, H. (2004) *Constitutional and Administrative Law*. London: Cavendish.

Beetham, D. (1999) *Democracy and Human Rights*. Cambridge: Polity Press.

Beetham, D. (2005) *Democracy: A Beginner's Guide*. London: Oneworld.

Beetham, D. and K. Boyle (1995) *Introducing Democracy: 80 Questions and Answers*. Cambridge: Polity Press.

Beetham, D., I. Byrne, P. Ngan and S. Weir (2002) *Democracy Under Blair: A Democratic Audit of the UK*. London: Politicos.

Birch, A. (1964) *Representative and Responsible Government*. London: Unwin.

Bogdanor, V. (2001) *Devolution in the United Kingdom*. Oxford: Oxford University Press.

Bogdanor, V. (ed.) (2003) *The British Constitution in the Twentieth Century*. Oxford: Clarendon.

Boulding, K. (1989) *Three Faces of Power*. Newbury Park, CA: Sage.

Bower, T. (2007) *Gordon Brown: Prime Minister*. London: Harbour Perennial.

Brazier, R. (1998) *Constitutional Reform*. Oxford: Oxford University Press.

Brazier, R. (1999) *Constitutional Practice: The Foundations of British Government*. Oxford: Oxford University Press.

Buckley, S. (2006) *The Prime Minister and Cabinet*. Manchester: The Politics Association.

Budge, I., D. McKay, J. Bartle and K. Newton (2007) *The New British Politics*. Harlow: Pearson.

Burns, B. (1978) *Leadership*. New York: Harper & Row.

Butler, D. (1983) *Governing Without a Majority: Dilemmas for Hung Parliaments in Britain*. London: Collins.

Byrne, P. (1997) *Social Movements in Britain*. London: Routledge.

Byrne, T. (2000) *Local Government in Britain*. London: Penguin.

Cole, M. (2006) *Democracy in Britain*. Edinburgh: Edinburgh University Press.

Cowley, P. (2005) *The Rebels: How Blair Mislaid His Majority*. London: Politicos.

Cowley, P. and D. Cavanagh (2010) *The British General Election of 2010*. Basingstoke: Palgrave Macmillan.

Coxall, B. (2001) *Pressure Groups in British Politics*. Harlow: Pearson Longman.

Crick, B. (2000) *In Defence of Politics*. Harmondsworth: Penguin.

Crossman, R.H.S. (1963) 'Introduction', in W. Bagehot, *The English Constitution*. London: Fontana.

Denters, B. and L.E. Rose (2005) *Comparing Local Governance: Trends and Developments*. Basingstoke: Palgrave Macmillan.

Denver, D. (2007) *Elections and Voters in Britain*, 2nd edn. Basingstoke: Palgrave Macmillan.

Dicey, A.V. (1959 [1885]) *An Introduction to the Study of the Law of the Constitution*. London: Macmillan.

Erskine May, T. (1997 [1844]) *Erskine May Parliamentary Practice*, 23rd edn. London: LexisNexis Butterworths.

Farrell, D. (2011) *Electoral Systems: A Comparative Introduction*, 2nd edn. Basingstoke: Palgrave Macmillan.

Fielding, S. (2003) *The Labour Party: Continuity and Change in the Making of 'New' Labour*. Basingstoke: Palgrave Macmillan.

Foley, M. (1993) *The Rise of the British Presidency*. Manchester: Manchester University Press.

Foley, M. (1999) *The Politics of the British Constitution*. Manchester: Manchester University Press.

Foley, M. (2000) *The British Presidency*. Manchester: Manchester University Press.

Gamble, A. (1994) *The Free Economy and the Strong State: The Politics of Thatcherism*. London: Macmillan.

Gamble, A. (2003) *Between Europe and America: The Future of British Politics*. Basingstoke: Palgrave Macmillan.

Geddes, A. (2004) *The European Union and British Politics*. Basingstoke: Palgrave Macmillan.

Giddens, A. (1998) *The Third Way*. Cambridge: Polity Press.

Grant, W. (1995) *Pressure Groups, Politics and Democracy*. Hemel Hempstead: Prentice-Hall/Harvester Wheatsheaf.

Grant, W. (1999) *Pressure Groups and British Politics*. Basingstoke: Palgrave Macmillan.

Griffiths, J.A.G. (1997) *The Politics of the Judiciary*. London: Fontana.

Hansard Society Commission Report (2001) *The Challenge for Parliament: Making Government Accountable*. London: Hansard Society.

Harden, I. and N. Lewis (1988) *The Noble Lie: The British Constitution and the Rule of Law*. London: Hutchinson.

Hay, C. (2002) *British Politics Today*. Cambridge: Polity Press.

Hay, C. (2007) *Why We Hate Politics*. Cambridge: Polity Press.

Hazell, R. (ed.) (1999) *Constitutional Futures: A History of the Next Ten Years*. Oxford: Oxford University Press.

Heffernan, R. (2001) *New Labour and Thatcherism: Political Change in Britain*. Basingstoke: Palgrave Macmillan.

Heffernan, R. (2008) 'Prime-Ministerial Predominance', *Politics Review*, vol. 17, no. 3.

Heffernan, R. *et al.*, (2011) *Developments in British Politics 9*. Basingstoke: Palgrave Macmillan.

Hennessy, P. (2000) *The Prime Minister: The Office and its Holders since 1945*. London: Penguin.

Heywood, A. (2000) *Key Concepts in Politics*. Basingstoke: Palgrave Macmillan.

Heywood, A. (2007a) *Politics*, 3rd edn. Basingstoke: Palgrave Macmillan.

Heywood, A. (2007b) *Political Ideologies: An Introduction*, 4th edn. Basingstoke: Palgrave Macmillan.

Holden, B. (1993) *Understanding Liberal Democracy*. London and New York: Harvester Wheatsheaf.

Holliday, I., A. Gamble and G. Parry (eds) (1999) *Fundamentals in British Politics*. Basingstoke: Macmillan.

Ingle, S. (2000) *The British Party System*. London: Pinter.

Jones, B., D. Kavanagh, M. Moran and P. Norton (2010) *Politics UK*. London: Longman.

Jordon, G. and W. Maloney (1997) *The Protest Business*. Manchester: Manchester University Press.

Jordon, G. and Maloney, W. (2007) *Interest Groups and Democracy*. Basingstoke: Palgrave Macmillan.

Kelly, R. (2008) 'Conservatism under Cameron: The New Third Way', *Politics Review*, vol. 17, no. 3.

Kennedy, H. (2005) *Just Law: The Changing Face of Justice and Why it Matters to Us All*. London: Vintage.

King, A. (2001) *Does the United Kingdom Still Have a Constitution?* London: Sweet & Maxwell.

Leach, R. (2009) *Political Ideology in Britain*, 2nd edn. Basingstoke: Palgrave Macmillan.

Leach, R., B. Coxall and L. Robins (2011) *British Politics*, 2nd edn. Basingstoke: Palgrave Macmillan.

Leonard, D. and R. Mortimore (2005) *Elections in Britain: A Voter's Guide*. Basingstoke: Palgrave Macmillan.

Lloyd, J. (2004) *What the Media are Doing to our Politics*. London: Constable.

Ludlam, S. and M.J. Smith (eds) (2001) *New Labour in Government*. Basingstoke: Palgrave Macmillan.

Lukes, S. (2004) *Power: A Radical View*. Basingstoke: Palgrave Macmillan.

Macintosh, J. (1962) *The British Cabinet*. London: Stevens.

Madgwick, P. and P. Woodhouse (1995) *The Law and Politics of the Constitution*. Basingstoke: Palgrave Macmillan.

Maloney, W. (2007) 'Interest groups in Britain', *Politics Review*, vol. 16, no. 4.

Mather, J. (2000) *The European Union and British Democracy*. London: Palgrave Macmillan.

Mazey, S. and J.J. Richardson (1993) *Lobbying in the European Community*. Oxford: Oxford University Press.

McCormick, J. (2007) *Contemporary Britain*, 2nd edn. Basingstoke: Palgrave Macmillan.

McCormick, J. (2011) *Understanding the European Union*, 5th edn. Basingstoke: Palgrave Macmillan.

McKenzie, R.T. (1964) *British Political Parties*. London: Heinemann.

Michels, R. (1959 [1911]) *Political Parties*. New York: Dover.

Miliband, D. (ed.) (1994) *Beyond Left and Right: The Future of Radical Politics*. Cambridge: Polity Press.

Miliband, R. (1982) *Capitalist Democracy in Britain*. Oxford: Oxford University Press.

Moran, M. (2011) *Politics and Governance in the UK*, 2nd edn. Basingstoke: Palgrave Macmillan.

Naughtie, J. (2002) *The Rivals: The Intimate Story of a Political Marriage*. London: Fourth Estate.

Norris, P. and C. Wlezien (eds) (2005) *Britain Votes 2005*. Oxford: Oxford University Press.

Norton, P. (2005) *Parliament in British Politics*. Basingstoke: Palgrave Macmillan.

Norton, P. (2008) 'The Constitution under Gordon Brown', *Politics Review*, vol. 17, no. 3.

O'Hara, K. (2007) *After Blair: David Cameron and the Conservative Tradition*. Cambridge: Icon Books.

O'Neill, M. (ed.) (2004) *Devolution in British Politics*. London: Longman.

Pulzer, P. (1967) *Political Representation and Elections in Britain*. London: Allen & Unwin.

Putnam, R. (2000) *Bowling Alone: Collapse and Revival of American Community*. New York: Simon & Schuster.

Rhodes, R. (1997) *Understanding Governance*. Buckingham: Open University Press.

Rhodes, R. and P. Dunleavy (eds) (1995) *Prime Minister, Cabinet and Core Executive*. London: Macmillan.

Richard, I. and D. Welfare (1999) *Unfinished Business: Reforming the House of Lords*. London: Vintage.

Richards, D. (2008) 'Challenges to the Westminster model', *Politics Review*, vol. 17, no. 3.

Riddell, P. (2002) *Parliament Under Blair*. London: Politico's.

Rogers, R. and R. Walters (2004) *How Parliament Works*. London: Pearson Longman.

Rosenberg, J. (1997) *Trial of Strength: The Battle Between Ministers and Judges over Who Makes the Law*. London: Richard Cohen Books.

Rush, M. (2005) *Parliament Today*. Manchester: Manchester University Press.

Russell, M. (2007) 'The House of Lords: Reform Past and Future', *Politics Review*, vol. 17, no. 1.

Sampson, A. (2005) *Who Runs This Place?* London: John Murray.

Seldon, A. and D. Kavanagh (eds) (2005) *The Blair Effect 2001–5*. Cambridge: Cambridge University Press.

Seldon, A., P. Snowdon and D. Collings (2007) *Blair Unbound*. London: Simon & Schuster.

Smith, M.J. (1999) *The Core Executive in Britain*. Basingstoke: Palgrave Macmillan.

Stevens, R. (1993) *The Independence of the Judiciary*. Oxford: Oxford University Press.

Stoker, G. (2006) *Why Politics Matters: Making Democracy Work*. Basingstoke: Palgrave Macmillan.

Street, J. (2011) *Mass Media, Politics and Democracy*, 2nd edn. Basingstoke: Palgrave Macmillan.

Sygan, J.A. (1998) *The UK Parliament and EU Legislation*. Dordrecht: Kluwer.

Thatcher, M. (1993) *The Downing Street Years*. London: HarperCollins.

Wadhurst, C. (2002) *Anatomy of the New Scotland*. Edinburgh: Mainstream.

Watts, D. and C. Pilkington (2005) *Britain in the European Union Today*. Manchester: Manchester University Press.

Webb, P. (2000) *The Modern British Party System*. London: Sage.

Wilson, D. and C. Game (2011) *Local Government in the United Kingdom*, 5th edn. Basingstoke: Palgrave Macmillan.

Wright, T. (2003) *British Politics: A Very Short Introduction*. Oxford: Oxford University Press.

Index

Bold = boxed material; *italics* = definitions in margin. f = figure; t = table.